THE TRANSFORMATION OF GOVERNANCE IN THE EUROPEAN UNION

The Transformation of Governance in the European Union provides a challenging contribution to the topical, ongoing governance debate. Governance is the new buzz-word aimed at catching the present-day complexity of political action. Coordinating actors that are both autonomous and interdependent is a growing matter of concern for governing within and beyond the nation state. It is of particular relevance to the EU because of the very properties of this system: highly sectoralised policy regulation has to be agreed in a multilevel framework.

The book presents a theoretically-informed typology of modes of governance which is tested in a careful selection of comparative country and policy studies. At the core is the question of whether the European Union is destined for a network type of governance and whether and how this type of governance will be translated into the member states. The individual chapters subject the governing patterns at European and national level to empirical scrutiny. Drawing on recent research findings in different issue areas – including monetary union, social affairs, environment, genetic engineering and market liberalisation in transport, banking, energy and professional services – the contributions highlight the impact of European activities in the policy-making process in the member states.

This book will give researchers in political science, European studies, international relations and policy-making a new perspective on the topical and controversial issue of governance. It will also be useful to those with a professional interest in the topic, from lobbyists, national civil servants and MEPs to Commission officials.

Both the **editors** are at the University of Mannheim, Germany. **Beate Kohler-Koch** is Jean Monnet Chair for European Integration, and **Rainer Eising** is Lecturer in the Department of Political Sciences. Beate Kohler-Koch has written widely on matters of international relations and West European integration, and is co-ordinating the six-year research programme of the German Science Foundation on 'EU Governance'.

ROUTLEDGE/ECPR STUDIES IN EUROPEAN POLITICAL SCIENCE

Edited by Hans Herman, *Vrije University, The Netherlands* and Jan W. van Deth, *University of Mannheim, Germany on behalf of the European Consortium for Political Research.*

The Routledge/ECPR Studies in European Political Science series is published in association with the European Consortium for Political Research, the leading organisation concerned with the growth and development of political science in Europe. The series presents high-quality edited volumes on topics at the leading edge of current interest in political science and related fields, with contributions from European scholars and others who have presented work at ECPR workshops or research groups.

1 REGIONALIST PARTIES IN WESTERN EUROPE
Edited by Lieven de Winter and Huri Türsan

2 COMPARING PARTY SYSTEM CHANGE
Edited by Jan-Erik Lane and Paul Pennings

3 POLITICAL THEORY AND EUROPEAN UNION
Edited by Albert Weale and Michael Nentwich

4 POLITICS OF SEXUALITY
Edited by Terrell Carver and Véronique Mottier

5 AUTONOMOUS POLICY MAKING BY INTERNATIONAL ORGANISATIONS
Edited by Bob Reinalda and Bertjan Verbeek

6 SOCIAL CAPITAL AND EUROPEAN DEMOCRACY
Edited by Jan van Deth, Marco Maraffi, Ken Newton and Paul Whiteley

7 PARTY ELITES IN DIVIDED SOCIETIES
Edited by Kurt Richard Luther and Kris Deschouwer

8 CITIZENSHIP AND WELFARE STATE REFORM IN EUROPE
Edited by Jet Bussemaker

THE TRANSFORMATION OF GOVERNANCE IN THE EUROPEAN UNION

Edited by
Beate Kohler-Koch and
Rainer Eising

London and New York

First published 1999
by Routledge
2 Park Square, Milton Park, Abingdon, Oxon, OX14 4RN

Simultaneously published in the USA and Canada
by Routledge
270 Madison Ave, New York NY 10016

Routledge is an imprint of the Taylor & Francis Group

Transferred to Digital Printing 2007

Typeset in Baskerville by
Curran Publishing Services

British Library Cataloguing in Publication Data
A catalogue record for this book is available from the
British Library

Library of Congress Cataloging in Publication Data
The transformation of governance in the European Union/
edited by Beate Kohler-Koch and Rainer Eising
336 pp. 15.6 x 23.4 cm (Routledge/ECPR studies in European
political science: 12)
Includes bibliographical references and index.
1. Political planning – European Union countries. 2. European
Union countries – Politics and government. 3. European Union.
I. Kohler-Koch, Beate, 1941– II. Eising, Rainer, 1964 –
III. Series.
JN32.T73   1999
320'.6'094dc21   99-22359
                                                  CIP

ISBN10: 0-415-21548-X (hbk)
ISBN10: 0-415-43037-2 (pbk)

ISBN13: 978-0-415-21548-0 (hbk)
ISBN13: 978-0-415-43037-1 (pbk)

Publisher's Note
The publisher has gone to great lengths to ensure the quality
of this reprint but points out that some imperfections
in the original may be apparent

CONTENTS

CONTENTS

FIGURES AND TABLES

Figures

Tables

CONTRIBUTORS

Mark Aspinwall is Lecturer in Politics at the University of Durham, United Kingdom.

Kenneth Dyson is Professor of European Studies at the University of Bradford, United Kingdom.

Rainer Eising teaches International Relations at the University of Mannheim, Germany.

Gerda Falkner is Associate Professor at the Institute for Government and Political Science, University of Vienna, Austria.

Andrea Lenschow is Lecturer at the Institute for Political Science, University of Salzburg, Austria.

Herbert Gottweis is Professor of Political Science at the University of Vienna, Austria.

Thomas Hueglin is Professor for Political Theory and Comparative Politics at the Wilfrid Laurier University, Waterloo, Canada.

Beate Kohler-Koch is Professor for Political Science at the University of Mannheim, Germany.

Jill Lovecy is Lecturer in the Department of Government of the University of Manchester, United Kingdom.

George Pagoulatos is visiting research fellow in the Hellenic Studies Program and South European Research Group, Department of Politics, Princeton University, USA.

Vivien Schmidt is Professor of International Relations at Boston University, USA.

Niels Christian Sidenius is associated Professor in Political Science at the University of Aarhus, Denmark.

Klaus Dieter Wolf is Professor of International Relations at the Technical University of Darmstadt, Germany.

PREFACE

By the series editor

If there is one topic in the mind and research of European political scientists at present, it is without any doubt the emergence and development of the European Union. The number of workshops, research meetings, master programmes, and other professional activities around the 'new Europe' is seemingly endless. In short, the EU as a political system *in statu nascendi* is not only a booming industry in teaching and research in political science, international relations and public administration, but also one of the greatest challenges to the profession. The challenge is less to describe and concomitantly assess the development from European economic co-operation and collaboration towards political and economic integration, which we now depict (and accept?) as a reality in modern Europe (i.e. the European Union as a political system) than to develop new frameworks of reference and related insights into the underlying mechanisms which can explain the EU as a political system *per se*.

All this has been widely discussed, described and analysed in many books, articles and other media. Yet, in my opinion, most of these publications – however important they are (or have been) as sources of information on a topic that concerns all Europeans – appear to be unable and insufficient to further our knowledge of what the history of European cooperation and integration really implies for the working and related effects of political life in Europe on whatever level of authority (internationally, nationally and intra-nationally) and, subsequently, of what impact it has on the everyday life of Europe's citizens.

Of course, there is a lot of debate about the 'democratic deficit' in the organisation of political decision making inside the EU, and the concurrent role of national élites, particularly with reference to their effect on the quality of democracy. There have been valuable contributions to the debate about the pros and cons of different modes of policy-making in the EU, in terms of effectiveness and efficiency, mutual gains, improving social and economic life, the emergence of (positive and negative) spillovers and externalities, and so on. And of course, the idea and reality of Europe as a forum for furthering common interests and as an irreversible political development is widespread as well as thoroughly documented. All this is true, and therefore much of the research and many of the related publications are quite valuable and relevant. Nevertheless, in my opinion, precious little advance has been made in the study of the European Union as a genuinely new political system, unlike any previously in existence in the way it works, how it performs, and even more, in what direction it is developing as a 'polity' and a 'machinery'.

In analysing and interpreting the polity of the EU – that is, the institutional design that is emerging and is meant to develop political decision-making across the European territory, which affects the choice of public goods enhancing the welfare of every citizen – many students of European politics tend to apply existing modes of statehood and democratic control and command as an analytical instrument or yardstick. This may have been helpful for taking stock of the (historical) development of the process of Europeanisation *per se,* and it may well have been conducive to the development of relevant research questions, but it appears to be a shallow basis for further research into EU decision-making as a political system *sui generis.*

In assessing and evaluating the performance of European policy-making as a machinery – that is, the process of policy-making and implementation within a political system which aims at allocating material and immaterial values across territories and functional categories (such as social welfare, transportation, environment, fiscal and monetary regulation) – most students of European integration tend to use existing models of policy analysis. Again, this may have been useful for descriptive analysis, but it is not adequate (any more) for understanding the present administrative procedures and subsequent policy performance of the EU machinery as a political system *sui generis.*

To be honest, it is easier said than done to develop a conceptual framework that enables the political scientist to analyse empirically the development of the EU as such, and its emergence as a separate political system. I consider therefore this volume of the European Political Science Series, published in collaboration with the European Consortium for Political Research, as a challenging step forward for the development of an empirically driven attempt to analyse theoretically the EU as a political system *per se.*

The book starts from the assumption that the EU can be neither analysed as a (territorially extended) state, nor considered as an equivalent of international organisations. Hence, notions such as 'federalisation' or 'regimes' are not appropriate to describe its features as a polity. Likewise the terms 'government' and 'representational bodies' do not appear adequate to describe the machinery of the EU. In short, a fresh approach to the EU as an institutionalised body of transnational politics is needed. In response to these observations the editors of this volume have proposed to give a central place in their conceptual framework to the notion of network governance. However – this is the strength of their argument – it is not considered as a container concept which covers all empirical features of the EU polity and machinery that cannot be classified otherwise. Rather, they see it as an extension of existing modes of government. These existing modes are, according to the editors, corporatism, pluralism and statism. Hence they depart from existing knowledge on the relationship between institutions (in a polity) and behaviour (as expressed in decision-making and policy-making), and add to that – as a specific mode of political regulation – network governance. In this way it is possible to combine two dimensions of politics: more or less vertical relationships in decision-making (territorially and functionally) and interest-driven behaviour, which reflects the balance between common and particular goals on the one hand, and the shared versus the adversarial interests of the actors involved on the other. This extended model of governance is theoretically developed in Part I of this book by comparing and combining it with existing concepts such as pluralism and corporatism, and all are confronted with the concept of statism.

In Part II the concept of network governance is applied to various cases of policy-making in Europe (such as the environment, social policy and the coming of the ECU). In Part III the focus is much more on the EU machinery in relation to national modes of policy implementation, and the question whether (in)congruence of regulation, differences in speed of development and subsidiarity in terms of competencies are important to policy performance as a result of network governance. Finally, in Part IV the results of the empirical investigations are discussed in terms of theoretical progress made and practical knowledge about the EU gained.

The overall conclusion of the editors is that the concept of network governance applied to the EU as a separate political system yields promising results. It appears to be an important heuristic device, which allows the investigator to analyse the EU polity and machinery and the related performance as a separate and autonomous system. The results further demonstrate that the focus on interests and actors within the institutional configuration of a multi-level system is capable of explaining the multifarious outcomes of European politics as a patterned variation of policy-making.

Of course, all this is a first step in the development of our knowledge of the Europeanisation of national politics. Further elaboration on the conceptual framework is necessary and amplification of empirical evidence is needed. Nevertheless, I think the steps made and the case studies presented in this volume are important. They certainly make this book a valuable asset and an indispensable companion to any student of European politics or European policy-making.

Hans Keman
Amsterdam, February 1999

PREFACE

By the editors of this volume

This book grew out of a workshop organised by Beate Kohler-Koch and Markus Jachtenfuchs within the framework of the European Consortium for Political Research (ECPR) Joint Sessions of Workshops at Oslo, in spring 1996. In the spirit of the ECPR joint sessions, the workshop brought together a group of 'senior' and 'junior' scholars carefully selected from a great number of paper proposals. The common objective was to test the new governance agenda with theory-guided empirical analysis. With the encouragement of the ECPR to pursue a publication, we joined for another meeting at Mannheim in January 1997 presenting and discussing the revised draft chapters. The volume is not only organised around a common subject but aims at conceptualising the transformation of governance in the European Union (EU). The authors are drawn from seven countries and different academic backgrounds, covering international relations, comparative government, policy analysis, and political sociology.

We are grateful to the European Consortium for Political Research, in particular Hans Keman who encouraged us to pursue this volume. The Stiftung Volkswagenwerk provided the financial support and the Mannheim Centre for European Social Research (MZES) the logistic support for organising the meeting at Mannheim. We are also grateful to a number of conference participants – Peter Bursens, Sander Dankelman, Markus Haverland, Markus Jachtenfuchs, Robert Ladrech, Amy Verdun, Alasdair R. Young – who are not represented in this volume for stimulating comments and advice both during the discussions and in reviewing individual chapters. In addition, we want to express our warmest thanks to Fiona Hayes-Renshaw for help in language editing (supported by the MZES), and to Ana Langer and Uschi Horn for help in consolidating the bibliography and in preparing the manuscript for the press.

Beate Kohler-Koch
Rainer Eising

ABBREVIATIONS

ARE	Arbeitsgemeinschaft Regionaler Energieversorgungsunternehmen
BDI	Bundesverband der Deutschen Industrie
BMBau	Bundesministerium für Raumordnung, Bauwesen und Städtebau
BMF	Bundesministerium für Finanzen
BMI	Bundesministerium des Inneren
BMU	Bundesministerium für Umwelt, Naturschutz und Reaktorsicherheit
BMWi	Bundesministerium für Wirtschaft
BoG	Bank of Greece
BRIC	Biotechnology Interservice Committee
CBI	Confederation of British Industry
CCBE	Commission Consultative des Barreaux d'Europe
CEDEC	Conféderation Européenne des Distributeurs d'Energie Public Communaux
CEEP	Centre Européen de l'Entreprise Publique
CTP	Common Transport Policy
Coreper	Committee of Permanent Representatives
DG	Directorate General (of European Commission)
DIHT	Deutscher Industrie- und Handelstag
DVG	Deutsche Verbundgesellschaft
EAP	Environmental Action Programme
EBCG	European Biotechnology Coordination Group
EC	European Community
ECB	European Central Bank
ECJ	European Court of Justice
ECOFIN	Council of Economic and Finance Ministers
ECOSOC	Economic and Social Committee
EdF	Electricité de France
EEC	European Economic Community
EECT	European Economic Community Treaty
EIA	Environmental Impact Assessment
EIRR	European Industrial Relations Review
EMI	European Monetary Institute

EMS	European Monetary System
EMU	Economic and Monetary Union
EnWG	Energiewirtschaftsgesetz
EP	European Parliament
ERM	Exchange Rate Mechanism
ESI	electricity supply industry
ESPRIT	European Strategic Programme for Research in Information Technologies
ETUC	European Trade Union Confederation
EU	European Union
EUI	European University Institute
EURELECTRIC	European Grouping of the Electricity Supply Industry
GATT	General Agreement on Tariffs and Trade
GDR	German Democratic Republic
GDP	gross domestic product
GEODE	Groupement Européen de Sociétés et Organismes de Distribution d'Energie
GMO	genetically modified organism
GWB	Gesetz gegen Wettbewerbsbeschränkungen
IEM	internal energy market
IGC	Intergovernmental Conference
IMF	International Monetary Fund
IPC	Inter-ministerial Privatisation Committee
MEP	Member of the European Parliament
ND	Néa Dimokratía
NEPP	National Environmental Policy Plan
NGO	non-governmental organisation
NTPA	negotiated third party access
OECD	Organization for Economic Co-operation and Development
OJ	Official Journal
PASOK	Panellínio Sosialistikó Kínima
RPR	Rassemblement pour la République
SEA	Single European Act
TEN	Trans-European Network
TEU	Treaty on European Union
TUC	Trade Union Congress
UDF	Union pour la Démocratie Française
UEAPME	European Association of Craft, Small and Medium-Sized Enterprises
UK	United Kingdom
UNICE	Union des Industries de la Communauté Européenne
US	United States
VDEW	Vereinigung Deutscher Elektrizitätswerke
VIK	Verband der Industriellen Energie- und Kraftwirtschaft
VKU	Verband kommunaler Unternehmen
WWF	World Wildlife Fund

Part I

THE CONCEPTUAL CHALLENGE OF EUROPEAN GOVERNANCE

1

INTRODUCTION

Network governance in the
European Union

Rainer Eising and Beate Kohler-Koch

During the last two decades, the scope and the density of the European Community (EC) rules have immensely increased and its institutions have been profoundly reformed. As a consequence, prominent commentators even came to regard the EC as a 'new' institution (Keohane and Hoffmann 1991; Sbragia 1992a).[1] In other words, it is well recognised that the EC activities have re-built the architecture of territorial rule in Western Europe (Grande 1994). To an ever growing extent, the European institutions are responsible for the authoritative allocation of values. However, there is also widespread agreement that the EC neither qualifies as a state, as it lacks legal sovereignty, nor can be reduced to an international organisation since its rules take precedence over domestic laws. Furthermore, the institutional configuration of the EC differs from both nation states and international organisations. In this sense, the European Community is a *sui generis* political system.

As the Community institutions are not likely to evolve into a federal state during the near future and yet play a growing political role in Western Europe, this volume addresses two pertinent questions: how are values legitimately allocated in the European Community and how do the ways and means of allocation, that is, the governance of the EC, impinge upon the member states?

Characterising the European Community as a system *sui generis* does not mean that our analysis needs to do without the theoretical or methodological tools that have been developed in international relations or comparative politics.[2] To analyse the nature of political processes in the European Community we have taken recourse to the concept of *governance* as developed in both *international relations and comparative politics*. In both sub-disciplines governance and not government is the focus of research because authoritative allocation takes place without or outside government. 'Governance without government' nowadays is a top priority on the research agenda (Rosenau and Czempiel 1992; Rhodes 1997). In international relations, the spread and the persistence of institutionalised co-operation in numerous issue areas, even despite contravening power relations or interest constellations, have provided the stimulus to this research agenda (Rosenau 1992). In short, the governance agenda in international relations centres on the structuring of state behaviour by international institutions. International regimes play a leading role in explaining the co-operation of actors.[3] In comparative politics, the governance concept forms a response to the growing segmentation of both society and the state resulting from socio-economic dynamics. The increased autonomy of social actors and the growing complexity of actor constellations attracted the attention of a broad range of literature on policy networks, sub-governments, and negotiation systems which have deprived the state of its authoritative position (Rhodes 1997). Despite their different origins and emphases, both strands of the debate have in common that they emphasise *new processes of governing*: they stress above all the absence of a central authority. State actors have lost their pivotal place above society. The political arena is populated by formally autonomous actors who are linked by multifaceted interdependencies. They suggest further that political arenas and societal sub-systems develop their own rationale and logic of decision-making and are only loosely coupled to other political arenas. And last, not least, they call attention to the maintenance of order and patterns of structured co-operation despite the absence of a central organising and regulatory authority. From a theoretical point of view, both sub-disciplines emphasise the role of ideas and the relevance of institutions for the structuring of expectations and behaviour, the shaping of interests and identities. As usual, the empirical findings and the theoretical interpretations of 'governance without government' are disputed but, nevertheless, these are the common themes.

Considering the concept's prominence in both sub-disciplines, it is of little wonder then that it has also been used to explore the interface of international relations and domestic politics, the European Community. However, so far it is not at all clear what is meant when we talk about governance in the European Community.[4] In a recent review article, almost anything falls under the label of 'the "new governance" agenda' (Hix 1998). Among others, Paul Pierson's historical institutionalist account of the EC as applied to social policy (1996), Giandomenico Majone's portrayal of the regulatory state in Europe (1996), and Fiona Hayes-Renshaw and Helen Wallace's analysis of Council decision-making (1997) are mixed into a cloudy 'new governance' cocktail. This does not come as a surprise. The few authors who have explicitly had recourse to the governance concept in their analyses of EC decision-making relied heavily on the concept's self-explanatory power and did without a definition or explicit elaboration of its elements (Bulmer 1994; Pollack 1996).

Its variegated and disputed use in international relations and comparative politics, and the confusion over what falls under the label of governance when talking about the EU, point out the need for clarification. In essence, 'governance' is about the structured ways and means in which the divergent preferences of interdependent actors are translated into policy choices 'to allocate values', so that the plurality of interests is transformed into co-ordinated action and the compliance of actors is achieved. It is quite evident then that, for us, governance is not synonymous with a new process of governing. Rather, we propose to distinguish between different ideal-types in terms of modes of governance: statism, corporatism, pluralism and network governance. It is only network governance, which in our opinion, bears several new characteristics. Building on the debates in international relations and comparative politics, these ideal types may be distinguished by the ways in which they combine four elements that are at the core of any kind of governing: the role of the state as compared to other actors, the rules of behaviour, the patterns of interaction and the level of political action.

The volume starts from the neo-institutionalist premise that the institutional and democratic properties of a political system shape but do not determine the mode of governance. The contributions test (and contest) the hypotheses, first that the European Community because of its systemic properties is governed in a particular way, namely in a network mode of governance, and, second, that this predominant mode of European governance disseminates into the member states. The concept of governance, in particular 'network governance', was elaborated by Beate Kohler-Koch in a draft paper for the conference and became a common point of reference. Nevertheless, individual authors had deviating research questions and we did not want to put them into a strait-jacket. In the introduction, therefore, we will point to variations in terminology.

The core idea of 'network governance' is that political actors consider problem-solving the essence of politics and that the setting of policy-making is defined by the existence of highly organised social sub-systems. In such a setting, efficient and effective governing has to pay tribute to the specific rationalities of these sub-systems. The '*state*' is vertically and horizontally segmented and its role has changed from authoritative allocation 'from above' to the role of an 'activator'. Governing the EC involves bringing together the relevant state and societal actors and building issue-specific constituencies. Thus, in these patterns of interaction, state actors and a multitude of interest organisations are involved in multilateral negotiations about the allocation of functionally specific 'values'. As a consequence, within the networks the level of political action ranges from the central EC-level to decentral sub-national levels in the member states. The dominant orientation of the involved actors is towards the upgrading of common interests in the pursuit of individual interests. Incorporated in this concept is the idea that interests are not given as it is assumed in ideal-type assumptions about pluralism and corporatism, but that they may evolve and get redefined in the process of negotiations between the participants of the network. (See Table 1.1.)

The book is divided into four parts. In the first part, the governance concept is elaborated in more detail. The second part explores whether or not there really is a dominant mode of EC governance and provides evidence from different policy areas and economic sectors. The individual chapters point out that across issue areas network governance is very present but that different modes of governance may co-exist in the EC, ranging from statism in monetary policy and corporatism in social policy to networks in market integration and environmental policy. Likewise, a mix of modes is found in some of these areas. The third section centres on

Table 1.1 Core elements of ideal types of governance

	Statism	Pluralism	Corporatism	Network
Role of the state	Authority	Referee	Mediator	Activator
Dominant orientation	Pursuit of common 'national' interest	Pursuit of individual interests	Integrating conflicting group interests	Co-ordinating related interests
Patterns of interaction	Command and control based on majority rule	Competition and bargaining to build minimum winning coalitions	Concerted negotiations to reach consensus	Multilateral negotiations to approximate positions
Dominant actors	State actors	State actors and multitude of interest groups and parties	State actors and functional peak associations	State actors and multitude of stake holders
Level and scope of political allocation	Central level covering all issue areas	Overall and issue specific at respective government level	National or sub-national level covering specific issue areas	Functionally specific agreements cutting across different levels

the transformation of national modes of governance in the context of EC integration. Congruence between EC-level governance and member state governance is a key issue in most of the chapters. The authors give a detailed assessment of the implications of differing degrees of congruence regarding the member states' attitudes towards EC governance, their openness for EC governance, and the repercussions of EC policies on domestic modes of governance. Despite evident variations, the contributions meet on common ground as the analyses deviate from previous studies which argue that national actors generally defend theirnational institutions and identities (Héritier *et al.* 1994; Caporaso, Green Cowles and Risse, forthcoming). In the fourth section, the concept of 'network governance' is contested from different theoretical angles. One claim is that despite a lot of networking the role of the state may not have changed at all and the other is that EC network governance may only be a euphemism for upper class rule. The final contribution gives a comparative assessment of the separate chapters.

In Chapter 2, Beate Kohler-Koch outlines the theoretical underpinnings of the governance concept which, in general, have informed the volume. Combining the analysis of policy-making in the EC and the literature on the democratic deficit, she relates the network mode of governance to the institutional organisation and the democratic properties of the European Community. She starts from the hypotheses that the network mode of governance is predominant at the European level and disseminates into the member states. Putting this mode of governance in a broader theoretical perspective she compares EC governance to differing modes of governance at state level. She identifies two core variables that discriminate between modes of governance: the constitutive logic underlying political systems (i.e. either the pursuit of individual citizen interests or a common purpose dear to a political community) and the organising principle of political relations (i.e. either majority-rule or consociation). The combination of these variables accounts for the single modes of governance. They result from strategic choices informed by 'belief systems' about appropriate ways of governing. According to her, network governance is distinct from corporatism, pluralism and statism in that it combines the principle of consociation with interest based politics. At the opposite end of the spectrum, statism is based on majority rule and common purpose. Reflecting on how the EC specific mode of network governance carries over into member states, she proposes to distinguish between three different ways: imposition by EC actors, involvement of state and non-state actors in EC policy practice, and incentives provided by EC institutions.

The contributions in Part II focus on the evolution of EC-level governance in individual policy areas and economic sectors. At the intersection between EC-level governance and national-level governance, Andrea

Lenschow (Chapter 3) analyses both the evolution of a new mode of environmental governance in the EC and its repercussions on a number of member states, namely the Netherlands, Spain, United Kingdom, and Germany. She places the emergence of network governance in world-wide debates on governance in general and on environmental policy in particular. In her opinion, a 'new, systemic understanding' of environmental governance has emerged which is 'rooted in a new awareness of insufficient problem-solving capacity' and constitutes a break from the almost statist style of EC-level governance in the past. She then points to recent 'institutional and procedural innovations' which, according to her, loosen horizontal boundaries and create networks between EC public and private actors. Qualifying these changes as 'extensions' to the old mode of governance rather than as a full-blown transformation of governance, she finds only 'moderate' pressure on the member states' own modes of governance. Like Vivien Schmidt, she points to the congruence between EC level and national level governance as an important factor influencing the receptiveness on the part of the member states for the EC mode of governance. While the Netherlands were a 'front runner' in new environmental governance, and therefore fit the governance model emerging in the EC rather well, this does not hold for the other member states which have greater difficulties adapting to the EC and, in part, also display an unwillingness to implement a 'new' mode of governance.

Herbert Gottweis (Chapter 4) departs from the institutional perspective and presents a post-structuralist view on governance in the European Community. Analysing the regulation of genetic engineering in the EC, he emphasises the 'importance of discursive practices' and regards EC governance as 'a field of political intertextuality', asserting that 'actors and structures' as well as 'interests and strategies' must be conceptualised as products and effects of discursive practices. In his detailed account of the emergence of genetic engineering regulation at EC-level, he calls attention to the role of the Commission in the shaping of EC-level discourse. He argues that, despite several competing viewpoints, the Commission's Directorate General XI (Environment) managed to gain a central position because it 'skilfully deployed a regulatory narrative which linked the precautionary regulation of hazards' to the metanarrative of the EC, namely market integration. This narrative provided the multitude of actors on the EC level – other DGs, national experts and bureaucrats, industry and environmental interest groups – with 'sufficient overlap' in their definitions of central problems and integrated them by an 'intricate process of successful enlisting and mobilisation . . . into a network of meaning'.

In Chapter 5, Gerda Falkner illustrates that EC governance may change considerably over time. She argues that the governance of social policy has been transformed through various stages into a close to corporatist mode of governance. Initially, EC social policy was almost a 'non-issue'. From the mid-1970s to the early 1990s, a pluralist mode of pressure politics rather than co-operation of employers and trade unions characterised EC social policy-making. Only the Social Protocol, an annex to the Maastricht treaty, has strengthened corporatist elements. In her reading, this evolution should be attributed, on the one hand, to the growing relevance of the 'social dimension of the internal market' in the context of the Internal Market Programme, which was propagated again and again by the Commission. On the other hand, the prospect of majority voting in social policy which became evident during the Maastricht Treaty negotiations induced the European employers' interest organisation, UNICE, to change their strategy. For the first time they accepted selective negotiations with the European representative of labour, ETUC. Consequently, the author notes interdependencies between the 'action capacity at the EC level' and the evolution of 'interest politics'. However, according to her, the Social Agreement does 'not replicate classic national corporatism'. First, its functional scope is restricted. Secondly, the social partners cannot themselves guarantee the implementation of their agreements. Finally, the EC as well as the social partners at the European level lack the organisational capacity for full-scale macro-corporatism.

In Chapter 6, Kenneth Dyson presents a deviant case because he argues that the governance of European Monetary Union 'is a study in core executive action'. Thus, EMU was almost brought about in a statist mode of governance by the national heads of state and government and a closed circle of other core executives from the national finance ministries and central banks. In a marked contrast to other policy issues, these actors shared an interest in retaining control over policy formulation. The negotiations were marked by the absence of consensus-building between state actors and civil society, and characterised by a great reliance on technical rationality. Based on the assumption that 'core executive' governance does represent an 'object for analysis rather than an analytical model or explanatory theory', the author tests several theories that generate models about 'core executives'. Kenneth Dyson maintains that these theories, such as bureaucratic politics or elite theories, capture only part of the elements that were characteristic for the EMU negotiations. They do not suffice as 'stand alone' explanations because they do not come to grips with the 'cross-national interlocking of core executives'. To emphasise this aspect of the negotiations, the author characterises the actors' behaviour as a special case of two-level bargaining games.

Chapter 7 is dedicated to analysing the governance of the transport sector and the shift towards EC liberalisation. Mark Aspinwall's point of departure is a puzzle: 'given that a common transport policy was always seen as an essential element of European integration, why did a new European-level governance system for transport only begin to take shape in the 1980s, and in the form that it did?'. He argues that, on the one hand, there was a continuous institutional 'pull', namely, the active role of both the European Court of Justice and the Commission throughout the evolution of market integration. On the other, he sees a political economy 'push' in the form of the evolution of national and international transport markets that turned out to become a major driving force towards a change in policy and the emergence of a new EC mode of governance. Within the broad contours of network governance, he distinguishes between three sub-sets: soft issue alliances, supranational regulatory frameworks, and domestic security networks. Thus, he departs from the other contributions in that he posits the networks at specific levels of government. These subsets of governance are distinguished by the actors involved, the level of governance, the degree of institutionalisation and the dominant values. Soft issue alliances only display a low degree of institutionalisation and are conceptualised as attempts by the Commission to mobilise support groups. Supranational regulatory frameworks are well-established networks governing the transport sector on the EC-level according to the 'rules affecting market access and competition'. Domestic security networks are responses of those member states and industries which oppose the neo-liberal reform agenda in the transport sector.

In Chapter 8, Jill Lovecy looks into the determinants of sectoral governance transformation in the health care and legal professions. As compared to the other chapters, she emphasises the role of law and the European Court of Justice (ECJ) in the transformation of governance. She locates her study in a neo-institutionalist framework, arguing that this approach best accounts for the 'path dependent' evolution of the heterogeneous regulatory systems established for each profession. Over time, the professions have attained 'entrenched' positions as policy 'insiders' at the national level and developed 'close relationships with their sponsoring ministries'. *Inter alia,* they formulate rules relating to market entry and behaviour, standards of conduct, and delivery of services. According to her account, the dynamics of market integration and EC regulatory policy since the mid-1980s plus the rulings of the European Court of Justice have then marginalised those actors 'resistant to relinquishing their traditional protections' from market-competition and 'most attached to preserving intact the national professional bodies' regulatory powers'. By providing the individual members of the professions with legal rights, the 'professions as collectively organised actors' were challenged to an unexpected extent. The European Court of Justice proved to be decisive in the transformation of governance. According to the author, the ECJ 'allows those who are "policy outsiders" at the national level to come centre-stage at the EC-level'.

Part III contains a series of chapters on the transformation of national governance in the context of EC integration. Highlighting the institutional settings and the interaction between state actors and interest groups as the main determinant and component of the modes of governance, Vivien Schmidt (Chapter 9) argues that the United Kingdom, France, and Italy represent member states with a statist pattern of governance and that Germany stands for the corporatist type. Compared to these, the European Community is closer to the United States with their pluralist type of governance. Looking at the large member states there is an obvious 'clash' between EC and national governance patterns and a particular high degree of adaptive pressure on statist and corporatist countries. Examining both the processes of policy formulation and policy implementation, she comes to the conclusion that statist countries have a 'markedly more difficult time adjusting than corporatist countries'. Hence, she presents a recurrent theme of the contributions, namely, that degree of congruence between EC level governance and national level governance is important for the response of the member states to EC action.

In Chapter 10, Niels Sidenius expounds the impact of European governance on the national patterns of interest intermediation in a single member state, Denmark. He puts forward two hypotheses: first, Danish business associations have become integrated into the European system of interest organisation and, secondly, as a consequence the national patterns of interest intermediation in Denmark have disintegrated. On the basis of survey data, the author confirms the validity of the first hypothesis supported by a growing number of contacts with the EC institutions, closer co-operation with EC-level interest organisations, and a growing number of offices in Brussels. However, this does not result in a progressive disintegration of established patterns of interest intermediation in Denmark. The number and the regularity of contacts between Danish business associations and state actors have in some cases even increased in response to EC-level policies. Thus, 'domestic features are supplemented, but not really substituted by international integration'. The interpretation of this finding centres on the path dependency of institutional developments. The author relates the ongoing integration of both business and labour into Danish policy-making to both the frequency of Social Democrats being in power and the 'tradition' of minority governments inclined to listen to interest organisations.

George Pagoulatos (Chapter 11) examines in detail how EC network governance affects patterns of statism on the national level. Comparing Greek banking deregulation and privatisation, he notes a differential degree of pressure in the two policy areas. The EC's influence on privatisation was 'considerably less powerful and direct' than in banking deregulation. Additional factors supported the reform efforts: the international spread of the neo-liberal paradigm, the dismal performance of the affected sectors, and the deterioration of the Greek fiscal system. In line with the arguments presented in the two preceding chapters he concludes that the implementation of EC policies met the EC objectives but were implemented in a way that left little room for anything but the traditional statist mode of governance. It depended 'upon domestically existing structures of governance, interest organisation, and their attendant normative conceptions'. In both reforms, the state actors 'regarded the maximisation of their own control of policy as vitally important' to ensure the effectiveness of implementation. According to the author's view, the Greek statist mode of governance is deeply rooted in 'dissensual' relations between the Greek state and the fragmented interest group system. Only after the reforms have been successful are there 'signs of a move in a sectoral corporatist direction' in the banking sector, but not in the privatised industries.

Chapter 12 is about the impact of the EC on sectoral governance regimes in the member states. Rainer Eising presents a case study on the liberalisation of the EC electricity supply industry and its repercussions on the German sectoral regime. He devotes his attention to changes in actor preferences concerning regimes and shifts in power between state and economic actors. First, he attributes to EC policy initiatives gradual changes in the preference of member states regarding their domestic governance regimes. Being exposed to the continuous flow of information about 'alternative governance regimes' and the close and structured interaction on the EC-level, state actors revise their position. He regards the German Federal Economics Ministry's change of attitude from outright opposition to emphatic support of the Commission proposal as an instance of such a change. Second, analysing the controversial discussion within the German Federal Government and the conflicts between state actors and sectoral firms, he finds evidence that supports the claim that EC integration contributes to strengthening national executives because of the central position they occupy in 'two level games'. However, he qualifies the argument because the effect is limited to the leading departments at national level and it is conditioned by particular institutional context factors. In addition, he regards the achievement of consensus on the EC-level as a necessary precondition for any significant strengthening of national departments. Finally, the specificity of EC rules is important.

Part IV presents antithesis and synthesis. First, network governance is challenged on theoretical and normative grounds, then a concluding chapter gives a comparative assessment of the contributions to the current debate. Klaus Dieter Wolf (Chapter 13) challenges the concept of network governance with its emphasis on consensus-orientated negotiations between state and non-state actors from an international relations perspective. He starts from a puzzle: the high degree of self-binding on the part of the member states on the one hand, and the lack of participatory rights granted to non-governmental actors (democratic deficit) on the other. Both phenomena can only partly be explained by international relations theories: realism can only account for the democratic deficit while liberalism can only explain the self-binding of states. To solve the puzzle, he conceives of states as strategic actors in both intergovernmental and state-society relations. In this perspective, the 'meta-strategy' of governments is their 'striving for autonomy', because it 'provides the room to make other, more concrete choices under more specific circumstances'. Consequently, the 'transfer of regulatory competencies to international or even supranational institutions' such as the European Union 'reflects the common strategic interest of governments in withdrawing their policies from the control of societal or sub-national actors'.

In Chapter 14, Thomas Hueglin subjects the practise of network governance in the EC to a trenchant normative criticism rooted in the study of comparative federalism. For him, federalism 'denotes a general principle of adequate societal structuration aimed at the recursively balanced organisation of unity and diversity'. Three elementary components are at the core of his concept of federalism: the pluralisation of governance, the consent requirement, and mutual solidarity. Judged by these criteria EC network governance can be regarded as a pluralised form of governance. However, there is no balance of pluralist interests. Rather, EC governance is dominated by a modernising coalition made up of 'policy entrepreneurs in the Commission, managers of multinational corporations, and the governments of the economically strong member states'. In the author's view, network governance favours economic core countries such as Germany and the prosperous regions to the detriment of the countries and regions at the periphery. Moreover, the consent requirement is undermined by a new EC constitutionalism, whose centrepiece is the European Central Bank which writes into 'constitutional stone the autonomy of European monetary policy from democratic scrutiny and control'. The EC thrives on 'ideological capture' centring around market and monetary integration. A seemingly neutral regulatory language draws a veil over winners and losers. As a consequence, mutual solidarity appears also 'eclipsed from essential policy fields'. To quote Schattschneider in his portrayal of American pluralism: 'the heavenly chorus sings with a strong upper-class accent'.

The final Chapter 15 by the editors brings together the arguments of the individual contributions and presents a comparative assessment of the evolution of network governance in the EC and the likely transformation of established modes of national governance.

Notes

1 The analysis is limited to the supranational pillar of the EU, i.e. the EC, based on the European Community Treaty.
2 For a contrary argument see Hix 1998.
3 For an excellent overview over the literature on 'international regimes' see Hasenclever, Mayer and Rittberger 1997.
4 William Wallace (1996: 439ff.) prefers to talk about 'government without statehood'.

2

THE EVOLUTION AND
TRANSFORMATION OF
EUROPEAN GOVERNANCE

Beate Kohler-Koch

Why talk about European governance?

European integration is about more than just building a common market; it is about political regulation as well. This lesson has been learned in the last decade. Since Maastricht, Community competence has been enlarged, covering many aspects of daily life. It is evident that European policy-making has an impact on substantive policies. Whether or not it has an impact on the ways and means of governing is another question entirely. In the long run, the most important question is whether European integration will bring about a change in governance. The term 'governance' refers to patterns of governing which, as we know, vary from country to country.[1] In essence, 'governance' is about the ways and means in which the divergent preferences of citizens are translated into effective policy choices, about how the plurality of societal interests are transformed into unitary action and the compliance of social actors is achieved.

The essence of governance just like that of government is to reach binding decisions. The difference between government and governance is that government is the organisation in charge of making binding decisions, resting on a constitutionally defined authority. A government is an agent furnished with explicit rights and subject to control according to established procedures. Governance will have different properties whenever it is enacted without government.

The European Community (EC) is governed without government and, therefore, it is bound to be governed in a particular way.[2] In addition, EC governance is penetrating into the political life of member states and its particular mode of governing may disseminate across national borders. These, in a nutshell, are the two hypotheses that will be tested. The first is that Europe's supranational Community functions according to a logic different from that of the representative democracies of its member states. Its purpose and institutional architecture are distinctive, promoting a particular mode of governance. The second is that the process of 'Europeanisation', that is extending the boundaries of the relevant political space beyond the member states, will contribute to a change of governance at national and sub-national levels. Being a member of the EU is concomitant with the interpenetrating of systems of governance; any polity which is part of such a 'penetrated system' is bound to change in terms of established patterns of governing.[3]

The European Community: a very particular system of governance

It is part of the conventional wisdom that the European Community is a '*sui generis*' polity, a political system which is far more than an international organisation and yet does not fit the notion of a federal state (Sbragia 1992a: 2). European integration has, indeed, taken us 'Beyond the Nation State' (Haas 1964) in two different ways: first by extending the realm of the political beyond the borders of the once sovereign nation states; and second, by building up a political system which is not – and, in the foreseeable future, will not be substituting for – the nation states.

One of the most characteristic features of this '*sui generis* system' is that it is governed without government. The 'sovereign people' are sovereign citizens only within the boundaries of their individual states. Representative democracy stops at state borders. There is no delegation of political power to a directly responsible top decision-making authority at the European level. Nevertheless, policies are decided at the European level and decisions have binding force on citizens within each member state. Although there is no government, citizens are governed. To put it in more general terms, governance is not just limited to actions taken by a government and, although it is embedded in a context of representative democracy, European governance does not conform to the norms of democratic rule. This much is obvious; what follows is the less obvious but plausible assumption that when there is no government and no democratic representation, the ways and means of governing will be different.

These two aspects must be seen in conjunction, in order to understand how the European Community is governed. Up to now, both aspects have been treated separately. Research has either looked at the institutional structure and administrative organisation of the Community, or it has focused on the 'democratic deficit' of the EC. In the latter case, the debate has centred mainly on the constitutional design of the Community, on the evolution of public support and on the so-called 'structural prerequisites' of a working democracy in terms of political identity, a political infrastructure of intermediary institutions, and a European-wide public debate. Little attention has been paid to the ensuing patterns of European policy-making.

Policy analysis, on the other hand, has provided us with innumerable case studies which link the institutional set-up and the legal framing of EC decision-making to the processes and outcomes of Community governance. In comparing policy studies, a deep insight is gained into the particular features of EC agenda-setting and the formulation and implementation of European policies. Despite some variations across policy areas, the findings coincide with the picture drawn by those who are interested in assessing the politics of EC governance. There is a broad consensus about the 'logic of common decision-making' (Kerremans 1996). The lesson to be learned is that the very properties of the EC system result in particular patterns of actor relations and decision-making routines and that this in turn feeds back on the characteristic features of the Community system (Eising and Kohler-Koch 1994).

This type of research is chiefly interested in the 'performance' of the European system. Empirical research as well as theoretical reasoning are employed to investigate those institutional mechanisms of the European multi-level negotiating system which might promote or endanger its capacity for efficient decision-making and effective problem-solving.[4] It is a functional rather than a normative debate. Normative deliberations arise when research touches upon the question of whose interests prevail in European politics and whether the system has a structural bias to privilege some group of actors over others. Even then the focus is not on the legitimacy of the Community system as such.[5]

Only recently has the discussion on the democratic fallacies of the 'negotiating state' reached EC policy research.[6] Up to now, those who have written about the democratic deficit of the European Community have hardly ever bothered to take a close look at how the system is administered, and those who know all the details of how policies are developed have not reflected generally on the legitimacy of being subject to European rule. Two camps of scholarly debate co-exist, and the participants live happily in a state of peaceful non-communication.[7]

However, in order to discover whether a particular system of European governance is likely to evolve, it is necessary to adopt both approaches. The policy-making process gains direction from the allocation of competence, formal and informal rules of decision-making, administrative routines and the working of 'comitology'. Nevertheless, this is only part of the picture. Governing is also directed by shared beliefs about what constitutes the legitimacy of a political system and what supports the claim to make binding decisions.[8] No balanced assessment about the likely emergence of a particular mode of European governance can be drawn up without considering the constitutional framework which supports or does not support expectations of legitimate governance. The system, after all, is operated by actors who are all too aware of the fragile legitimacy of their joint enterprise. Therefore, the first hypothesis is that European governance is not just determined by the structural properties of the EC system but also influenced by actor's perceptions of legitimate organising principles.

The second hypothesis is that supranational integration and efforts to satisfy demands concerning efficiency and accountability will produce a very particular type of polity. The constitutional logic of the EC has never been clear. It may be seen as an intergovernmental enterprise, a supranational technocracy or a political community in its own right. Depending on which view is held, its legitimacy rests on the democratic quality of member state governments, on output performance or on the consent of the governed. The general assessment – although one may take issue with it – is that in the early years of the European Economic Community the policy programme laid down in the Treaty, in combination with the Commission's right of initiative and the unanimity rule in the Council, reconciled the first two competing paradigms of political legitimacy.[9] The EEC Treaty provided for an action programme which would be implemented best by an independent body of European experts. Political regulation extending beyond 'negative integration' was under member state control because any member state could use its power of veto.[10]

With the deepening of the European Community, the conditions for ensuring the legitimacy of the system changed. A series of institutional reforms aimed to take account of the transformation of the basic conditions without upsetting this delicate mix of legitimacy. The introduction of majority voting was a response to demands to unlock the decision-making process. The capacity to act became both more difficult and more important in a larger Community which now embraces a wider range of responsibilities. Majority voting, however, infringes upon the sovereign right of the partners to ultimately decide what is and what is not acceptable to their home constituency. Introducing elements of democratic accountability through the European Parliament in compensation for the loss of intergovernmental and technocratic legitimacy will not help, because of the inferior representative quality of that parliament.[11] In addition, there is a fundamental incompatibility between the democratic norm of giving equal rights to citizens to state their views and the federal principle of giving equal representation to the collective members of the union.

The architects of the union are stuck in the democratic dilemma of supranational integration with no blueprint available to get out of it. The more salient the issues to be decided, the greater the need to keep them under member state control, and the more emphatic the demands for democratic accountability. The domestic constituencies have made it clear that they are not content with a purely elitist system. The message to member governments and Community bodies alike from the referenda on the Treaty of Maastricht was that they had to bring the European Union 'closer to its citizens'.[12]

Any move towards a more democratic system has strengthened the unitary character of the system. Different strategies have been designed to increase the responsiveness of Community policy-making. The principle of 'partnership' has been introduced into various programmes to give the people affected a say in the framing and programming of Community policies. In particular the Commission has established routines to draw upon the expertise of public as well as private actors in order to ensure that its proposals are approved of by the governed. For years it has supported transnational interest formation and played an active role in 'networking', that is, building up transnational policy communities around those policy issues which the Commission has an interest in promoting. The Commission has often been characterised as a 'political entrepreneur' which manages to give policy issues a European dimension and brings subnational actors into the game, whether for the sake of promoting European integration or for the sake of its own political standing *vis-à-vis* the member states. These strategies would not have been successful without a widespread acceptance that European policy-making is not just an intergovernmental affair. The permissive attitude of governments and the responsiveness of societal actors rests on a shared, if diffuse, understanding that a mix of complementary elements – functional representation, technocratic regulation, institutionalised deliberation – will increase the legitimacy of European governance. Each of these elements has been part of EC governance from the very beginning. Functional representation is institutionalised in the Economic and Social Committee (ECOSOC) and other advisory bodies with socio-economic representation.[13] Their actual importance and the assessment that functional representation is a means of compensating for the democratic deficit has been varying over time and is now on the increase.[14] The same holds true for 'non-majoritarian institutions', for elements of 'deliberate democracy' which have been disclosed within EC comitology (Joerges and Neyer 1997), and for 'bridgeheads' of civil society extending to the core of the EC bureaucracy (Heinelt 1998).[15] Supported by legal provisions for 'openness' and 'transparency' the mix of these elements is intended to serve two aims: first, to make up for the weakness of parliamentary legitimacy and second, to prove the appropriateness of a different type of governance. The message is that the EC is, by nature, a non-majoritarian system. It is a negotiating system which embraces Community institutions as well as economic and social actors and defines the role of the 'state', that is member state governments and the Commission, not as the apex of a decision-making hierarchy, but as a mediator in the common endeavour to come to terms with competing interests and an activator pushing for designing common policies.

The foregoing account may be read in two different ways. The first sounds quite familiar. It highlights the role of the Commission in decision-making, that is its capacity to forge alliances with non-state actors to push reluctant governments to come to agreements. The second reading is less common. It is about system building. By bringing in social actors and forging advocacy coalitions the Commission takes an active part in redefining the boundaries of the European polity. What is at stake is the transformation of the Community system in terms of the transition from a compound of member states, a Staatenverbund , into an overarching transnational political space that is becoming a polity, both in and for itself.[16]

The Commission is active as an actor – although not the only one – interested in redefining the boundaries of the European political space. Its interests coincide with those of two different kinds of actors. First, there are the territorially based, that is sub-national, actors who hope to improve their own autonomy, or at least to gain the right to be represented and to gain political influence in European affairs. In recent years, a redefinition of boundary rules has been apparent. Regions (and later also municipalities) have been accepted as relevant units of political action. At first their political recognition was limited to a particular policy field, namely that of EC structural policies. Today, the representation of territorial collective identities within the individual member states has been accepted as a general principle, and is institutionalised in the 'Committee of the Regions'.

Established boundary rules are also contested by functional collectivities. Just as transnational mergers of companies gave rise to an increased number of truly European corporate actors, so interest associations have been created which are not just federations of national associations, but are genuinely transnational in terms of organising interests irrespective of territorial provenance and taking the EC as the relevant playing field.

But corporate and resourceful actors are not alone in challenging traditional boundaries. Community law empowers each individual citizen to cross national borders. This is not just a matter of mobility and the right of establishment. It extends to challenging the supreme power of national sovereignty. Member state citizens have the right via Community law to take legal action against their governments. In this way, the European Community has been institutionalised as the *référentiel collectif* (Jobert and Muller 1987) for individual citizens. Community decisions open windows of opportunity, and citizens may reach out to take advantage of them irrespective of the rulings of their national governments.

Together, the Single Market and Community law have transformed the 'compound' into a 'political unit' on a sector basis. A compound system is governed through inter-system negotiations, while a political unit develops different modes of intra-unit governance (Scharpf 1991: 58). To the extent that the member states no longer define the range of political options, alternative ways of interest representation gain legitimacy. The member state governments can no longer claim a monopoly on representing the interests of their citizens. Other avenues are open to them, and other non-national actors are competing for the position of legitimate interest representative.

To sum up: the European Community system is both a compound and a unit at the same time. Agents of the state together with Community bodies are engaged in inter-unit negotiations. Notwithstanding this, individual, corporate and collective actors are also legitimate participants in the political process and take the EC as one single playing ground. Will this support the emergence of a particular mode of governance?

A typology of modes of governance

What we need is a heuristic instrument to identify different modes of governance relating to particular features of political systems. A typology will help in two ways: first, to characterise the most prominent features of the EU system, and second, to classify the various member states, in order to know where to place them so that, in turn, we can show how much they differ and in what respect EU integration might impact on the mode of national governance. Precisely because such a classification system has to cover diverging types of governance, the categories on which it is based must encapsulate the essence of governing, namely the transformation of the plurality of individual preferences into collectively binding decisions.

The typology I would like to propose draws on elements of Lijphart's well-known typology of democratic regimes (1977), although in defining the criteria I am closer to Lehmbruch (1967; 1991) than to Lijphart.[17] Lijphart based his typology on two criteria: the structure of society and elite behaviour (Lijphart 1977: 106). In my reading of the working of institutions structural settings do not translate directly into modes of governance and elite behaviour is more of a dependent variable which may oscillate across diverging types of governance. Cross-national and cross-sector variations of governance types cannot be explained by looking at the properties of the constituent elements of a system. Attention should rather be paid to patterns of relationships and regularities in the interactions between these constituent elements (Lehmbruch 1991: 124).[18] Structural contingencies as well as 'task contingencies' have a constraining effect.[19] Nonetheless, 'collective actors involved have some latitude for *strategic choice*, in the design of inter-organizational relations' (ibid.: 132). This choice depends on the strategic orientations of actors who are guided by collective interpretations of social reality. Understanding a particular governance system requires 'the reconstruction of meanings and interpretations that support their institutionalization'; they 'have to be understood as products of collective historical experience' (ibid.: 148).

In this Weberian tradition, I take 'constitutional conceptions' as the basic criterion by which to differentiate distinct types of governance. They embrace 'belief systems' about 'pertinent' (based on causal beliefs), 'appropriate' and 'exemplary' (based on normative beliefs) ways of governing. (See Table 2.1.)

Table 2.1 Constitutional conceptions supporting different modes of governance

Relating to the organising principle of political relations		*Relating to the constitutive logic of the polity*	
majority rule	consociation	common good	individual interest

The typology is based on two categories: one refers to the *organising principle of political relations*, the other to the *constitutive logic of a polity*.

There are two opposing *principles of organising political relations*: majority rule and consociation. They have been linked to distinct structural settings. Majority rule is supposed to be best suited to a homogeneous political environment and a pragmatic orientation of political elites (Almond 1958: 398–9) which makes it compatible with an adversarial style of political discourse. Consociation is located in a pluralist society marked by deep cleavages which can only be bridged by a coalescent policy style and all-embracing grand coalitions. By their sheer existence, however, structural settings do not produce particular patterns of actor relations. They rather give way to a particular understanding of a given situation and the choice of matching strategies. Concepts of 'good governing' are developed in historic situations, interpreting contextual conditions in view of how best to deal with the problems and challenges which arise.

Interpretations are hardly ever unequivocal, and in the European context it would be misleading to expect a direct translation from structure to governing concept. There are two good reasons for this. First, European history is rich in political thinking and institutional experiments and thus will nourish competing world-views on constitutional politics. Furthermore, there is a variety of national traditions accounting for quite divergent practical experience. Second, the EU as a 'polity' is still in its formative phase, and its very 'nature' – not to mention its *finalité politique* – is still contested. Concepts will differ, depending on the interpretation chosen as to what sort of political animal the EU is, or ought to become.[20] Therefore, it is difficult to predict which will become the dominant interpretation. Research is challenging because the concepts which emerge in today's politics tend, over time, 'to petrify into ideological sediments that guide much of the interpretation of later crisis and structural adaptations' (Lehmbruch 1991: 148). This 'emerging concept' will, however, not merely aggregate the divergent national and partisan beliefs about legitimate types of governance. It will be 'path-dependent' in terms of taking up what was written into the founding treaties and subsequent institutional reforms. Intergovernmental high-level agreements and daily practice have over time established an institutional system which constrains future choices. In addition, actors are oriented by divergent belief systems, have competing interests and a different perception of their own mission. Member state representatives by definition are guardians of the constituent elements of the EU system whereas the Community institutions (the European Court of Justice, the European Parliament, and the Commission) are agents of the 'European interest' and an emerging European polity.

To put it in a nutshell, consociation and majority rule are not organising principles born out of a given structural situation, but the result of strategic choices taken over time and driven by some fundamental beliefs about the legitimacy of specific patterns of governing. Consociation is a conscious concept to bridge the heterogeneity which is supposedly incompatible with (even temporary) subordination of a minority to the wishes of a majority. Majority rule, on the other hand, expresses the belief that forming the 'minimum winning coalition' (Riker 1962: 32-33) is the best way of securing efficient government.[21] Subordination is accepted because it is in the logic of political competition that government is a temporal affair. Compliance rests on the assumption that, in the event of poor government performance, the minority will attain the majority position.

The second dividing line between types of governance is that which marks different conceptions of the *constitutive logic of a polity*. This 'constitutive logic' is a boundary rule of a particular kind. It defines the grounds and reasons on which a legitimate political unit of action will be formed. The answer may be given in two alternative ways. Collective political action may be considered to be legitimate because it is based on uniting those who are 'bound together'.[22] Politics is an investment in a common identity which is expressed and will be reproduced in the political process. According to this line of thinking, the pertinent concept of governing is the pursuit of a collective purpose, acting on behalf of a community of citizens. The contrasting concept builds on 'premises of individualism and self-interest' (March and Olsen 1995: 5). Governing has to reconcile the competing preferences of self-interested individuals in an institutionalised system of peaceful conflict resolution. The legitimate right to have 'voice' is not confined to members of a given community, but is extended to all who are 'affected' by a policy.[23] Anybody with a 'true interest' and anybody who has the capacity to improve the quality of a decision is a legitimate partner in politics. Heterogeneity is the hallmark of the system, and matching interests will be organised along functional rather than territorial lines.

When these two categories are combined, four modes of governance can be distinguished: first, 'statism' based on majority rule and supported by a dedication to a 'common purpose', second, 'corporatism' which includes competing social interests in consensus formation in order to achieve the common good, third, 'pluralism' which combines majority rule and the individualistic pursuit of interests, and fourth, 'network governance' which

Table 2.2 A typology of modes of governance

		Organising principle of political relations	
		Majority rule	Consociation
Constitutive logic of the polity	Common good	*Statism*	*Corporatism*
	Individual interests	*Pluralism*	*Network governance*

also builds on self-interested actors and aims at 'upgrading common interests' in the process of negotiations.[24]

When looking for empirical cases which fit into a typology of governance, the most common approach is to look merely at the organising principles of political relations.[25] In this perspective the 'British model' matches the 'majority rule' type and the 'Swiss Model' corresponds to the consociation type.[26]

The characteristic features of these two models are well known: In the 'British model' the composition of government is 'unitary' by nature, that is a majority is in power and the minority in opposition.[27] Politics is ruled by competition and political discourse is adversarial. Precisely because competition is the rule of the game, majority governments are based on 'minimum winning coalitions'. The system thrives on a pragmatic approach to conflict resolution which is most likely to exist in a culturally and politically homogeneous environment.

The 'Swiss model' is less well known but easy to bring to mind. It is founded on and is perpetuating a well-known cultural and social plurality.[28] The most characteristic feature of such a system is a coalescent style of politics aimed at consensus formation. Broad coalitions and a right of veto for minorities are the rule and not (as in the British model) the exception. It is in the logic of the system that all significant segments of society co-operate in governing the polity. This holds true for political systems segmented by deep cultural or social cleavages as well as for federal systems in which – independent of the nature of societal cleavages – the political body is segmented along territorial lines. The German case nicely illustrates the fact that, in federal systems, territorial segmentation does not necessarily coincide with a cultural or social segmentation of society. Nonetheless, the particular political organisation of parts of a largely homogeneous society gives rise to political segmentation. Again, it is not structure which determines governing patterns. The Federal Republic of Germany is considered to be a typical example of a consociational democracy, whereas the United States, despite having a federal construction, belongs to the majoritarian camp.

The second divide, that is differentiation according to the criteria laid down for what constitutes the logic of the polity – a drive for a common purpose or for individual interest materialisation – is most pronounced in state-society relations. France is viewed as the most typical example of the *étatist* philosophy. Based on the notion of *état-nation*, the 'state' is responsible for preserving the identity of the nation and for giving expression to the 'national interest'. Politics according to this logic is by nature 'expressive', it is the perpetual reproduction of the core *référentiel*, that is, the national will. Private interest groups lobbying the government to push partial interests are a reality of life but not appreciated, because lobbying is considered to be incompatible with the system. The authority to govern does not rest on successful interest intermediation but on electoral voting and a strong state bureaucracy. Those who are in power are not in an exchange relationship with segments of society, they are in command. Government has the legitimacy to demand subordination. The United States is in the opposite camp. Politics is not about creating and giving expression to the 'national will'. It is an interest-driven game about who decides what. Anybody who is in command of resources and skills has the right to exert influence on the 'authoritative allocation' of material and immaterial goods.

Consociational systems differ along the same line. The belief that politics must pursue a collective purpose is the guiding concept of (neo-)corporatist systems. It governs inter-group relations and is also embodied in intra-group relations. The essence of corporatism is that a strong state is bargaining with a limited number of encompassing associations that enjoy representational monopoly and control membership behaviour (Schmitter 1979: 13,21). Their coherence and their capacity to secure compliance will not come about just by the simple aggregation of interests. Cohesiveness is supported by common aspirations; an aim is at stake, not just matching interests. Partisan allegiance, which provides the cement, has a strong ideological component. Interest groups are institutions which shape the identity of members. Membership has connotations of belonging, and 'exit' is not just a matter of individual cost-benefit calculation. Cohesiveness is the necessary condition for a collective group to turn into a 'corporate' actor. Compliance is a powerful resource in exchange relations. When associations lose their *weltanschauliche* attraction, the corporatist system starts to crumble.

When compared to other systems, the most obvious feature of a 'network' system is that politics is not about the reproduction of identity but of managing differentiation. This is most pronounced in the case of the EU. It lacks a unifying ideology which would give collective action binding force. Referring to the concept of 'Europe' has never been anything more than a vague allusion to a common, though very divisive history and an

24

overarching cultural tradition of Christianity, Roman law and enlighten-
ment. Its reason for being is purely functional. It is based on the
assumption that institutionalised co-operation, when properly handled,
may turn into mutual benefit of its members, be it for peace, security or
welfare. Common institutions have been designed to give the system dura-
bility and to support the 'up-grading of the common interest' in
inter-group negotiations.[29] Governing involves reaching agreement in a
highly interwoven negotiating system with two main actors, the Council
and the Commission, who are not politically accountable in any direct way.
Putting aside the democratic implications for the moment, the result is policy-making without politics. There is no voting mechanism which could
mobilise a sense of political dedication to the European enterprise or give
partisan support to a majority position on vital issues. 'Political primacy',
therefore, is alien to the EU system. It is a system based on the recognition
of a plurality of interests and it is linked to a reductionist concept of legitimacy which is equated with efficient performance.

Since *consociation* is the widely accepted governing principle and *interest*
is both the rationale for exchange relations and the genuine reason for lasting agreements, the EC is well equipped as a network type of governance.[30]

What is special about 'network governance'? First of all, it is not just an
academic concept, used as an analytical tool in scholarly research; it is a
political concept as well. The core idea is that politics is about problem-solving and that the setting of policy-making is defined by the existence of
highly organised social sub-systems. It is evident that, in such a setting, efficient and effective governing has to recognise the specific rationality of
these sub-systems. Governing is about fitting new regulatory mechanisms
into an environment which is functioning according to its own regulatory
logic and has so far been unwilling or unable to change. European integration is a project of transformation in a highly complex constellation.
Introducing new and sometimes quite deviant regulatory principles cannot
be done by unilateral steering. Neither the institutions nor the predominant ideas of European co-operation allow for a hierarchical system of
governance. Optimising performance calls for a sympathetic treatment of
target groups. This is not meant to imply that their partial interests should
prevail but rather that it is reasonable to proceed in a way which makes
them adapt in a productive fashion to the new situation. The Community
tends to be a negotiating system, specifically a negotiating system with a
variable geometry because, depending on the issue at stake, different actors
have to be considered. It is not only member governments who negotiate;
various public and private actors are also part of the game.

Second, 'network governance' may be constructed as an ideal type useful for heuristic purposes. In drawing up a general picture of 'network
governance', four characteristic features stand out: the role of the state,
rules of behaviour, patterns of interaction and levels of political action. The

'state', in terms of the most relevant public actor within a political system, is no longer an actor in its own right. Its *role* has changed from authoritative allocation and regulation 'from above' to the role of mediator and activator.[31] Governing involves bringing together the relevant actors of society. Networking is a principal task and it is best accomplished when offering institutional frameworks which reduce transaction costs and give stability to self-regulatory agreements. The public administration is an actor which mainly organises the arena for political exchange and agreement.

Rules of behaviour and the prevailing decision-making style within a 'negotiating state' (Scharpf 1993) will differ from those prevalent in a hierarchical state or those in an anarchical 'self-help system'. Without suspending the assumption that actors are self-interested and rational, it is plausible to assume that the structure of their situation will have an effect. Actors are tied up in a stable negotiating system which puts a high premium on 'Community friendly' behaviour. Nevertheless, it is best compared to a 'mixed motive' constellation because parties involved have common as well as competing interests.[32] Joint problem-solving is usually linked to the distribution of benefits. The commitment to a collective good, therefore, is as much part of the game as is the pursuit of partial interests.

Distinct *patterns of interaction* evolve, too. Hierarchy and subordination give way to an interchange on a more equal footing. The once clear-cut borderlines between the private and the public spheres become blurred. Multiple overlapping negotiating arenas emerge. The 'state' is not a unitary actor but is divided into functionally differentiated sub-structures which are part of sector 'policy communities' and drawn into various 'issue networks'.[33]

The *level of political action* embraces higher levels of co-ordination and lower levels to include those who are affected by a policy and whose active support is needed for implementation. 'Joint problem-solving' will by necessity be functionally more specific. Any policy that is geared to the 'mobilisation of indigenous resources' and 'joint learning' has to be decentralised and carried out in smaller units at lower levels. 'Subsidiarity' is a core principle in network governance. The controversial discussion that followed its introduction into Community law highlights the ensuing difficulties. Conceding more autonomy to the 'local' level gives rise to provincialism and the exploitation of the general interest.

When types of governance meet

Let us assume that within the Community system a network type of governance is likely to emerge. What is the impact of EC governance on the established governance systems within the member states?

At first sight it is obvious that governance patterns across EU member states vary considerably.[34] A first simple, but plausible hypothesis is that the readiness with which national systems of governance might adapt will depend on the 'match' of systems and on parallel developments, whether in response to domestic or to international forces. Furthermore, in view of the well-known inertia of long-established and complex organisations it is more likely that innovations will succeed as 'extensions' to rather than a replacement for traditional patterns (Héritier *et al.* 1994). Last but not least, there is a good deal of evidence that 'Europeanisation of national governance is compatible with the maintenance of very distinct national institutional arrangements' (Goetz 1995: 93). Is path dependency telling the whole story then?

Matters are not that easy. There is first the question of the scope and range of the possible impact of European governance. The EC has by no means universal competence. Does it make sense to assume that governing patterns prevailing in only a few, but central economic policy areas, will spill over into the system as a whole? Or is it more likely that changes will be contained within specific policy sectors? Keeping in mind the fact that EC policies are highly sector specific, a 'meso-level' approach might be most promising. Looking at individual sectors would also take into account the fact that EC policies are at different stages of development, that is that their maturity differs from one issue area to another.

By examining the various policy areas, we will certainly get a more detailed picture. But knowing more about the variations in governance practices still does not tell us anything about what makes a system change. In order to follow in a systematic way how a particular mode of governance is transmitted from the European to the national level, three distinct avenues may be considered: imposition, involvement, and attraction.[35] *Imposition* is the one-way flow from the European to the national level, whereas involvement and attraction see the recipient playing a more active role. Being involved means being confronted with the European type of governance in practice. Experience may or may not change the appreciation of particular modes of governance and the readiness to adapt. The Community is offering new concepts of governing that will attract attention whenever demands are met and actors find it suitable to incorporate them into their own strategies. Because the EC is a political space open to all, it provides opportunities for various actors who are looking for outside support and encouragement. To just look for 'impact' would obscure the active and interactive dimension that supports the diffusion of modes of governance.

It is worth differentiating between three different ways of dissemination for yet another reason. Governance has an ideational dimension as well as an organisational one. And the impetus to change either one of them is passed on in a different way. The ideational dimension relates to shared concepts of what legitimate governance is about. It relates to belief systems about what is appropriate and exemplary in the ways problems are solved, how conflicts are mediated and how public-private relations are organised. Belief systems can hardly ever be 'imposed'. They may change because learning takes place or because the discourse organised around a new policy contributes to produce a new 'guiding concept'.[36] On the other hand, belief systems are certainly not immune to power politics. A different concept may become dominant due to a shift in the balance of power between competing advocacy coalitions. Imposition is more likely to occur when it comes to the more tangible parts of governance, that is the organisation of the political process. This relates to the admission of actors, the allocation of competencies, the fixing of formal rules and procedures and the definition of the boundaries of a policy.

Imposition is closely related to EC sector policies. It takes place whenever a European policy regime is established which links the objectives that have been agreed to a particular set of regulatory procedures and a distinct group of actors to be included in that policy domain. The provisions for implementing the EC's regional policies are a good example of how a programme has been linked to a procedural logic. 'Partnership' is the formula which stipulates taking sub-national as well as social actors on board in the framing and implementing of structural fund projects. Programmes, however, are not the most convincing case for imposition. They are of limited scope and apply only to those who are eligible and willing to participate and accept the strings attached. Regulatory policies, on the other hand, leave no room for escape. They have binding force although they leave some latitude for national variations when formulated as directives. But even regulatory policies are not a clear-cut case for imposition. By following the history of a directive, it becomes quite obvious that changes in governance are hardly ever imposed. Adaptation is a process which develops along with the protracted negotiations of a policy. Pre-emptive moves are more likely to occur than subordination. Adaptive moves occur before and not after a directive has been issued.[37] Subordination to legal enforcement once a policy has been established tends to be the exception, and indicates opposition locked into a particular (national) context.[38]

Negotiation entails the exchange of information, defending preferred policy options on grounds of optimising regulatory problems, etc. This is an ideal situation in which to initiate learning processes or to ease adaptive behaviour. In the EC context, *involvement* may be considered to be the most effective way of bringing about change in governance. 'Involvement' in the EC context is not a private affair in terms of inviting individuals with particular properties to become members of a network.[39] Networks embrace organisations, and operating a network means managing inter-organisational co-ordination. Due to the complexities of inter-organisational systems, particular strategies have been developed. Although no 'unequivocal design norms' (Alexander, E.R. 1995: 325) may exist, management strategies may be transferred into a different context. With the multiplica-

28

tion of autonomous actors at the national level, structural similarities spread and invite transfer behaviour. Changes of whatever sort come about in an incremental and mainly bottom-up process of adaptation. They involve a multitude of actors seeking direction under the pressure of rapidly changing conditions brought about by Europeanisation and globalisation simultaneously. Being involved in the formulation and implementation of European policies and in the concertation of transnational interests, they become socialised to new practices. Being involved implies being part of an institutionalised learning process. Experience will teach the deficiencies and/or the attractiveness of a particular mode of governance.

Attraction sounds like the least active strategy: the Community sets an example in best practices of governing and elaborates more or less convincing governing concepts. It would be overselling the case to expect this kind of supply to trigger change. A constructivist approach helps to conceptualise how ideas and political practice spread (Gottweis 1998, Kohler-Koch and Edler 1998). The formulation of European policies enmeshes national and Community actors in a complex discursive process. It incorporates a shared understanding of the basic rationale of the aims and purpose of European political regulation. This has a structural dimension. EC policies are usually developed by extending existing Community competence. In this way, new policies are functionally closely related to established ones, which explains why they are so much in line with established philosophies. What looks like a well-designed strategy and proof of the dedication and entrepreneurial capabilities of the Commission is, in fact, built into the system. Extending the scope of competence from one field to another meets less opposition when it is done according to the logic of supplementing rather than inventing a new policy, and when it is in line with tried and tested principles and regulatory patterns. In 'post-structuralist' language, developing governance systems is a 'contested process of introducing organisation and order into an unstable discursive environment' (Gottweis, this volume: 63). Such 'processes of introduction' tend:

> to incorporate images, representations and value systems which refer to a larger context of legitimate symbols, statements and norms. Such representations link a particular policy to other fields of policy-making and to domains of social and cultural interaction.
> . . . The rationale behind a policy and political programme needs to be situated within a larger framework of meaning.
>
> (Gottweis, this volume: 64)

Discursive affinities do not only spread when actors are physically involved in Community interaction. The drafting of a new Community directive is bound to stimulate discussions which, on the one hand, are nested in the national context and, on the other, relate to a transnational discourse. The Community institutions allow the Commission to take the lead and endow it with the capacity to:

> organis[e] differences, [to] creat[e] links between different discourses which initially seemed to be hermetically closed off from one another, and thereby [to] position itself and other actors in the policy-making process in a way which would be generally acknowledged as fair and appropriate.
>
> (Gottweis, this volume: 68)

Negotiating Community policies is always a competition about what Gramsci called 'hegemonic concepts', defining legitimate objectives and appropriate ways and means of sector governance. Supplying a persuasive concept is one side of the picture. The other is the gate-keeping powers of those who want to control the supply and demand of concepts. In an open society, it is difficult to control public discourse. The best way to do so is to limit the scope of the policy under discussion. Control is exerted by manipulating the arena in which concepts will be taken up for discussion. By defining the policy issue in a particular way, the policy arena will be open or closed to particular kinds of actors.[40] It is the 'core executives' which police the boundaries of an issue area.[41] In so doing, they determine which actors may legitimately claim to be affected and take part in the discussion. It is this kind of 'border politics' which opens or closes the gates to the spread of conceptual ideas.

Establishing the framework for empirical research

In order to provide an answer to the question of whether the European Community is bound to develop a network type of governance and transpose it into the governing systems of its member states, an analytical framework is needed that will grasp the complexity of an ongoing process of change. For this very reason, this chapter has introduced a typology of systems of governance which allows us to differentiate between modes of governing, and provides us with a basic understanding of the underlying logic of the diverging types of governance. It has sketched out the most characteristic features of governing in networks because it has been argued that it is plausible to assume that the purpose and institutional architecture of the European Community may be best suited to a network type of governance. In addition, this chapter gives a systematic account of different ways of disseminating governing patterns among European and national political spaces. There are good reasons to believe that such a spread will occur under the pressure of shifting perceptions of legitimacy both within the European and member state polities. The deficiencies of parliamentary democracy raise the value of functional representation and expert participation in politics. And it will take place within the realm of individual policies, which is why most of the following chapters are dedicated either to scrutinising a single policy field or to comparative policy analysis.

The emergence of a particular type of governance will certainly be shaped by the constitutional framework of the EU and its members. Limits are imposed by nested contexts. Changes in sector governance must take account of governing patterns in adjacent sectors. Contingencies may spur on or retard the dissemination of new types of governance. Nevertheless, it is not simply a case of 'historic institutionalism at work'. Adaptation occurs in the shadow of the market. Both the single European market and globalisation are reshaping the context in which actors formulate their preferences and strike bargains. Shifts in power and preferences may make different modes of governance more attractive. Governance change, after all, involves actor strategies taking into account the operational costs of change and the legitimacy of a regulatory logic as compared to established rules and procedures. The shadow of the market can be felt in another way. Faced with the inherent complexity of a network system of governance, conceding even more allocative powers to the governing mechanism of the market may become attractive.

When considering actor strategies, power in terms of a policy-specific capacity to act should not be underrated. The construction of the European Community may not change patterns of traditional interest mediation, simply because actors at national level lack the capacity for transnational interest representation. Weak actors may be condemned to provinciality because they do not command the necessary resources to become a European player in the EC polity. Enlarging the policy space discriminates against actors who are affected but incapable of becoming a partner in the new game. Intergovernmentalism, that is strengthening the components of the system, may be a very attractive alternative for them. The Commission, on the other hand, has a vested interest in upgrading the unitary character of the system and drawing in many different types of actors. Defining the realm of the Community is shaping the architecture of the polity and will consolidate particular patterns of governing. Though institution building touches on the prerogatives of member state governments many other actors take part in it. However, whenever actors disagree, it becomes quite obvious who the 'core executives' are. The national governments are the final arbiters. 'Border politics' delineates the policy field and, in so doing, opens or closes the arena to economic, social or other forces. As a result, decision-making may remain a strictly intergovernmental affair, controlled by top executives. Monetary affairs, foreign and security policy and co-operation in criminal law are not examples of network governance. Public and private actors cannot move easily between levels of decision-making and become engaged in transnational coalition-building. Here again it must be remembered that 'European governance' is not an all-embracing stable pattern, but varies over time and across policy areas.

Two questions lie beyond the scope of this book. First, despite a careful selection of policy areas and a large number of cases, more comparative research would be needed to answer the question of whether or not the sector pictures add up to a coherent pattern of European governance. Particular attention will have to be paid to variations between policy types, namely regulatory and distributive policies as compared to redistributive policies. Therefore, we hope that this volume will contribute to a scholarly debate which will attract others to engage in a systematic treatment of this issue.

Second, normative questions about the democratic quality of network governance have not been addressed. This chapter has argued that governing strategies are influenced by the awareness of elites that the democratic quality of the EC does not live up to public expectation. The 'democratic deficit' may be a driving force for deliberate changes in patterns of governance. It is quite another question, however, whether the instruments chosen will increase responsive and responsible policy-making. There is no easy yardstick by which to evaluate the democratic quality of a penetrated system of governance such as the European Community, which is operated in a network type of governance. The conventional wisdom is that the yardstick of parliamentary control will not suffice to evaluate the democratic character of the European system. All the categories so often applied to the European Community, such as transparency, accountability, etc., are closely linked to the nation-state model of representative democracy. It is open to debate whether, even in this context, they are applicable or not. Referring to the British system, Rhodes has argued that:

> to call one institution to account for how it has operated is to disregard key features of the differentiated polity. Policy is the responsibility of no one institution but emerges from the interaction of several. Criticizing the processes of one institution is to disregard the major process, inter-organizational conflict and bargaining.
>
> (Rhodes 1988: 404–5)

The European Community is certainly a highly differentiated polity. It is difficult to predict the nature of a 'postnational democracy' (Curtin 1997) and the normative categories which would fit it. Consequently, we have been reluctant to extend our argument beyond the question of the evolution and transformation of governance.

Notes

I am grateful for stimulating comments by Theodor Barth, Luigi Graziano and Josef Melchior.

1 In this contribution, the term 'governance' is not synonymous with a new process of governing, as suggested by Rhodes (1997: 15), but embraces all different modes of governing patterns.
2 The analysis is limited to the supranational pillar of the EU, i.e. the EC, based on the European Community Treaty. We did not test whether it applies to the Common Foreign and Security Policy or to EU Co-operation in Justice and Home Affairs.
3 This refers to an understanding of 'penetration' as developed by Rosenau (1969), i.e. the right of external powers legitimately to take part in authoritative decisions.
4 See in particular Fritz Scharpf's work; for the general argument, see Scharpf (1997).
5 In the interests of brevity, I do not differentiate here between two distinct lines of debate which hardly ever meet in actual research. First there is the discussion about the relative importance of member states versus Community agents, and thus the normative question about preserving member state autonomy versus the pursuit of common European interests. The notion of 'two-level games' has introduced some new arguments into the intergovernmental debate (see Wolf, in this volume), while the neo-institutionalist approach has highlighted conditions for 'Community friendly' negotiating strategies and the empowerment of Community agents. The second line of debate concerns research which looks into the shift between private and public actors and the in-built bias in favour of particular groups of organised interests. The institutional properties of the EC system are conceptualised as constituting a particular 'logic of influence' which invites private actors to enter the game and privileges some actors over others.
6 This topic has been highlighted as one of the central research questions to be dealt with in the research programme sponsored by the German Science Foundation (see Kohler-Koch and Jachtenfuchs 1996) and has been developed in particular by Benz 1998.
7 This is a deplorable state of the art because evaluating the democratic deficit should take into account both the input and the output side of a political system.
8 This argument refers to the neo-institutionalist approach as put forward by James March and Johan P. Olsen; see in particular March and Olsen (1994). For a more elaborate account of the argument presented here see Kohler-Koch (1996).
9 'The early years' refers to the period up to the completion of the customs union and the free market.
10 'Negative integration' is the removal of trade barriers to allow market forces to penetrate markets as compared to 'positive integration', i.e. regulatory intervention to enforce a particular kind of integration (Tinbergen 1965).
11 There is a broad consensus in the scientific community that a parliamentarisation of the EC system will not improve the democratic quality of the system. The argument is best presented by Kielmansegg (1996) and Grimm (1995).
12 This is a quote from the Turin (1996) declaration of the European Council meeting.
13 For example, the Standing Committee on Employment; in these committees both sides of industry are represented, whereas in other committees – whether Commission or Council committees – functional interests are only invited at the discretion of the Community institution in charge.

14 ECOSOC, in particular, and with it the idea of institutionalised functional representation lost standing, and has been crowded out by interest group lobbying. In recent years, however, the idea has gained new ground in politics (most obviously in the EC-sponsored 'social dialogue'), and in political science, with the debate about 'post-parliamentarian democracy' (Richardson and Jordan 1979).

15 The political importance of non-majoritarian institutions has increased in the wake of the creation of the single market, one telling example being the committees on standardisation; the scholarly debate has been illuminated in particular by the contributions of Majone (1996). For a comparative evaluation of how these three different elements may or may not improve the EC's democratic quality, see Kohler-Koch (1998a).

16 'Staatenverbund' has been coined by the German Constitutional Court in its decision on the Treaty of Maastricht.

17 Lijphart wrote on comparative government, not on international relations. Nonetheless, he borrowed the term from Althusius and when Althusius wrote about 'consociatio' he applied the concept to a federation of states. Lijphart himself wrote that the consociational model 'stands between the unitary British model and the model of international diplomacy' (Lijphart 1977: 43).

18 Lehmbruch only referred to interactions of organisations and public bureaucracies since he was interested in interest inter-mediation.

19 In the EC, with its segmented system of policy-making, the notion of 'task contingency' which has been elaborated in research into industrial organisations is particularly relevant.

20 It is somewhat surprising that five decades of discourse on governing the European Community has hardly changed the views of national elites on the nature and most appropriate way of governing the emerging European polity. National differences are more pronounced than partisan ideological inclinations. This evidence has been produced by a comparative research project just concluded at Mannheim (Jachtenfuchs 1999).

21 'Minimum winning coalitions' are based on the assumption that any party which wants to govern will only take as many coalition partners on board as are absolutely necessary to assure a majority decision because, with each new partner, new demands have to be taken into consideration.

22 I am not referring to any concept of 'primordial' communities which rests on inalienable properties of the members but rather to concepts of 'communities of will'.

23 'Voice' and 'exit' when put into quotation marks refer to the concept of Hirschman (1970).

24 'Upgrading of common interests' has been a central topic in neo-functionalist writings to catch the kind of positive-sum solutions which are arrived at through co-operation without aiming at a preconceived 'common good'.

25 When referring to empirical cases, it should be remembered, first, that reference is made to political systems as they developed in a specific period of time and, second, that the description aims to highlight the characteristic features distinguishing one system from the others.

26 Both models have already been dealt with in depth by Lehmbruch (1967) and Lijphart (1977).

27 Many would argue that the 'British' or 'Westminster' model bears little resemblance to today's reality. Rhodes (1997) argues that there has been 'a shift from the Westminster model to the differentiated polity' (24), i.e. '[i]t replaces strong cabinet government, parliamentary sovereignty, HM's loyal opposition and ministerial responsibility with interdependence, a segmented executive,

policy networks, governance and hollowing out' (ibid.: 7). According to him: 'the unitary state is a multiform maze of interdependencies' (ibid.: 16), best characterised as 'the differentiated polity' (ibid.: 7).

28 Most obviously expressed in its four linguistic communities.

29 It should be recalled that EC institutions were deliberately designed to strengthen the 'common interest', not just to reduce 'transaction costs'.

30 The ideas which follow have already been developed in Kohler-Koch 1996: 369–72; they are summarised here because they were a point of reference in the group's discussion.

31 This does not imply that government is just another group among the multitude of pressure groups nor that, from a methodological point of view, the concept of 'group actor' has not been applied to government before; see Richardson and Jordan (1979: 17).

32 For a thorough treatment of the general argument, see Scharpf (1997).

33 The terminology follows Marsh and Rhodes 1992.

34 See Vivian Schmidt's contribution in this volume.

35 For a more detailed account, see Kohler-Koch (1998b: 21–3).

36 That this is not the same as 'learning' is convincingly argued in the contribution by Gottweis to this volume.

37 See the contributions by Aspinwall, Eising and Lovecy in this volume.

38 For a long time, German vine-growers could be taken as a typical example: Locked in a position of structural minority they had no chance of pushing their interest at the European level whereas at the national and, in particular, the local level they could expect indulgence through exemptions. This is why for a long time they never engaged in pro-active strategies.

39 Even when a particular kind of expert knowledge is needed, the expert invited to a committee is the one who is supposed to represent a scientific community.

40 The recent Intergovernmental Conference gives a good example of agenda management in order to keep arenas separate. Monetary issues were deliberately kept off the agenda to avoid any attempts of mingling issues.

41 Dyson gives in his contribution a telling example of how a policy issue has been kept under the control of core executives. For the concept of 'core executives', see Dunleavy and Rhodes (1990).

Part II

THE TRANSFORMATION OF EUROPEAN GOVERNANCE

Variations on a theme

3

TRANSFORMATION IN EUROPEAN ENVIRONMENTAL GOVERNANCE

Andrea Lenschow

Introduction

With 'the transformation of governance' this volume is returning to a theme that has preoccupied scholars of the European Community since the early days of its existence. Early analyses focused on the shifting power relations between different levels of government and in public-private relations as the primary dimension of governance (the leading works being Haas 1958 and Hoffmann 1966). In the light of an increasingly acute awareness of, on the one hand, the complexities of the process, interactive structures and the institutional design in Europe, and, on the other, a growing concern with the *problem-solving capacity* of national and supranational governing authorities confronted with the complex, diverse and dynamic nature of 'modern' policy problems (Kooiman 1993b), recent studies of European governance have begun to examine not only the distribution of competencies but also modes or practices of governance (Jachtenfuchs and Kohler-Koch 1995; Kohler-Koch 1996).

The present chapter investigates the emergence and diffusion patterns of new governance structures and practices with respect to one specific 'modern' policy area, namely environmental policy. European environmental policy represents a regulatory and sector-transgressing policy field. Its complex nature and extensive scope, with implications for the appropriate role and internal organisation of the state and its governing style, place environmental policy in the centre of the present re-evaluation of governance models (see the so-called 'Molitor report' for an evaluation of the structure and mode of environmental policy in terms of its problem-solving capacity (Commission 1995a)). The recognition of a considerable implementation gap has served to further highlight the limits to governability in the relationship between the EC and the national (implementing) level, across policy sectors due to failing policy co-ordination and integration, and over time by allowing practices unsustainable in the long term.

Reflecting upon the widened scope of the governance debate, the concept is defined here as consisting of two dimensions:

1   *Structural elements* with reference to *organisational features* (vertical and horizontal distribution of responsibilities) and *state-society relations* or forms of interest intermediation (authoritarian role of the state versus corporatism versus competitive pluralism versus networks/partnership). This dimension encapsulates the 'traditional' power-related understanding of governance, whereas the following category responds to the new emphasis on governing practice.
2   *Regulatory style:* following van Waarden (1995), I distinguish between three sub-dimensions, namely the routine *intervention mode* (hierarchical/interventionist versus co-operative), *routine procedures* (legalistic versus flexible/pragmatic, adversarial versus consensual); and *routinely created policy networks* (exclusive versus inclusive, formal versus informal).

A particular choice of *policy instruments* is related to the respective regulatory structure and style and will be included in the analysis as an indicator of the respective mode of governance. In brief, a shift away from command-and-control (top-down) policy instruments towards market-oriented, self-regulatory and communicative 'learning' tools tends to correspond with more open governing structures (networks, partnerships) and the adoption of a facilitating, co-operative and consensual rather than imposing mode of governance.

The following section situates the debate on European environmental governance in the ongoing general as well as policy-specific (environmental) global discourse on governance. The purpose of this discussion is merely to elaborate on the features of the ideal-typical 'new' mode of governance in the environmental area. Although it is my assumption that European governance is embedded and responsive to global pressures as well as a global exchange of ideas, the analytical focus of this chapter is limited to, first, the extent to which such a new mode is emerging with respect to EC structures and policies, and, second, the degree and mechanisms of its diffusion in the member states.

The global discursive context of the transformation of European environmental governance

European considerations regarding the transformation of environmental governance take place in the context of a general and a policy-specific governance debate. These, I suggest, are distinct in the specificity of the observed problem-solving deficiency, but overlap in the types of governance structures and practices that are being identified as governance solutions, namely the shift from hierarchical to inclusive network structures and towards a co-operative, consensual and facilitating governing or regulatory style.

To elaborate briefly on the two concurrent debates, the issue of general governance focuses on the often cited 'crisis of the state' and loss of problem-solving capacity of central governments (see Wolf, in this volume). The perception of crisis goes hand in hand with a broader, more systemic understanding of the nature of today's policy problems and has led to several 'global responses' to these new concerns, ranging from the 'pooling of responsibilities' in supranational and international fora, or attempts to change the forms of governmental 'management' and state-society relations (see Scharpf 1988, Mayntz 1993). The so-called steering debate (*Steuerungsdebatte*) – reinforced by the concurrent 'neo-liberal' economic debate – has triggered plans for institutional reforms, aimed at slimming and unburdening the central state, accompanied by changes in governing practices and a choice of policy instruments, for example, moves toward deregulation, market liberalisation or 'new public management' (Hood 1995, Wright 1994b).

The evolution of European environmental governance is influenced equally by a global debate on the content and structure of environmental policy (WCED 1987, UNCED 1992). This debate, while focusing on the interpretation of the political, socio-economic and scientific reality, has structural – that is, governance – implications in its own right which currently resonate in EC and member state programmatic documents (e.g. the Commission's Fifth Environmental Action Programme (Commission 1993a) and the Dutch National Environmental Policy Programme). The emerging recognition of the complexity of the policy *problématique* is implied in a new, systemic understanding of the role of environmental protection in economic development. Governance failures are identified along two dimensions, one touching on intra-state and the other on state-society relations, with implications for governance structure, style and instruments.

First, fragmented policy-making structures have led to 'insulated' environmental and economic governing activities, despite the inherently horizontal nature of the environmental policy field. This has prevented effective policy co-ordination leading to optimal policy outcomes across policy fields (i.e. the minimisation of costs inflicted by one policy on the other) and even the exploitation of complementary policy objectives (rooted in the realisation that environmental protection and economic development are mutually dependent on one another in the long term).

Second, the traditional choice of a legalistic, hierarchical policy style with corresponding top-down regulatory policy instruments, and the failure to systematically include a wide spectrum of societal actors in policy formulation and implementation, was based on the assumption of a smooth transposition of policy objectives into policy practice through legal imposition. Implementation failures have highlighted the fact that environmental protection ultimately depends on changes in attitude and hence the behaviour of every member of society. Thus the limited problem-solving capability of authoritative regulation (and technological solutions) suggests a more co-operative, consensual and inclusive policy style aimed at gaining the acceptance of business actors and ordinary citizens concerning environmental policy objectives and their responsibility for the collective (economic *and* environmental) good. The perception that successful policy depends on economic and private actors 'internalising' their environmental responsibility has further consequences for the choice of policy instruments, implying a more limited role for top-down regulatory instruments and a more prominent role for market-oriented, self-regulatory as well as informational and communicative instruments.

It is clear that the seemingly environment-specific concerns about governance structures and style resonate with the above-mentioned general issues concerning the overall capacity loss of the state. We detect 'conceptual borrowing' across the general and policy-specific debates. The steering debate and the environmental governance debate have led to similar calls for a shift from reactive and narrowly conceived policy-making to problem-solving (Scharpf 1988), the replacement of hierarchical state-society relations with network structures formed by a negotiating (Mayntz 1993) and jointly learning (Kohler-Koch 1995) set of actors, and a facilitating and mediating state. The use of communicative and informational policy instruments corresponds with 'modern steering'; whether market-oriented and self-regulatory instruments may equally represent an attempt at 'modern steering' by conferring greater responsibility for the collective good on societal actors depends on the larger context in which these instruments are embedded (though they may reflect ideas derived from the economic debate on neo-liberalism as well).[1]

Having elaborated on the interplay between general and environment-specific governance in the context of the ongoing global debates, we now turn to the actual emergence of 'new' modes of governance in European environmental politics. The global debates just discussed move 'backstage' in the following analysis and the focus shifts first, to a 'stocktaking' of the mode of European environmental governance, in contrast to the features of 'new' governance identified above, and then, to the diffusion of 'new' governance structures and style in the EC member states. The question is posed to what extent and under what conditions the EC example is followed in the member states (keeping in mind that each level will have been influenced by global developments as well as playing a role in shaping the global and European processes). A first attempt will be made to trace the EC impact on national transformation processes as well as policy performance. Figure 3.1 serves to highlight the specific focus of this analysis (thick arrows) within a complex international institutional and ideational context.

In the analysis of the top-down impact of EC governance structures and practices on national patterns, we can formulate the null-hypothesis that no domestic transformation occurs. In contrast, if we detect a convergence towards a new mode of governance on the supranational and the national level, we can think of this process in terms of European push or member state receptiveness to new influences.[2] In other words, the transformation process can be hypothesised as the result of the interplay of *transformation pressure* (necessary condition), on the one hand, and *receptiveness* (sufficient condition), on the other.

The level of European push depends first and foremost on the institutionalisation and internal consistency of the European example, encompassing a clear perception of the policy problem and a corresponding model for governance structures and practices deemed capable of

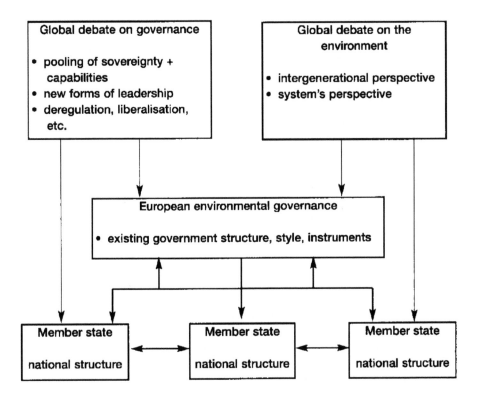

Figure 3.1 The context of the transformation of environmental governance

problem-solving. Receptiveness, I argue, depends on ideational and institutional factors. I have suggested above that new structures and modes of governance are rooted in a new awareness of insufficient problem-solving capacity, which in turn arose from a new problem definition (on a general level the complexity, dynamic and diversity of 'modern' policy issues; in the case of the environment, its inter-sectoral, inter-generational and societal dimension). The 'new' problem definition may have been more or less adopted in the member states, affecting its drive to engage in governance reforms (for a similar reasoning see Haas 1990 and Jachtenfuchs 1996a). The move from ideational to governance transformation is further influenced by institutional resistance to change. In DiMaggio and Powell's words 'institutional models are quite unlikely to be imported wholeclothed into systems that are very different from the one in which they originate' (DiMaggio and Powell 1991: 29); hence we expect 'proposals' for new modes of governance in the European or global arena to be re-interpreted in the given national context. In other words, member state receptiveness also depends on the gap between 'new' (European) and already existing domestic patterns as well as the density, extension and stability of the latter.

A new mode of governance in EC environmental policy-making

The old mode of governance: fragmentation and legalism

On the EC level there is evidence that the wider and more systemic environmental problem perceptions formulated in global environmental fora are taking root. The associated new structures, style and instruments of governance are equally gaining currency on the Brussels level of European environmental policy-making. This section shows that currently they *supplement* rather than replace traditional governance structures. In other words, Europe is sending 'mixed signals': a mediating factor with respect to the transformation pressure created for the member states.

Environmental policy in the EC began as an opportunistic policy in the 1960s, exploiting policy niches 'unclaimed' in the established policy areas on the European level and relatively non-controversial or non-politicised among member states. In Hildebrand's words, this early European environmental policy, which then lacked a formal legitimation in the EC Treaty, was 'incidental to the overriding economic objectives' (Hildebrand 1993: 13) although in the 1970s and early 1980s it became increasingly 'responsive' to a greening public opinion (spurred on by concrete environmental disasters) and the realisation of the often transnational effects of pollution (ibid.: 20–8).

Even though several policy principles were proclaimed in the first European Environmental Action Programmes, such as the principles of prevention, polluter pays and policy integration, in reality these principles were compromised and no distinct policy philosophy or general problem perception supported by a coherent governance structure emerged on the European level. Nevertheless, especially in contrast to the new mode of governance sketched above, several general features of early EC environmental policy can be detected.

First, the nature of the environment-specific problem-solving *problématique* remained elusive, hindering the emergence of coherent governance structures. The EC's *ad hoc* creation of environmental policy, resulting in a policy patchwork rather than an integrated system, played an important role in this respect. In part due to the very restrictive opportunity structure for systemic environmental policy-making (Knill and Héritier 1996; Lenschow 1996) environmental policy emerged in those 'niches' which were non-controversial among member states or had escaped political attention. This was reinforced by the EC's legal structures which did not provide an explicit legal basis for environmental policy. Thus, environmental measures were placed primarily in the context of the internal market and evaluated according to their costs (re-regulating liberalised market processes) and benefits (through the harmonisation of standards) for the market.

Second, the largely vertical structure of Community institutions resulting in limited interaction between horizontal (e.g. the environment) and sectoral policy fields intensified the patchwork character of the set of ideas guiding EC environmental policy (Lenschow 1996). The European policy level was perceived as the top layer in the policy-making chain. The formal (legal transposition) rather than practical implementation of EC legislation was the primary concern of EC-level 'guardians' in the Commission; as a result, co-ordination with the implementing national or regional level was low. Furthermore, the ad hoc style in policy 'appropriation' hindered a systematic division and co-ordination of responsibilities along vertical and horizontal lines. In terms of state-society relations, a clear structure of interest intermediation on the European level has not been detected, its characteristics fluctuating between corporatist and pluralist patterns.

Third, on the basis of this formal structure in environmental policy-making, an interventionist and legalistic policy style developed. Access for societal actors tended to be informal and favoured economic interests; trilateral or multi-lateral partnerships constituted an exception to this rule. The network structures that emerged around the Commission operated merely in the early policy formulation phase, and therefore performed as an instrumental device for the Commission. They were short-term in their impact, rather than elements of a new mode of governance based on co-operative partnerships. Nevertheless, the process of policy formulation was relatively consensual in order to reduce the level of conflict in the subsequent competitive decision-making phase.

Fourth, corresponding to this interventionist and legalistic style, EC social regulations are traditionally *command-and-control measures,* establishing material or procedural standards to be followed in the member states. To this day the EC has adopted more than 200 binding pieces of environmental legislation (Haigh 1990).

The emergence of a network mode of governance in the EC?

Since the mid 1980s, the EC has slowly departed from this traditional pattern of governance in the environmental policy field. Past implementation problems had alerted policy makers to the insufficient problem-solving capacity of the system and triggered a debate on policy and institutional reform. On the basis of the globally emerging new understanding of environmental protection as constituting the basis for economic development, the governance problem became identified as one of policy integration and learning. Accordingly, the Treaty on European Union (TEU) lays down that 'environmental protection requirements must be integrated into the definition and implementation of other Community policies' (TEU, Art. 130r,2), strengthening the formulation chosen in the SEA. Policy integration as a structural requirement for realising the complementary nature of economic and environmental policy goals represents the central message in the latest EC Environmental Action Programme (Commission 1993a) and features in Commission programmatic publications, such as its White Paper on Growth, Competitiveness, Employment (Commission 1994a) or its Communication on Trade and Environment (Commission 1996a).

Institutional and procedural innovations by the Commission reveal its attempt to adjust governance structures to the new problem perception. To this end, horizontal policy boundaries have been loosened and networks created to connect public authorities and society. These networks reach beyond the existing policy-specific networks and focus beyond the immediate and narrow policy formulation stage. To be specific, three dialogue groups have been established: a consultative forum, including representatives of regional and local authorities (four members), consumer and environmental organisations (five), trade unions (two), industry (nine), agriculture and agri-food organisations (two) and independent personalities (nine), to provide a general sounding-board on the general direction of EC environmental policy and its relation to economic development; an implementation network, made up of Commission officials and representatives of relevant national authorities involved in the implementation of EC policy; and a policy review group, composed of the environmental Directors General in the member states and Commission officials, aimed at developing a mutual, cross-national understanding and the exchange of views and information on environmental policy and specific measures.

The Commission too, indicating an emerging belief in policy integration and the problems inherent in organisational fragmentation and insulation, has begun to engage in internal administrative and procedural reforms as well. In an internal communication (Commission 1993b) the Commission announced its readiness to:

- clarify 'the mechanisms for internal consultation, in particular to stress that the services responsible for environmental policies in the Commission are consulted at the early stages of definition of Community policy and action';
- practice environmental impact assessments (EIA) of its own actions;
- strengthen its internal mechanisms by: preparing an annual integration report based on a self-evaluation by all DGs of their performance; designating in each DG a senior official with responsibility for ensuring that policy and legislative proposals prepared in that DG take account of the environment; and establishing a special unit in DG XI with the task of co-ordinating and monitoring the implementation of the fifth EAP;
- communicate its integration efforts through the annual work programme and the annual report and prepare a code of conduct for its own practices.

The Commission as a whole has also announced a number of measures designed to enhance the transparency of its work. The package includes the earlier publication of the Commission's annual work plan, allowing for more effective discussion with the other institutions and potential revisions, more structured procedures and broader consultation with affected interests and a code of conduct on access to information supported by technological innovation (Peterson 1995).

The implications for governance of these internal changes, once completed, are twofold. First, they are intended to improve the legitimacy and accountability of the Commission in the area of environmental policy through the adoption of self-regulating measures and a higher level of transparency, in the absence of democratic controls. Second, in order to facilitate systemic/sustainable policy-making, they constitute an attempt to break down boundaries between policy areas, so prevalent at EC level, and broaden as well as deepen communication channels between previously insulated policy makers.

Other boundary-breaking initiatives introduced by the Commission involve links with civil society. DG XI, in particular, has stepped up its efforts in this area, developing its own support network beneath the public authorities in the member states but also enabling societal actors to play a more equal role in policy-making at domestic and EC level. In addition to financially supporting the operation of several Europe-wide environmental organisations, a process common in other policy areas, the Commission engages in regular – increasingly high-level – contacts with them. 'New' funding goes to specific NGO policy projects that are aimed at developing and mobilising an environmentally concerned element in civil society within the member states as well as outside EC territory (e.g. in Eastern Europe). Through financial support, consultation services and the facilitation of cross-national exchanges of information and cooperation, the Commission has also been instrumental in the setting up of, for instance, the 'European Partners for the Environment' (providing a platform for industry and NGOs to meet and discuss ways of achieving sustainable development) and the 'Car Free Cities Club,' thereby facilitating the development of a mutual understanding among segments of society and, in the long run, attitude change.

Similarly, the process of challenging the traditionally legalistic, command-and-control approach to environmental policy-making is visible in the beginning of a shift in the choice of policy instruments. They are aimed at improving the amount and quality of information (data collection, research), the consideration of spatial and temporal environmental impact (spatial planning, environmental impact assessments, integrated pollution control), integrating policy objectives by 'getting the price right' (economic analysis and instruments), and changing producers' and consumers' attitudes and hence behaviour (education, training, information, incentives). The new European Environmental Agency plays a central role in supporting and co-ordinating these efforts. In general, these new instruments and institutional innovations will perform the function of facilitating problem recognition and resolution, rather than of imposing a diagnosis and prescriptions from above. The emphasis on information collection and provision, research and education help the creation of equal partnerships in policy-making, joint learning but also mutual control. The plurality of actors associated with the different instruments will result in a new complexity in territorial and public-private terms, counteracting old hierarchical chains of command.

Despite the impression of a significant transformation of governance in the EC, it must be emphasised that the innovations just described are taking place as 'extensions' to, rather than replacements for, traditional structures, styles and instruments. The integrative structures continue to be weak and often ineffectual, due to the persistence of horizontal policy divides; similarly, the new formal networks created after the adoption of the 5th EAP have not yet emerged as main contributors in the policy-making process (Commission 1995b, Favoino 1997, Lenschow 1996). On the other hand, many issue-specific policy networks are growing and beginning to play an important role in the Commission's work as well as national policy-making practices (Interviews Bundesministerium für Umwelt, Naturschutz und Reaktorsicherheit (BMU) March 1997). Command-and-control legislation by far outnumbers the existence of new policy instruments.[3]

As regards the institutionalisation of new governance structures at EC level, it is revealing to briefly examine the position of the European Court of Justice (ECJ) with regard to the new problem perception and the associated governance structures.[4] The ECJ has been instrumental in legitimising EC environmental policy-making, but has not succeeded in clarifying the connection between environmental and economic objectives (Koppen 1992) and, on this shaky ground, considers environmental issues on a case-by-case basis. In this way, the ECJ has contributed to the perpetuation of fragmented governance structures, an adversarial rather than consensual patterns of conflict resolution and exclusive network structures. For instance, by limiting the right of environmental organisations to legally pursue non-compliance with EC environmental law (admissibility to the Court is premised on a violation of individual rights), and thereby resisting a broad definition of 'access to justice', the ECJ has prevented the establishment of more open governance structures and practices.

In conclusion, while a shift in the policy discourse is quite apparent, especially within the Commission, neither the impact of organisational and procedural innovations, nor the shift towards new policy instruments, nor the 'constitutional' status of new governance elements are unambiguous. Rather, the present status of EC environmental policy should be characterised as a mix of old and new policy philosophies, structures, styles and instruments. To the extent that a trend towards new practices can be observed, such a trend is currently most prevalent in DG XI and the Environment Committee in the European Parliament. From the analytical perspective of this chapter, the necessary condition for a transformation of governance in the member states – EC push – is not clearly satisfied, even though a trend can be identified.

The European Community and the governance of the environment in the member states

It can therefore be concluded, based on the foregoing discussion of the governance pattern at EC level, that the overall pressure for transformation is only moderate. What has been a mix of governance features from the start has now become even more mixed through the addition of new elements. It is nevertheless worth analysing the diffusion of these new elements.

To this end, this section examines experiences in Germany, the Netherlands, Spain and the UK. They represent a wide spectrum of national governance traditions in general, and specifically with respect to environmental policy (Badie and Birnbaum 1983, Dyson 1980 and 1992, Knill 1995, van Waarden 1995), hence we can expect to gain some insight into the patterns of national responses to EC transformation pressure.

Before turning to the individual transformation processes, there is general evidence that member states have adopted the EC rhetoric of a new problem definition regarding a new system of environmental governance. Also, in structural terms they participate in and have imitated some of the organisational innovations visible at EC level. According to the recent progress report of the fifth Environmental Action Programme, *all* member states have followed the Commission in creating organisational arrangements for policy integration, ranging from environmental units in other ministries and inter-ministerial committees (e.g. Germany, the Netherlands and the UK) to sectoral conferences (Spain). The actual impact of these organisational adaptations to date appears weak (Commission 1995b: 104), probably because they constitute institutional extensions rather than indicate a deep institutional transformation – a pattern repeated with respect to societal structures and matters of policy style and instruments.

The Netherlands

The Dutch National Environmental Policy Plan (NEPP), published in 1989, has many parallels with the fifth European Environmental Action Programme. They share a policy philosophy (problem definition) and problem-solving approach, and differ mainly in terms of emphasis and degree. For instance, the Netherlands emphasises the need for 'internalisation' over that of 'integration'; hence the structure and practice of state-society relations form the centrepiece in the Dutch strategy.

In line with traditional EC thinking and practice, Dutch environmental policy used to be shaped by the notion of a trade-off between economic and environmental policy objectives, with policy problems identified with respect to concrete issues rather than within a general framework. Consequently, mainly regulatory/legalistic measures were adopted under political pressure from environmental advocates within the government operating in an alliance with mobilised societal actors (Bressers 1997). But evidence of continuing policy failure, reinforced by critical public opinion, the Queen's unusual intervention in her 1988 Christmas Address and the innovative policy-making style of two subsequent ministers for the environment in the 1980s (Weale 1992), triggered closer co-operation between government and business in order to improve environmental performance (Bressers 1997) and the major policy reform in 1989.

There is evidence to suggest that new structures and modes of governance are crystallising in Dutch environmental policy-making. The NEPP and its successors are shaped by the clear perception of human activity as the source of systemic malfunctions in the ecological system and resulted in a new problem-solving approach focusing on the attitude and behaviour of all societal actors (the so-called *verinnerlijking* strategy). With respect to the appropriate choice of policy instruments, the mere imposition of legal standards seemed insufficient to produce the necessary educational and learning processes required for the effective internalisation of environmental responsibilities (Le Blansch 1996). Instead, target groups convened by public authorities and composed of societal actors are formed and are involved in the definition of policy objectives and the selection of policy instruments. In these new network structures, actors join together in order to create a public good in a way that is complementary with, but not determined by, particularistic interests (Mayntz 1993). While the traditional perception of a conflict between economic and environmental interests has not disappeared and the state continues to assume top-down steering responsibilities, Glasbergen and Driessen (1994) cite several examples (the Genre Valley, the Green Heart, Schiphol Airport) of relatively successful new governance practices, termed 'network management'.[5]

Hence, from a governance perspective, the Netherlands fits the governance model emerging at EC level. This is far from surprising, however, considering that the Netherlands was actually a front-runner in integrating new environmental governance features in the national system. Influenced by the *global* environmental debate culminating in the Brundtland report, the Dutch reform process preceded (in fact shaped) transformation processes at EC level. Consequently, EC-induced transformation pressures were minimal; at most, EC developments amplified on-going national processes.

The experience in the Netherlands raises interesting questions about the future of 'new' environmental governance, however. Given the actual environmental performance in the country, ambiguities remain concerning the effectiveness of 'target group' or 'network management' for the protection of the environment. Van der Straaten and Hajer are leading critics of the 'new' governance approach, pointing out that the Netherlands remains one of the most polluted countries in Europe and that vested industrial interests tend to prevail within the network structure, due to the absence of commanding and sanctioning mechanisms (Hajer 1992, van der Straaten and Ugelow 1994). In contrast, Haverland (1997) traces a relatively successful waste packaging policy to new structures in state-industry relations and the use of self-regulatory policy instruments. But even here, consensus-building seemed finally to depend on developing a more exclusive network structure than initially intended. In other words, the Dutch experience points to the evaluative question regarding the impact of new governance practices on policy performance. Further insights into the general problem-solving capacity of the new modes of governance may be gained by comparing the environmental case with other issue-areas analysed in this volume.

Germany

The policy perception and associated problem-solving approaches in Germany are distinct from the understanding at which the EC and the Netherlands have arrived. On the basis of the existing overlap in terms of problem perception, a clear approximation of the policy rhetoric of the EC and Germany can be observed; the persisting ideational distinctions are reflected in the more selective adoption of new governance structures, styles and instruments.

In effect, it is not the failure of societal actors to accept and take responsibility for the environmental good, but the notion that business can gain from activities in environmental protection which lies behind the German perception of 'no trade-off' between environmental and economic objectives. This perception has its roots in the German regulatory tradition and its impact on industrial behaviour. Domestic industry was faced with challenging, i.e. technology-pushing, regulatory standards, and indeed developed products and production processes capable of meeting these relatively high standards. Particularly when harmonisation of environmental standards at EC level took place at the level of German domestic standards, 'clean' German industry possessed a comparative advantage and was able to exploit new market opportunities in the rest of Europe. The temporary cost of meeting environmental policy standards turned into long-term business opportunities and gains. Hence, the problem-solving approach, developed on the basis of a recognised mutual dependence between economic and environmental goals, is one-sided and instrumental; it is not rooted in a holistic 'life cycle' interpretation as in the Netherlands.

This perception has implications for environmental governance structure and style, particularly since it excludes large parts of the business sector as well as society. Weidner (1996) has named the resulting structure of state-society relations 'ecological neo-corporatism' (*ökologischer Neokorporatismus*) or 'industrial-bureaucratic environmental policy network' (*industriell-bürokratisches Umweltpolitiknetzwerk*), in other words, a relatively exclusive network structure which is innovative in its relative openness to environmental business interests as well as scientific experts, but offers only limited access to the interested public at large. The role of the state in this structure is that of an authoritarian facilitator; i.e. operating through network contacts on the basis of the ever-present threat of command-and-control legislation (Müller 1989).

The overall legalistic and interventionist policy style with a preference for policy instruments that provide clear, material standards for public administration, business and the ordinary citizen is firmly rooted in the German state and legal tradition (van Waarden 1995, Dyson 1992) and is reinforced by a fragmented (federal) political structure requiring the existence of harmonising legislation. The constitutional character of this tradition and the presence of a dense legal framework already developed on this basis make Germany quite resistant to change.

For this reason, Germany has been slow to implement policy instruments implied in 'new' governance, aimed at public participation and joint learning, i.e. the introduction of 'soft' regulatory measures directed at behavioural change, such as self-regulatory codes of conduct, as well as measures to improve the transparency of, and access to, policy-making processes. Already in the formal transposition of EC policies representing new governance practices, there have been problems in Germany. For instance, the latest Implementation Report by the Commission (Commission 1996b) speaks of conformity problems in Germany with the Freedom of Access to Information and the Environmental Impact Assessment Directives. The former Directive has been transposed into German law with more than one year's delay, and in its application poses doubts as to whether it conforms with the spirit of EC law (Scherzberg 1994, Lenschow 1997a, b). Comparing the Dutch and German information strategies, Knoepfel and Weidner concluded more than a decade ago that the German system for information access, which compensates restrictive assess in the policy formulation phase with relatively open access to administrative courts subsequently, 'mainly serves the function of creating legitimacy for the regulatory outputs produced, while the substantially more open Dutch system is more appropriate for reconciling conflicting interest positions' (Knoepfel and Weidner 1983: 208). The underlying concept of state-society relations still prevails.

Nevertheless, changes in governance structure, style and instruments can be detected in Germany. Jänicke and Weidner find 'changes in direction towards consensus building, a broader form of cooperation that includes scientists and members of environmental organisations critical of current environmental policy' (Jänicke and Weidner 1997: 140) as well as 'modernised... instruments... stressing the role of information and negotiation' (ibid.: 139). For instance, eco-auditing and eco-labelling are seen as potentially useful *complements* to top-down regulation, though not as alternatives (see also Héritier, Knill and Mingers 1996). Despite the emergence of communicative tools in the context of dispute resolutions (e.g. mediation) and self-regulatory instruments such as voluntary agreements (Rehbinder, talk at the EUI 1997), new instruments for environmental policy have been most extensively implemented – and internalised in German policy culture – where they do not conflict with the constitutional and administrative tradition, that is, in the area of fiscal policy (Cremer and Fisahn 1998). Taxation measures operate within a general legal framework, complementing sanctioning regulations with market correctives. They do not imply changes to administrative and state-society structures and procedures. While they do relieve public authorities in the context of an increasingly complex world which is difficult to regulate centrally, they do not imply adaptations to socio-political structures.

While these changes can in part be attributed to a process of 'internal' policy learning (from past policy failures), EC legislation, implying market-oriented, self-regulatory and communicative instruments (most of them first opposed by Germany) seem to strengthen a growing willingness to adapt past practices, i.e. EC influence boosts the process of internal learning (Interviews BMU). Furthermore, transformation or adaptation processes must be seen in the context of other policy developments, that is, *general* efforts to de-bureaucratise the state. EC legislation on eco-audits, for instance, is being implemented enthusiastically (despite initial opposition), due in part to the promise it holds for future de-regulation (Lenschow 1997a, b). This linkage of 'new' agendas continues to be shaped by traditional, relatively exclusive, network management in Germany, however, as current de-regulation measures tend to occur at the expense of public participation (Cremer and Fisahn 1998).

The United Kingdom

In contrast to Germany, the British traditional style of environmental policy-making was quite different from traditional EC patterns. Hence, the UK government tended to resist the regulatory measures proposed by the Commission, often under German influence, because the implied legalistic command-and-control policy style was foreign to the prevailing pragmatic and flexible British practice (Knill 1995, Weale 1997). British policy-making in general is characterised by the absence of a strong interventionist tradition on the part of the state (a 'state-less society', Nettl 1968), and the common law tradition, which favours a case-by-case approach over universally applicable rules and regulations derived from fixed (constitutional) principles. Primary legislation establishes the administrative framework for specific regulations and standards, which are often developed through a process of public consultation and extensive negotiations between public authorities and the actors to be regulated (Weale 1997: 92). The state and the economically powerful segments of civil society interact in an informal and flexible manner to find a regulatory consensus based on a liberal market logic; democratic control and participation through political channels are marginal.

Confronted with the German-influenced command-and-control legislation – establishing firm, material and typically emission-based standards – Britain was forced to augment its pragmatic, flexible policy style and 'cosy' relationships between public authorities and industry with more formal statutory practices. Since the late 1980s, Britain has been attempting to avoid such pressure to adapt by behaving more pro-actively in the EC policy formulation process, pushing for the British regulatory approach to be adopted at EC level. The eco-label regulation represents one successful example (Héritier, Knill and Mingers 1996).

The new governance patterns emerging at EC level, while sharing some stylistic and instrumental elements with the UK tradition, differ from it significantly, however, in terms of the underlying problem perception and governance structures. Given the British state and legal tradition, the notion of the conceptual development and universal application of a systemic problem analysis with associated problem solving approaches is quite foreign. While the state may have become a more autonomous authority since the Thatcher era, 'clubby' state-industry relations still dominate in the environmental field; neither the pre-Thatcher nor the post-Thatcher type of state-society relations corresponds with the newly envisioned structure in the EC, in which the state plays the role of facilitator, mediating between an inclusive set of actors aiming for a common problem perception (internalisation) and mutually agreeable solutions on that basis. The British consensual and pragmatic style, therefore, differs from the 'new' governance style in its implied market logic and absence of a collective 'problem-solving' dimension.

Nevertheless, in its rhetoric the British government has firmly adopted the notion of sustainable development articulated in the Brundtland report, including its implied institutional consequences. The 1990 White Paper *This Common Inheritance* established several inter-departmental ministerial committees to pursue environmental questions (HMSO 1990, Weale 1997: 103). The UK strategy on sustainable development, published in 1994, calls for the integration of environmental priorities into other areas of policy-making and proposes partnerships between the public and private actors in developing new initiatives; thus it hints at problem-solving through wider policy networks. More concretely, it announced the formation of a Roundtable on Sustainable Development and a citizens' environmental initiative, intended to improve the quality of the debate and build an understanding at the local level of policy issues and linkages (Christie 1994). The impact of these high-level, formal institutional innovations on the 'deep' governance structure in Britain remains to be seen, however; their creation must be understood in the context of similar institutional developments globally and in Europe.

The none the less limited degree of the *Europe-induced* transformation of governance in Britain becomes more apparent when analysing the choice of policy instruments. The shift towards market-oriented and self-regulatory measures in the UK is not rooted in a new belief in modern governance practices, based on public-private partnership relations and the recognition of a shared responsibility in a common good. It is rather due to a domestic preoccupation with *laissez faire* governance through market mechanisms and accountable government (Knill 1995) which, in turn, can be situated in the context of a global neo-liberal trend. Similarly, access to information policy in the UK has its intellectual roots in an attempt to curtail discretionary state actions and to legitimise conservative reform in the UK (ibid.); it was not intended to facilitate equal partnerships, joint learning and problem-solving. In other words, in terms of governance style and instruments, a 'merger' of the global socio-economic debate can be observed, rather than the 'steering debate', with themes raised by 'new' environmental governance.

The notion of policy effectiveness needs to be the subject of future analysis, as to whether similar tools based on different leading ideas show significant differences in their performance. Christie has cautioned that 'so far development of the political culture for sustainability is on a very small scale, and can only be described as marginal in terms of public investment, political debate and public awareness' (Christie 1994: 17–18). With that statement he raised the question whether a formal comparison of governance structures, styles and instruments has any potential for leading us beyond the analysis of transformation processes to conclusions regarding the impact of certain governance patterns on policy effectiveness.

Spain

Upon joining the EC, Spain decided to incorporate all EC legislation enacted before 1986 into national law. Apart from quickly causing severe implementation problems and 'administrative blockage' (Pridham 1996: 67), Spain effectively adopted a package of environmental regulations which was still characterised by *ad hoc*, fragmented and legalistic top-down policy-making in Brussels. This early 'strategy' corresponds with the observation made by La Spina and Sciortino that 'Southern European states generally do not advance proposals of their own, nor do they obstruct proposals made by others. This acquiescence is a way to overcome national decisional paralysis, or better, let the EC overcome it' (La Spina and Sciortino 1993: 208).

With respect to the adoption of the ideational basis and institutional principles of modern governance since 1986, this view needs to be modified, however. Aguilar has characterised the present Spanish stance in EC policy-making as 'defensive' (Aguilar 1993: 231), especially where the notion of a complementary relationship between environmental and economic policy goals and policy integration is concerned. Arguing that EC environmental policy would have severe repercussions on its economic development, Spain has succeeded in extracting large sums of money from the EC budget for environmental protection, for instance via the Cohesion Fund (Lenschow 1997a, b). Limited institutional adaptation is to be expected because of the limited convergence at the ideological level, even though EC structures and instruments are likely to be imitated where the national context constituted a *tabula rasa*.

Given that environmental policy institutions are more likely to be missing in Spain than an overall governing style, it is not surprising to observe some evidence of convergence with respect to formal institutions for sustainable development and modern governance (see Commission 1995b), but a persistence of the traditional statist tradition in Spain, providing little access for civil society to the policy-making process. Spanish environmental policy remains characterised by the 'pre-eminence of public actors'

(Aguilar 1993: 236–7) controlling rather than facilitating the building of relatively exclusive networks with and among elements of civil society (mostly industry). Due to EC influence, formal contacts between government and industry are now increasing and voluntary 'environmental pacts' have been created; however '[s]tate intervention and a resistance to private government persists . . . [and] the weakness of the system of interest mediation favours the persistence of the statist design' (ibid.: 240–1). Nevertheless, in part due to the Commission's 'clientelistic' policy and transnational NGO activities, an environmentally aware segment of civil society is emerging and seeking to influence Spanish and EC policy (Interviews Europe offices of WWF and Friends of the Earth, 1994).

The administrative structures in Spain represent the primary hindrance to cross-sectoral integration and problem-solving in open networks. The Inter-ministerial Committee for the Environment was dissolved in 1987, and had previously been largely ineffective in terms of facilitating policy integration. In addition, the transformation of Spain into a 'state of autonomous regions' with the latter taking over large amounts of responsibility for environmental matters has resulted in highly deficient administrative co-ordination (Aguilar 1997). Philosophical conflicts, with the state adopting a longer-term and systemic understanding of the environmental *problématique*, and the regions pursuing shorter-term and particularistic interests, disrupt state-regional relations. However, there is evidence to suggest that new governance signals sent from Brussels are resonating in the more economically advanced autonomous regions of Spain, such as Catalonia (Boerzel 1997), which are more receptive to the idea and problem perception behind new governance structures and practices.

Conclusions: patterns and results of transformation processes

This overview of the transformation of governance structures and practices at EC level and in the member states indicates change as well as continuity in Europe; i.e., the null-hypothesis of 'no change' can be discarded. As regards change, continuing diversity in outcome is discernible at national level, confirming that aside from European transformation pressure, the nature of national receptiveness to problem definition and institutional fit or malleability needs to be analysed.

Despite discarding the 'no change' hypothesis, a good deal of continuity is perceptible, suggesting that the necessary condition of transformation pressure has not been fully satisfied. Indeed, with respect to new modes of environmental governance, it is doubtful whether EC governance in the field of environmental policy is sufficiently comprehensive, coherent and stable to trigger a decisive and uniform response. Despite the leadership of some member states in shaping EC environmental policy, and imposing their national policy 'paradigm' on the European level, EC policy has emerged as a patchwork of national styles rather than a coherent whole. The introduction of new governance features since the late 1980s may signify a trend, but these transformation signals arrive in an inchoate rather than paradigmatic form in the member states.

In examining the member states, the clearest evidence of change is visible at the level of policy rhetoric, suggesting the infiltration of common policy ideas and problems, small-scale institution-building and the diversification of policy instruments. As argued at the beginning of this chapter, the change in environmental rhetoric must be viewed within the global and European environmental debate as ideas circulate freely and, more concretely, national policy programmes are formulated in compliance with international and EC agreements. The penetration of new ideas into the 'deep structure' of the European consciousness, or the core of the prevailing policy paradigm (Hall 1993), remains varied, however. In the Netherlands, the external impetus combined with a high level of internal dissatisfaction with the status quo, triggering a convergence of the international and Dutch problem perception even prior to the crystallisation of the European 'environmental idea'. In Germany, components of the newly-defined environmental *problématique* corresponded to, and were interpreted within, the framework of a more narrowly perceived, pre-existing variant. In the UK, the new environmental rhetoric appears symbolic and independent of a clear policy programme, in tune with the pragmatic national policy culture. This new rhetoric resonates with the more deeply-rooted neo-liberal paradigm in Britain, however, and corresponding governance responses need to be understood in that light. Finally, in Spain the new definition of the environmental problem, namely the notion of an economic-environmental win-win situation, has not been accepted. Hence the ideational basis for new governance structures, styles and instruments is missing.

Despite these differences at the level of problem perception, similar institutional responses can be observed in each of the countries, following in many respects the example set by the European Commission. Here it is important to note that these institutional innovations have not yet replaced, nor even undermined, traditional organisational or interest intermediation structures; they have tended to be 'add-ons' rather than to constitute substantial reform elements. In addition to a certain degree of institutional imitation that seems to occur independently of a shared problem perception (most notably in Spain), the empirical evidence suggests that the direction of change signalled in Brussels has the most impact on governance structures and style if it resonates with concurrent, though possibly independent, transformation processes at the global or domestic level, such as the global debate on de-regulation or domestic moves towards more transparency (Knill 1997). In such cases, EC pressure for transformation seems to amplify on going transformation processes, even if there has not yet been a convergence at the ideational level. Overall, the level of institutional imitation in the EC is quite impressive and its impact on the long-term institutionalisation of ideas will be important to follow.

The dimension where the clearest influence of the EC on national patterns is visible is that of policy instruments. This makes sense from an institutional perspective, suggesting that policy instruments are easier to change than core ideas (Hall 1993). It could equally be due to the nature of the transformation pressure exerted at the European level. In contrast to merely setting institution-building examples at European level, legislation (implying the use of policy instruments) needs to be implemented at national level, and consequently is capable of exerting direct pressure for change in the member states. Recent empirical research has shown that the shift towards a new structure and mode of governance (i.e. going beyond the mere use of new instruments), set in motion through the implementation process, is mediated by national legal, political and administrative traditions, acting as filters in this transformation process (Knill 1997).

Finally, a word on the link between governance structures and policy performance. Experience with different mixes of governance types in the member states does not provide clear evidence of their comparative capacity to produce solutions for environmental problems. In particular, given the differences in national culture and socio-economic and political structure among the member states, as well as differences in the type and severity of the policy problems, 'good' governance may imply different structures depending on the exact situation. Hence, a wider *repertoire* of governance strategies rather than transformation towards a uniform, new mode of governance may be most desirable from a normative point of view.

Notes

I am grateful to Peter Bursens, Rainer Eising, Markus Jachtenfuchs, Markus Haverland, Christoph Knill and Michèle Knodt and all participants in the ECPR workshop meetings in Oslo and Mannheim for valuable comments on earlier drafts of this chapter.

1 Such concurrence of debates poses obvious analytical problems which, due to limited space as well as empirical breadth, could not be tackled systematically in this chapter.
2 It should be noted that the focus on the influence of EC governance patterns on domestic governance reflects a restricted analytical perspective rather than an underlying assumption that global impact is insignificant, or that no feedback from domestic structures and politics to EC practices occurs. A systematic analysis of the interplay between the three levels of analysis would have far exceeded the space provided as well as the scope of this volume.
3 No normative judgement is implied in this statement. It may very well be that

command-and-control instruments are superior in reaching environmental objectives compared to market-oriented, self-regulating or informative/communicative instruments. Several authors have pointed out the limits of self-regulatory measures in particular (e.g. Hajer 1992, Lübbe-Wolff 1996, Scharpf 1992, van der Straaten and Ugelow 1994, Weidner 1997).

4 Weiler in particular has emphasised in his work that the Court's rulings have had a significant effect on polity building and governance in the past.

5 Much in line with the mode of modern governance described in this chapter, he defines 'network management' as a:

> multi-actor system, consisting of various government agencies and societal organizations, each carrying particular objectives and interests. These actors however need each other's help to solve the [environmental] problem. Management by government must mobilize this multi-actor system into co-operative action, and a structured process of interaction and communication must be brought about. In this process, actors will have to learn from each other how to realise outcomes that can both bring environmental objectives within reach and create opportunities for those actors affected by these objectives.
>
> (Glasbergen 1994: 31, citing Zillessen *et al.* 1993)

The same kind of thinking lies behind the formation of the dialogue groups at EC level (even though they exist only on a general level of policy) and corresponds with the use of communicative policy instruments.

4

REGULATING GENETIC ENGINEERING IN THE EUROPEAN UNION

A post-structuralist perspective

Herbert Gottweis

Introduction

When political scientists write about the European Community, they often describe the impressive process of European integration since 1957. But the same authors could also tell a second story emphasising the difficulties, setbacks and as yet unachieved steps of shaping an integrated Europe and its identity. Certainly, these two stories about the European Community are not mutually exclusive; they merely feature different sides of the same process. In this paper I am more interested in the second story and the tendencies which point to the fragile and tentative character of EC political development (Gottweis 1998).

The case study developed in this paper focuses on the making and implementation of two important directives regulating genetic engineering in the EC. The first directive deals with the contained use of genetically modified organisms (GMOs), the second with the deliberate release of GMOs into the environment. I will emphasise the importance of discursive practices for policy-making, and argue that the political space of EC governance in the field of regulating genetic engineering can be better described in terms of a field of political intertextuality rather than in the divisive language of 'the state' versus the 'supranational.'

EC governance: a post-structuralist approach

Simon Hix has recently maintained that approaches to EC politics in the sub-fields of international and comparative politics can be neatly divided into those emphasising either structure or agency in the explanation of the political process (Hix 1994). While the international politics theory discussion in particular has tried to 'solve' the 'actor-structure' problem (Doty 1997), today's dominant models of EC governance seem to be characterised by a distinction between a concentration on and favouring of either actors or structures in their explanatory efforts. For example, the state-centric model of EC governance presents states as the ultimate decision-makers and describes policy-making as being constrained by political interests nested within autonomous state arenas which connect sub-national groups to European affairs (Marks, Hooghe and Blank 1995). By contrast, the multi-level governance model asserts that the state no longer monopolises European-level policy-making and that supranational institutions consequently have an independent influence in policy-making which cannot be derived from their role as the agents of state executives. Both approaches share a number of analytical interests and characteristics. While state-centric approaches tend to reify institutions as independent variables, the desegregation of the state in multi-level models focuses on actors with unquestioned stable identities and driven by utility maximising rationality. Furthermore, both approaches seem to subscribe to a model of EC governance where the EC institutions are somehow located 'above' and at the same time 'outside' the nation state.

While the different schools which study EC politics concentrate on either actors or structures in their accounts or try to 'solve' the 'actor-structure problem', the post-structuralist perspective developed in my paper suggests a different approach: instead of seeking to identify the 'true nature' of actors and structures and their interactions in politics, we should rather conceptualise actors and structures as effects of discursive practices. As a result, we should focus on how these effects are produced, rather than assuming their existence. This analytical strategy is in line with arguments in recent social theory, which have stated that today's post-modern conditions seem to be characterised by a mood of uncertainty and the absence of analytical and political guarantees, privileged political positions and agents, and by the co-existence of a plurality of political spaces and social logics through which various forms of social and political identify are constituted.

One important expression of this post-modern constellation which has enormous implications for policy-making is the perception of a blurring of the boundaries between phenomena in a variety of different social and political sectors (Smart 1992: 219; Latour 1993). Examples of this process are the increasingly unclear boundaries between experts and non-experts in scientific decision-making, the collapsing boundaries between nature and technology, and the great difficulty encountered in identifying the boundaries between national economies and the international economy. Scientific expertise does not enjoy the same legitimacy as it did some decades ago. Frozen embryos appear to be a form of life, but also of technology. Processes of globalisation undermine traditional notions of what constitutes the economy of a nation state. While these processes may already have been going on for some time, they have only recently become the focus of attention. Political science analysis needs to concentrate on conceptual tools which are capable of bringing the contested and 'fluid' character of social and political phenomena into focus.

Post-structuralist political analysis puts forward a number of important theoretical arguments which help to reconceptualise the study of EC governance (Gottweis 1998: 11–18). First, it argues that there is no such thing as a theory-neutral observation language. Whereas the (neo-positivist) representationalist/ correspondence theory of truth claims that 'there is a truth out there' which can be represented through the neutral medium of language, the anti-representationalist view of post-structuralism rejects such a 'picture theory' of language (Rorty 1989; Daly 1994: 167–8) Consequently, the 'truth' of an event, a situation or an artefact will always be the uncertain outcome of a struggle between competing language games or discourses which transform 'what is out there' into a socially and politically relevant signified. Thereby, human agents introduce order into their world and strive to give sense and coherence to the otherwise confusing or contradictory realities of political life (Laclau and Mouffe 1985; Linstead and Grafton-Small 1992: 343).

But the agents which create structure and order are by no means 'simply there'. From a post-structuralist perspective, subjects or actors cannot be viewed as the origin of social relations. Actors do not have stable subject identities but constantly develop their subjectivity in a discursive exchange (Laclau and Mouffe 1995: 115; Smart 1992: 135). This is not a 'cultural dope' conception of human agency, but a perspective which points out that human agency is produced reality. Also, this perspective does not imply that 'there are no human actors' in politics or that we have to stop to talk about agency as we analyse political processes. But we have to understand that actors depend on the specific discursive conditions which make them possible.

Following this constructivist perspective, governance can be conceptualised as an 'empty space' until demarcated and partitioned in boundary-drawing struggles which, for example, determine who has the right to participate in a policy-making process, and who does not (Gieryn 1995). There 'is' no such thing as 'society,' or 'politics,' or 'the European Community' which constitutes a totality and as such is linked together or 'sutured', to form a unity of some kind and capable of 'interactions', such as between the 'European Community' and a 'member state'. Rather, social, economic, and political 'reality' are constructions made possible through spoken or written practices (Cooper 1989; Reed and Hughes 1992; Hassard and Parker 1993). From this standpoint, EC governance can be thought of as a contested process of introducing organisation and order into an unstable discursive environment. Regimes of governance are locations where people, individuals, nature and artefacts are transformed into objects of interventions and become 'governable.' The objects of government (such as pregnancy, genes, the economy, or global warming) co-emerge at a number of different locations which are not necessarily considered to be 'political' (such as in hospitals or research institutes), but nevertheless are sites where significant influence can be exerted on the logic and the rationales of a policy field. Accordingly, the question of the 'level' of governance (regional, national or supranational) seems misleading and appears to be not so much a question of institutional or territorial 'realities' as a question of boundary construction. What I suggest is that the multiple regime of EC governance involves the systematic collapsing of the different 'levels' of governance through discursive practices which transcend any institutional or territorial logic (Ruggie 1993), but follow the logic of discursive construction and articulation.

Processes of introducing organisation and order into a discursive environment do not happen in a cultural vacuum. Policy-making tends to incorporate images, representations and value systems which refer to a larger context of legitimate symbols, statements and norms. Such representations link a particular policy to other fields of policy-making and to domains of social and cultural interaction (Jobert and Muller 1987: 52). The rationale behind a policy and political programme needs to be situated within a larger framework of meaning. Narratives are a central means of organising a polity and its identity. At the most general level, 'narrativity' is the representation of real events which arises out of the desire to have these events display the coherence, integrity, fullness, and closure of an image of life that is and can only be imaginary. Narratives bring elements of clarity, stability, and order into what usually tends to be the complicated and contradictory world of politics. Two critical articulations of narrativity in political discourse are political metanarratives and policy narratives. Political metanarratives describe general concepts and values of the social order. Metanarratives offer a conceptual framework that provides a polity and its subjects with an imagined collective political identity situated in historical time. Policy narratives are more specific and describe the frames (Goffman 1974: 10–11) or plots used in the social construction of the fields of action for policy-making, for governmental activities from environmental to technology policy.[1] These frames or plots are the principles of organisation which govern events. They describe a structure of relationships which endows the events contained in the account with a meaning by integrating these events into a narrative. In short, they make governance possible.

Changing metanarratives and new regulatory policy frames in Europe

The importance of discourse and narratives for the construction of the actors, institutions and goals of policy-making in the EC can clearly be seen when we try to understand why and how the EC became involved in the shaping of European genetic engineering regulations. There was nothing obvious about the EC emerging as one of the central actors in genetic engineering regulation in Europe. Rather, a number of critical, not necessarily related but mutually reinforcing discursive changes, prepared the ground for administrators and agencies at EC level to get involved in the regulatory policy-making process.

First, there were a number of important changes in western political discourse at a more general level. In the early 1970s, the environment had become a topic of political debate and intervention (Hajer 1995). After a period of framing environmental issues as incidental problems requiring *ad hoc* solutions, the 1980s witnessed an important modification of the metanarrative of modernisation, which began to incorporate cognitive frames which were often summarised by the interchangeable slogans 'ecological modernisation' and 'sustainable development.'

The latter concepts became the two major indicators of the new ecology discourse (Spaargaren and Mol 1992: 328–9). The academic discourse on ecology, sustainable development, and ecological modernisation was gradually disseminated throughout the mass media and public culture, but it also found its way into the policy statements of parties, interest groups, and the state. The central elements of this discourse became part of a new political metanarrative which developed in tandem with the emerging new environmental ethics on the cultural level (Tesier 1993; Tschannen and Hainard 1993).

Furthermore, the scientific debate on the environmental risks related to genetic engineering proved important for the emerging debate on genetic engineering regulation (Levin and Strauss 1991). Some of the main lines of the (scientific) arguments developed in this debate became textual devices for the (political) framing of the emerging genetic engineering controversy in Europe.

These changes at the level of scientific discourse and political metanarrative constituted a new context for EC policy-making (Wägerbaur 1992; Smith and Hunter 1992; Wright 1991; Freestone 1991). The emergence of Community environmental policy (see Lenschow in this volume) was closely linked to one of the central economic objectives of the EC political metanarrative: that is, economic harmonisation. In the Single European Act (SEA), Articles 100a and 130r, s, and t gave formal recognition to Community environmental policy. Article 130r defined the objectives of EC environmental policy as being to preserve, protect, and improve the quality of the environment; to contribute towards protecting human health; and to ensure a prudent and rational utilisation of national resources. However, the very same SEA stated that all its objectives, not just its environmental protection ones, should be attained. Consequently, member states cannot adopt environmental protection measures which conflict with secondary Community legislation, such as the free movement of goods. Examples of limited regulation are Articles 100a and 130t which grant member states the right to maintain or introduce national environmental standards stricter than those approved by the EC, provided that they do not constitute a form of 'hidden protectionism' and are otherwise compatible with the Treaty of Rome.

Hence, the substantial shift at the level of EC political discourse towards a comprehensive and integrated environment policy was inseparable from a re-articulation of environmental policy as a device used in the formation of the common market. As I will show, it was the construction of genetic engineering regulation around one of the major elements of the EC metanarrative – the creation of a common market – which was to play a critical role in the emergence of a group of administrators in DG XI as the dominant actors in the policy-making process.

The EC becomes an actor in recombinant DNA regulation

While in the 1970s the European Community had remained rather inactive in the shaping of recombinant DNA policies, this situation changed in the mid-1980s, when representatives of various departments (Directorates General – DGs) in the Commission began to define the European Community as a central player in the regulation of genetic engineering. This involved the utilisation and mobilisation of various and varied policy stories which were found in the repertoires of available political discourse. This early process of policy negotiation was rather informal, and involved meetings of actors from a number of DGs. At the same time, the policy actors in Brussels were aware that in a number of member countries such as Denmark, Germany, and Britain, moves were underway to draft national genetic engineering regulations.

At a first, important inter-service meeting in November 1984, an agreement was reached that some Community action in the field of genetic engineering regulation was necessary. But the representatives of different DGs offered divergent readings of the genetic engineering issue. These readings were as much contributions to an emerging game as attempts by a number of policy actors to position themselves in the policy-making process. Both DG III (Industrial Affairs) and DG XI (Environment) pointed to the need for regulatory action, though they disagreed on how to proceed. DG III maintained that 'regulations and authorisations in respect of process controls and field trials should be administered by those responsible for the regulation of the eventual *product*'.[2] In this approach to the genetic engineering issue, DG XI would have played a minor role, whereas other DGs, such as Agriculture or Trade and Industry, would have had a central role, since it was these DGs which tended to have responsibility for the regulation of *products*.

DG XI, on the other hand, contended that risk regulation should not focus on the final *products* of biotechnology, but on the *processes* involving genetic engineering by which biotechnology products were produced. Policy actors from DG XI on the one hand, and DGs III and XII on the other, supported three quite different strategies based on different definitions of the reality of genetic engineering: Both DG III and DG XII supported a product-oriented approach towards regulation, but whereas DG III seemed to support at least some new form of a regulatory regime, the DG XII approach was strongly oriented towards the US model of recombinant DNA work, which shunned special legislation and regulation, and supported regulation by scientific advice only. In contrast to DG XII's risk discourse, which was strongly influenced by a technological definition of risk, DG XI espoused a regulatory approach broadly based on ecological notions which required the establishment of special process-based legislation.

Obviously, the different actors espoused conflicting definitions of the nature of genetic engineering: what constitutes a hazard, where to demarcate the boundary between 'naturally' occurring biological processes and those modified by genetic engineering technology, and what regulatory developments abroad were deemed significant. Certainly, these different positions reflected the different interests of actors in a policy negotiation. At the same time it is crucial to bear in mind that these different positions were based on elements of larger models of reality which carried assumptions about prerequisites for industrial development, the nature and identity of Europe, and the proper role of the different DGs in the overall context of the Commission. These different discourses suggested different actor constellations and institutional arrangements for constituting and influencing regulatory decision-making in Europe.

In July 1985 a 'Biotechnology Interservice Committee' (BRIC) was set up, its function being to co-ordinate the individual services. DG III and DG XI were designated as the principal departments, and the position of chairmanship was to rotate between them. CUBE (DG XII) would become the secretariat of the Committee.

Around this time, a new and important group of spokespersons for genetic engineering emerged in the regulatory game: representatives of the European Parliament. Particularly since the Maastricht Treaty, EC political discourse had begun to emphasise and expand the influence of the European Parliament. This changed discourse was reflected by the fact that, by the mid-1980s, despite limited powers in comparison with the weight of the Commission and the Council, the Parliament was widely viewed as being representative of 'public sentiments on issues', a fact which led BRIC to pay considerable attention to its activities where genetic engineering was concerned.

On 20–21 November 1985, the Parliament organised a hearing on the general aspects and implications of biotechnology. In Benedict Haerlin, a Green Party representative who had been appointed by the Committee on Social Affairs and Employment to draft its opinion of the statement on biotechnology produced by the Committee on Energy, Research, and Technology, the European Parliament had found its most outspoken and influential critic of biotechnology.[3] Haerlin suggested a number of radical measures, such as warning Third World countries of the possibility of genetically engineered organisms being deliberately released in their territories. He offered a policy counternarrative which refused to allow the recombinant DNA debate to be limited to issues of safety risks and which was reminiscent of the positions put forward by the critics at national and regional level in countries such as Germany and Britain (see below). Indeed, Haerlin had already played an important role in the European politics of genetic engineering by initiating and supporting the Gen-Ethic Network in Germany, a highly influential umbrella organisation for critics of biotechnology, and he was about to inform the French public about an unauthorised and deliberate release of a genetically modified organism in Dijon. With his report for the EP, he launched his campaign against genetic engineering at EC level.

Haerlin's intervention is a good example of the complexities of EC policy-making. Haerlin as an actor cannot be simply ascribed to the European Parliament, nor is he simply an important actor and organiser in the French or German political context. Rather, he was an important nodal point in a complex emerging network of meaning which began to define the EC as a site for genetic engineering regulatory policy-making. A number of events – Haerlin's GRAEL (Green Alternative European Link – a sub-group of the Rainbow Group in the European Parliament), the

German Greens, the ongoing German and Danish preparations for national recombinant DNA regulations, the development of the biotechnology industry, the (Maastricht-inspired) EC political discourse attributing heightened importance to the EP and the newly-emerged EC environment policies – were not necessarily all causally related, but they nevertheless constituted important elements in the construction of a new policy narrative in whose co-ordination DG XI played an important role.

DG XI's plan was to position itself at the centre of regulatory activity. But this could not be achieved by simply claiming responsibility or mobilising potential allies. The key to DG XI's power was in organising differences, creating links between different discourses which initially seemed to be hermetically closed off from one another, and thereby positioning itself and other actors in the policy-making process in a way which would be generally acknowledged as fair and appropriate.

Local arguments about recombinant DNA regulation

While the actors and agencies of the emerging policy negotiations began to take shape at the level of EC regulatory policy-making, a number of stories about genetic engineering regulation began to be deployed at the level of national policy too. These policy stories, together with EC narratives, constituted a regulatory intertext which structured and guided regulatory policy development in the European space.

At the national level, for example in Britain and Germany, regulatory initiatives came to be interpreted not as contradictory, but as reinforcing regulatory efforts at EC level. In the shaping of national regulatory networks of meaning, the notion that the 'EC is preparing directives for the contained use and the deliberate release of genetically modified organisms' turned into an important point of reference. The governments of these countries did not put pressure on the EC to become active in the field of genetic engineering regulation; nor did they refrain from national regulatory initiatives, even if regulatory initiatives at EC level were expected sooner or later.

Why had a number of EC member states become active in the field of genetic engineering regulation? The regulatory initiatives in particular in Germany, France, and Britain had much to do with the discursive politics of genetic engineering in the mid 1980s.

When, in the early 1970s, genetic engineering technology became available, the following argument about the risk issue became dominant: Although the risks of genetic engineering cannot be denied, there are ways of controlling them. The increasingly dominant regulatory narrative argued that, provided appropriate precautions were taken, the expected enormous benefits of genetic engineering would far outweigh the expected risks. This approach to the risk issue of genetic engineering resulted in the passing of recombinant DNA regulations, first in the United States and Britain, then in most other industrialised countries. In the late 1970s, many of the initially stringent regulations for genetic engineering work were abolished, and it seemed as if the genetic engineering risk debate was history. The argument which had gained dominance was that many of the initially adopted regulations were exaggerated, and that the progress made in the understanding of genetic engineering justified deregulation (Wright 1994).

But from the mid 1980s onwards, the old policy narrative about the risks involved in genetic engineering lost credibility and explanatory power and was challenged by a number of new competing or counternarratives. These challenges came from different directions and gave a new meaning to the biotechnology issue. Activists from animal protection groups, representatives from Ministries of the Environment, and feminists and professors from ecology departments – to name just some of the spokespersons – began an uncoordinated though mutually reinforcing dialogue on genetic engineering which eventually, through a process that redefined some of the key issues and goals of biotechnology policy, led to a proliferation of new actors in the biotechnology networks, the shaping of new group identities, and attempts to change the operating procedures of the biotechnology policy networks.

The considerable weight of the critical voices must be understood in the context of the changed discursive constellation of the 1980s, in which the environment had become a core value in the political arena. This discursive change provided the critics with their subject position as relevant policy actors. The new discursive situation allowed the critics to legitimately position themselves *vis-à-vis* the already established actors in the policy field. The various social movements and groups launching the new genetic engineering controversy were not simply 'against' genetic engineering. They were not just voicing grievances about potential dangers, such as the deliberate release of genetically modified organisms into the environment. Their 'grievances' were not merely background factors which had come to the forefront, but were discursively produced (Buechler 1993: 222). The new environmental discourse, the rise of environmental policy as an important field of state activism, the emergence of a number of new actors in genetic engineering regulation, such as new social movements and Green parties, along with a series of other events and developments had created a new context for genetic engineering regulation (Gottweis 1997).

In Germany the Greens (in close collaboration with many citizens' groups and movements) had a critical influence on the convening of a parliamentary Commission of Inquiry on genetic engineering (Catenhusen and Neumeister 1987). One outcome of the Commission's work was a set of suggestions concerning the regulation of genetic engineering and a recommendation to ban deliberate releases of genetically modified organisms into the environment. On 6 November 1989, the High Administrative Court in Hessen decided, in response to a citizens' group's intervention, that there was no legal basis for industrial production of genetically-engineered products in Germany and that Hoechst, therefore, had to discontinue its insulin project until such a legal basis had been established. This decision was not only relevant to Hessen: the legality of industrial production using genetic engineering methods was put in question for the whole of West Germany. With these developments, the diffusion of genetic engineering into the economy and society was severely threatened. After stormy debates and bitter controversy, the new German Genetic Engineering Act was approved by the Bundestag in March 1990 and came into force on 1 July 1990.[4]

In Britain, as was the case in Germany, the perception that the existing regulatory 'business as usual' framework was insufficient to deal with the complexities of genetic engineering in the 1980s had gained ground. The preparation of changes in the British regulatory approach towards genetic engineering was closely related to a number of developments. According to the new environmental discourse, modernisation and environmental precaution were increasingly defined as mutually reinforcing principles. This discourse had stabilised in the emergence of a number of new and powerful actors in British environmental politics, such as the Royal Commission on Environmental Pollution and the Department of the Environment, which were about to become central players in the shaping of recombinant DNA regulations. Finally, the challenge from social movements, political organisations, and consumer groups had outlined an approach towards genetic engineering which went beyond demands for regulatory reform and called for the establishment of new principles of decision-making for biotechnology policy. Groups like the UK Genetics Forum and the Green Alliance emphasised more ecological research, but in their counternarrative they also demanded a number of other important reforms, such as strict enforcement of regulations, tighter scrutiny and monitoring, a consent-based system of regulation, strict liability for originators and producers of GMOs, greater access to information and greater public participation (Wheale and McNally 1990).

A number of events and developments – such as context the outbreak of salmonella from infected eggs in 1989 and an outbreak of BSE, a deadly brain disease, which by 1990 affected about 10,000 cows – contributed to the perception that genetic engineering was in the grip of a serious crisis. Alarmed administrators began to compare genetic engineering hazards with BSE and salmonella.[5] Finally, in 1990 the deliberate release of genetically modified organisms was regulated by the 1990 Environmental Protection Act.

France, like Britain, did not experience a level of political mobilisation against genetic engineering comparable to that in Germany. But, despite the fact that France did not pass any legislation comparable to the German 'Genetic Engineering Act', closer inspection reveals that the French policy on genetic engineering was also marked by a substantial reconfiguration of the dominant policy narrative. By the mid 1980s, the Ministry of the Environment was established as an important player in the field of biotechnology regulation, which had so far been dominated by the Ministries of Research and Agriculture.

A Ministry of Industry initiative led to the creation of the 'Groupe Interministeriel des Produits Chimiques', the Inter-ministerial Group for Chemical Products , which was initially set up in 1981.This Group came to the conclusion that, in the field of genetic engineering, France had a 'regulatory puzzle in need of reform.[6] But unlike the German and British governments, the French government did not pass any legally binding regulations on biotechnology. This refusal to pass such regulations probably reflected a situation in which the government had to refrain from imposing anything on resistant constituencies, particularly since a regulatory decision was expected soon at EC level. But despite the apparent absence of policy-making activities on the surface, France was also undergoing a transition to a new regulatory narrative which had been in preparation since the mid-1980s.

Hence, in all three countries we see the re-emergence of the question of recombinant DNA regulation of research, development and production, a question which had appeared to be settled by the early 1980s. Practices of regulatory policy-making had created highly specific and nationally diverging local discursive contexts and systems of governance which were to play an important role in the creation and implementation of the EC genetic engineering directives. In the mid 1980s, the first drafts of these directives were prepared by the Commission.

Policy frame conflicts in the European Community

On 23 October 1986, while the controversy over the approach to the genetic engineering issue was in full swing at national level, DG XI was allocated the task of drafting a 'prevention of accidents contained use' directive, and it took until 10 March, 1987 to produce its proposal. This proposal, together with a subsequent one for a deliberate release directive, constituted the critical step in the elaboration of a new regulatory policy narrative which would eventually shape EC legislation on genetic engineering. It became the object of intense conflict and discussion between actors inside and outside the Commission. With the drafting of this proposal, DG XI emerged as the central co-ordinating agency in the shaping of the EC's directives in this field. The regulatory narrative of the contained use draft proposal hardly represented a particularly radical approach, from an environmental policy perspective being oriented around goals of integrated pollution control. However, as we will see, it was precisely this depiction of the contained use of genetic engineering as an object for precautionary environmental regulation which was to give rise to substantial disagreements.

The most contested directive, however, was the proposal for the 'deliberate release' directive. According to the proposal, any person, before undertaking a deliberate release into the environment of a genetically modified organism, would have to notify the competent national authority. According to the proposal, deliberate release also implied the placing on the market of a product.[7] If a release posed a risk to a third country, the competent authority would immediately send a copy of the notification to this third country and the Commission. In particular, the provisions which stipulated substantial regulatory co-operation between countries went well beyond what was in the process of being elaborated in Germany and Britain at national level.

In the meantime, DG XI had received support for its position from the European Parliament. In a resolution on biotechnology in Europe, the EP had demanded that deliberate releases into the environment be banned until binding Community safety directives had been drawn up.[8] Inside the Commission the conflict continued. Whereas DG XI's approach, derived from arguments made in ecological studies, emphasised the uncertainty of the risks of genetic engineering and therefore the importance of precautionary regulations, DG XII marshalled scientific arguments from other disciplines such as microbiology in order to support its own reasoning. DG XII was not the only one to be unconvinced by DG XI's draft. Individual experts from the member states meeting to discuss the directives were very critical of the proposal. In particular, they criticised what they saw as a departure from 'what is accepted world-wide,' namely singling out genetic manipulation from the context of biotechnology hazards.[9] This narrative had a number of discursive links to industry's position on the genetic engineering regulations, such as the European Biotechnology Co-ordination Group's position (EBCG).[10]

Following this informal meeting of the individual experts convened by DG XI, the first meeting of the national experts – a typical procedure for the preparation of directives – took place on 11 and 12 May 1987. These meetings of the national experts became an important forum for discussions about the genetic engineering risk problem at national and EC level. The experts did not simply represent coherent and well-defined country positions, but also stood for approaches or aspects of approaches to the genetic engineering issue which were derived from a variety of places, such as scientific disciplines or local controversies. Again, the meaning of genetic engineering was at the centre of the debate.

In the summer of 1987, after the approval of the higher echelons of the EC hierarchy had been received and the member states had been informed of the impending action, the first drafts of the directives were drawn up. The member states, the directorates and leadership of the Commission, experts and industry agreed only that something ought to be done concerning the regulation question, but there was hardly any agreement on particular strategies. Neither was there an agreement on what to regulate nor on how to regulate it. Different policy approaches had created different political realities. However, it became clear that some member states, particularly Denmark and Germany, had either already adopted or were in the process of adopting national legislation. There was increasing pressure on the Commission to act, but at the same time still enough room for different approaches. Once a formal proposal for a directive had been sent to the European Parliament and the Council, the Commission would have lost most of its room for manoeuvre.

With the onset of time pressures and the need to find a compromise within BRIC, a new turn of events took place in mid-October 1987. DG III and DG XI agreed to co-operate on a new draft directive. As a member of DG III put it, although scientifically it made no sense to differentiate between genetically modified and unmodified organisms, it was DNA recombination which worried people, and therefore political priority had to be given to it. Hence, along with the 'truth' statements on the nature of genetic engineering, other considerations such as 'public sentiment' became critical elements in the emerging regulatory narrative. DG VI supported this approach and an agreement was reached that the draft would be applicable in instances involving processes of genetic engineering where no EC legislation existed. As regards DG XII's idea to establish a European Bio-Safety Science Committee, more and more doubts and criticism were raised.

This new co-operation between DG III and DG XI was a critical development. Apparently, the efforts of DG XI to construct a narrative stabilising the field of genetic engineering politics were beginning to be successful. This situation can hardly be explained by interest group or institutional arguments. DG XII, the biotechnology industry, all the major science organisations, a number of member states, and the Commission's experts' meetings seemed to share an approach based on the naturalisation indicator, which broke down the boundaries between nature and genetic engineering. As a result, there was a tendency to opt for a regulatory approach which de-emphasised the need for comprehensive legislative action. But in the second half of the 1980s, a discursive constellation had developed which had placed DG XI in a better position to articulate a new dominant definition of the regulatory requirements. DG XI had not simply advocated a restrictive regulatory strategy. On the contrary, it had outlined the need for comprehensive, precautionary regulatory action as a prerequisite for the creation of a strong European biotechnology industry. This approach was linked to industry's view of the need for regulatory action and harmonisation. Another important element of linkage in DG XI's approach was the view of critics of genetic engineering, who were pressing for much more radical legislative action. Furthermore, important EC member states which already had, or were in the process of adopting, genetic engineering laws (i.e. Germany and Denmark) could be easily enlisted into DG XI's discursive network, since they had become involved in the EC regulation debate at the level of national policy-making. In addition, DG XI's language and approach fitted into the current, broadly accepted ecology discourse, which had helped shape environmental policy in the EC since the 1980s. This new approach towards environmental policy was part of a larger narrative on social regulation, which dominated the EC's discourse in the 1980s: despite the fact that social regulation, such as environmental policy, was never a primary concern for the EC, the gradual extension of Community policy can be observed during the 1970s and 1980s in a variety of policy fields (Dehousse 1992). Hence, DG XI's position on recombinant DNA regulation mutually reinforced a number of other discursive practices, having established its meaning in reference to important elements of the EC political metanarrative. What emerged in this complex discursive constellation was a 'dominant feeling' of the 'right way to proceed,' that is, an expression of successful hegemonic articulation at that time.

In the second week of December, sharp notes from DG III and DG VI also raised substantial concerns about the deliberate release directive encompassing not only the regulation of deliberate releases in the stricter

sense of the term, but also including the placing on the market of genetically engineered micro-organisms. With provisions focusing on the process
of production rather than on the characteristics of products, there was a
threatened shift in responsibility from DGs such as DG III and DG VI to DG
XI. Process regulation was a critical element of DG XI's political rationality.
For the central policy actors of DG XI, there was only one appropriate way
to regulate genetic engineering – by defining it through its application,
whether or not the outcome (product) displayed traces of genetic engineering. This representation of genetic engineering implied that DG XI
would be in charge of many of its applications and uses. Whenever methods of genetic engineering were used, DG XI would be involved in the
game, while other DGs, which used to have regulatory responsibility for
products such as pesticides, would not.

The draft goes to the Council and the European Parliament

What we have followed so far was a relatively informal process of decision-
making in the Commission. As I have showed, it was already obvious at this
stage that it was difficult to clearly separate those interpretations of the
genetic engineering issue which had been developed at national level and
those which proliferated at EC level. The emerging EC governance of
genetic engineering risk involved a large number of actors operating from
different institutional sites and supporting different versions of the reality
of the risks of genetic engineering. From the very beginning, DG XI had
outlined a regulatory narrative which sought, at the same time: to include the
other DGs, national experts, and countries such as Germany; to take into
account the larger EC political metanarrative; and to try to define roles, identities and pathways of action for the policy-making process. If everything
worked according to plan, the sphere of genetic engineering regulation
would conform to DG XI's model. What followed was the more formal
process of Community legislation, a process with a more defined structure of
rules and procedures which were mobilised by the various actors who
attempted to define the reality of the genetic engineering question.

Obviously, for DG XI's regulatory model to become reality, the skilful
manipulation of the highly enmeshed system of EC governance involving
hundreds of actors was necessary. What happened over the next few years
was an astounding process of negotiations, characterised by constant stalemates, reversals of positions, the reshaping of actor coalitions, crises,
accusations, and animosity. This process involved a multitude of players,
from the Socialist group in the European Parliament to a group of Nobel
laureates in France. As successful as DG XI's conceptualisations of the
genetic engineering issue had been in previous years, it was far from certain in early 1988 that its draft policy meaning would actually expand from a
definition of reality to a reasoned statement of objectives, taking the form of
an institutional-legislative framework and related policy instruments.
Industry, science, and a number of member states were certainly not in

favour of special legislation, and a blockage of the deliberate release directive was as much a possible scenario as, it would later turn out, a ban on all deliberate releases in Europe. Furthermore, any of the regulatory measures proposed in the DG XI drafts were open to revisions which, in sum, had the potential to shift the directive in a more or less stringent regulatory direction.

However, as I will show in the rest of this paper, the discursive affinities between the positions of DG XI, actors within the European Parliament and various green pressure groups, national representatives of countries such as Germany and national experts had given rise to a situation where these actors, without any explicit agreements or formal meetings, 'collaborated' in the sense of defining a reality which allowed for a successful translation of the DG XI policy narrative into a new system of regulation. Neither DG XI, actors in the European Parliament, nor various green groups necessarily agreed on all the definitions of the central problems involved in recombinant DNA legislation or ideas concerning regulatory measures. But there was sufficient overlap in the definition of problems to create a common discursive constellation which was critical for the ensuing successful dominant approach. Furthermore, occasional disagreements were often only temporary and motivated by strategic deliberations, which eventually lost their relevance. In addition, a second 'hegemonic layer' was constructed due to the fact that DG XI's approach was already closely related to positions strictly opposed to it. In this context, the 'regulation-as-market-harmonisation' indicator played a fundamental role in the process of defining the dominant approach. Throughout this process, DG XI adopted a 'middle of the road position' which, in turn, created discursive links to positions held by industry and other member states. Finally, it is important to note that the narrative of the central actors of DG XI was not simply some sort of policy goal they pursued, but reflected the operation of a complex discursive constellation which had given the environment a new status in the policy process. While actors from DG XI had interests and acted in a strategic way, both interests and strategies were discursive products which connected DG XI to the operation of a larger discursive economy of policy narratives and political metanarratives.

The proposals for the directives on 'contained use' and 'deliberate release' (COM (88) 160 final) viewed genetic engineering hazard regulation as a problem for environmental policy-making that could be solved by instruments and institutions borrowed from ecological discourse. By including products involving genetically modified organisms under the deliberate release guidelines, the 'process' approach prevailed over the 'product' approach. Following the framework of integrated pollution control, genetic engineering was regulated comprehensively from laboratory work to experimentation and diffusion into the economy and society. Public information and access to the decision-making process concerning the implementation of recombinant DNA regulation were integral features of this approach. Furthermore the directive had truly transnational features: the member states not only had to implement the directive, they also had to provide the resources for an EC-system of mutual notification and information with respect to recombinant DNA work, which also gave them the right to influence features of experimental design and production involving recombinant DNA in other countries.

After the proposal had been presented, it was sent to the Council of Ministers, the European Parliament (EP) and to the Economic and Social Committee (ECOSOC). In June 1988, discussions on the two Commission proposals began in the Council's Environment Working group. At the same time, various interest groups and individuals continued with the informal process of influencing the decision-making process. On 8 September 1988, the industry's European Biotechnology Co-ordination Group (EBCG) issued its comments on the Commission proposals, which demonstrated a critical shift in EBCG's line of reasoning. Its comments showed a certain acceptance of DG XI's approach to the regulation issue, for it was now supportive of the proposal. Apparently, the 'inevitability' of a regulatory model with DG XI as the central agency had begun to dominate EBCG's perception of political reality.

On 24 November 1988, the Council discussed the two directives and, after a review of the different positions and the progress made up to that point in the negotiations, the Environment Ministers stated unanimously that high priority should be given to the biotechnology directives.[11] In the meantime, another important player had entered the game. Various committees of the German Bundestag had examined the proposed directives and made an overall recommendation that the Federal Government should press for stricter provisions than those foreseen by the directive.[12] This position restated that of the 'northern country coalition' which, by demanding regulations which went beyond DG XI's requirements, helped to position DG XI as an intermediary force within the policy-making process.

Two weeks later, the Socialist Group of the European Parliament also demanded stricter regulations than currently proposed by the Commission. At a colloquium on the 'Ethical and legal problems of genetic engineering', the Socialist group demanded, among other things, that the release of genetically modified organisms be prohibited without exception.[13] This indicated a development at parliamentary level which went well beyond DG XI's position.

The meetings of the Council's Environment working group continued on 13 January 1989. The patterns of reasoning established at previous meetings persisted, with the politics of signifying genetic engineering still at the centre of the debate. Ostensibly, this was a debate between those demanding strict regulations and those in favour of a more relaxed system of regulation. However, behind these positions lay different approaches to the nature of genetic engineering, such as: what 'is' a genetically modified organism, or what is the difference between a product created by means of genetic technologies and a product produced by other means? In the course of the negotiations, the different actors mobilised scientific arguments in support of their respective cases. These scientific arguments were inseparable from political ones; for example, it was argued that special legislation for products produced by means of genetic engineering would somehow brand these products in an unfavourable way and would damage industries of the future. Depending on the position taken, precautionary regulations could be part of this negative symbolism or, in contrast, could help to make genetic engineering more acceptable. Political reasoning, therefore, was always supported by reference to scientific arguments, while scientific reasoning inevitably relied on arguments from the political discourse. Thus, scientific theories, experiments, ideologies of industrial development, genetically engineered products and theories of consumer behaviour were all part of this highly complex policy-making process.

Compared to three years previously, the genetic engineering debate had stabilised significantly and the importance of EC-wide binding regulations had become generally accepted. However, the different policy narratives of the central actors in the negotiations were still too divergent to allow for the adoption of the directives. The overall picture had remained unchanged. The representatives of the Netherlands, supported by those from Germany and Denmark, urged a stricter regulatory course of action, with the majority of the other nations having reservations about such a move. As regards the 'deliberate release' directive, the main conflict still focused on the scope of the directive: what is it and what should be regulated? This question, of course, was inseparable from such others as: what is genetic engineering, and how can we know or see that a product was produced by means of genetic engineering? Hence, the main dissension concerned the question as to whether the directive should contain provisions relating to the deliberate release of GMOs in products.

By the time the European Parliament was ready to deliver its opinion on the Commission's proposal concerning the two directives, it had become clear in the negotiations within the Council and in those between the Council and the Commission that the initial Commission proposal would undergo considerable revision. This was especially true for the 'contained use' directive, on which, were it not for Germany's opposition, almost a complete compromise had been reached by early March; it was true to a lesser extent for the deliberate release directive. As a result, the reaction of the Council and the Commission to the Parliament's opinion was not what it purported to be. In fact, the legal requirement to respond to the Parliament provided the Council with the procedural opportunity to change the initial Commission proposal, and a formal way of integrating the results of the political negotiations into a modified proposal.

For the developments which followed, it is important to know that one country, Germany, continued to oppose the compromise that had been reached. This would have created a serious obstacle to the passing of the directive under Article 130s, which requires unanimity in the Council. This legal basis was widely favoured by the member states, albeit for different reasons. For the Danes, it meant the possibility of adopting stricter national rules; for the French it meant the chance to block any measures they considered to be too strict. But even under Article 100a, the opposition of only one country in the Council could create a serious obstacle because, in the case of the EP rejecting the Commission' s proposal and adopting amendments by majority, the overruling of this position requires unanimity in the Council. Furthermore, it is interesting to observe that, throughout the negotiations, the 'Northern Alliance' within the Council had taken up and supported positions held by DG XI throughout the preparation of the BRIC directives, and some of DG XI's ideas which were shelved during the BRIC negotiations began to re-emerge in the Council sessions. It became increasingly obvious that a coalition existed between member state representatives in the Council, DG XI, the Parliament, the Economic and Social Committee, and various green pressure groups, an alliance which allowed DG XI to reassume positions it had been forced to give up in previous negotiations.

On 28 April 1989, the European Parliament's Environment Committee tabled reports on the 'contained use' and 'deliberate release' directives, the most far-reaching element of which was a proposed ban on all releases in the Community except those for research purposes.[14] This suggestion was nothing less than a ban on the launching on the market of products involving genetic engineering. These two reports and the more than one hundred amendments attached to them, mainly on the ban on releases, constituted a policy counternarrative which created a serious challenge to both the Commission and the member states in the Council. However, the reports adopted by the EP's Environment Committee had to be finally adopted by the plenary session of the Parliament, and it was at this stage that some of the more far-reaching changes proposed by the Committee were dropped. Before the votes on the two directives, a wide-ranging lobbying effort was launched focusing especially on the members of the conservative groups in the EP.

The proposed banning of the commercial release of genetically engineered products in particular had stirred the emotions. The lobbying had its impact, although the vote in the Parliament could hardly have been narrower. *Nature* reported, 'Europe avoids moratorium. The European Parliament in Strasbourg on 25 May narrowly avoided imposing a five-year moratorium on the sale of certain products of genetic engineering. The moratorium . . . was defeated by a single vote'.[15] The proposed ban on the production or release of high risk genetically modified organisms was also narrowly rejected. The Environment Council finally agreed by consensus on the two draft directives on 22 Mar 1990, and the final adoption of the directives occurred during the meeting of the EcoFin Council of 23 April 1990.

Rewriting the EC directives

Five years of fierce negotiations had come to an end. The regulatory narrative of DG XI, several member countries, the ECOSOC, a variety of green groups, and the European Parliament dominated the conceptualisation of the genetic engineering issue which was now stabilised in an institutional-legal framework. DG XI's regulatory model, first sketched five years earlier, had turned out to be a highly successful instrument for integrating differences, and in the end it was this DG whose definition of reality dominated the policy-making process. This was not the *result* of any powers DG XI had within the highly complex framework of EC governance. There was nothing in the institutional set-up of the Commission which would have privileged DG XI over DGs XII or III; nor can we say that the Commission is always the dominant actor in the EC policy-making process. Finally, it was not even obvious that the EC should get involved at all in the drafting of directives regulating genetic engineering. Rather, DG XI's institutional status and power was the *effect* of a long and intricate process of successful enlisting and mobilisation of individuals, agencies, procedures, and positions into a network of meaning which, at a certain point in time, began to consolidate and gained coherence and structure. To this end, DG XI skilfully deployed a regulatory narrative which linked the precautionary regulation of hazards of genetic engineering to market harmonisation policies, successfully portrayed European industry as lacking a common regulatory framework as a prerequisite for the 'biotechnology revolution', and described the current political situation in terms of the mounting public mistrust of genetic engineering and the rise of critical groups all over Europe, a situation exacerbated by the rise of the green parties in many of the national political systems. Important political events, such as the EP's narrowly defeated motion to impose a ban on the commercial release of GMOs, became critical elements in this debate. A number of privileged nodal points were thus linked into a system of meaning which provided the dominant definition of the genetic engineering regulation question at that particular point in time. Representations of nature, such as genes and their properties, were important elements in such networks of meaning. At the same time, the actors in DG XI were not operating autonomously or without constraint in their deployment of a regulatory narrative. Rather, the positions of the central actors in DG XI were themselves a discursive effect, as they were constituted in a complex discursive web which gave language, meaning and rationality to the kind of opinions and strategies which DG XI was advancing.

The fact that the ECBG and DG XII believed they could settle the regulatory debate by the repeated assertion that there is no scientific evidence for the difference between processes involving recombinant DNA and 'naturally' occurring processes gives reason to believe that they had not studied Saussure in sufficient detail. According to Saussure, language is a system of differences without positive terms; hence, the meaning of a term is always purely relative and determined only by its opposition to all other terms. Hence, the power of a particular representation of genetic engineering technology in a particular historical situation emerges within a matrix which involves other stories, such as those told by ecologists or by animal protection groups which, independent of true/false considerations, become part of the decision-making process concerning the meaning and credibility of dominant reality definitions. Neither ECGB nor Benedict Haerlin could subscribe to all the elements and their combination in DG XI's regulatory narrative. But this was not the point. The point was that DG XI's narrative provided sufficient linkages and affinities to other positions for them to be credibly enlisted into a framework for policy action. The 'actors' (or 'actants') in this network were certainly not 'Germany' or

'ECBG' as a whole. Actor identities are not unitary, but are the result of processes of enrolment and coalitions which create identities that are subject to constant change and negotiation. Hence, the identity of Germany as an actor in the regulatory process was the result of a complex process of negotiation at national and, simultaneously, at EC level. These negotiations gave rise to the positions and strategies adopted by Germany in the Council for example, and allowed for its integration within DG XI's narrative. Countries such as Germany,France, and Britain had felt that there was a need for regulatory action in the field of genetic engineering. But it was not the case that 'these countries were pushing Brussels' to become active. Rather, the national controversies and debates reinforced the arguments of those groups within the Commission which were trying to propose the EC as a site for the drafting of genetic engineering regulations. At the same time, such proposals at EC level strengthened those actors at national level who supported preliminary domestic regulatory initiatives. Such constructions of meaning were also predicated upon a complex discursive constellation which included the dominant EC discourse on social and economic regulation in the Community, and a political metanarrative which aligned modernisation policies and precautionary environmental policies as highly compatible projects.

This shows that EC governance cannot be understood in isolation from its constituent political, scientific, and economic discourses. Ascribing different meanings to the European Union will result in different readings of legitimate patterns of EC governance. Although we speak of the 'European Union', it is not clear what is meant by this term. Where are the boundaries of this European Union? Is it synonymous with Delors' vision of Europe as an 'organised' regulatory space, or with the idea of an Anglo-Saxon style deregulated free-trade area? What constitutes the territory of the European Community? Such questions are far from settled, and hence need to be treated as open and unresolved issues.

The importance of debate for patterns of EC governance also becomes clear from the implementation process of the two genetic engineering directives. The two directives were implemented differently in Britain, France and Germany which – overall – led to substantial and significant differences in the national regulatory situations.[16] Thus, the adoption of EC legislation did not imply the disappearance of local arguments over genetic engineering. Nationally divergent constructions of the boundaries of administrative responsibilities and of risk assessment, for example, created stark contrasts in local readings of the genetic engineering issue. The choice of the so-called 'competent authority' responsible for responding to release notifications and for representing the national viewpoint at EC level played a critical role in the implementation of the directives. In Germany, the competent authority was the Department of Health, which did not seek any dialogue with the critics of genetic engineering. By contrast, in Britain the new statutory authority was assigned to the Department of the Environment, which sought to accommodate environmentalists by enhancing their regulatory role. Such institutional boundaries also affected the boundaries of legitimate expertise in the evaluation of the risks of recombinant DNA experiments. Whereas in the UK the Department of the Environment emphasised the ecological uncertainties about the behaviour of known genetic inserts (and thus responded to the ecologists' concerns), in France, the competent authority (the Ministry of Agriculture) focused in its authorisation practice on the risks of genetic imprecision, a concern which had little apparent relevance to environmental concerns. Such multiple readings played a critical role as they became elements of competing networks of meaning which socially construct the political realities of EC governance.

Hence, the EC regulatory narrative was not simply adopted in France, Germany and Britain. Like all texts, it became the object of a process of reading and rewriting as soon as it was published. These regulation stories were introduced into the various national discursive economies. Since any successful stabilisation of a policy narrative depends on the terms of the dominant political metanarrative for its expression, the dominant political discourses, the prevailing concepts of social order and legitimacy, the dominant state models, and the current practices of democracy in Britain, France and Germany were crucial elements in the implementation of the EC directives.

Such intertextualities, however, are neither an indication of the 'strength' of the nation state nor of the 'weakness' of supranational institutions. They describe highly contested models of EC governance and practices of drawing the boundaries of the political architecture of Europe. What is at stake in the creation of this European political space are boundaries of governance such as those between nature and technology, or those between scientists or experts and the public, which are either permeable and allow for the negotiation of the risks of genetic engineering, or are constructed in such a way that the determination of the genetic engineering risks are the prerogative of experts only. Such boundary work is always an articulation of power relations, as it links individuals, structures, and institutions together through processes of legitimation, classification and control. In Europe's newly-emerging political system, such boundary work occurs in a space which extends beyond the nation state without being synonymous with 'the supranational'. This space is populated by a heterogeneous mixture of artefacts, theories, ideologies, individuals, countries like Germany and France, and institutions such as DG XII or the Department of the Environment. Uncertainty and fluidity are the central characteristics of this post-modern regime of EC governance, which the discursive constructions and semantic stabilisations of micro-political practices of boundary construction seek to overcome.

Notes

1 I follow in my usage of the term 'plot' the distinction made in literary theory between 'story' (the pre-literary sequence of events providing the writer with the raw material), and 'plot' (the literary re-ordering of this sequence).
2 DG III, Regulation on Biotechnology, 4 June 1985, Memo, Brussels.
3 European Parliament, Committee on Social Affairs and Employment. Draft

Opinion for the Committee on Energy, Research and Technology on matters relating to biotechnology. Draftsman B. Haerlin, May 14, 1986, PE 105.015, Brussels, 4.

4 Gesetz zur Regelung von Fragen der Gentechnik, 20 June 1990, Bundesgesetzblatt 1080–1095.

5 Interview, MAFF, London, 27 July 1989.

6 République Française. Premier Ministre. Groupe Interministeriel des Produits Chimiques, Reglementation des Biotechnologies. Etat actuel et propositions soumise au premier ministre, 7 juin 1989, Paris, Memo, 10.

7 DG XI, Council Directive on the Deliberate Release into the Environment of Genetically modified organisms, Draft, 29 September 1987, Brussels.

8 European Parliament, Resolution on biotechnology in Europe and the need for an integrated policy. Doc. A2-134/86, Official Journal of the European Communities, 23 March 1987.

9 Statement of the individual experts meeting, 29 April 1987, Memo, Brussels.

10 EBCG, Safety Evaluation through Risk Assessment in Biotechnology, Memo, Brussels, March 1987, 2.

11 Commission of the European Communities, Council, Résultats des Travaux du Conseil 'Environnement' du 24 novembre, 1988, Minutes, Brussels.

12 Deutscher Bundestag, 11th legislative period, Recommendation for a decision and report drawn up by the Committee of Research and Technology, Proposal for a Council Directive on the contained use of genetically modified micro-organisms-COM (88) 160 final-SYN 131, Publication 11/3563, 24 November 1988.

13 Socialist Group–European Parliament, Colloquy, Ethical and legal problems of genetic engineering, 6 December1988, Memo, Brussels.

14 European Parliament, Session Documents, Series A, Document A2–141/89 SYN 131 Cooperation procedure (first reading), 28 April 1989, Report drawn up on behalf of the Committee on the Environment, Public Health and Consumer Protection on the proposal from the Commission to the Council (COM/88/160-C2-73/88) for a directive on the contained use of genetically modified microorganisms. Rapporteur: Mr. Gerhard Schmid, Brussels. Then, European Parliament, first reading on deliberate release, 28–29.

15 *Nature*, 8 June, no. 339 (1989): 413.

16 See for the following: Les Levidow, Susan Carr, Rene Schomburg, David Wield, Deliberate Release Directive 90/220: EU-Level Policy Issues. GMO Releases: Managing Uncertainty about Biosafety. A study of the implementation of Directive 90/220. DG XII/E-1 horizontal programme Assessment of the Ethical and Socio-economic Effects and Technological Risks from Biotechnology, Brussels, December 1995.

5

EUROPEAN SOCIAL POLICY

Towards multi-level and multi-actor governance

Gerda Falkner

Introduction

This volume is concerned with changes in European governance. In EC social policy, such changes were manifold and even occurred at the level of formal Treaty changes in the 1990s. The move towards co-operative public-private governance was only the most prominent aspect, the process of change having concerned basically all characteristic elements of a 'system of governance' (see Kohler-Koch, in this volume). Thus, innovation occurred at the levels of:

- belief systems about appropriate principles of action (shared responsibility between the European and national levels according to horizontal and vertical subsidiarity principles);
- actor constellations (a few privileged interest groups were incorporated into EC decision-making on public policies);
- decision-making routines (very specific processes were established), and
- boundaries (territorial exclusion of the UK; functional exclusion of various aspects of social policy).

This chapter will first outline the traditional patterns of EC social policy and briefly analyse failed efforts towards more cooperative governance patterns during the 1970s and 1980s. It was only when a major change in EC social policy was deemed inevitable during the 1991 IGC that employers agreed to participate in a quasi-corporatist mode of governance. The changes in EC social policy governance brought about under the Maastricht Treaty will then be outlined before their operation in practice is discussed. Finally, the changes will be assessed in the wider perspective of European governance.

In seeking an explanation for the most singular element in the EU context of the change in governance under review here, i.e. the development of quasi-corporatist patterns of decision-making under the Social Agreement (indeed, a 'corporatist policy community' developed; see

Falkner 1998 in more detail), the hypothesis of a co-evolution of political and associational structures will be tested. It was put forward by Eichener and Voelzkow (1994a) but is deemed to rest on rather weak empirical foundations so far (see Kohler-Koch 1997a). The question is whether the EU's developing statehood (in the sense of action capacity) results in a reorganisation of the system of interest representation, while in turn being influenced by the relevant organised interests (Eichener and Voelzkow 1994a: 17).

The 'old patterns': social policy governance under the EEC Treaty

As a background to the changes which have occurred, it is important to understand the main characteristics of the initial system of EC social policy governance. It was based on national competence and on hierarchical relations between public and private actors.

The social chapter of the 1957 EEC Treaty (EECT) lacked explicit competence for EC-level intervention. The dominant philosophy was that welfare would be provided by the economic growth stemming from the economics of a liberalised market and not from the regulatory and distributive capacity of public policy (e.g. Kohler-Koch 1997a). To the extent that social provisions were included at all, they concerned the cost aspect of social policy and constituted small concessions for the more interventionist camp (e.g. Art. 119 EECT on equal pay for both sexes; the establishment of a 'European Social Fund' to co-finance professional training programmes). The only explicit Community competence for social policy regulation under the original EECT arose under the freedom of movement for workers, as part of the Treaty's market-making activities (Art. 51 EECT). In principle, EC citizens were only being ensured equal treatment in social security via EC co-ordination, while the national social systems remained autonomous in principle (but see Leibfried and Pierson 1995 on losses of sovereignty and spillovers).

The original procedural patterns laid out in the EC social policy chapter were exceptional within the Treaty. The Commission was assigned 'the task of promoting close co-operation' between member states (Art. 118 EECT). However, while in other areas of EEC activity the Commission was empowered to present legislative proposals with a view to the Council deliberation of binding EC law, the Commission could only 'act in close contact with Member States by making studies, delivering opinions and arranging consultations both on problems arising at national level and on those of concern to international organisations' in the social area (Art. 118 EECT). It is important to note that the organised interests of labour and industry were not given a special role in the social realm in the 1957 Treaty. The Economic and Social Committee, which includes nationally nominated representatives of employers, workers, and various other interests, had a merely consultative function as in most other areas of European integration. Until the Maastricht Treaty was introduced, therefore, the constellation of actors in EC social policy was no different to that of other functional realms.

To sum up: the EECT provided for a rather hierarchical mode of governance in social policy. The member states had almost exclusive competence in this area. To the extent that EEC level action was allowed, the formal political institutions established under the Rome Treaty were the exclusive masters, and the Council was obliged to decide unanimously. As the following section will show, however, from the early 1970s onwards the EC institutions tried to introduce change alongside the incremental development of a 'social dimension' of European integration.

Early efforts towards changes in governance in the 1970s and 1980s

During the first fifteen years of their existence the European Communities concentrated on the realisation of goals formulated in the founding Treaties. Consequently, social policy was almost a non-issue. But during the late 1960s, the relevant political climate changed. As soon as social policy (mainly in terms of labour law harmonisation) became an issue of debate, efforts to include the two sides of industry in the policy process began.

At their 1972 Paris summit, the EC Heads of State or Government solemnly declared that economic expansion should not be an end in itself but should lead to improvements in the living and working conditions of the populace. With a view to relevant EC action, they recommended that a catalogue of social policy measures be elaborated by the Commission. The 1974 social policy action programme (OJ 74/C 13/1) represented a milestone in EEC social policy, and several of the proposed measures were adopted by the Council in the years leading up to the early 1980s (e.g. on equal treatment at the workplace; labour law minimum standards such as early warning in cases of mass redundancies; on details see e.g. Hantrais 1995; Gold 1993).

It is interesting to note that one of three central goals of the action programme, along with full employment and the improvement of living and working conditions, was the growing participation of the social partners in the economic and social policy decisions of the Community. The Council demonstrated its support for those employees' representative bodies which participate in the activity of the Community by *inter alia* establishing a European Trade Union Institute. This was an important signal to the European Trade Union Confederation (ETUC) which had only been founded in 1973. Furthermore, the Council planned, depending on the circumstances in the individual member states, to facilitate the conclusion of European collective pay agreements in appropriate areas. This pledge, made as early as 1974, shows the long history behind invitations to the social partners to conclude European-level agreements.

In 1974 also, 'Tripartite Conferences' were established as a new public–private forum for social policy issues. It was hoped that this institution would not only allow for consultation of the major interest groups, but also for interest aggregation. The Economic and Social Committee had proved unsatisfactory in this regard. The ideological split between, and the lack of internal coherence and structure within, the three groups (employers, employees, and various interests) have, in many cases, deprived the Committee of a good basis for compromise. In practice, this has meant that the results of cumbersome decision-making processes have lacked coherence and/or any definitive status (for a case study see Falkner 1991 on the so-called 'EC Social Charter'). In the 'Tripartite Conferences' European-level representatives of labour and industry were invited to participate for the first time, alongside national social partners, the Council and the Commission. These conferences met six times between 1974 and 1978, at which stage ETUC withdrew due to the reluctance of the employers' side to conclude agreements. The consequences of this decision for the employers were not serious, as the European trade union organisation was only in its infancy and incapable of significant collective action. Furthermore, the Council's social policy impetus of the early 1970s had already stalled, and many important legislative projects remained blocked.

Moves towards cooperative governance were made when Jacques Delors came into office as Commission President in January 1985 and prompted a period of Euro-activism. Delors had a well-known personal history of trade union leadership and was strongly in favour of social dialogue – as were his major collaborators (e.g. Ross 1995a: 150). They launched the so-called 'social dialogue' between the umbrella organisations of labour and industry at EC level (ETUC, UNICE and CEEP) at the Val Duchesse castle outside Brussels. The Commission's plan was to reach common views which would subsequently be presented and discussed with the two sides of industry in each member state. This should, in turn, lead to new topics being discussed at Community level, with a view to reaching common views. Consequently, it was hoped, the stalemates in social policy discussions in the Council would be circumvented or ended. However, because of the employers' refusal to enter into binding agreements, the 'Val Duchesse social dialogue' never went beyond non-binding joint opinions.

With the 'Europe 1992' project, Delors successfully pressed for EEC reforms. The price, however, was that it only applied to economic integration at first. In the absence of a consensus among the governments, the White Paper on the Internal Market Programme did not include a social policy chapter. The 1986 Single European Act also contained very few social policy innovations. Nevertheless, the first explicit Community task was inserted within the EECT's social provisions, i.e. to improve worker health and safety, notably at the workplace. This was even allowed to happen on the basis of qualified majority voting which had never before applied to social policy issues. Furthermore, the Commission President was successful in getting formal backing for the Val Duchesse social dialogue as initiated by him: the possibility of Euro-level collective agreements was explicitly being mentioned, and the Commission was solemnly attributed the task of endeavouring to develop the dialogue between management and labour at European level (Art. 118b EECT).

While the practical implementation of the Internal Market was progressing, the lack of a 'social dimension' was increasingly being politicised. Actors such as the EP, ETUC, and the Commission argued that open economic borders created the need for EC action to prevent 'social dumping' (Falkner 1993). In 1988 the Commission published several discussion documents on what was called the 'social dimension of the Internal Market'. It called for the creation of a code of minimum social standards, for some thought to be given to Euro-level labour relations, and the deepening of the social dialogue (e.g. Social Europe 1988/1: 74). Although the Commission could not expect high ambitions from the employers in the Val Duchesse talks at the time, it still hoped that the social dialogue could result in innovative social policy. The national governments joined the Commission in pressing for collective Euro-agreements. By the late 1980s, several European Council meetings would, in the presidency conclusions, refer not only to EC social policy in general, but also to the desirability of social partner involvement in particular (see EC Bulletin 1988/12: 9–10).

All these invitations were in vain while social policy was in the doldrums. At the very end of the 1980s, however, new activism was prompted during debates on an improved legal basis for EC social policy. Due to British opposition, the EC 'Social Charter' was only adopted as a non-binding joint declaration by the other eleven governments in December 1989. It nevertheless constituted another milestone for European social policy. Minimum rights were solemnly assured in various areas, and selective EC action was envisaged. 'Social partnership' was again a central topic (points 10–13). The Charter's implementation was perceived to depend on the active participation of the EC social partners in many areas (Preamble).

Formulae for involvement of the social partners similar to the later Maastricht innovations were presented for the first time in the Commission's working programme to implement the Charter (Commission 1989). The Commission, together with the two sides of industry, wanted to 'examine the extent to which and under what terms the former could agree to participate, in the framework of the social dialogue, in preparing certain legal instruments which the Commission would subsequently submit to the Community bodies concerned' (ibid.: 29). The Commission furthermore proposed to consult the two sides of industry systematically on the numerous legislative proposals contained in the action programme. It was no surprise that UNICE voiced concerns about the volume of initiatives proposed and the thrust of some of the proposals (UNICE position paper of 22 March 1990). The Commission's tactics to employ 'sticks' (envisaged social regulation) as well as 'carrots' (participation of the social partners therein), however, was already successful (Ross 1995b: 377): UNICE made clear that, despite its opposition to most EC-level legislation, it wanted to have a say in the details of any measures discussed:

> UNICE requests that it should be properly consulted before the final detail of an initiative is decided by the Commission, as well as on formal proposals to Council. . . . In some cases, it may be appropriate for the social partners to have an opportunity to

debate the issues involved in the social dialogue at an early stage, prior to the Commission adopting a formal proposal. However, this should not replace or delay direct consultation of UNICE by the Commission.

(UNICE position paper, 22 March 1990)

Although UNICE warned on that occasion that 'too much regulation and central control will stifle initiative and demotivate the social partners' (ibid.), later developments leading up to the Maastricht Treaty demonstrated the reverse: Euro-level interest politics developed alongside the increased 'state' capacity of the EC in social policy. This shows that the process of European integration draws political actors into a new game where they are induced to redefine their strategies (Kohler-Koch 1996: 366). While a pluralist mode of pressure politics rather than co-operation of private interests had characterised EC social policy-making up to the early 1990s, once the EC's capacity for action grew, industry found itself involved in a process of change. As will be shown below, UNICE even became an active co-actor when the Intergovernmental Conference (IGC) preceding the Maastricht Treaty finally put in place a network type of governance for EC social policy, which includes characteristics of what is known as a 'corporatist' set-up at member state level.

The 1991 IGC: a 'whip in the window'

The establishment of the central features of the new pattern of social policy governance was, in fact, due to the major European interest groups' *anticipation* of significant changes in the EC social policy provisions.[1] The provisions (which are outlined in detail below) were suggested by the three central social partner organisations ETUC (workers), UNICE (employers) and CEEP (public enterprises). Following an initiative by the Commission in February 1991 (Cassina 1992: 13), these three peak associations sat down with the Commission (Schulz 1996: 86) to formulate proposals to the IGC. In a letter to the Council President dated 28 June 1991, they informed him 'of the progress of the social dialogue ad hoc working group on the role of the social partners and of [their] willingness to make a timely contribution to the work of the Intergovernmental Conference' (Social Europe 2/1995: 138). At their meeting of 31 October 1991, ETUC, UNICE, and CEEP reached an agreement on how to strengthen the role of the social partners in the new Treaty. On the basis of earlier inputs to the IGC by the Commission and the Belgian government, they drafted proposals for the wording of Articles 118 (4), 118(a) and 118(b) of the draft Treaty under discussion (published in Social Europe 2/1995: 138–9). This input to the IGC received much public attention and was obviously accorded prime importance by the governments. The social partner proposals were indeed accepted by the Dutch presidency and subsequently by the signatories of the Social Agreement.

During the eight months of negotiations on this social partner agreement important developments occurred on both sides of industry.

Originally, neither of the partners had unequivocally perceived themselves as a potential collective negotiator at the European level. Influenced by certain of its member organisations, even ETUC had *de facto* rather feared formal obligations resulting from collective negotiations. But at the May 1991 Congress, important changes were decided in the wake of the internal market and the increased competitive pressures which made joint European action ever more pressing. Voting by two-thirds majority was reformed to be more effective, and the European Industry Committees were given full voting powers (except in financial and statutory matters; Ebbinghaus and Visser 1994: 239). Both territorial and functional interests are now directly represented under the umbrella of ETUC. Further amendments to the ETUC constitution were decided during the May 1995 Congress. The Executive Committee now has a responsibility to 'determine the composition and mandate of the delegation for negotiations with European employers' organisations', and to 'ensure the convergence at European level of the demands and contractual policies of affiliated organisations' (Art. 11).

For the employers' group, the likely switch to majority voting in the realm of social affairs changed its perception of how best to pursue its self-interest (see also e.g. Keller 1993: 593). Assuming that it was better to keep the steering-wheel in one's own hands, UNICE's former tactics of non-co-operation at the Euro-level no longer went unquestioned. The CBI, however, constituted a special problem because it demonstrated extreme resistance to collective bargaining at the EU level. Reportedly, two aspects helped to unlock the situation: the more cooperative attitude of several other national employers' organisations, most of which had experienced intense social partner co-operation at home; and the lifting of the blockade by the CBI who (wrongly) expected that the British government would block social policy reforms at Maastricht anyway (Cassina 1992: 14; Ross 1995a: 151). With the Maastricht Social Protocol (see below) in place, several internal reforms were made to enable UNICE to meet its challenges. In June 1992, the organisation was formally assigned the task of representing its members in the dialogue between the EC social partners (Art. 2.1 of the Statute). Further innovation arose from the failure to reach a collective agreement on European works councils (see below). According to an internal agreement of April 1994, the CBI continued to participate but did not have a right of veto in negotiations under the Social Agreement, but nor was it bound by a rejected agreement.

To sum up: the internal interest group structure of the two major Euro-players both anticipated the changes in governance under the Social Agreement and reacted to them later on. Without the joint social partner proposal to the 1991 IGC, the actual features of the new Treaty basis would probably have looked different. A pattern of interdependence is thus discernible between action capacity at the EC level on the one hand, and the development of relevant interest politics on the other. According to Eichener and Voelzkow (1994a), this constitutes a co-evolution of the structures of the state and of organised interests respectively. The evidence presented here furthermore endorses the hypothesis that European integration has over the past decade been a polity-creating as well as a market-deepening process (Hooghe and Marks 1997).

The Maastricht Social Agreement as a change in governance

Social policy was one of the crucial areas in the 1991 IGC. The originally envisaged extension of the provisions in the EEC social chapter could not be realised because of strong opposition from Great Britain. In order not to endanger the rest of the IGC's compromises, the UK was finally granted an opt-out from the social policy measures agreed by the rest of the member states. In the 'Protocol on Social Policy' annexed to the Treaty on European Union (TEU), the other member states were authorised to have recourse to the institutions, procedures and mechanisms of the Treaty for the purposes of implementing their 'Agreement on Social Policy' (see e.g. Falkner 1996a). As already outlined in the introduction, this so-called Social Agreement represents a significant change in governance if compared to the earlier Treaty provisions. By now, it has been included in the EC-Treaty by the Amsterdam IGC.

Innovations under the Social Agreement concern the full range of major governance components as outlined above. Thus, there is now an explicit Community competence for a wide range of social policy issues, including working conditions; information and consultation of workers; equality between men and women with regard to labour market opportunities and treatment at work; and the integration of persons excluded from the labour market (see Art. 2). Consequently, both the EC member states and the Community share the power to act in the social realm, and both are now in that sense partial governance systems. Action under the Social Agreement can in most areas even be taken under the supranational mode of qualified majority voting, for example in the area of information and consultation of workers. Thus far, however, the new social policy provisions do not depart from patterns established in other issue areas in EC politics.

This is not the case where the boundaries of this sub-system of EC governance are concerned. In geographical terms, the full opt-out of one member state is unprecedented. Another interesting feature is that the functional boundaries are explicitly restricted: excluded from the scope of the Agreement are matters of pay, the right of association, and the right to strike or to impose lockouts (Art. 2.6). Under the EECT, by contrast, the subsidiary competence provisions allow for practically any action which is deemed necessary for reaching Treaty goals, notably market integration.

The changes to the policy-making process constitute probably the most innovative aspect of change. The Social Agreement contains three layers of social partner participation in the policy process. first, a member state may entrust management and labour, at their joint request, with the implementation of Directives adopted pursuant to the Social Agreement. Second, the Commission now has a legal obligation to consult both management and labour *before* submitting social policy proposals. And third,

90

but most significantly, management and labour can, on the occasion of such consultation, inform the Commission of their wish to initiate negotiations in order to reach agreements instead of EC legislation. Such agreements may, at the joint request of the signatory parties, be implemented by a Council decision on a proposal from the Commission.

The Euro-level representatives of labour and industry are thus included in a pattern of co-operative policy-making. They may jointly act instead of, or in conjunction with, the EC institutions – depending on their options concerning the specific issue. The actor constellation in social partner negotiations under the Social Agreement is hence sharply distinct from what is usually characterised as the classic EC pattern, namely, a multiplicity of lobbies which try to influence the Commission independently of each other. The Social Agreement provides for 'corporatist' co-operation of interest organisations and public authorities (Lehmbruch 1982: 8) rather than for 'pluralist' pressure politics (which will however continue during the early phase of a policy proposal). The interest associations are incorporated within the process of authoritative decision-making and implementation (see the famous definition of neo-corporatism by Schmitter 1981: 295).

Collective agreements even enjoy primacy on the path towards social legislation. That constitutes the 'double principle of subsidiarity' (Commission 1993c). First, the principle of subsidiarity as laid down in Art. 3b ECT shall be applied to the social field, too. It implies that the Community shall take action only 'if and in so far as the objectives of the proposed action cannot be sufficiently achieved by the Member States'. But second, even if EC action is taken, social partner agreement is sought in the first place. Thus, the national level has priority over the European one, and the level of collective agreements is preferred to that of traditional EC legislation.

As regards the actor constellation too, a pattern reminiscent of 'neo-corporatism' was prompted by the Social Agreement where private interest representation was concerned. Two decision processes have so far been completed under the new rules. In both cases, the negotiations were monopolised by the three major cross-sectoral interest federations (ETUC, CEEP and UNICE), with the backing of both the Council and the Commission.[2]

In the following, I shall outline the practical developments under the Social Agreement to date, in order to underline the fact that the *practice* of decision-making has also undergone significant changes.

Cooperative policy-making under the Social Agreement

The first application of the new procedures concerned the establishment of European Works Councils. UNICE had always strictly rejected any EC-level initiatives on employee information and participation in the enterprise on the grounds that they might cause 'unnecessary and intolerable complications' and have a 'negative impact on investment' (UNICE 1991: 2).

It was, therefore, a major innovation when UNICE declared itself 'ready to sit down with the Commission and/or the European unions to develop a . . . procedure for information and consultation that is acceptable to all parties' (EIRR 238: 13), when the Social Agreement entered into force in autumn 1993, and the Works Councils Directive became the test case.

ETUC was sceptical as regards the employers' presumably tactical new approach. It therefore suggested initially having only preliminary talks on the possibility of entering into formal collective negotiations. After two exploratory meetings between the three cross-sectoral peak federations during the spring of 1994, an exchange of conditional offers to negotiate began. The crucial point was the 'need for the negotiating parties to adopt a flexible approach and to examine alternative methods and procedures' (Hornung-Draus 1994: 4). This was regarded as indispensable by UNICE and CEEP, and was opposed by ETUC, which wanted explicit rights (for employees of transnational enterprises), obligations (for central management), and rather centralised fall-back provisions. An *ex ante* agreement on the latter ideas would, in the employer federations' eyes, have left purely 'technical details' for proper negotiations (ibid.). Nevertheless, three days before the closing date of the second phase of consultation, UNICE and CEEP broadly conceded to ETUC's principles (Gold and Hall 1994: 180), after crucial mediation by the Commission. There was also agreement to submit the envisaged final pact to the Council for implementation as European law.

Just before the end of the deadline, however, the stance of the British organisations, the TUC (Trades Union Congress) and CBI (Confederation of British Industry), changed the situation. The British employers' federation withdrew from the negotiations (on details see e.g. Ross 1995a: 381ff.; Falkner 1996b). By the spring of 1994, UNICE seemed as yet unprepared to outvote its British member organisation, while ETUC considered the participation of the CBI to be indispensable. A significant sign of the changes which occurred under the Social Agreement is that, in their official statements, both UNICE and ETUC conferred the responsibility for the failure of the 'talks about talks' (Gold and Hall 1994: 181) on each other. This indicates that although there is clearly no obligation to arrive at specific agreements under the Social Agreement, these organisations felt bound by their earlier commitment in principle: under the conditions of institutionalised co-operation (which is typical of EU governance), behavioural norms have a tendency to become binding (Kohler-Koch 1996: 363). The Works Councils issue was subsequently settled by a traditional Council Directive.

The second decision-making process under the new social policy regime has already resulted in a Euro-collective agreement among the three major federations. As was the case with worker information and consultation, the issue of parental leave had been discussed since the early 1980s, and had turned out to be extremely controversial. On 14 December 1995, ETUC, UNICE, and CEEP nevertheless established a framework agreement which provides for an individual right of a minimum of 3 months parental leave while employment rights are maintained. These standards are low if compared to what the more advanced member states already had before, but constitute significant progress, say, for Ireland, and advances in detail for several other countries. (Incidentally, the same is true for most EC Directives adopted by the Social Affairs Council.) On the suggestion of the social partners, the Commission subsequently proposed a draft Directive with the aim of rendering their Agreement binding. Political consensus within the Council was reached within only two months, and the Directive was formally adopted on 3 June 1996 (for details see Falkner 1997).

The main actors reportedly perceive their collective agreement as only a first step. ETUC Secretary General Gabaglio considered the parental leave agreement as 'the point of departure for the establishment of a European industrial relations system as required by the single market and European economic integration' (indirectly quoted in *Agence Europe* 15 December 1995: 9). CEEP President Castellano thought that it represented 'remarkable progress that will . . . signify that other agreements may be reached' (quoted in *Agence Europe* 16 December 1995: 9). For UNICE President Périgot, 'this negotiation proves that there is a contractual space at the European level that there must be a will to take care of' (quoted in *Agence Europe* 16.12.1995: 9). It should be noted that, in the second half of the 1990s, it is no longer only ETUC which is pleading for a 'conventional dimension' of European integration; in solemn declarations, at least, the employers' representatives are doing so as well. Indeed, a third social partner agreement, on part-time work, was reached in 1997 and a fourth, on fixed-term work, in 1998.

Conclusions: the Social Agreement and the transformation of governance in Europe

EC social policy has indeed experienced a change in governance. Although most social policy decisions are still taken at the national level (notably those regarding costly social benefits), there has been some degree of Europeanisation, particularly during the 1990s. The now commonly agreed and even formalised principle of action is co-operation and shared responsibility for social policy goals, between, on the one hand, the various levels of governance (mainly national and European) and, on the other, various actors at the Euro-level (social partners and EC institutions). The developments under the Maastricht Social Agreement are thus a good example of what has been described as the transformation of governance evolving around (but not exclusively at) the EU-level: a shift away from a hierarchical towards a network style of governance, which is characterised by cooperative rather than competitive interaction patterns among a large variety of actors. The recent developments in EC social policy fit well into the trend outlined by Beate Kohler-Koch (Kohler-Koch 1996): there are mutually dependent but, at the same time, autonomous actors and blurred borderlines between the private and the public. The above overview on the development of EC social policy governance has shown that both problem definition and the setting of respective preferences are influenced by the process of interaction. Governments still try to reign, but they have shared their power with one another, with the Community institutions, and (formally under the Social Agreement) with the major private interests.

How did this change in governance come about?

And: why did change occur only during the 1990s, although efforts had already been made long before that? The evidence points to two interdependencies: between economic integration and social policy; and between EC action capacity in social affairs and social partner participation. There is no space to elaborate the first argument, but it is obvious that the increased market integration prompted many calls for a 'social dimension' which, at least eclectically, resulted in EC Directives (see Falkner 1998 for details). And it was indeed the (anticipation of) increased regulative activity rather than solemn invitations which finally prompted the qualitative leap in social partner involvement. The developments under the Social Agreement are thus a prime example of the co-evolution of political/administrative structures (what might be called 'the state' at the European level) and interest politics. As long as the 'social dimension' lagged behind economic integration, due to a lack of competencies and to the frequent unanimity requirements, the employers' representatives were successful in blocking any involvement in EC social policy-making which went beyond classic lobbying or non-binding consultation. UNICE had no negotiation mandate from its members and did not aim to get one because its organisational weakness was indeed a strength in its relationship with ETUC (Streeck 1995a: 116). This tactic was revised as soon as the Maastricht negotiations made qualified majority voting in EC social policy only a matter of time. UNICE's new attitude and the subsequent joint social partner proposal to the 1991 IGC were in turn essential contributions to the forthcoming reform of the Treaty basis for EC social policy. This points to an interdependence of state capacity and interest group developments, as argued by Eichener and Voelzkow (1994a).

From the mid 1970s onwards, the Commission (often supported by specific Council presidencies) once again acted as a political entrepreneur by sponsoring the idea of cooperative social policy-making. The basic reasoning was that the major interest groups might develop and legitimise specific social policy measures at the EU level with a view to ending or circumventing stalemate in the Council. It seems that the constant presentation of 'social partnership' as a good practice of governance finally made even those governments in the Council without a national tradition of corporatism agree to the new approach (except, that is, for the UK). Increasingly, the problem of EC social policy would not only be identified with Council stalemate, but also with a 'decision gap' at the level of organised interests (Streeck 1995a). But institutional activism alone was not enough to make the employers come to the bargaining table. Only the 1990–91 IGC offered a 'window of opportunity': the employers supported collective negotiations as a lesser evil when compared to increased EC legislation.

Democratic legitimacy and fit with national patterns

It is interesting to note that the growing 'statehood' of the EC is paralleled by patterns well-known in some member states. It has already been mentioned that the new mode of EC social policy governance displays some similarities to 'neo-corporatism'. Once again, 'the state' (in this case: the EC institutions) has an interest in sharing the burden of governance with the major interest groups. A particularly important feature in the case under discussion is the striving for increased public legitimacy for the EU via 'social partnership'. This is against a background of widespread criticism regarding the meagre social dimension of European integration and the EMU, whose convergence criteria *de facto* put increased pressure on social expenditure in the member states. It is hoped that the social partners bring EC social politics closer to the citizens by strengthening one type of representation, in addition to the pre-existing forms at EC level: there is political representation of citizens based on direct elections to the EP; there is indirectly legitimated representation of the member states in the Council; and now, under the Social Agreement, there is a powerful functional representation of the major societal interests (i.e. employers and employees). In line with recent suggestions to develop a mix of democratic elements with a view to creating a working post-national democracy (i.e. to employ both direct and various representative mechanisms, e.g. Zürn 1996; Grande 1997), such an additional link between the citizens and EC decision-making is to be welcomed.

To date however, the innovations of the Social Agreement as regards increased democracy are by no means unequivocally positive. As with corporatist systems at the national level, functioning intra-group democracy as well as the adequate representation of a wide range of other interests (e.g. the unemployed) cannot be taken for granted. Furthermore, a typical but much criticised feature of classic (neo-)corporatism, namely the bypassing and downgrading of parliaments (e.g. Streeck and Schmitter 1991), is repeated under the Social Agreement. The directly elected European Parliament is not involved in decisions taken by the social partners, and has no power of co-decision if collective agreements are implemented by a Council Decision.

Although some characteristics of corporatism have been detected, the patterns evolving under the Social Agreement cannot replicate classic national corporatism. In short, major differences commence with the restriction of functional scope to social policy only. This limits political exchange and thus the political clout of the arrangement in overall terms, particularly if compared to national corporatism at the macro-level during the 1970s. As recent concertation attempts with a view to employment policy ('Essen Follow-up') and studies in other EC policy areas show (see e.g. Greenwood *et al.* 1992a; Eichener and Voelzkow 1994b), the Social Agreement is not the only field where more cooperative public–private governance is under way. Nevertheless, due to the extremely fragmented system of EC politics, with extreme divergence both in sectoral policy regimes and in patterns of interest representation within the individual sectors (e.g. Eising and Kohler-Koch 1994: 182–3), one should not expect a coherent cross-sectoral pattern. The emergence of cross-sectoral macro-corporatism at the EU level is therefore not on the agenda (see also Traxler and Schmitter 1995: 213; Kohler-Koch 1992: 103; Streeck and Schmitter 1991).

Another difference from corporatism at the national level is that, so far, the EC-level social partners cannot themselves guarantee the implementation of their agreements (e.g. Keller 1995; Obradovic 1995; Traxler and Schmitter 1995). Implementation via a Council Directive, however, provided a pragmatic solution to this – similar to the existing '*Allgemein-verbindlichkeitserklärung*' in several European countries, an extension of collective agreements to parties which have not signed them. It should also be noted that recent EC social policy Directives have typically only outlined a general framework. Further specification of standards (and implementation as such) happens in a 'cascading'-like pattern where politics filter down from the supranational to the national, sectoral and even enterprise-level. The Social Agreement provides that, at all these levels, the social partner organisations may be the decisive actors. This regulative pattern gives incentives for the inclusion of the social partners in public policy-making at the member state level too. This might, to a certain extent, reinforce existing patterns of national corporatism, or even bring about more cooperative patterns of public–private interaction in pluralist or statist member states. Due to the punctual character of current EC social regulation one should, however, not expect a significant effect on the very diverse national systems *soon*.

A further difference between the recent EC social policy patterns and national corporatism is well known from the literature: there is less cohesiveness and centralisation of the interests represented at the European level, notwithstanding the fact that interest group form has followed function to a significant extent in recent years. Last, but not least, a sort of balance of power between labour and management was assumed for corporatist arrangements. It is certainly still the case that there is formal parity between the two sides of industry at the negotiation table. But, with open economic borders and increased competitive pressures, the political resources of labour are devalued if compared to capital's exit option. An even stronger backing from 'the state' (that is to say, under the Social Agreement, from the Commission and the Council) is needed to give labour an effective voice at least in restricted issue areas.

The future of EC social policy

As regards the problem-solving capacity of EC social policy, the increased participation of the social partners *per se* will not bring about significant innovation. Here, the above-mentioned interdependence of 'state' action capacity and interest group politics is of renewed relevance. Only 'in the shadow of law' (Bercusson 1993) were the employers willing to negotiate. Without pressure from other political actors, in turn, there is little chance of agreement between management and labour. Thus, the success of an 'unburdening' of the EC Social Council will depend to a large degree on the governments' own willingness and capacity to make progress in the 'social dimension'. For those who deem EC-level action indispensable for the future survival of the welfare state in Europe, the fact that EC goals in social policy as well as majority voting were significantly extended at Maastricht gives some hope that EC social policy might exceed 'neo-voluntarism' (Streeck 1995b). However, innovative and acceptable concepts for appropriate measures which go beyond regulatory eclecticism still need to be developed.

A rather gloomy scenario is conjured up by the hypothesis that stalemate in the Social Council might persist in the future despite the improved Treaty basis. The social partners can now be brought in as an alternative route to arrive at EC social standards, but they might also become the scapegoat for the failure of a 'social dimension' of European integration if they cannot arrive at agreements. If the citizens perceive the EC-level involvement of the 'social partners' as symbolic politics only (notably under conditions of further increased unemployment and continuing redistribution to those who are already better off), the legitimacy deficit of European integration might in the end be aggravated. In addition, a growing legitimacy deficit of trade unionism in the eyes of what used to be called the 'working class' could lead to the further strengthening of right-wing and nationalist forces.

The above indicates that cooperative public–private governance as well as multi-level governance may at best offer opportunities to be seized. They are *no solution as such* for any of the social problems arising in times of increased internationalisation and competitive pressures on the markets for capital, goods, services and labour. The Europeanisation of public and private action capacity in social affairs may increase the overall problem-solving potential of our societies. If theory is not turned into practice, however, the loss of unilateral action capacity of the member states will lack a counterbalance.

Notes

1 This follows established knowledge. With regard to the growth of European interest group federations, Kohler-Koch (1994: 171) observed that they did not develop parallel to an increase in the EC's policy-making powers, but rather, 'the anticipation of a growing importance of the EC in a rather vague sense ... stimulated the establishment of transnational organisations [and not] the actual transfer of powers'; see also Greenwood *et al.* 1992b: 244.

2 Indeed, in autumn 1996, the excluded Euro-association of small and medium-sized enterprises UEAPME brought an action against the EC Council which was however not successful (case T-135/96, decided 17 June 1998).

6

ECONOMIC AND MONETARY UNION IN EUROPE

A transformation of governance

Kenneth Dyson

Introduction

This chapter explores the character of the governance of the process of Economic and Monetary Union (EMU) in Europe; in what ways there has been a transformation of governance in EC economic and monetary policies; the kind of normative issues that have been thrown up relating to the legitimacy of this process; and the ways in which the governance of this sector can be explained. The basic argument is that, whilst EMU has undergone a process of transformation, the sector is better understood as a type of 'core executive' governance than as 'network' governance. Its central attributes are an increasingly intensive interlocking of 'core executive' actors, a pronounced 'territorial' instinct in relation to controlling policy, and the momentum imparted by a sense of shared ownership of an historic policy project.

The defining character of the governance of EMU is provided by shared understandings that economic and monetary policies constitute a 'special' and privileged domain. There is no sense that it is the responsibility of officials to share power with social and economic interests or to referee contests among those interests. It is recognised that governance of this sector is ultimately political. It involves striking politically acceptable deals that satisfy strategic interests of member state governments and that can be ratified in different domestic political arenas. But, at a deeper level, there is an understanding that constructing EMU is a cognitive issue. It is about putting in place an EMU that will 'work', that will be technically viable and durable. Hence the governance of EMU has a strongly technocratic, problem-solving face. It involves a narrow, exclusive and privileged set of actors who gravitate around the monthly meetings of ECOFIN, the Council of EC economic and finance ministers; the EC Monetary Committee, to which each state sends a senior finance ministry official and a senior central banker, and which prepares the work of ECOFIN in the strictest confidence; and the European Monetary Institute (EMI), which brings together the EC central bank governors and was created with Stage Two of EMU. The 'territoriality' of the policy process expresses itself in a shared interest in retaining control of policy development within this narrow world. In that way the primacy of a technical definition of EMU problems can be retained.

The authority of the voice of finance ministry and central bank officials in the governance of EMU bestows a technical legitimacy on the process. Policy proposals carry conviction because they are likely to 'work'. At the same time technical legitimacy does not exhaustively deal with the normative issues raised by the way in which EMU is governed. There is a problem of fitting the dictates of technical legitimacy – like an independent European Central Bank (ECB) and tough budget discipline – with inherited conceptions of political legitimacy. As in France, such conceptions may bestow primacy on the political direction of economic and monetary policy and seek a strong political 'pole' to balance a strong monetary 'pole'. This problem of legitimacy highlights the paradox of the strength and weakness of the governance of EMU. Its strength derives from a conception of technical legitimacy, from a belief that only a particular set of institutional arrangements and policy rules will 'work' in the context of globalised markets. Its weakness comes from its exposure to contesting conceptions of political legitimacy.

The evidence of transformation

The process of EMU in Europe seems *prima facie* to offer promising ground for identifying a transformation of governance. Economic and monetary policies are being 'Europeanised' in conformity with the requirements laid down in the Maastricht Treaty. This process of transformation can be traced back to the establishment of the Delors Committee in 1988 to study how EMU might be realised; to the work of the Guigou Group in 1989 in identifying the key questions for a future IGC; to the preparations begun in the EC Monetary Committee (e.g. on excessive deficit issues) and in the Committee of EC Central Bank Governors (notably on the ECB's draft statute); to the IGC on EMU and the final agreement of the Treaty on European Union at Maastricht in December 1991; to the negotiations on the stability pact for Stage Three in 1995–7; and to the final decisions on transition to Stage Three in 1998. By 1997 EMU had progressed from Stage One to Stage Two; the EMI had replaced the Committee of EC Central Bank Governors in 1994; and the ECB, operating a single monetary policy for Europe, and a system of co-ordinated budgetary discipline were imminent.

Additional evidence for transformation comes from the effects of 'Europeanisation' on national political agendas, policy processes and the distribution of power. Meeting the convergence criteria contained in the Maastricht Treaty put the requirements of economic stability at the forefront of domestic political agendas. It empowered controllers of public expenditure over service providers, the interests of savers over those in need of public services. Issues of privatisation and of welfare state reform were shifted to the centre of the political agenda across all EC states. In short, the Maastricht Treaty became an instrument for radical change to domestic policy agendas. National governments were emboldened to push through domestic reforms, even at the price of mobilising public dissent – as in France in November/December 1995.

The specific features of governance in this sector were also made manifest by the high level of intensive preparation for the IGC on EMU, compared to that dealing with political union in 1991 and then again in 1996–7. Actors in the sector were tied together by a set of shared beliefs, both normative and causal. The key normative belief involved a primacy to economic stability; the main causal beliefs identified exchange rate discipline and central bank independence as the main variables explaining economic stability. In this respect there were elements of an 'epistemic community' in evidence. The common experience of inflationary shocks and deteriorating economic performance in the 1970s had generated a dissemination of ideas from 'strong' to 'weak' performers. This dissemination meant in effect the common acceptance of the 'German model' as the basis for constructing EMU. The learning process involved a very limited number of 'privileged' actors in national finance ministries and central banks. It meant that their interactions were reasonably well-structured and predictable: that their preferences were well-defined; that they knew each other extremely well; and that issues and rules of decision were clearly understood. The sector had its own historical memory on which to draw for common references, looking back to the Werner Report on EMU in 1970 and to the experience of the European Monetary System (EMS) and of the Exchange Rate Mechanism (ERM) crises, notably that of 1983. The process of EMU involved a cohesive policy network, tied together by shared belief and experience and with an acquired instinct for co-ordination. It was far removed from the 'garbage can' model of policy making, in which ill-defined preferences and contradictory problem definitions compete for attention (Cohen, March and Olsen 1972). Indeed, the governance of EMU can be said to have more of the aspects of a policy 'community' than of a policy 'network'. Shared beliefs and a shared historical memory endowed it with a striking cohesion and sense of identity.

The preferred pattern of conflict resolution and problem solving in the sector evolved as highly accommodative. The key driving force at work here in transforming governance was the political drive for EMU unleashed by the heads of state and government meeting as the European Council. In essence, the shared maxim in ECOFIN and the other technical arenas was: better an agreement between us than imposition of an agreement by the European Council because of our failure to agree. This accommodative attitude reflected also a marked sense of 'territoriality'. ECOFIN wanted to retain control of policy *vis-à-vis* the EC foreign ministers and the EC Commission as well as the European Council. The more active these other arenas became, the stronger was the sense of 'territorial' ownership in ECOFIN. Hence the dynamic for accommodation was reinforced.

However the political drive from the European Council could not explain another key feature of the governance of EMU: the structure of shared beliefs that evolved. Here there is a prime explanation – globalisation – and a secondary but increasingly important explanation, the impact of the institutionalisation of co-operation. The mounting scale and speed of change of global financial markets was the source of a powerful learning process within finance ministries and central banks. At the heart of economic policies in the EC was the use of expanding intra-EC trade as an instrument of output and employment growth. The speculative pressures unleashed by globalised financial markets put that objective at risk. In the 1970s and 1980s, EC economies under-performed in output and employment growth. They also became vulnerable to exchange rate crises. Hence the first stage in the learning process was a recognition of the value of co-operation in exchange rate management. This recognition took the form of the creation of the EMS and of the ERM in 1978-79. Thereafter the EC Monetary Committee and ECOFIN became important institutional arenas for policy learning. By 1983–87 the ERM was evolving into a more powerful informal institution, being used as an instrument for domestic fiscal discipline and for promoting economic convergence among member states. In this way EC member states were trying to reduce the risks that they faced in relation to the global financial markets. The return of EMU to the agenda in 1988 was an extension of this learning process. A single currency and a single monetary policy offered the prospect of a more cohesive and purposeful approach to financial markets. It was part of a longer-standing process of upgrading the value of co-operation and extending and deepening joint action. The trigger was globalisation; the institutional mechanisms for operating the ERM took on the role of sustaining and channelling the subsequent learning process.

Governance and 'path dependency' in EMU

The EMU negotiations avoided becoming a 'garbage-can' decision situation because of the degree of structuring imparted to its governance as a sector. This 'path dependency' derived from two fundamental developments that were deeply affecting the policy processes of West European states by the 1980s and forcing adaptive behaviour on their governments.

First, the governance of EMU can be seen as a response to underlying economic and social changes in Western Europe: notably, the liberalisation and globalisation of financial markets; and the social and cultural effects of the accumulation of savings and of demographic change towards an ageing population dependent on the value of accumulated savings. These interrelated changes helped to account for a new political valuation on price stability.

Most potently of all, global financial markets were inflation-averse and capable of imposing severe sanctions, even on anticipated inflation. The experience of the French government in paying high penalties in the form of three devaluations between 1981 and 1983 represented a learning experience for the French about the virtues of an economic policy of *rigueur* to support a *franc stable*. A subsequent convergence of economic policy ideas between France and Germany, and the strengthening of France's economic performance and its convergence with Germany, notably on inflation, created the context within which the French government could act as a more credible *demandeur* for EMU, which appeared a more viable policy option. Global financial markets acted as a force for convergence of both economic ideas and performance. In so doing, they undermined the reservations of those who saw convergence as a precondition for reopening EMU as an agenda issue. A French government pursuing 'competitive disinflation' had greater credibility as a bargaining partner for a German government committed to the traditional priority of 'stability policy'.

In this respect the historic significance of the EMU agreement struck at Maastricht rested on two characteristics. First, it represented a recognition that, individually, member states were less and less able to be, or even pretend to be, masters of their own destiny in the new context of global financial markets and of the consequences of freedom of movement of goods, services and capital as the EC's single market became a new reality. The Maastricht Treaty was a new framework for recognising and responding to this situation of mounting interdependence: not least for putting in place more suitable arrangements for securing monetary stability in the interests of a more efficiently functioning single market, and better adapted to more volatile financial markets.

In addition, the Maastricht Treaty reflected and embodied a change of economic policy paradigm since the mid-1970s, based on a new emerging consensus that stable money matters. It conveyed to politicians and the public the message that the prime economic value was sustainable low-inflationary growth resting on low budget deficits and public debt levels. It was one thing to try to resolve the political problems of the 1970s by piling up public debt levels from initially low levels of indebtedness. But the lesson of the Maastricht Treaty, reinforced by the German 'stability pact' proposal of 1995, was that member states could not go on in this way. They faced serious risks of harsh penalties imposed by the financial markets, not just in the form of exchange rate crises and devaluations but also of punitively high long-term interest rates. Without a new framework of discipline, member states risked the loss of electoral support as they failed to meet the aspirations of savers as well as deteriorating investment performances. It was the convergence of domestic policy preoccupations consequent on these changing economic and social foundations of the EC member states that made possible the EMU provisions of the Maastricht Treaty: possible, that is, but by no means inevitable. Member states were at least led to consider whether EMU might provide them with a less crisis-prone means of reasserting some control over economic and monetary events, even if only in the form of sharing power at the EC level rather than retaining the formal attributes of national sovereignty in this policy area.

Second, the phenomenon of 'path dependency' underpinning the governance of EMU was sustained by the nature of the institutional structures at EC and national levels through which the debate about EC economic and monetary policies was conducted. At the EC institutional level it was possible to discern the phenomenon of 'path dependency' at work (North 1990). Finance ministry officials and central bankers became locked into consideration of the implications arising from past policy commitments (notably the single market programme and the liberalisation of capital movement). These commitments raised unavoidable questions about the EC's capacity to sustain stable exchange rates via the EMS in its present form and about the value of a single currency to safeguard and make more efficient the single market (Padoa-Schioppa *et al.* 1987). These questions were inexorably forced on reluctant finance ministry and central bank officials in the EC Monetary Committee and on central bank officials in the Committee of Central Bank Governors. The outcome was a privileging of the role of central bankers in the debate about the direction of European integration after the single market and a capacity to structure the content of bargaining on their terms.

The most potent source of structuring came from the institutional dynamics created by the operation of the ERM since 1979. This mechanism for achieving exchange-rate stability was judged by the late 1980s to have been a success story in reducing the number and scale of realignments and in promoting convergence in inflation performance, budget deficits and interest rates. The path of building on this success by moving towards 'locked' exchange rates (i.e. EMU) was tempting to follow. At the same time the ERM had developed not as an ECU-based system but as a system anchored *de facto* to the D-Mark. In consequence, German monetary policy set the standard for the system, and Germany was in the position to act as broker of any EMS reform and EMU deals. Most importantly, the Bundesbank had a structurally privileged position. Its preferences were always likely to count for more than those of any other actor in an EMU bargaining process – which meant that an independent ECB, with a clear mandate to safeguard price stability, was a predictable outcome of EMU bargaining (Giavazzi and Giovannini 1987).

'Path dependency' in the governance of EMU involved more than a pre-structuring of its contents. It also involved a powerful 'locking-in' to a particular line of development. Globalisation and liberalisation of financial markets is crucial in understanding the nature of the path into which European integration became locked in this sector. The locking-in was then secured by the nature of the institutional structures concerned with developing EMU, the inheritance of past EC policy commitments and the 'sunk costs' involved in its development.

But one should beware of an 'over-determined' picture of the governance of EMU. In one sense, the economic and institutional factors were primary. Without them political motivations would have been channelled into different directions or, perhaps, in no particular direction at all. Strategic political visions of EMU had always to be tailored to the changing structures of incentives and constraints posed by market and institutional realities. Thus the Genscher Memorandum on EMU of February 1988, the turning point in the relaunch of EMU, was grounded in a perception of strengthening convergence and a transformation of French economic policy towards market discipline. Similarly, French diplomatic interest in pressing EMU post-dated the adoption of 'competitive disinflation' as a domestic economic strategy and the financial market liberalisation programme post-1984. As a French diplomatic objective, EMU would have lacked any serious credibility in their absence.

At the same time the transformation of the governance of EMU was driven by political motivations and strategic visions of European political leadership. At issue were such factors as France's political leadership of Europe; German diplomatic concerns to reduce tensions with her neighbours (consequent on the diplomatic costs of the functioning of the ERM as a 'DM-zone'); the development of the Franco-German axis as a factor of security and stability in Europe; and Europe's voice in the world. In particular, from autumn 1989 onwards, German unification and the collapse of Soviet hegemony over eastern Europe were to add decisively to the importance of political leadership in transforming this policy sector. Indeed, the events of 1989-90 gave what was to prove to be the decisive political impetus to the fixing of dates for the IGC on EMU (at Strasbourg), of the date for Stage Two (at Rome 1) and the final date for Stage Three (at Maastricht).

The crucial point is that, however powerful 'path dependency' appears to be as a conditioning factor, the governance of EMU was by no means simply routinised and predictable. So reluctant were finance ministries and central banks to go down the path to EMU that it took firm political leadership 'from above' to put EMU back on the agenda at Hanover in 1988, and then strong leadership to keep them on track to the final outcome. In fact, the EC's institutional structures left scope for the reassertion of political leadership over EMU: namely, through the European Council where heads of state and government, accompanied by their foreign ministers, could – and did – bypass their finance ministers and central bankers, as for instance at Hanover, Strasbourg and Rome 1.

At the same time, the governance of EMU remained in the hands of the institutional structures attached to ECOFIN: in particular, the EC Monetary Committee, the Committee of EC Central Bank Governors and the IGC on EMU during 1991. This organisational structuring of EMU governance kept employment and economics ministers, with their closer contact to the 'real' economy, out of – or peripheral to – the main negotiations. Through the EC Monetary Committee and the Committee of Central Bank Governors the central bankers were assured a privileged access; indeed, the negotiation of the draft statutes for the ECB and the EMI was essentially delegated to them. This support structure for ECOFIN and for the IGC helps to explain the focus on 'nominal' rather than 'real' convergence criteria as tests for entry into Stage Three, and the emphasis on the financial and monetary aspects of EMU over the economic aspects.

The EC central bankers had the additional advantage that they had older and more intensive patterns of co-operation than the other actors involved; that the operation of the ERM had intensified that co-operation and a mutual learning process about policy objectives and instruments; and that they had acquired key attributes of an 'epistemic community', of a group of policy actors united around shared normative principles (price

stability), shared causal beliefs (that inflation was a monetary phenomenon, that credibility and reputation were the prerequisites of a successful
counter-inflationary strategy, and that in the long-run there was no trade-off
between unemployment and inflation) and a common policy project (central bank independence). Central bankers possessed a combination of
professional mystique, mutual familiarity, shared policy beliefs and privileged
access that ensured them a significant influence on the governance of EMU.
In this way the negotiation and implementation of the Maastricht Treaty
became locked into a set of policy assumptions and practices that were institutionally anchored(Dyson, Featherstone and Michalopoulos 1995).

'Core executive' governance

What was perhaps most striking about the governance of EMU was the
absence of elaborate attention to consensus-building between state and
civil society. The major organised groups, like employers' associations and
trade unions, or banking associations, were not drawn into the development of EMU policy positions (not at least until the implementation stage
in the form of the technical preparations for Stage Three). Neither the
Giscard d'Estaing-Helmut Schmidt initiative for a Committee for Monetary
Union in Europe, nor the Association for Monetary Union in Europe
gained any kind of privileged, insider status in the policy process. There
was no serious attempt to co-opt such groups into a process of joint learning and problem-solving with state actors. In other words, there is no
substantial evidence that the negotiation of EMU emulated the characteristics of 'governance' via networks as a model of how EC policy is made
(Kohler-Koch 1995).

The actors in the member state executives and EC executive concerned
with EMU were far removed from the image of brokers between the relevant economic and social actors. They did not treat the executive power as
simply an arena, in which state actors were acting as partners or mediators
with organised groups. More accurately, the governance of EMU was confined to members of the 'core executive', understood as embracing the
central banks, though with a clear distinction – even in the German case –
between the technical, advisory role of the central bank and the formal
responsibility for negotiations which rested firmly with finance ministries
and heads of government. Hence the object of analysis is not 'network' governance by joint public-private problem-solving but 'core executive'
governance. In so far as there was an exercise in co-optation and joint
learning and problem-solving, it involved the central banks: and, in so far
as there was a network, it involved the EC central bankers.

In this respect the governance of EMU is a study of core executives in
action: 'of all those organisations and procedures which co-ordinate central government policies, and act as final arbiters of conflict between
different parts of the government machine' (Rhodes and Dunleavy 1995).
The key actors are heads of state and government, their advisers, cabinets
and their committees, inner circles of ministers and officials, bilateral

meetings, inter-ministerial working parties, and finance ministries, each vying for a role in the processes of co-ordinating bargaining positions. The decision routines comprised procedures of bureaucratic co-ordination, unwritten understandings about the division of work within the executive on different issues, the exercise of departmental power not least by finance ministers, inter-ministerial mechanisms for political clearance of proposals, and the claims to authority of heads of state and government. We are looking at a small, enclosed world in which the relative power of actors shifted over time and across specific issues.

Theories of 'core executive' governance

In itself, the concept of 'core executive' governance does not take us very far. It represents an object for analysis rather than an analytical model or explanatory theory. This limitation can be overcome by applying various theories of governance to generate models for the study of core executives (Rhodes and Dunleavy 1995).

A first model to consider is that of *constitutional behaviour*. This model is associated with the theory of legitimacy, focusing on how ideas about legitimacy structure and inform relationships within the governance of EMU. It draws attention to the way in which formal institutional structures within the core executive condition behaviour: in the weakest sense by placing constraints on which actors may do what; in the strongest sense by being internalised by ministers and officials and playing a constitutive role in their behaviour. Both these senses clearly operate in the major EC states. In the British core executive the principle of collective responsibility remains potent, making the notion of cabinet government a key axiom on which goverment business is premised. Its influence on the way in which British positions for the IGC on EMU were prepared was striking, notably through the importance ascribed to the relevant cabinet sub-committee OPD (E). The idea of EC policy as part of the French President's privileged domain legitimated an interventionist role by Mitterrand and his most trusted advisers, whilst in Germany respect for the Chancellor principle (the 'guidelines competence') and the principle of departmental responsibility meant that co-ordination gravitated around Kohl, Genscher and Waigel and their key officials and did not involve a significant role for cabinet. At the same time constitutional principles tend to provide only general and often vague guidance, and politicians and officials may be tempted to exploit the consequent potential for flexibility in the functioning of the core executive to the full (and possibly even beyond). This type of behaviour was most notable in the British case under Thatcher where EC policy, and notably the issue of ERM entry, was highly centralised around small ministerial cliques and kept off cabinet agendas.

Another aspect of constitutional behaviour involves the effects of EC institutional structures. The location of final responsibility for EMU bargaining in the European Council created a common pressure for heads of state and government to be well briefed on EMU issues. In the particular case of Franco-German relations the fact that the Elysée assumed responsibility for this relationship as part of the privileged domain of the President created a pressure in Bonn to centralise the responsibility for this relationship with the Federal Chancellor. By this means Kohl was drawn into EMU bargaining by the institutional exigencies of the Franco-German relationship.

A second model, derived from the pluralist theory of politics, is 'bureaucratic politics' (Allison 1971). This model stresses the internal complexity of the governance of EMU, involving a range of actors, each with their own distinctive (often agency) interests. In particular, it points to the absence of an authoritative source of strategic direction. The metaphor of 'collage' is used to characterise bargaining positions which are pictured as adopted in a piecemeal and reactive manner in response to urgent, often unanticipated pressures. Relationships within the governance of EMU are seen as a complex sequence of moves and counter-moves within the core executive as different bureaucratic interests fight wars of position for control over executive territory. A typical manifestation of 'bureaucratic politics' was 'turf-fighting' for control over EMU policy development, for instance between ECOFIN and the EC Monetary Committee, on the one hand, and the Council of Ministers and European Council, on the other; or, at the national level, between foreign and finance ministries and between finance ministries and central banks. Central banks too were motivated by threat to corporate interest (to the power of the *Bundesbank*) or by perceived corporate gain in the form of institutional independence (notably in the case of the *Banque de France*). To a significant extent the development of EMU bargaining positions in France was influenced by the attempt of the *Trésor* to find ways to maintain its powers and the attempt of the *Banque de France* to gain its independence.

The model of 'bureaucratic politics' understates the degree of strategic direction and control that was achieved in the governance of EMU. Bureaucratic politics is, in part, constrained by considerations of legitimacy (for instance, the *Bundesbank's* belief that EMU is a matter for the federal government with its role being that of technical advice). In particular, Kohl and Mitterrand were prepared to exert their political will on behalf of particular outcomes (central bank independence and fixed dates for Stage Three, respectively).

Third, other models emphasise the relationship between the governance of EMU and the structure of the economy. They focus on the constraining and/or shaping role of economic forces but differ in their accounts of how the economy operates. According to both neo-liberal and neo-Marxist accounts of this relationship, business interests are central to the way in which EMU is governed, irrespective of whether they are formally involved in the process. Otherwise, these two theoretical accounts are radically different.

In one, the *neo-liberal* theory of the state, the market is presented as the arbiter of EMU policy positions and outcomes, sanctioning 'irresponsible' behaviour in the form of high interest-rate premiums and currency crises and rewarding 'responsible' behaviour with the benefits of a 'strong' currency. According to this theory, EMU bargains were informed by attempts to second-guess the financial markets, for instance in designing criteria to define excessive deficits. Hence, those close to the markets – the central bankers – came to hold a strategic position in the governance of EMU. The financial markets can be seen as defining and altering the patterns of incentive and constraint to which actors in the core executive respond. The test of policy positions on EMU is their credibility to the financial markets, which act to promote the interests of savers against the risks of economically irresponsible behaviour by governments as they come under the influence of the 'political business cycle' and are induced to reflate before elections (Dyson 1994).

The other key models that focus on how the economy shapes the governance of EMU derive from the body of *neo-Marxist* theory. At one extreme this type of theory sees core executive actors in EMU as simply instruments of dominant capitalist interests. More persuasively, it represents the 'core executive' governance of EMU as an arena in which a struggle for power within capitalism is being conducted. Its actors are presented as arbiters between different 'fractions' of capital, for instance between multinational companies (which have an interest in the reduced transaction costs associated with a single currency area) and small and medium-sized companies (which are more concerned about transition costs to a single currency). EMU can be viewed as part of a wider struggle for hegemony between different fractions of capital, represented in the British case by the contrast between the broadly pro-EMU Confederation of British Industry and the anti-EMU Institute of Directors. Interest focuses on the nature of the social forces that form the 'hegemonic bloc' favouring global restructuring (of which EMU is seen to be a part) and the nature of the social forces that oppose it. According to this account, the governance of EMU is part of a more fundamental struggle about the relationship between politics and markets in a global economy (Cox 1987).

Fourth, 'New Right' and elitist theories give more attention to the theme of political leadership in the governance of EMU. In 'New Right' theories the stress is on the role of *'policy entrepreneurs'* within the core executive. Typically elected politicians, they are looking out in a self-interested way for opportunities to promote new ideas, initiatives and alliances which will give them political credit, benefit their personal position and further their own career interests (Frohlick, Oppenheimer and Young 1971). Jacques Delors can be interpreted as a policy entrepreneur on behalf of EMU, seeing it as a means to bolster the role of the EC Commission and his personal position. By putting EMU on the agenda in early 1988 the French Finance Minister, Edouard Balladur, sought to identify himself with the pro-European wing of the RPR–UDF coalition and establish his profile there. Hans-Dietrich Genscher's espousal of the cause of a European central bank and EMU in 1988 becomes linked to the search for personal political profile within the Bonn coalition, following his strengthened personal position after the 1987 elections; whilst Pierre Bérégovoy saw in the strategy of 'competitive disinflation' and the policy project of financial market liberalisation means to advance his personal reputation as a reformist Socialist finance minister who had never devalued. This model sensitises us to the role of the motives of leading politicians and officials, notably their career ambitions and public profile, in shaping the governance of EMU.

Fifth, elite theories identify in political leadership a dimension that goes beyond more mundane technical issues of EMU governance. Governance also involves the manufacture of consent both by projecting an image of competence and authority and by appealing to shared historical experiences and identities. The model of *symbolic politics* draws attention to the way in which 'core executive' governance is shaped by considerations of leadership imagery (Edelman 1964). Thus Helmut Kohl's embrace of EMU just before the Hanover summit in 1988 can be attributed to his desire to escape from the shadow of his predecessor Helmut Schmidt as the champion of EMU. His policy position on EMU in 1990–1, notably on the issue of dates for Stages Two and Three, and 'automaticity' of entry into the final stage, is explained by reference to his overriding desire to project an image of a 'Europeanised Germany' rather than of a 'Germanised Europe' and to consolidate and extend the leadership competence that had been attributed to him during the process of German unification. Within the same context of the Bonn coalition government, Theo Waigel as Finance Minister sought to identify his own party, the CSU, with the Erhard tradition of 'stability policy', by focusing on the principle that the single currency must be at least as stable as the D-Mark. For President François Mitterrand, the issue of the dates for the IGC on EMU and for Stage Two became symbolic of a determination to project a leadership image that would enable him to dissociate himself from the mistakes of the interwar period in handling the problem of Germany. In a different, but familiar way, Margaret Thatcher's handling of the issues of ERM entry and EMU were subordinated to the political symbolism associated with her image of a 'conviction' politician; and John Major's different style on these issues was part and parcel of his attempt to project a contrasting image of leadership. On the other hand, both of them united in linking EMU policy debate to the symbolic issues of sovereignty and nationhood.

Another type of elite theory focuses on the knowledge which actors carry in their heads as a determinant of 'core executive' governance. Changes in this knowledge (learning) serve as a factor in the redefinition of problems to be solved and of the interests at stake, as well as in the way that power is exercised (Haas 1990). In order to understand the governance of EMU we need to know more about how beliefs and knowledge lead actors to frame problems in particular ways, thereby restricting policy choices. The role of cognitive processes of learning is captured in the concept of epistemic communities, defined as professionals who share certain normative and causal beliefs, who are committed to a common policy project, and who seek to monopolise access to strategic decision-making positions (Haas 1992). In the case of EMU, the closest approximation to an epistemic community is provided by the central bankers and by the way in which monetarist economic ideas, and credibility theory in particular, endowed them with a new confidence and legitimacy as actors. A cluster of monetary economists was important in disseminating a set of ideas that supported the use of the 'hard' ERM as a counter-inflationary device (borrowing the credibility of German monetary policy via the exchange rate) and that identified in central bank independence the precondition for stable, low inflation. The governance of EMU can be seen as embodying a cluster of normative beliefs (the primacy of price stability) and causal beliefs (relating to 'nominal' convergence criteria) as well as a shared commitment to central bank independence as a policy project.

Each of these explanatory models of 'core executive' governance behaviour is persuasive in the sense of highlighting particular aspects of the governance of EMU. But they remain problematic as stand-alone explanations. For instance, though symbolic issues intruded into the governance of EMU, often in a powerful way, the governance of EMU was also preoccupied with 'technical' issues of the viability of EMU. The governance of EMU was, in part, an exercise in solving the problems of creating a sustainable EMU. Crucial then was the way in which problems were defined by reference to policy beliefs and the underlying role of theoretical knowledge in the governance of EMU. Part and parcel of the governance of EMU was a dissemination of ideas about how to tackle substantive policy issues relating to the design of, for instance, central banking structures, exchange rate management and fiscal policy arrangements. Given the technical nature and complexity of these issues there was a strong preference for dealing with them by delegation to finance ministry and central bank officials who possessed the appropriate technical knowledge.

Similarly, the limitation of the policy entrepreneur model, stressing for instance the role of Genscher in Germany, is that it evades the importance of technical knowledge about substantive issues of 'viable' policy as a basis of power in the governance of EMU. Quite simply, politicians have an interest in being associated with policies that will work: again, they either become directly involved at this technical level or (as over EMU) delegate. There is no question that factors of policy entrepreneurship drove forward the EMU agenda and that symbolic politics injected a sense of larger purpose into its governance. But one should not confuse occasional involvement and influence on key issues, whether for entrepreneurial or symbolic reasons, with power over the decision-making routines of the EMU sector.

The analysis of power within the governance of EMU highlights the importance not just of cognitive variables but also of bureaucratic politics and 'turf-fighting'. Thus, for instance, the French *Trésor* was motivated by its desire to avoid ceding power to an independent *Banque de France;* and the German *Bundesbank* was preoccupied by the threat to its corporate power and interests. Not least, for EC finance ministers retaining control over the governance of EMU, and hence power over the outcomes, a central interest was at stake. In order to limit foreign ministry access to IGC issues in the EMU negotiations of 1991 a series of techniques was employed involving delegation of specific issues to the EC Monetary Committee and the Committee of Central Bank Governors, as well as to an IGC technical level group during the Dutch presidency.

At the same time, the story of the governance of EMU involved the overruling of *Trésor* resistance and of *Bundesbank* opposition by determined political leadership. Governmental leaders were, on the whole, content to delegate the multitudinous and complex technical issues to finance ministries. But, for various reasons, they did not wish to remain too aloof. First, they were sensitive to issues of legitimacy and their constitutional prerogatives. Their responsibility for negotiations at the level of the European Council meant that they needed to be fully briefed on EMU. Second, government leaders operated with a sense of a 'segmented' decision structure, in particular that certain issues were reserved to them as they were of such strategic political importance. The most important such issues were dates for the IGC and for Stage Two; and final dates for Stage Three and procedures for qualification. Third, government leaders were particularly sensitive to the symbolic aspects of EMU, to its wider historical and political dimensions. This aspect encouraged them to 'nest' EMU in a larger context and to transform the way in which the issues at stake and negotiated outcomes were perceived. Most strikingly, at Hanover, Madrid, Strasbourg, Rome 1 and Maastricht, finance ministries were taken by surprise at the will to seize the political initiative displayed by heads of state and government. In the governance of EMU, French *Trésor* and German *Bundesbank* officials exhibited profoundly constitutional behaviour, deferring to the ultimate political authority of the President and the federal government.

EMU as interlocking 'core executive' governance: how EMU governance operates

The main argument of this chapter is that EMU has involved the transformation of the governance of economic and monetary policies in Europe; and that this transformation has taken the form of an interlocking of 'core executive' actors. The interlocking has been manifested at the level of beliefs: there has been a shared learning experience and dissemination of ideas that have given a new coherence and shared identity to the actors involved in the governance of EMU. It has been exhibited in the intensity of personal interaction and intimacy within the small cluster of actors involved. It has been reinforced by a shared ownership of the EMU project, a sense of historic as well as legal responsibility to pilot the EMU project safely through a dangerous pregnancy, birth and childhood. There is, in effect, a 'locking-in' to a path of policy development.

Interlocking 'core executive' governance has two other attributes. There is a preference for a technical problem-solving style that involves a respect for the quality of argument, a disposition to reflect and learn within the policy process, and a style of mutual accommodation. In addition, the actors involved have a strong sense of territorial boundaries. This sense involves keeping other actors away from the resolution of EMU issues. Its principal effect is that EMU has been designed as a 'stand-alone' project, with the objective of retaining control of the policy process.

The limitation of existing explanatory models of 'core executive' behaviour is that they do not capture this process of interlocking and its implications for the governance of EMU. With the exception of state-economy models, they are fixated on the domestic basis of, and constraints on, core executive action. Hence the models considered in the previous section remain inadequate from the point of view of understanding the governance of EMU.

In order to better understand the governance of EMU, it is useful to see the behaviour of its actors as a *special* case of 'two-level' bargaining games (Putnam 1988). This analytical perspective represents a variant of, and development on, two theories of international relations: the Realist theory, with its focus on the role of political leaders in mobilising national preference formation behind international objectives; and the Liberal theory, with its stress on how interdependence in trade and investment has eroded the reality of sovereignty and made the achievement of domestic goals, like price stability, dependent on international negotiations. At the same time EMU is a special case in the sense that the EC's institutional structure and policy scope represent a uniquely intensive blending of international and domestic factors and a disposition to define EMU policy games as iterative rather than 'one-off'. An absence of constructive engagement in negotiations is deeply problematic as leaders are faced with the trade-off between opting out to avoid the perceived high costs of EMU, and the risks of loss of EC influence as a consequence (the British case).

As an analytical framework,'two-level' bargaining games offer two important insights into the governance of EMU. First, they offset the tendency to see the formation of actor preferences on EMU exclusively in terms of domestic factors. Preference formation is intertwined with the two phenomena of 'reverberation' and 'synergistic' linkage. These phenomena draw attention to the way in which negotiators manipulate their own and other states' domestic politics to make EMU deals possible. An instance is provided by acceptance of the principle of central bank independence in France, despite the fact that it ran counter to core tenets of the republican tradition. By 'synergistic issue linkage' the project for EMU was used by the *Banque de France* to alter radically the parameters of economic policy-making in France. In Germany, Finance Ministry and *Bundesbank* officials found themselves caught up in a dynamic of EC policy-making, notably with and after the Delors Committee, that forced them to reconsider traditional positions on EMU. The Delors Report had major 'reverberation' effects on the nature of the German debate on EMU, changing its parameters. 'Reverberation' and 'synergistic issue linkage' are important aspects of the governance of EMU. They draw attention to its role as an instrument for transforming governance at the national level.

Second, 'two-level' bargaining games highlight the potentially creative role of actors in the governance of EMU. Opportunities to play such a role derive from the fact that they are operating simultaneously in two contexts: the context of EC negotiations and the context of domestic politics. Both contexts interact in their minds and their strategic and tactical calculations, in ways that can not only produce problems but also generate new opportunities for leadership and problem-solving. An instance was provided by the way in which Kohl hitched the EMU project to German unification and to the implications for Germany and Europe.

Domestic politics remains a crucial element in the analysis of the 'core executive' governance of EMU. Never far from the minds of its actors are problems of domestic ratification: defined in the German case as the problem of getting the Bundesbank on board and behind the EMU project, and persuading a reluctant public to swap the trusted D-Mark for a new, untried currency. This problem is highlighted in the analysis of 'two-level' bargaining games in the form of the concept of domestic 'win-sets' (i.e. policies around which a winning coalition can be built). The governance of EMU is constrained by the nature of the agreements that domestic political systems will ratify.

There are three key questions in relation to EMU: first, whether domestic 'win-sets' overlap so that an agreement is possible; second, the size of the 'win-set' in different member states, that is, the range of potential agreements that would be ratified domestically as opposed to the status quo of no agreement; and third, whether in some states the 'win-set' is narrower, in which case those states are in a position to force more concessions on others. 'Win-sets' become the key determinant of the feasible range of outcomes in the governance of EMU. In Germany the 'win-set' remained narrow and problematic as long as the threat of costs to stability from an EMU agreement compared to the benefits of the *status quo* remained. For France, by contrast, the 'win-set' was wider: the benefit of an EMU agreement over the *status quo* was the prospect of greater influence over monetary policy. Clearly, the relative size of domestic 'win-sets' shaped the pattern of incentives for, and constraints on, achieving an EMU agreement and the substantive terms on which it had to be concluded if it was to be safely ratified by all partners. The greater problems for Germany of ratifying an EMU agreement translated into a stronger bargaining position than that of France.

However, importantly, the actors involved in the governance of EMU are not impotent in the face of the size of domestic 'win-sets'. They can attempt to alter perceptions about the 'win-set' by redefining what is at stake in EMU: notably, by focusing on political gains in terms of European security that transcend technical calculations of economic costs and benefits. For Kohl, EMU was about German security in Europe and about a particular kind of Germany in Europe. Unlike Major, he had the opportunity to mobilise a wider basis of political support for European union, within his own party and right across the German political establishment. At the same time, Kohl had a major domestic ratification problem: the *Bundesbank*. He tackled this problem by drawing the *Bundesbank de facto* into participation on the technical design of EMU by getting the central bank governors appointed 'in their personal capacity' to the Delors Committee. In effect, Kohl was using the technique of co-opting the major threat to domestic ratification into the governance of EMU. Co-option of the Bundesbank was used by the German government throughout the EMU negotiations as a means of reassuring German industry and finance and the wider German public about the low prospective costs of an agreement. In that way the

Bundesbank was drawn into considering EMU as a European and international issue rather than seeing it as pre-eminently a domestic issue. This participation crucially affected the outcomes of the EMU bargain, in Germany's favour, whilst relaxing the constraints on Kohl's domestic 'win-set'.

By contrast, as in the British case, the 'win-set' can be presented as so narrow that the head of government feels enabled to reject EMU in principle (the approach of Thatcher) or constrained to agree negotiating positions line-by-line in cabinet and seek prior authorisation via Parliament (the approach of Major). The strategy of emphasising his interest in an agreement (in being at 'the heart of Europe') whilst binding his hands in this way enabled Major to strengthen his bargaining position in 1991.

At the same time the governance of EMU was by no means a one-way process in which narrow 'win-sets' – and hence the prospect of ratification difficulties – were used to bolster EC power by claiming that one's hands were tied in domestic politics. There was a reverse process at work. Broad public support for European integration could be a resource on which to draw in order to justify the 'requirement' for domestic transformation in governance patterns. For Italian and Spanish politicians and officials, and many in the French élite, an EMU agreement had an attraction: as a means of enforcing domestic economic discipline, not least through strict convergence criteria, thereby precipitating a long overdue and fundamental reform of the state and of its relations to the economy. Such transformation extended beyond the specific provisions of the Maastricht Treaty to include welfare state reform, privatisation and wage and price flexibility, all fields of reform in which action could be legitimated by the requirement to conform with the disciplines of EMU. The appeal of EMU rested in its synergistic effects in opening up new opportunities and leverage for domestic political and policy transformation that otherwise seemed closed.

Faced with the choice of strategies within the context of 'two-level' games, the preferences and approaches of heads of state and government become important (Moravcsik 1993a). For Mrs. Thatcher, her approach as a 'conviction politician' combined with her absolute priority for parliamentary sovereignty to make her adopt a 'hawk-like' bargaining style, leading to her isolation in EMU negotiations. Major represented another type of leadership style: the leader as agent, his behaviour driven by the very narrow domestic 'win-set' within which he found himself and the search to take up a median bargaining position within that context. In both their cases British bargaining strategy remained the same: to tie one's own hands by emphasising and even dramatising the tightness of the domestic 'win-set'.

By contrast, the attachment of Andreotti, Kohl and Mitterrand to the principle of European union was deeply rooted in their personal biographies and went along with a dove-like bargaining style. Their approach to EMU was characterised by a position of some distance from domestic considerations of ratification and of proximity to each other's policy and political problems. The result was a high degree of Franco-German collusion and Italian complicity in the final EMU agreement. There was a mutual concern to enhance each other's domestic standing and, by appropriate policy signals, to expand the other's 'win-set'. An instance was to offer countries like Belgium, Ireland, Italy and Spain a 'side-payment' in the form of attaching allowance for 'trend' performance in debt levels onto the convergence criteria, and, for Spain, Greece, Ireland and Portugal, a 'side-payment' in the form of new 'cohesion fund' money. French concessions on an independent European central bank as a precondition for EMU bargaining were an example of policy signalling designed to create a 'reverberation' effect in Germany to alter the balance of domestic opinion there.

Despite this scope for political leadership, the truth was that heads of state and government could not completely control the governance of EMU. Other actors too, notably finance ministers and their officials, central bankers, and foreign ministers and their officials, were involved in their own 'two-level' bargaining games: via ECOFIN, the EC Monetary Committee, the Committee of Central Bank Governors, the General Affairs Council, the Delors Committee, the ICGs at ministerial and personal representatives' levels, as well as in a host of bilaterals. This complexity of interaction reflected, in part, the high degree of technical specialisation required to deal with the specific issues in the sector, in part, the phenomenon of competing agency interests (and consequent bureaucratic politics), and, in part, the role of policy entrepreneurs, as individual ministers sought to enhance their own public profiles and career interests. Core executive actors were each involved in their own 'two-level' games.

Conceptualising the governance of EMU as a 'two-level' game has an additional advantage besides focusing on the complex interactivity of domestic and EC levels as a force for transformation within the policy sector. It also helps to identify the specific mechanisms by which core executive actors are interlocked in the governance of EMU. By cultivating and using 'cross-governmental' alliances and 'cross-level' interaction, core executive actors are able to manipulate their counterparts' domestic 'win-sets' to their advantage. By these two means, they can attempt to influence agenda-setting in other member state governments and the kind of policy positions adopted. A key theme in the governance of EMU is the attempt by actors to reshape political perceptions in both their own and their counterparts' domestic arenas.

The strategy of cross-governmental alliance building comes into play when a government is internally divided on EMU, and actors in another government seek to bolster the influence of a like-minded faction in that government. In the case of EMU, agenda-setting in 1988 before the Hanover summit was influenced by the close relationship between Dumas and Genscher, the French and German foreign ministers, over the problem of German monetary power in Europe. Dumas' direct persuasion of Genscher to take up the issue of EMU was critical to the agenda-setting. On the vexed and, for Germany, internally divisive issues of the date for the IGC and the date for Stage Two, direct Elysée (Elisabeth Guigou and Hubert Védrine) and Federal Chancellor's Office (Joachim Bitterlich) contacts were crucial to unblocking intra-German resistance. On the later question of who would control the IGC on EMU, Pierre Bérégovoy, the French finance minister, enlisted the support of Waigel, the German finance minister, to pressurise Kohl, who would in turn persuade Mitterrand, who was deeply suspicious of finance ministries.

Less important was the strategy of cross-level interaction. Cross-level strategies involved key actors in the core executive of a member state communicating directly with domestic publics in other states. In January 1990, for instance, Karl-Otto Pöehl, president of the *Bundesbank*, used a speech in Paris to appeal directly for French recognition of central bank independence as a precondition for EMU. In a similar vein, Jacques de Larosière, governor of the *Banque de France*, used opportunities to persuade German banking and industrial audiences and, in 1991, the *Bundestag* finance committee, of the attachment of France to economic stability. Pöehl was important in linking EMU to a specific policy proposal which in turn was highly relevant to the problem of how economic stability could be reinforced in France. His initiative enabled de Larosière to take up the issue of central bank independence directly with the French President. In this case the strategy was successful because Pöehl's proposal was attuned to policy debate in France itself about *désinflation compétitive.* It served to strengthen the position of de Larosière within that debate.

Though this type of interlocking was to play a vital role in the governance of EMU, and was to act as a force for transformation, the capacity to interlock by forging cross-national alliances was unevenly distributed. In this respect, the Franco-German relationship represented a special aspect of the governance of EMU. Founded on the Élysée Treaty of 1963, this bilateral relationship has taken on an intense form in economic and monetary policy. Its main effects are apparent in a capacity for building cross-national alliances between the Elysée and the Federal Chancellor's Office, and between the two foreign ministries, that has sustained coherence and momentum to the governance of EMU. But, over time, that coherence and momentum have been increasingly provided by the respective finance ministries and central banks of the two states. Their capacity to play this role has been augmented by: collaboration in operating the ERM and managing its crises, especially in 1992–93; from 1988 onwards, the institutional focus of the Franco-German Economic Council; the role of the confidential Franco-German bilaterals in agreeing Treaty texts alongside the negotiations in the IGC on EMU; and the sense of joint interest in, and responsibility for, implementing the Maastricht Treaty provisions on EMU. At the same time, in forging this special inner relationship in the governance of EMU, the French and German finance ministries were conscious of how far they lagged behind the offices of their heads of state and government and the foreign ministries in cross-national alliance building. Between 1988-89 and the mid-1990s, the French and German finance ministries moved from a defensive, reactive posture to a more promotive role.

Conclusion

This chapter has highlighted the way in which transformation of the governance of EMU was structured by the development and implications of global financial markets, the policy inheritance of the EMS/ERM, the single European market, and the specific institutional arrangements of the policy sector. Each in its individual way influenced the governance of EMU. The effects of globalisation, as mediated through ERM crises, triggered a learning process about the value of price stability as a guiding belief. Repeated exercises in saving the ERM helped instil a sense of shared ownership and identity. The institutional arrangements of the policy sector privileged a particular set of actors, preoccupied with the financial and monetary aspects of overall economic management. This structuring of the governance of EMU is suggestive of the explanatory power of a neo-liberal theoretical interpretation. Certain political strategies – notably reliance on central bank independence and tough convergence criteria – and certain actors – in particular, central bankers – were privileged in the governance of EMU (Jessop 1990).

At the same time there was nothing inevitable about the agenda-setting process or about the momentum that was given to EMU. Agenda-setting in 1987–8 depended on the specific skills and political capacities of policy entrepreneurs, especially Genscher. The continued momentum owed everything to the way in which Kohl and Mitterrand 'nested' EMU in a wider historical and political setting of symbolic politics. The policy sector was transformed at the pace that it was because political leaders chose to engage themselves and behaved with consummate strategic skill in binding in EC central bankers to the process. Political leadership accounted for the setting of dates for the IGC on EMU and for the date for Stage Two and the final date for Stage Three.

Despite this element of creative political direction, the constraints on political leadership in the governance of EMU appear awesome. They include: the consequences of past actions of EC political leaders, notably in liberating capital movements; the degree of economic convergence or divergence among member states; the strength of domestic economic performance; the complexities of bureaucratic politics; personal rivalries about political profile; and the degree of public support for European union. These constraints have influenced the potentiality to achieve coherence and momentum in the governance of EMU and determined whether individual actors negotiate on strong or weak terms.

This chapter has tried both to conceptualise and to theorise the governance of EMU. Conceptually, EMU is best seen as a case of 'core executive' governance. It does not possess the attributes of 'network' governance. EMU comprises a process of conflict resolution among nationally defined interests with a process of joint learning and problem-solving about the conditions for a viable and sustainable EMU. The challenge is to theorise about this type of governance. Here different explanatory models of 'core executive' behaviour have been examined and assessed, notably, cognitive, bureaucratic politics and symbolic politics models. More importantly, it has been argued that existing explanatory models fail to identify a key aspect of the governance of EMU: the cross-national interlocking of core executives. Cross-governmental linkages have been a potent mechanism for transforming the governance of EMU, and the capacity and skill of actors to make creative use of those linkages has been a salient factor in their relative effectiveness.

Explanatory models of 'core executive' governance offer some limited insight into another set of key issues thrown up by the governance of EMU, namely, normative issues relating to the source of political authority over economic and monetary policies, to the beliefs that should guide those policies, and to the design of the institutional mechanisms through which EMU is to be governed. At the domestic level, traditional ideas about the appropriate management of economic and monetary policies have been divergent. Thus the French republican tradition has stressed the primacy of political direction over policy; ultimately, the source of political authority is to be found in the sovereign people. Postwar German beliefs centre on the need to depoliticise the management of monetary policy in order to safeguard the people and democracy from the irresponsible use of power by politicians. French economic policy beliefs have had a more mercantilist bias, German a more market-oriented bias. Hence the governance of EMU is bedevilled by the potential for destabilising debate and action generated by the appeal to different political traditions. For German negotiators, the legitimating formula is a 'stability community', rooted in a wholly independent ECB pledged to price stability as its objective; for French negotiators, legitimacy requires a strong 'political' pole to balance the 'monetary' pole in the form of an 'economic government' at the EC level. The governance of EMU is held together at technical working levels by a set of shared normative and causal beliefs. But, when one delves further, a deeper realm of inconsistent formulae of legitimacy is exposed. In that sense the long-term threat to the governance of EMU stems from the lack of a parallel political union.

Note

This paper is based on a project funded by the UK Economic and Social Research Council (ESRC) Grant R000 234793, entitled 'The Dynamics of European Monetary Integration'. It studies the negotiation of the Maastricht Treaty provisions on EMU, comparing France, Germany, Italy and the UK.

7

PLANES, TRAINS AND AUTOMOBILES

Transport governance in the European Union

Mark Aspinwall

The purpose of this chapter is to trace the changes that have occurred in the European Union (EU) transport policy, account for them, and attempt to describe the emerging system of governance in EU transport. The challenge of accounting for the development of a common transport policy (CTP) and describing the emerging governance system in transport must come to grips with the following puzzle: given that a common transport policy was always seen as an essential element of European integration, why did a new European-level governance system for transport only begin to take shape in the mid-1980s, and in the form that it did? The answer to this puzzle has two parts. The first part has to do with the timing of the change and the second part with the nature of the change.

The timing of the change was caused by the confluence of institutional and political economy factors. Until sufficient institutional 'pull' existed at the EU level, actors were not persuaded that a CTP was viable and in their interests, and consequently not only were they unable to support a common policy, but more importantly, they did not begin to establish the governance system that would later become a feature of EU transport. Institutional pull refers to the authority of the supranational institutions over policy areas. For nearly three decades, the authority contained in the EU institutions was insufficient to overcome the many obstacles to collective action. This authority is expressed in the 'constitutionality' of the sector, which vests power in the supranational institutions by virtue of the Treaty of Rome. Where authority exists (and as policy output accumulates), a growth in collective action occurs, followed in the transport case by the establishment of a governance system to manage policy oversight and continually reassess priorities. The stakes for all actors are raised in policy areas which fall within the purview of the EU institutions, creating strong incentives for greater European-level collective action among interests thus affected, leading in many cases to permanent policy networks capable of, and interested in, governing this emerging system.

The EU institutions exercise this authority by drafting proposals, making decisions, gathering information on the implementation and enforcement of these decisions, and allocating funding. However, in addition to the exercise of authority necessary to create specific policies and programmes, the supranational institutions also provide multiple access and veto points for information and influence on the part of interests. Divided institutions, fragmented policy competencies within each of the institutions, the lack of a large and well-resourced bureaucracy, and a tradition of relative openness to input all create a potential vacuum to be filled by private interests prior to and in the wake of new policies. These interests have emerged in the transport field and hardened into a new governance sub-system, but it only occurred after the supranational institutions had acquired the legitimacy and authority necessary to attract them.

Institutional pull was only one factor behind the emergence of a new transport governance system in the EU. The other was a 'push' generated by the convergence in the political economy of transport from the 1980s. Until that time there was a distinct lack of convergence among transport actors and member states sufficient to 'push' them toward common solutions. These divergences were caused by market segmentation, ideology, and national security, for the most part based upon the historically distinct evolution of national economic systems. National systems of transport were organised around the principles of cohesion, security, employment, and public service in some member states (particularly France and Germany), while liberalism – in which transport acted as a trunk service to industry – was the organising principle in other member states (notably Britain and the Netherlands). Until a consensus emerged on one or the other set of principles, it was not possible to say that convergence existed. This consensus was finally forged in the 1980s as new methods of production and retailing, and a new assimilation of liberal ideas, brought change. Member states had committed themselves to the single market and to a CTP; changes in the political economy of production and lower transport costs helped opinion to congeal around the liberal approach. The convergence that occurred represented the ascendance of consumer values at the expense of cohesion values.

Thus, preferences in transport are shaped and changed by the pull of European institutions and the push of the international political economy. Considering that transport policy was one of only two 'constitutionalised' policies (with agriculture) in the Treaty of Rome, it may seem odd to characterise the failure to agree a common policy as one of insufficient institutional authority. Yet the lack of agreement among member states and market actors on basic principles continued until a combination of ideological change and a restructuring of the international economy began to produce a new approach to transport. The liberalism versus social cohesion dichotomy between member states was resolved in favour of the former, due in part to the deregulatory agenda originating in the US and UK. But in addition, new methods of production and retailing, which rely on cheap transport, changed the preferences of industrial transport consumers and even prompted the creation of EU-level pressure groups to advocate change. This occurred at the same time that a number of EU institutional developments – European Court of Justice (ECJ) cases, the Single Market programme, the adoption of qualified majority voting, and European Commission and Parliament advocacy – increased the 'pull' of Brussels. The 'output failure' that characterised transport policy in the 1960s (Lindberg and Scheingold 1970) had finally given way to progress.

The pushing and pulling metaphor takes us a long way toward an explanation of why governance transformation took place when it did, but it does not explain the nature of that transformation. For an answer to this question we must look to the specific features of institutions in Europe and the agents who inhabit them. The most important feature is the nested character of institutions in the EU. State institutions are nested within an EU institutional context. It is from the pre-existing state governance systems that all new EU governance systems are wrought, and yet differential state–society relations among member states ensure different responses to the challenge of European integration. Where the state reaches deep into society, owning monopoly enterprises and consummating hierarchical relationships, the reaction to change is likely to be far different than for states ordered in a more horizontal manner. In the latter states, economic actors are more open to outside competition, and have developed closer links to foreign producers and consumers. Hierarchical states are more likely to view issues as in the national interest, and so will be more resistant to negative – or liberalising – integration.

A second feature of European institutions is that their structure privileges certain types of policy over others. Transport policy competence is shared between the Transport Directorate (DG VII) and the Competition Directorate (DG IV). In general, DG VII has represented carrier interests and DG IV has represented consumer interests, though there are exceptions to this. For example, highly competitive carriers such as British Airways and the Greek deep-sea shipping companies have found their interests more closely resembling consumers than fellow (protected) carriers. In addition, the existence of these two principal directorates with shared competence over transport policy marginalises other interests. Environmental advocacy and labour advocacy (to the extent that it diverges from company interests) did not play a large part in the transformation of transport policy from the national to the EU level. Nor do these interests feature in the ongoing EU-level governance of transport. In addition, the role of the Transport Council in decision-making has had an impact favouring carriers. It has encouraged the formation of carrier interests at the supranational level, and also the formation of consumer interests, who have attempted with only limited success to rally ministers in the Industry Council to their cause.

Finally, the agency role of EU actors is crucial to an understanding of governance transformation. The European Commission and the European Court of Justice (ECJ) actively constructed a European competence in important ways, through rulings, proposals, and alliances with actors at various levels across the EU. In the case of the Commission, this activity is ongoing through an identification of new issues and problems, proposed solutions, and the establishment of new alliances. Through its work, the

Commission strives to legitimise itself and create a demand for European-level public goods in transport. This activity contributes to what I call a 'pre-governance system', in which the institutions have begun to gather the participants in a possible future governance system. Whether this results in the transformation of governance to the EU-level depends on the acquiescence of the member states and the continued participation of non-state actors in EU-level policy networks.

The new *acquis transport*: what happened in the 1980s?

Institutional change: the catalyst for transformation

The Treaty of Rome divided transport sectors into inland modes (road, rail, and inland waterway), and international modes (maritime and aviation). Under Article 84 (2), the latter were excluded from a CTP until such time as the member states decided to include them. The purpose of this bifurcation was the belief that market distortion in the international modes would not hamper creation of the customs union; there was also concern over effects upon non-European trading partners of a disruption to the bilateral system of market segmentation (degli Abbati 1987: 38). In the inland modes, the fear was that transport tariffs would act as discriminatory barriers to trade, and thus would counteract the common market (Winters 1993: 34). Regardless of the rationale behind this division, however, none of the modes proved susceptible to serious common action until the 1980s.

A series of institutional developments beginning in the 1970s (but becoming more potent in the 1980s) heralded the beginnings of a new system of transport governance. First, in 1974 the ECJ ruled in the French Seafarer case that the general provisions of the Treaty of Rome (those outside the transport title, such as competition policy and freedom of movement) applied to shipping automatically, unless the Council of Ministers acted to exclude them (ECJ 1974). This ruling was prompted by a challenge to French policy excluding non-national seafarers from employment on French vessels, and the Court ruled that it was in conflict with Article 48 of the Treaty of Rome.

This left air transport – the other mode to be specifically excluded from the common transport policy – in some ambiguity until the Court entered the same judgement in the Nouvelles Frontières case in 1986 (ECJ 1986). These judgements were a vindication of the Commission's position that, despite the apparent exclusion of air and sea transport from the common transport rules, other Treaty provisions did apply to them automatically. The Court took an expansive view of the general rules of the Treaty of Rome, arguing that they applied to all economic activity in the Community, and that 'far from involving a departure from these fundamental rules, the object . . . of the common transport policy is to implement and complement them by means of common action' (ECJ, 1974: point 25).

These were important rulings, but the Court was not finished. On 24 January 1983, the European Parliament brought a case against the Council of Ministers, accusing it of failing to adopt a CTP as required by the Treaty of Rome, and specifically mentioning sixteen of the Commission's proposals relating to harmonisation, market operation, and infrastructure, among others. The Court found that the Council had indeed neglected its duty; it ruled that 'in breach of the Treaty the Council has failed to ensure freedom to provide services . . . and to lay down the conditions under which non-resident carriers may operate transport services in a Member State' (ECJ 1985: 1601; on the implications of this case for the institutional balance of power in the EU, see Dashwood 1985). Though it was not decided until 1985, this case, along with the French Seafarer and Nouvelles Frontières cases, helped galvanise opinion that more effective action in transport was imperative.

The single market programme begun in 1985 provided a ready-made vehicle for encouraging action in transport. Among the nearly three hundred White Paper measures were several related to transport. The Single European Act, which established a deadline for completion of the single market, also changed the voting rules in transport from unanimity to qualified majority, thus lowering the threshold for common action. Together these developments brought to an end an era of stagnation in EU transport, colourfully described by two scholars in 1970 as 'a dismal story of false starts, of politically inept Commission proposals, of persistent Council inaction, of divided government views, and of an apparent drift in the direction of more nationally directed policies' (Lindberg and Scheingold 1970: 143).

The changing political economy of transport

The political economy of transport in Europe has undergone profound change since the early 1980s.[1] This change has occurred both internally and externally, and many factors appear to be behind it, including ideology, technology, productivity and competition, and demographic change. Member states began with radically different approaches to transport policy, which raised serious obstacles to early common governance. There was by no means a consensus that market principles ought to apply; France and Germany in particular believed that transport was part of a wider social system, and that it contributed to geographic and social cohesion. This was reflected in the state ownership of railways and the preservation of domestic road haulage for national companies, as well as the strict system of price regulation. Other countries, notably the Netherlands and Britain, have traditionally seen transport as a trunk industry, serving the needs of manufacturers and industrial consumers (Molle 1990: 340).

Despite this inauspicious beginning, major convergence has occurred in the praxis of transport. The inland transport system of the EU has seen a rapid shift from public to private transport and from rail and inland waterway use to road use. This has occurred against a backdrop of rising transport demand in both freight and passenger services: 70 per cent of EU transport of freight and passengers takes place on roads, and roads account for more than 50 per cent of the increase in transport over the past twenty years (Commission 1994b: 3). It is important to note that these changes happened in virtually every member state, representing a convergence in economic and demographic change across the EU which fed into the transport systems. Moreover, these changes are underpinned by the rapid increase in foreign direct investment (FDI) and trade, both within the EU and more widely. Factor-based investments have made integrated production and sales systems necessary, with firms adopting 'just-in-time' delivery in order to reduce inventories. The decline of Fordist production techniques in favour of lean production, greater product differentiation, the use of information technology to design and plan products have all contributed to the trend (UNCTAD 1994).

Thus, common management and production practices, a focus on cost-cutting (especially during recession) and global competition, new alliances and markets formed in the wake of the Single Market, and an ideological recognition of the importance of consumer interests have all led to transport being inextricably linked to economic success. Furthermore, convergence was not limited to the EU. Liberalism, deregulation, and privatisation were US-driven to some extent, and cognitive links between the American and European versions of competition policy and deregulation are clear. Officials from DG IV in the European Commission (the directorate responsible for competition policy) have for many years shared information with their counterparts in the US. In both, a normative adjustment took place towards open and liberal systems of production, exchange, and transport which widened the choice for industrial and individual consumers.

The contours of governance in the 1990s

Is it possible, based on what we know about transport, to categorise these emerging forms of governance? In this section I suggest that two governance subsystems now exist: the domestic security network and the supranational regulatory network. In addition, a pre-governance sub-system has emerged, which I refer to as soft issue alliances. I also suggest that which of these is most relevant depends not only on the policy issue, but also on the time continuum: early in the life of a policy the Commission dialogue with interest groups predominates in a soft issue alliance; later, as agreement is worked out, a supranational regulatory network takes shape. However, much conflict remains unresolved, and remains the province of a domestic security network concerned with preserving national economic or military advantage, cohesion, or some other national priority. Moreover, even where a supranational regulatory network is created, member states have the opportunity to fine-tune policies to national cultural and legal contours in the implementation and enforcement stages. This means that governance transformation in decision-making does not always imply governance transformation in administration.

In taking this line, I borrow from the network governance approach (Kohler-Koch 1996). The latter stresses the role of government as an arena rather than as an actor, and it illuminates how networking offers 'the institutional framework within which transaction costs can be reduced and successful self-regulation can be supported' (Kohler-Koch 1996: 371). The key features of network governance are the autonomy of actors combined with their mutual dependence, the bargaining process they undertake, and the fact that actor preferences are formed within the context of their inter-action (ibid.: 369–70). This approach is particularly helpful in understanding the supranational regulatory network that has emerged in transport. Within the member states' domestic security network, however, the picture is more varied; governance methods differ dramatically depending on the state, the mode, and the time. Statist policy-making sys-tems remain entrenched, and state-producer relationships in which other actors are marginalised continue to be the norm in some cases.

Governance sub-system one: the domestic security network

The first governance sub-system exists within individual member states, whose 'many indigenous cultural, physical, and geographical factors' pre-clude adoption of a comprehensive common transport policy (Fokkema and Nijkamp 1994: 140–1). National priorities are the key underlying norms in this sub-system. I have termed this a domestic security network. The most important values associated with this sub-system are national security, cohesion, public service, and occasionally safety and environmen-tal issues. This governance sub-system predates EU governance, and it is from the domestic security network that new sub-systems are forged. Transformation can only occur when there is agreement, based upon the push and pull described earlier. Thus, we find the domestic security pattern where public goods remain nationally-based. Although there is insufficient space to treat this issue in detail, the emergence of a new governance sub-system at the EU level has begun to transform domestic security sub-systems in important ways, though not uniformly across member states and modes.

Examples of nationally-based public goods include transport service in the Aegean, which is constantly under the cloud of poor Greek–Turkish relations. Greece, despite its generally liberal attitude towards shipping, sought to protect this trade from foreign competition in order to ensure continuity of service and the presence of a domestic fleet. In addition, Austria's concern over transit traffic in the Brenner Pass, which is highly polluting and benefits mainly Italian-German trade, led it to seek exemp-tions from the liberalised policy on trucking. In aviation, the Commission has found that its efforts to gain authority to conclude trade agreements on aviation rights with third countries is undermined by member states taking unilateral action.

Moreover, large differences exist between member states in policies regarding vehicle taxes and excise duties on fuel, both of which affect the demand for road transport haulage (Camerra-Rowe 1994; Young 1994). These differences exist not simply because of different environmental pri-orities, but also because member states are loathe to part with fiscal autonomy, and the minimum standards that have been set have not required great change among member states. More formal harmonisation measures – such as the carbon tax – have failed precisely for this reason. Thus, the national approach to fiscal policy undermines the formation of policies at the EU level.

The actors involved in this sub-system are predominantly the carriers and national bureaucrats, though differences exist between modes and member states. In aviation and rail, dominant nationally-owned carriers have enjoyed particularly close relations with bureaucratic elites, while in the maritime and trucking sectors the fragmentation of carrier interests, with more competition among smaller, privately-owned firms, has weakened them in a relative sense. In addition, transport consumer interests are generally better developed in northern states, providing a countervailing voice and partially undermining the statist policy-making orientation of state-level transport governance.

These differences are reflected in the resilience of the domestic security governance sub-system. State ownership of monopolies tends to fossilise national policy communities of bureaucrats, producers, and national parliaments in such a way that they are resistant to both domestically-driven change (from consumer groups, new producers, and non-functional 'generalist' ministries) and foreign-driven change (from foreign producers, the EU, and other international organisations). 'Fossilised' policy communities are less visible in the modes (and states) characterised by competition, openness, and private ownership. It is partly for these reasons that northern member states have adapted more readily to the emergent supranational regulatory network. Hierarchical, statist governance systems do not lend themselves easily to supranational influence, particularly when the cohesion values embedded within them are at odds with the prevailing supranational liberal values. Thus, the governance sub-system associated with domestic security has proved resilient and only marginally transformed.

In addition to differences based upon policy-making systems and state-society relations, there remain distinct cultural differences in approach based upon ideology and national legal systems. The liberalism–protectionism debate is resurrected with each new infusion of state capital into ailing flag-carrier airlines. Idiosyncracies in national legal systems mean that implementation and enforcement create wide scope for differential application of EU policies, even where the EU has competence (see Majone 1993b). The lack of commitment to EU policies on the part of some member state domestic security networks has led to backsliding on agreements, incomplete implementation, and even blatant refusal to incorporate new norms into national law. Thus, governance transformation at the decision-making stage of EU policy-making does not always lead to governance transformation at the implementation stage.

Governance sub-system two: the supranational regulatory network

The second sub-system of governance, which I call the supranational regulatory network, governs the now well-established rules affecting market access and competition in all the modes.[2] The EU has been most success-ful in establishing common rules in these areas, which in turn has drawn affected actors into the governance sub-system. The Commission, eco-nomic interests (mainly consumers and producers), and national bureaucrats run the system and fine-tune it to work out problems (on the growth of EU interest groups and the implications, see Greenwood and Aspinwall, 1998). For example, industrial consumer groups organised rapidly in the 1980s (particularly in aviation, road, and maritime). This occurred in the wake of the Single European Act as the perception among consumers grew that a policy network detrimental to their interests was hardening between DG VII and carrier groups.

The dominant mode of policy-making has been negative – market inte-gration and competition policy – reflecting both the ascendant normative bias of liberalism and the structures of EU institutions, which privileged negative over positive integration (for a discussion of how the decision-making apparatus encouraged negative integration, see Scharpf, 1988). This governance sub-system is supported by the peculiar features of the EU decision-making system: divided institutions, multiple points of access, and in particular by the fragmented nature of the Commission, with the Transport Directorate (DG VII) often at odds with the Competition Directorate (DG IV). The institutional division of labour has actively encouraged the voice of producers and consumers, and helped to harden and make permanent the supranational regulatory network. It also dis-courages active participation by labour and environmental interests, who are marginalised by the structure of Commission DGs. The Council of Ministers (where the Transport Council takes the lead on transport) fur-ther narrows the window of opportunity to carriers, while consumers have in the past relied on the half-hearted attempts by the Industry Council to exercise power on their behalf.

The dominant values of this governance sub-system are liberalism, com-petition, and private ownership. We see this in the language of the Treaty of Rome (Articles 85 to 87) and in the strong role played by DG IV. This fact privileges consumers relative to their position within the domestic security sub-system, and also liberal carriers relative to protected ones. In addition, the fragmented structure of the governance sub-system, with its divided institutional competencies, helps erode the statist pattern of policy-making visible at the state level, replacing it with a more pluralist pattern. It is also relevant that each of the modes has been subject to liberalising policies, and unlike the domestic security sub-system, none are accorded special status except temporarily. Change has been slowest in those modes that provide the most important cohesion function (particularly rail, but also some ferry services), and in those parts of the EU where cohesion val-ues retain the greatest legitimacy (principally the Mediterranean). Thus, liberal ideas have not completely supplanted cohesion ideas, and this makes the operation of the supranational regulatory network somewhat messy in practice.

Furthermore, the actors within this governance sub-system also partici-pate in the domestic security governance sub-system, and the differences noted earlier between the member states in their domestic security sub-systems have two important implications for the operation of the supranational regulatory network. First, the realm of the supranational regulatory network is highly contested. While clear rules have been laid down by which participants are to behave, the implementation, enforcement, and national administration of these rules are uneven. The slow progress in opening formerly protected internal shipping markets in the Mediterranean states, for example, is evidence of slow adaptation to the new rules. The same is true of subsidised airlines. While the competition rules permit state aid under circumscribed conditions, the Commission has bowed to political pressure and permitted capital infusions to state-owned airlines which go beyond the scope of its own guidelines. The proposed alliance between British Airways and American Airlines is further evidence of the contested terrain between these two sub-systems: both British Airways and the UK government have challenged the European Commission's jurisdiction over the case.

Second, certain actors are more active in the EU supranational regulatory network precisely because the open, pluralist structure and the liberal values underpinning the sub-system favour them. Consumers as a broad class of interest are not uniformly attracted to the EU level, but rather consumers from the states where the policy-making pattern and governance sub-system is more open, less hierarchical, and where liberal reforms have been instituted prior to EU action. The same is true for carriers: those operating without subsidies tend to benefit from the EU sub-system and take a more active part in its governance.

The network that has emerged – two Commission DGs, a series of producer and consumer groups, and occasionally the European Parliament and the Council of Ministers – focuses its attention mainly on competition policy and to a lesser extent the market access rules. Competition policy is in constant need of interpretation because of the cartel behaviour of some transport companies. There is a reflexive tendency for these actors to turn to one another in the first instance, rather than their domestic security subsystem. This has resulted in a fairly stable set of policy networks, such that new cleavages have emerged between actors at the EU level, which often are more stable than inter-state cleavages based upon intergovernmental negotiations. Problem-solving occurs in Brussels, with minimal state–state interaction.

'Pre-governance': soft issue alliances.

A third sub-system consists of issue alliances in malleable areas where the EU does not have clear jurisdiction. I label this 'pre-governance' to reflect the fact that these are not yet permanent enough to be thought of as governance sub-systems in their own right. The EU institutions act both as a structure and as an agent, and it is this agency role that is crucial in preparing the ground for possible future governance sub-systems. The Commission has promoted an agenda of linkage, attempting to expand EU competence into new areas by stressing the economies of scale and the ability of transport projects to solve related problems. It has actively sought to draw new actors into these projects in a variety of ways (Cram 1997), and it is no accident that it has focused on those policy areas where the EU does not have clear competence but which are related to transport liberalisation, and in which the key ideas are not liberalism, competition, and private ownership, but rather 'post-material' values such as environmental protection, congestion relief, and improvements in intermodal transport connections for passengers.

Thus, a linkage is made between transport liberalisation and various negative externalities, such as environmental, safety, traffic management, and congestion problems. Notwithstanding its long-held belief in liberalisation, the Commission has consistently advocated a shift of passengers and freight to water and rail modes as the scale of environmental damage and congestion becomes apparent (Commission 1992; 1994b). It has also urged adoption of major transport infrastructure projects both as a means of continued integration of the EU and also to relieve unemployment. The Channel Tunnel, TGV, airport construction projects, new highway construction, and inland waterway linkages all provide job opportunities in addition to being components of the much-vaunted Trans-European Networks (TENs). It has also sought to extend TENs to eastern Europe in order to integrate their economies into the EU. The fact that there is wide scope for conflict between the Commission's environmental objectives and its job-creating, infrastructure-promoting objectives has been pointed out by Lenschow in this volume.

The Commission has pushed the positive agenda in a number of ways. First, through research, it has identified the social and environmental cost to the EU, which Transport Commissioner Neil Kinnock estimates at ECU 120 billion simply for increased car use (Commission 1996a). Second, it has highlighted best technology and best practices in the EU, including intermodalism in freight and passenger transport, and high-speed trains. Third, it has actively sought partnerships in industry and consumer groups to help it bring about change. The Commission helped establish the Citizens Network in early 1996 to advise it on best practice, and it brought two task forces – on the train of the future and intermodalism – to bear on these problems in late 1995.

The Commission's frequent publication of reports and studies – such as *The Future Development of the Common Transport Policy* (Commission 1992) – enable it to define both the problem and the potential solutions. It also attempts to co-ordinate funding between Member States. The Commission estimated funding requirements for transport projects at ECU 220 billion by 1999 (Commission 1994b: 49), and while accepting the need for a public–private partnership, it has advocated the use of capital loans from the European Investment Bank and the European Investment Fund, as well as leftover funds from the common agricultural policy.

The Commission's interaction with industry and consumer groups is helping it establish a constituency in the newer, undefined areas of transport policy, which are not yet regulated at the European level. The implications for governance transformation are potentially significant, but the networks that have been established are not yet hardened. The Commission is helping condition social groups to the norm of EU-wide public goods in transport (on the agency role of the American government in promoting economic governance transformation, see Lindberg and Campbell 1991). By engaging these groups in ongoing research and discussion, the Commission is also helping to define the nature of the problem: its parameters and characteristics. Of course, it is also in a position to offer potential solutions, and indeed it is the key EU institution capable of proposing them. It is, in the words of two scholars, shaping the 'beliefs, paradigms, codes, cultures, and knowledge' of actors in the field of transport (March and Olsen 1989). Thus, the Commission appears to be the most active agent in the search for a new governance system for the as yet non-EU policy areas.

The timing and nature of governance transformation

The timing of change

Why, then, did EU transport policy come about when it did and take the shape it did? To return to the point made earlier in this essay, the timing of change can be attributed to the 'pull' of institutional change and 'push' of change in the global political economy. The decisions of the ECJ, the single market programme, the new voting rules: all created new incentives and opportunities for collective action (or reduced the old opportunities to avoid collective action). These seemingly minor changes to the institutions provoked a logic that culminated in the liberalisation of transport markets, a decision that many countries, particularly the Mediterranean ones, would not have made independently of this logic. The Court of Justice, in three decisions, demanded a common transport policy from the Council and removed both shipping and aviation from the *lex specialis* protection of the transport title. While it is true that the Court was established by the member states in order to reduce the transaction costs of agreeing to common rules (Garrett 1992), it would be an understatement to say that many member states did not welcome these decisions. The concessions extracted by protectionist states in agreeing to liberalisation, the backsliding on commitments, the incomplete implementation and enforcement, all bear witness to their hostility to liberalisation. As Krasner has pointed out, initial choices cannot be taken back easily; these decisions tend to 'canalize future developments' and limit the range of options available to decision-makers (Krasner 1984: 240).

The single market programme held out the prospect of increased growth for many member states. In order to accelerate the decision-making process related to the single market, a system of qualified majority voting was established. Transport policy was made a part of the single market and was subject to the qualified majority voting rules. Thus, a commitment by member states to establish the single market and undertake decision-making reform brought European-level public transport goods into being, a development that some of the member states would clearly have opposed given an ability to rationally act on exogenous preferences outside this new context. They did extract what concessions they could, but their options were limited. Indeed, the preservation of important elements of national interest through safeguard clauses shows that member state prerogatives did matter.

However, though institutional change provided the 'pull' for new governance mechanisms in transport, the 'push' came from a convergence in the political economy of transport, which changed the calculus among actors in favour of collective action. Specifically, there was growing agreement among many (but not all) actors that liberal transport systems were preferable to protected systems serving social goals. This agreement occurred because of a new dynamism across all transport sectors caused by global economic change and also because of ideological shifts within the EU. By the 1980s the new dynamism had begun to dissolve national policy communities and introduce a new logic of competition. Transport deregulation and privatisation spread slowly from the US and UK to other parts of Europe; growing foreign direct investment, trade, and new methods of production and retailing put increased emphasis on transport. Economic recession increased the pressure on manufacturers to reduce transport costs. Thus, both public and private actors began to see competitive challenges and opportunities in the same light. The 'beggar-thy-neighbour' approach of separate national policies created an EU-wide void in that public goods at the regional level were undermined by national industrial protection. Apart from threatening to scuttle the single market, this was also a sub-optimal welfare outcome, and the growing recognition of this provided increased incentives for EU-level collective action on market regulation.

We see this convergence in thinking beyond simply the transport sector, and we see it in both functional and geographic actors. The 'push' of convergence helps explain why the large member states decided in the 1980s to support the Single European Act (Keohane and Hoffmann 1991; Moravcsik 1991; Garrett 1992). Moreover, it is now widely accepted that converging views among economic actors, particularly large firms faced with declining competitiveness *vis-à-vis* American and Japanese firms, led to a concerted effort to promote and guide the single market initiative (Sandholtz and Zysman 1989; Green Cowles 1995).

The nature of change

To understand fully the nature of governance transformation in this sector we need to dig a little deeper into the special features of the EU and member state institutions. In particular, three institutional factors are crucial to an understanding of the development of the CTP. First, the 'nested institutional environment' of the EU and member states shaped the formation of preferences and strategies by crucial actors in a way that conditioned them to seeing a CTP as a viable strategy. Second, the structure of the EU institutions privileged certain actors over others, and this contributed to the negative integration bias of the CTP. These first two factors are familiar from Hall's work (Hall 1986) on state economic institutions in Britain and France. Finally, the third factor is the agency role of the EU institutions themselves who, over a period of time, are actively creating the conditions suitable for an increased level of competence for the EU. Some work has been done on the agency role of the Commission and Court (Cram 1997; Burley and Mattli 1993; on the role of agency in governance transformation, see Campbell and Lindberg 1991: 327), and the perspective adopted here gives strong emphasis to these roles of the institutional agents. These institutional factors were the context, or filter, through which actors responded to specific economic and political changes: the push and pull in the transport sector.

Nested institutions

Nested institutions affect outcomes because only some issues are ripe for resolution at the EU level. Global and state institutions have legitimacy as well, and this robs the EU of potential authority. Clearly one could argue that the reason these issues have not been handed to the EU level is that the actors involved in such a decision have not rationally calculated that such a transfer is appropriate. Equally, it is possible to argue that the historical evolution of institutional competence over important issues by global regimes or states predates the formation of the EU by (in some cases) a very long time, and they are thus embedded in a particular context which defies change, regardless of the 'appropriateness' of such change.

There is another way in which the nested nature of institutions affects outcomes. The differential state–society relations in member states has an impact on the development of the common transport policy. As Hall has noted, 'structural consistencies [lie] behind the persistence of distinctive national patterns of policy' (Hall 1986: 18). Where hierarchical patterns exist, replicated through state ownership, protected markets, and other traditions, economic actors are less likely to represent themselves beyond the state. This is particularly the case for consumers, despite the existence of a directorate devoted to the promotion of consumer interests. Thus, while in law transport liberalisation applies equally to all member states, in practice there are differences in application, enforcement, and interpretation. The boundary between the supranational regulatory network sub-system and the domestic security sub-system is not neat, but varies by time, by geography, and according to mode. These differences are due to the historical patterns of culture and institutional arrangement in the member states.

Structural bias

A second way in which the institutional character of Europe shapes the evolution of transport governance is through the structure of the EU institutions. Decisions are made on transport in the context of these institutions, and it is instructive to examine the ways they may privilege certain actors and ideas over others. The fragmented decision-making system, and especially the competing directorates in the Commission, presents multiple 'voice-fora' where private interests may thrash out alternative views. As March and Olsen explain, the 'establishment of public policies, or competition among bureaucrats or legislators, activates and organizes otherwise quiescent identities and social cleavages' (March and Olsen 1989: 18).

The fact that the transport and competition directorates have the principal influence on the drafting of EU legislation is extremely important to its outcome. Of course, other institutional and ideological factors come into play – the single market initiative, the Treaty of Rome, and the general acceptance in most quarters of liberal principles also circumscribed what was possible – but the constant involvement of these two directorates in both the drafting and oversight of transport creates a system in which the principal conflict is between producers and consumers, although there are also conflicts between liberal and protected producers as well. Other actors are disadvantaged, including environmentalists and (to the extent their views differ from those of firms) labour. Likewise, decision-making by the Transport Council has had an impact on policy that favours producers at the expense of others.

The agency role of the European institutions

Finally, the EU is more than a structure. The Commission in particular has become an agent of change, as we have seen in its repeated efforts to achieve policy linkage, create new symbols, identify problems and solutions, and attract new interests. This agency role must be brought in as an analytical tool in the discussion of institutions (Cram 1997; Bulmer 1994; Lindberg and Campbell 1991). The agency role of the Commission, moreover, has not attracted simply functional interests, but territorial ones (Jachtenfuchs and Kohler-Koch 1995; Hooghe and Keating 1994). In addition to the Commission, the Court has also acted to promote a European *acquis*, not simply through the judgements discussed here but also occasionally in other spheres as well (Burley and Mattli 1993). Its activism is limited by political expediency, but nonetheless it plays a role in creating the institutional context which in the future determines the shape of EU governance systems.

Conclusion

I have sought to identify the parameters of two distinct governance subsystems in EU transport: domestic security and supranational regulatory network. I have also identified a 'pre-governance' sub-system: soft issue alliances. The EU has been more successful in establishing a governance subsystem in market regulation than it has elsewhere in transport. There were three basic changes which brought this about. The first was a partial globalisation of west European economies, including trade, investment, and production. These combined with steadily lower transport costs to produce pressure to open transport regimes to competition, reduce or eliminate cartels, and offer greater choice. The second was the spread of liberal ideas, and their adoption throughout the EU, which privileged certain options over others, and even removed some options altogether. Thus, the fundamental and long-lasting tension underlying state traditions in transport in western Europe – the tension between consumerism and choice on the one hand and cohesion on the other – began to break down as the latter lost its sense of legitimacy. Finally, the third change was the actions of the European institutions themselves. The Court removed the exceptionalism from transport and demanded a common policy. The Commission offered the means of doing so by delivering the proposed Single European Act and single market initiative, to which a common transport policy would be attached.

Ironically, it seems that success in negative integration has partly created the need for positive integration, but much less success has graced the attempts to address the costs of a burgeoning transport system. The Commission has sought repeatedly to create a consensus on social, fiscal, and environmental solutions to problems of congestion, pollution, and competitive disadvantage, but without notable success. Much of the reason for the slow progress is that the domestic security governance sub-system retains a great deal of legitimacy in these areas.

Governance change has always been driven by the European institutions, but it is a non-linear process. The timing of transformation depends on the resolution of the dynamics of institutional 'pull' and convergence 'push.' Where both dynamics are working in favour of EU solutions, we are likely to see integration occur, followed by the hardening of a governance mechanism made up of interested players. The nature of the transformation depends on several institutional characteristics spelled out in this paper: nested institutions, structural bias, and agency. Governance also depends on where along the policy continuum action is taking place. In the early stages, supranational, national, and interest agitation is likely to lead to a soft alliance around core values; later, as policies are implemented and enforced, the domestic security network is likely to imprint its own governance style. For the time being, transport firms remain prone to the fragmented, divided nature of governance: market regulation in Brussels, tax and environmental regulation in national capitals, some investment at the local level.

Notes

1 For early views of European transport, see Despicht 1964; Lindberg and Scheingold 1970; for later views consult Erdmenger 1983; Whitelegg 1988; degli Abbati 1987; for a discussion of the economics of European transport, see Molle 1990; Gwilliam and Mackie 1975.
2 Space does not permit a detailed analysis of policy change in transport. Interested readers should consult the following works: in rail, Molle 1990; Degli Abbati 1987; Commission 1994b. In road transport, Commission 1994b; Young 1994; Papaioannou and Stasinopoulos 1991; Camerra-Rowe 1994. In inland waterway Molle 1990. In aviation, Vincent and Stasinopoulos 1990; Kassim 1994. In shipping, Aspinwall 1995; Bredima-Savopoulou and Tzoannos 1990.

8

GOVERNANCE TRANSFORMATION IN THE PROFESSIONAL SERVICES SECTOR

A case of market integration 'by the back door'?

Jill Lovecy

Introduction

This chapter explores the complex processes of governance transformation which have been engendered by the project for European market integration in the field of services subject to professional accreditation. This is a sector which has in the modern period come to encompass an extensive and very diverse range of service activities in the member states of the EC. The study focuses on what can be identified, in this as in other areas of economic activity, as a long negative integration policy cycle initiated by the 1957 Treaty of Rome (Davidson 1989; Scharpf 1996). However, what sets the professional services sector apart is that negative integration here was from the outset centred on securing the removal of discriminatory rules based on the national origins of such services and their providers, by applying the principle of mutual recognition to the member states' systems of professional qualifications and diplomas (de Crayencour 1982; Séché 1988; Orzack 1991).[1]

It is this which gives a case-study of this sector its special interest. Professional services were, in effect, the only area of economic activity where the original signatory states to the Treaty of Rome had formally committed themselves to implementing mutual recognition by the end of the twelve year transitional period laid down in the Treaty. This policy instrument has of course much more recently come to be placed at the heart of the EC's system of sectoral governance. But this was only possible once the application of mutual recognition had been extended through the expansive jurisprudence of the European Court of Justice, with its landmark ruling in 1979 in the *Cassis de Dijon* case (Nicolaidis 1993; Rasmussen 1986), and had then been incorporated into the 1986 Single European Act as the key policy mechanism for securing the implementation of the Internal Market Programme (Garrett 1992; Keohane and Hoffmann 1991).

The processes of governance transformation that have been associated with the adoption and implementation of policies of negative integration in this sector have had three notable features. The first has been their protracted and tortuous character. That this has been no less true of professional services than it has of other sectors, *despite* the incorporation of mutual recognition into article 57 of the Rome Treaty and the original deadline set for its implementation in 1970, certainly demands some explanation. Indeed negative integration in this sector has only some forty years later been completed, with a further Directive on legal practice enacted in 1998.[2] The second feature concerns the intra-sectorally differentiated character of the outcomes of these processes of sectoral governance transformation. What has been established here are effectively three separate systems of governance for professional services, each organised around its own distinctive rules on EC-wide mutual recognition. These have, moreover, each resulted from very different kinds of policy process at the EC level and have emerged at differing points in time over the last twenty-five years. The third, and at first sight somewhat contradictory, feature concerns the emergence, at the end of this long negative integration policy cycle, of governance structures which are quite closely aligned to the network-governance model and have a quasi sector-wide remit, across all professions in each of the member states. This model, it has been argued (Kohler-Koch 1996), exemplifies an underlying logic of governance transformation embedded within the European project for regional market integration.

How then can we best account for these patterns of sectoral governance outcomes in the professional services sector, marked as they are by such sharp contrasts in the timing, coverage and structures of the three governance systems, and in the mutual recognition rules which they each manage? And what have been their major consequences for the national systems of professional regulation already established in the member states of the EC? In addressing these questions the study presented here will draw on and assess the respective explanatory capacities of two different theoretical approaches: historical institutionalism and the rise of a European 'regulatory state'. The first of these, along with globalisation theories, has been used extensively in studies of separate sectoral policies and of sectoral policy-making in the EC (Greenwood and Aspinwall 1998; Mazey and Richardson 1993c; Coleman and Underhill 1995). In contrast, sectoral studies drawing on the theorisation of the EC as an emergent regulatory state have as yet been confined to a quite limited and recent body of work (notably Majone 1992, 1994 and 1996).

Analysis of the empirical findings on governance developments in this sector focused on these two approaches is presented infra. Centrally the study argues that the course of this first policy cycle of negative integration for professional services has been informed and shaped primarily by the interaction between two contrasting and analytically distinct logics of governance, the one characterised by *intra-sectorally differentiated* and the other by *sector-wide* processes and outcomes. The first of these is most effectively addressed by the historical institutionalist and globalisation approaches. Here the analysis will concentrate on the first of these, leaving to one side the specific factors associated with globalisation. The latter are best able to account for the two separate, and strongly contrasting, governance systems that developed for health-care and legal services in the 1970s (Loveccy 1995).

However, it is by developing analytical and conceptual tools from within a regulatory state perspective that this study is able to locate the key role played by what will be characterised here as processes of market integration 'through the back door'. It is thus a second transformative logic of governance, focused on a distinctive mode of policy sectorisation, which will be shown later in this chapter to be crucial to any account of the overall trajectory of governance transformation for professional services. This, it will be argued here, can only be fully elucidated by working within a theoretical framework identifying those state-like properties of the EC which most set it apart, as an arena of governance, from the liberal-democratic institutional arrangements of its member states. The present sectoral study is thereby intended to contribute to a fuller understanding of this emergent type of state formation.

'Unpacking' governance transformation in the professional services sector: a preliminary assessment

The priority assigned to the task of 'unpacking' the processes of governance transformation is designed to enable this study to engage with a set of inter-related methodological and theoretical issues that arise in analysing the EC as an arena of multi-level governance. This section will therefore offer some preliminary comments on the research methodology adopted here, by identifying a range of different causative logics that are involved in shaping sectoral policies and sectoral governance outcomes within the EC, and then focusing on the specific forms each of these has taken within the professional services sector. Subsequent sections of the chapter will seek to elucidate the differing patterns of structured interactions operating between these differing causative logics over time.

In effect, a number of different types of explanatory strategy are available for an EC sectoral policy study of this kind. Three strategies locating the independent variable of analysis within the political economy and/or governance systems at three different levels would seem to be most salient, namely at the levels of the member states; or of the EC itself; or externally, in dynamic competitive processes within the international political economy. Historical institutionalism and the rise of a European 'regulatory state' respectively represent two of these three types of explanatory account and were selected for this study because of their individual salience to the professional services sector.

As a middle-level theory, historical institutionalism offers general propositions of very broad applicability, centring on the path-dependency of governance institutions in contemporary states. Analysis developed from within this framework therefore focuses on the extent to which such institutions, through their embeddedness within a broader complex of political, economic, legal, social and cultural arrangements, serve to shape and sustain specific patterns of behaviour, attitudes and goals among both individual and collective actors (Steinmo *et al.* 1992). The enormous value of such an approach when applied to the comparative analysis of professional services, their political economy and their characteristic forms of governance has been amply demonstrated in recent work (Rueschmeyer 1989; Burrage and Torstendahl 1990). What it offers when applied to the development of EC governance structures in this sector is an explanatory account focusing not so much on a transformative logic, but rather on the projection into the European arena of the entrenched features of intra-sectoral differentiation that have characterised this sector's governance and political economy in the member states in the modern period. It is this logic of intra-sectoral differentiation which will be examined in some detail elsewhere in this chapter.

In contrast, the *regulatory state* literature has been concerned with directly theorising the process of regional economic and political integration in Europe as being constitutive of a new type of state formation. Such an approach focuses on identifying those properties of the EC's governance system that most explicitly characterise it as the exemplar of an emergent regulatory state. Most notable here are the quite limited funding and personnel resources on which EC governance can draw; the restrictive range of policy instruments available to it; and, in consequence, the role of central importance that has accrued within this multi-tiered governance system to legal procedures – and in particular to the expansive jurisprudence of the European Court of Justice – on the one hand, and on the other, to reliance on authorities and agencies organised within the member states at the national or sub-national levels, for securing the application of EC-wide rules (Majone 1991 and 1994; Dehousse 1992).

At the same time the mode(s) of legitimation on which these EC governance arrangements draw are also distinctive, offering significant elements of contrast with those modes of legitimation associated with the member states' institutions, with their characteristic properties *qua* liberal democratic states (Majone 1996: 283–300). However, such regulatory-state elements co-exist with others that are more closely aligned to those constitutive principles of political citizenship and elective mandates on which modern representative democracies have been based. This is largely because of the intergovernmental components that have been sustained and developed within the EC's *sui generis* governance arrangements and have been reinforced with the introduction of direct elections to the European Parliament from 1979. Nevertheless, it is possible to design a research strategy focusing specifically on these regulatory state elements in order to identify their institutional dynamics, and the role which these have played in shaping sectoral policies and governance outcomes.

In applying this approach, the section on the regulatory state elements engages with those governance mechanisms which most clearly exemplify the second logic at work, that of sectorisation. The effect of these governance mechanisms has been to circumvent those actors most resistant to the integration of markets in professional services across borders who are entrenched at the national level. The material presented here takes the form of a double case-study: the first part centring on the European Court of Justice and its jurisprudence; the second centring on the distinctive policy procedures introduced to implement the Single European Market programme.

Finally, the third body of literature on globalisation embraces a quite varied range of theoretical propositions, but what globalisation theorists share is the critical importance they attach in the contemporary period to a quite distinct set of factors. These are exogenous, and in part technologically-driven, competitive processes making for new modes of transnationalism within the international political economy and re-articulating the relationships between local, regional and global actors and institutions (Dicken 1992; Hirst and Thompson 1996; Perraton *et al.* 1997; Petit 1994). When applied in relation to EC sectoral policies and governance outcomes, such an approach points to new patterns of inter- and intra-sectoral competition which are now feeding into and re-shaping those actors, interests and epistemic communities which have hitherto been organised within the framework of the established liberal democratic nation states. In this period such forms of inter- and intra-sectoral competition are also shaping new constellations of actors and interests around the EC's structures of governance, along with new epistemic communities at the regional and global levels.

This approach will be drawn on in this study only to supplement the main lines of analysis developed from within the other two approaches. As has been noted, and as I have argued elsewhere, in the period covered by this study, up until the late 1980s, what this approach is best able to address in its own right are the two most strongly contrasting governance outcomes in this sector covering health-care professionals and lawyers (Lovecy 1995). In part for reasons of space, but also because the concern here is rather with accounting for the eventual alignment of governance arrangements in this sector on the network-governance model, these developments and the explanatory capacity of globalisation theories in respect of them will only by referred to quite briefly here.

However, before proceeding with these two differing accounts of the causative processes informing the European regional integration project, the following section first provides a summary of the key empirical findings of this study, outlining the main characteristics of each of the three systems of governance that have developed at the EC level for professional services.

Three governance systems for professional services in the EC

The most important of the three is undoubtedly the most recently established, which dates from the 1989 First General Systems Directive (Directive 89/48/EEC). It was only with this Directive, commonly referred to as the Diplomas Directive, that legislation on mutual recognition was finally enacted encompassing the bulk of the professions where entry is dependent on a minimum of three years of formal post-secondary education. In the fifteen member states of the EU today, this amounts to some two hundred separately organised professions.

What this Directive put in place was a light-touch regulatory regime operating under the aegis of a responsible unit within the relevant Directorate General of the Commission (now DG XV). In effect, its governance structures are organised around a flexible framework of both bilateral and multi-lateral linkages, bringing together a mix of public and private actors drawn from the sub-national, national and European levels. Their central remit is to co-ordinate and monitor the common procedures for mutual recognition introduced by the Directive, enabling qualified service providers to establish on a permanent basis in a member state other than the one in which they gained their professional accreditation. These regulatory arrangements were also designed to facilitate the resolution, on a co-operative basis, of the greatly increased numbers of individual problem cases and disputes which were expected to arise as practitioners belonging to the broad band of professional occupations covered by the Directive availed themselves of their 'right of establishment'.

The contrast between this *quasi sector-wide* governance system, closely aligned to the network-governance model, and the two other forms of sectoral governance created earlier on could hardly be greater, even though all operate under the aegis of the same Directorate General of the

Commission. (At the time when these two earlier systems were established, the relevant Directorate General was DG III.) The first of these dates from a series of Directives in the mid-1970s, which put in place separate sets of profession-specific governance structures for six health-related professions: doctors (Directives 75/362/EEC and 75/364/EEC), dentists, midwives, nurses, vets and pharmacists (de Crayencour 1982). Here governance centres on a highly formalised system of tripartite representation, with the relevant national ministries, statutory professional bodies and other voluntary associations or trade unions in each of the member states being statutorily represented on the separate sets of European committees established for each of these professions. The operational costs of such a cumbersome and bureaucratic governance system (Orzack 1991: 143) have inevitably proved to be high, in terms of time and money. These governance arrangements, organised on a common pattern, and adopted for a whole group of professions, are taken here to together constitute a *group-specific* governance system.

This designation serves to differentiate these governance arrangements for health-related services from another set of profession-specific structures which have developed, quite uniquely, in the area of legal service provision. It is this third system, confined to Europe's lawyers, which will therefore be classified here as a *profession-specific* governance system. For most of the period since the mid-1970s, when it first began to take shape in the preparatory phase for the 1977 Lawyers' Services Directive (Directive 77/249/EEC), this has been organised on an almost entirely informal basis, centring on a private law body, the Council of European Bars and Law Societies (CCBE).[3] In recent years however, as we shall see, the pivotal role of the CCBE has been increasingly eclipsed, in part because arrangements for legal services have been put on a more formalised footing, with the 1989 enactment of rules on mutual recognition.

In its heyday, as a federation of national voluntary and statutory professional organisations, the CCBE was able to operate as the main arena for preparing – on a quasi-delegated basis on behalf of DG III – the initial drafts of what came to be a series of legislative texts covering legal services. For all the other professions, the negative integration policy cycle has been firmly centred around either a single Directive or, in the case of the health professions, a set of parallel texts enacted at roughly the same time. In contrast, for legal services this policy cycle has straddled these two periods and beyond, and this has resulted in governance arrangements in this sector also having an unusually evolutive character. Here a first Directive in 1977 (on temporary cross-border services, there being no parallel legislation for any other profession) was followed by a specific exemption for the legal profession from the main provisions of the 1989 Diplomas Directive and, more recently, by a projected profession-specific Directive on 'registered' lawyers. The initial draft of this Directive was adopted by the CCBE in

September 1992; in a modified form it was adopted through the post-Maastricht co-decision procedure between the Council of Ministers and the European Parliament.

Historical institutionalism and the dynamics of embedded intra-sectoral differentiation

It is in relation to the first two of the three key empirical findings noted in the introduction – the delays in enacting legislation on mutual recognition for professional accreditation, and the pronounced elements of intra-sectoral differentiation which have marked the processes and outcomes of sectoral governance transformation – that the explanatory capacities of historical institutionalism are clearly the greatest.

Historical institutionalist accounts of the professional services sector centre on the path-dependent heterogeneity of the separate regulatory systems that have been established for each profession at the national and sub-national levels, this heterogeneity itself being rooted in the twin features of market-closure and market-segmentation around which the professions' project has been constructed in the modern period. The public interest considerations underpinning such arrangements, in terms of protecting service recipients in market situations characterised by informational asymmetry, have historically provided a rationale for regulatory bargains between the state and individual occupational groups. Such bargains have secured for the latter a 'claim to jurisdiction' (Abbott 1988) over a defined area of service provision and the usage of a corresponding professional title. These core features of the sector's political economy have had the effect of insulating service providers from market competition and entrenching rent-seeking behaviour; they have, furthermore, resulted in the virtual exclusion of those crucial agencies of modern capitalism, the incorporated firm and waged employment, from extensive areas of service provision until the close of the twentieth century in the member states of the EU (Lovecy 1995: 515).

First and foremost, therefore, the historical institutionalist approach serves to underline a fundamental non-congruence between these features of the sector's political economy at the national level, and the European regional market integration project. It thus points to the formidable obstacles to integrating markets in professional services across borders that are posed by structural rigidities entrenched at the national and sub-national levels. Equally it points to the resistance that could be expected from national bodies seeking to maintain their profession-specific governance arrangements, and from those within the professions most attached to retaining restrictions on competitive market behaviour.

Within this general framework, it is the impetus towards intra-sectoral differentiation projected into the processes and outcomes of governance transformation in this sector which this approach is able to address most fully and effectively. It does so by locating this in the highly disaggregated and particularistic forms of private interest government found at the national level. In effect, public interest considerations have resulted in the presence of a quite distinctive kind of collective actor in this sector: para-public regulatory bodies. These have been established for each profession, in most cases on some kind of representative basis, and enjoy a range of powers in respect of what are, again in most cases, legally enforced closed shops based on professional accreditation systems, and a variable array of legally enforceable restrictive practices.

Here the analysis is further complicated because significant cross-national, as well as cross-professional, contrasts pertain to the status and powers of such regulatory bodies. In effect, in much of continental Europe, professions are subject to forms of state licensing, in terms of their institutional arrangements and the legitimising norms on which these draw. In the UK and in Ireland, on the other hand, a greater reliance on self-regulation has been sustained until the contemporary period. Such differences are of course important – although it is true that in both sets of countries the resort in practice to more hybrid arrangements has made such contrasts between national regulatory styles rather more muted and less clear-cut, in this sector at least (Vogel 1986). In the UK, for example, most professional regulatory bodies have a statutory basis – the most notable exceptions being the Bar in the UK prior to the 1990 Courts and Legal Services Act (White 1991), and professions operating in the financial services sector prior to 'the Big Bang' (Moran 1994). Equally, many state-licensed professions in other member states enjoy substantial elements of self-regulation. This has been especially true of the legal professions (Lewis and Abel 1989; Suleiman 1987).

Nevertheless, for the purposes of the present study it is what these various types of regulatory body share that is of rather greater significance than what sets them apart from each other. These professional bodies together with other voluntary representative associations – where these are separately organised – effectively occupy the place taken in other sectoral arenas by non-governmental actors, such as major firms or trade associations. Even where they enjoy a pronounced element of self-regulation, their participation in a set of relatively stable, closed policy networks has served to promote a close working relationship with their 'sponsoring' ministries. The long period of expansion of governmental responsibilities in this century has, moreover, favoured a steady, incremental process of policy accretion, extending the range of issue arenas in which major professions have been able to play an active role as policy 'insiders', either through their regulatory bodies or through other voluntary representative associations.

Arrangements such as these have put a high premium on sustaining unity within each separately organised profession. They have at the same time ensured that the collective organisations of the professions are also the arena for recurring competitive struggles, both for disputes *within* professions, centring primarily on the forms of market restrictions that should apply to the members, and also for conflicts *between* 'neighbouring' professions, over boundary issues. It is such intra- and inter-professional struggles, located within historically embedded institutions, which could be expected to be fuelled in new forms, as globalisation processes alter the market opportunities for different professions and for particular strata within them.

Globalisation theory could therefore be expected to be of particular relevance, even in the earlier part of the period covered by this study, from the early 1970s, for those areas of professional services, such as accountancy, financial services and law, most closely bound up with servicing industrial, commercial and financial trading, transnational take-overs and mergers, and foreign direct investment. It is certainly this perspective that is most helpful in explaining the efforts put in by elements within the leaderships of the national professional organisations for lawyers to recreate, through the CCBE, and to sustain at the European level the kind of professional unity that has underpinned professional organisations at the national level. This is because the task to which it has been primarily geared has been that of containing the competitive struggles arising over access to these emergent and lucrative regional markets for European legal services, by enabling representatives drawn from the national professions to jointly manage and police such competition.

In contrast, the strongly intergovernmental framework within which the preparatory consultations and negotiations for the health-care sector were managed, and the highly formalised governance system which these put in place, organised around tripartite representation, are themselves testimony to the entrenched and relatively impermeable boundaries between national health-care markets due to the different national systems for funding health-care that had been introduced in these states in the second half of the twentieth century (Esping-Andersen 1990). Health-care professionals were thereby insulated, at least until relatively late in this first negative integration policy cycle, from any significant element of regional market integration and from direct regional and global competitive pressures.

Nevertheless the professions, as collectively organised actors, enjoy close relationships with their sponsoring ministries and an entrenched position as policy 'insiders' at the national level; they have also been able to base their claims for participation in the preparatory phases of the policy process at the EC level on their status as sources of both expertise and representation. All this would point towards them having the leverage to secure the reproduction at the EC level of at least some profession-specific elements of governance, along with market-closure and some forms of the restrictive practices which they have hitherto been able to maintain at the national level.

Indeed a number of forms of profession-specific differentiation were initially written into the Treaty provisions adopted in 1957. The most important of these involved protection accorded to (profession-specific) host state rules, and thus to the professions as collective actors enjoying some powers of self-regulation. This was done, first, by according a right of establishment (article 52), through the mutual recognition of professional diplomas, which requires the migrant professional to register as a member of the relevant host state profession, practise under host state title and conform with host state rules. Second, the 'double-deontology' rule of article 60 requires those providing cross-border services on a temporary basis (i.e. *mobile* rather than *migrant* professionals) to adhere to the rules of the relevant host state profession, even though in providing cross-border services they continue to operate under their home state title under the terms of article 59 (and are therefore still subject to their home state profession's rules, too). These two provisions in combination would appear to rule out the development of more dynamic and far-reaching forms of regulatory competition that would arise if mobile (or migrant) professionals, whose home state rules were more liberal than those of the host-state profession, were able to provide services on a more long-term basis under their home-profession's rules.

The second significant element of intra-sectoral differentiation written into the Treaty of Rome has served to reproduce at EC level the special status accorded to health-care services within the member states. This took the form of a requirement, incorporated in article 57 para. 3, that mutual recognition be implemented for the health-related professionals, exceptionally, on the basis of a prior harmonisation of the member states' accreditation and training requirements. Finally, the Treaty potentially allowed for further elements of profession-specificity to be translated into EC governance, on a case-by-case basis, by providing for exemptions to be made to these general sector-wide rules on quite broadly defined public interest grounds.[4]

A key consequence, moreover, of the presence of so many different sets of profession-specific governance structures within the member states has been the degree of overload this imposed on the responsible unit in Directorate General III. Indeed, given the legal complexities and tactical and strategic problems that faced the Commission staff as they sought from the mid-1960s to manage preparatory consultations on implementing mutual recognition in this sector, it might be argued that a 'no-win set' – or, at the least, very extensive delays – was indeed the outcome that should have been expected. Nevertheless, despite the explanatory capacity of historical institutionalism in all these respects, what this perspective cannot engage with at all effectively is precisely the fact that such a 'no-win set' did not in the end prevail.

It is at this point therefore that the focus of analysis needs to switch to those developments which testify, instead, to the operation of a powerful impetus towards sectorisation within EC policy and governance arrangements, over-riding these highly differentiated forms of private interest government entrenched at the national level. This is what the regulatory state literature on the EC is able to offer.

Europe's regulatory state and market integration 'by the back door'

With the inauguration of the Single European Market programme, it became possible to characterise the European project as being essentially an exercise in regulatory reconstruction (Pelkmans 1989; Majone 1991 and 1992; Dehousse 1992). Arguably, however, an underlying regulatory approach was from the outset inherent in the Treaty of Rome's strategy of building 'an ever closer union of the peoples of Europe'. This was designed to use legal procedures (through binding Treaty commitments and a European Court of Justice to enforce them) to pursue an *economic* project, of regional market integration, by according sets of collective rights to individual economic actors. Freedom of movement for goods, services, labour and capital were founding principles of the 1957 Treaty of this type. The dynamic role which this strategy assigned to legal processes and actors, the expansive jurisprudence which these have gone on to produce, and the structured interactions that have developed between legal actors and institutions located at the national, sub-national and European levels, are all features of the EC governance system which have been the subject of much specialist commentary and debate (Cappelletti *et al.* 1986; Rasmussen 1986; Keohane and Hoffmann 1991; Weiler 1991).

What this approach most crucially offers for the analysis of governance transformation in the professional services sector is the identification of those governance mechanisms, and corresponding modes of legitimation, which have been available at the EC level to insulate the making of policy, and policy outcomes too, from key actors and interests organised at the national level in the member states. Such governance mechanisms have served to promote new forms of market integration 'by the back door', by bringing into play a distinctive logic of policy sectorisation.

In the case of professional services, the European Court of Justice and the Internal Market Programme have each operated in contrasting ways to circumvent the elements of complexity, overload and resistance deriving from the sector's political economy and governance arrangements at the national level. The former achieved this by its marginalisation of those actors most resistant to relinquishing their traditional protections from market-competitive behaviour or most attached to preserving intact the national professional bodies' regulatory powers in respect of accreditation and service delivery. The latter did so by drastically reducing the number of member states policy 'insiders' with a claim to participate in the consultation and policy preparation phases for the 1989 Diplomas Directive.

Of these, it was the European Court of Justice's role which was to be of decisive importance in this negative integration policy cycle centring on mutual recognition. Crucially, its shaping impact came into play some twenty years before the new policy procedures introduced by the Single European Act. However, as has been previously noted, it was to be these latter procedures – combined with the January 1993 deadline which the Act set for completing the Internal Market Programme – which finally enabled sectoral policies to be enacted in codified legislative form, and enabled governance structures aligned on the network-governance model to be put in place.

In accounting for the operation of these two governance mechanisms in the professional services sector, we are led back to the distinctive patterns of policy sectorisation constitutionalised under the 1957 Treaty's project for regional market integration. By according rights to specified categories of *individual* economic actors, the Treaty established policy objectives which cut across the patterning of policy sectors that had previously been institutionalised at the national level. In the case of the professions, this has served to undercut the primacy which policies and governance structures at the national level had hitherto accorded to the professions as collectively organised actors.

In effect, member state policies for professional services have been underpinned by processes of aggregation operating around profession-specific core-governance structures, with each profession having its own linked sets of rules relating to entry, standards of conduct, practice organisation and the delivery of services. In contrast, the Treaty's market integration objectives have involved disaggregating such profession-specific clusters at the national level, and replacing them at EC level by a quite different pattern of aggregation, on a cross-professional and cross-state sector-wide basis, around discrete policy issues such as Europe-wide mobility and competition. The negative integration policy cycle explored here has in this way centred on establishing the equivalence of national professional qualifications for market entry, although only in so far as entry rules affect mobile and migrant professionals (Lovecy 1994). For such services the European regulatory state has thereby operated to secure rights for *individual members of the professions* (and also the rights of individual purchasers and recipients of services) which challenge national professional regulations based on the member states' accordance of rights to the professions as collectively organised actors (Eidenmüller 1990).

As a result, the structure and substance of policies developed for professional services at the European level, and their associated forms of legitimation which link principles of fairness and individual rights to the pursuit of more competitive economic performance, have been fundamentally erosive of those unifying organisational forms, alliance strategies

147

and representations of professional identity which have been so character-istic of the 'professional project'. It is these elements of EC governance most clearly denoting it as a nascent regulatory state which have been bound up with new forms of regulatory competition within and between professions in this period (Lovecy 1995: 523–7). Modernising strata within individual or cognate professions have been able to take advantage of this context to promote liberalising reform strategies at the national level, and in the case of the legal professions, quite exceptionally, at the EC level too.

It is here that the ECJ has played a critical role. Operating as an arena which allows those who are 'policy outsiders' at the national level to come centre-stage at the EC level, it has enabled individual members of the pro-fessions (or individual service recipients) to challenge and, when successful, overturn the kinds of entrenched national and sub-national restrictive practices which have been the product of alliance-building between those who are 'policy insiders' within the member states' sectoral governance structures. In doing so, the Court has of course been con-cerned to give due weight to the broad public interest considerations, centring on the protection of the purchasers and recipients of professional services, which have underlain these collective rights of market closure and restrictions on market-competitive behaviour at the national level. Nevertheless, as the site of special kinds of decisional output within the EC's governance system, taking the form of case law rulings and an expand-ing body of jurisprudential principles, the ECJ has built on the approach laid down in the Treaty of Rome and focused on the rights assigned to indi-vidual economic actors. Two such jurisprudential principles are worth some brief comments here: direct effect and proportionality.

The first of these affirmed the direct applicability by the end of the transi-tion period of key Treaty commitments, despite their not having been translated into due legislative form. The principle of direct effect was origi-nally established by the Court in 1963 (Case 26/62 *Van Gend en Loos* v. *Nederlandse Administratie der Belastingen* 1963). It has been of central impor-tance to the nascent European regulatory state, providing a mechanism radically counteracting the failure of the formal policy process managed by the Commission and the Council to translate Treaty commitments into codi-fied legislative form. The first cases in which this principle could be applied to the article 57 mutual recognition provision, however, only reached the Court from the late 1960s onwards (with Reyners 1974 and van Binsbergen 1974). Once they did so, the Commission came under renewed pressures to expedite its drafting of legislation on mutual recognition. However, it only proved pos-sible to proceed at this stage with the preparation of profession-specific legislative texts. Paradoxically, these ECJ rulings on mutual recognition, with their inherently sector-wide applicability, served to trigger two forms of pro-fession-specific governance structures, the one developed for the group of six health-care professions and the other for Europe's lawyers.

148

The proportionality principle, that had been built from the late 1960s on the article 30 prohibition on measures having 'equivalent effect' to quantitative restrictions on imports, affirmed that the means employed by member states to safeguard, for example, public interest concerns, could only provide grounds for breaching general Treaty obligations and other EC legislation where such means were proportional to the ends to be achieved. This was reaffirmed with new force in the 1979 *Cassis de Dijon* judgement and related jurisprudence. Once applied in cases relating to professional services, this has had the effect of over-riding those protections for host state rules on the delivery and organisation of services which were written into the 1957 Treaty's provisions for both mobile and migrant professionals (Mattera 1991). Combined with competitive struggles driven by regionalisation and globalisation, this has opened up professional services and the economic actors within this sector to new processes and forms of regulatory competition between and within national professions (Lovecy 1995: 523–7).

The translation into codified legislative form of the ECJ's earlier rulings on professional mobility and direct effect, with their broad sector-wide applicability, only came in the wake of the intergovernmental 'package-deal' agreement on the Single European Act (SEA) and adoption of the Internal Market Programme (themselves triggered by the ECJ's ruling in the *Cassis de Dijon* case). The SEA, moreover, modified the institutional environment for the negotiation and adoption of policies falling within the Single European Market programme through the introduction of majority voting rules in the Council. It was in the preparation and subsequent implementation of this much delayed Directive, applying mutual recognition rules to the bulk of the sector, that new sectoral governance structures embodying the distinctive sectoral logic of the EC as an emergent regulatory state were finally put in place at *both* the EC and the national levels.

Because the Directives' central provisions covered all those professions where accreditation involved a minimum of four years post-secondary education and training, DG III was able to manage the preparatory phase in a way that cut across the separate arenas of private interest government within the member states, linking each profession to its policy-related ministry. This was achieved by bringing the member states' national education ministries centre-stage at the EC level, as the lead ministry with a sector-wide negotiating remit. The result was to confer on the national Ministries of Education a direct sector-wide co-ordinating role at the national level of a kind which had not previously existed; and the bulk of the affected national professions were thus excluded from access to the preparatory phase, except via their national education ministries. At the European level, the by now burgeoning constellation of European federations of national professions also found themselves excluded from what were essentially intergovernmental negotiations. The sole exception here was the CCBE which, in alliance with the national Ministries of Justice, won exemption for the legal profession from one of the Directives' key provisions.

The new rules enacted in the 1989 Diplomas Directive equally marked a sharp departure from those embodied in the national systems of professional regulation. Of course, in line with what was previously noted as the Treaty's generally protective stance in respect of the regulatory role of host state professions, the Directive did not provide for automatic equivalence between member state professional qualifications. Instead, qualified professionals seeking to establish in another member state from the one in which they had gained their professional qualification are required either to complete two years of practice, supervised by a qualified practitioner registered in the host state, or to sit a special examination set by the relevant host state accrediting body. Crucially, however, the right to choose between these two procedures was assigned to the individual professional. What were thus affirmed here, as in previous ECJ jurisprudence on cases concerning professional services, were not the rights of the professions as collective economic and regulatory actors, but rather the rights of individual mobile practitioners challenging that 'claim to jurisdiction' over market entry (and over the terms on which qualified practitioners are able to provide their services) which has been constitutive of professional identity and organisation in the modern period.

Finally, the establishment of new light-touch regulatory structures, for monitoring and co-ordinating the implementation of these rules, in turn consolidated the earlier break with traditional patterns of profession-specific administrative arrangements at the national level that had occurred in the preparatory phase. New co-ordinating agencies within each member state were now designated, enjoying a sector-wide remit paralleling that entrusted at the EC level to Unit E2 within DG XV. In the case of the UK, the designated civil servant is located in the Department of Trade and Industry, whereas in France the position was attached to the SGCI.[5] Implementation has thus required national sectoral governance to incorporate a key element of the EC's own pattern of policy sectoralisation. This has been reinforced by the designation within each member states' Permanent Representation of a desk-officer dealing with issues of professional mobility, again on a sector-wide basis, to provide an interface between these other two levels.[6] At the same time, these new cross-level and quasi sector-wide EC governance structures have also absorbed, for the purposes of supervising and co-ordinating mutual recognition itself, those two other areas of service provision, in health-care and legal services, for which alternative governance structures had previously been developed.

150

Professional services and the analysis of sectoral governance transformation within the European Community: some concluding remarks

The focus of this study has been limited to both a quite specific sector and a specific time-scale, covering the implementation of the Rome Treaty's initial set of negative integration objectives. As a result, the new competitive pressures and forms of regulatory competition arising from globalisation but taking shape at the local, national and European levels, and whose increasing prominence has marked the period since the mid- to late 1980s, have fallen largely outside of the remit of this study. Despite these limitations, both the methodology adopted here and some of the study's main findings should have wider applicability to other areas and aspects of sectoral governance in the EC, and should contribute to the debate about the EC as an emergent regulatory state. The two explanatory strategies that have been explored in some detail here, focusing respectively on factors and processes operating at the national and the European levels, have each been shown to provide distinctive contributions to our understanding of the processes and outcomes of governance transformation in this sector. These, it has been argued here, have been informed by the structured interactions between two contrasting governance logics, of intra-sectoral differentiation and of sectorisation.

Most centrally, this study has pointed to the gulf between, on the one hand, the policy objectives and instruments of European regional market integration laid down initially in the Treaty of Rome's provisions and, on the other, the policies and governance structures that have been constructed at the national level around systems of professional regulation within the framework of liberal democratic states. The latter, it has been seen, have centred on insulating service providers from market competition, and legitimised this as a way of securing the public interest responsibilities of national governments. The governance and political economy of professional services at this level have also been married, somewhat uneasily, into the broader framework of the liberal democratic state, partly though the representative structures that have been built into the para-public bodies regulating the separate professions. In markets characterised by a high degree of informational asymmetry, the interests of the majority have been deemed to be best secured not by their exercising their individual rights as (inadequately informed) consumers of such services, but by the state establishing a framework in which regulated professions and their members will give a primacy to the exercise of their professional judgement and expertise, untrammelled by the pressures of full-blown market competition.

In contrast, the 1957 Treaty and key governance mechanisms of the EC have been concerned with affirming and securing the rights of individual economic actors to mobility and choice within an enlarged European market, and legitimising such rights more broadly in terms of their fairness as well as their expected contribution to rising levels of economic competitivity and prosperity and, in the long term, to the goal of achieving an 'ever-closer union of the European peoples'.

The interplay between causative processes operating at two levels has thus been recast here as processes informed by two contrasting forms of state, each with the potential to operate across both the national and the European levels. What this study therefore suggests is that the complex patterns of institutional and actor interactivity between member state, sub-member state, and European levels of governance – and the transformative dynamics they give rise to – can be most fruitfully elucidated by reconceptualising these as centring on the interaction between established liberal democratic nation states and an emergent European regulatory state, each with their own characteristic, and fundamentally different, properties.

Notes

My thanks to those colleagues who attended the 'Transformation of Governance' Workshop held at the University of Mannheim in January 1997 for their constructive comments on an earlier draft of this chapter and for first formulating this title for the study.

1 The provisions applying to professional services are grouped together under Title III Free Movement of Persons, Services and Capital, in chapter 2: Right of Establishment (articles 52–58) and chapter 3: Services (articles 59–66).
2 This new, Directive (98/5 EC) allows lawyers a permanent right to practise under home-title in another member state and facilitates admission to host-state professions for lawyers having 'regularly pursued an activity for a period of at least three years in the host Member State' (article 10, OJ No. L77/36 1998).
3 The *Commission Consultative des Barreaux d'Europe*, founded in 1960 (Donald-Little 1991: ch. 3).
4 Under articles 56 and 66, 'on grounds of public policy, public security or public health'. In addition, activities 'which (in any given Member State) are connected, even occasionally, to the exercise of official authority' are also excluded, under articles 55 and 66.
5 Secrétariat géneral du comité interministériel pour les questions de coopération économique européenne. Interview with Mme J. Minor, Head of Unit, DG XV-E2, Brussels, November 1995.
6 Interview with UK Permanent Representation desk officer, July 1992.

Part III

THE EUROPEAN UNION AND THE TRANSFORMATION OF NATIONAL PATTERNS OF GOVERNANCE

9

NATIONAL PATTERNS OF GOVERNANCE UNDER SIEGE

The impact of European integration

Vivien A. Schmidt

Introduction

In recent years, scholars have focused increasing attention on the nature of European institutions and their impact on those of member states. Scholars concerned in particular with the structure of EU governance tend to disagree over whether the EU is best elucidated as a collection of unitary states (Taylor 1991; Moravscik 1991; Garrett 1992) or as a quasi-federal state (Sbragia 1993: 28). Among those who consider the EU as a quasi-federal governance structure, most tend to describe a 'dynamic confusion of powers' (Schmidt 1997a) instead of the traditional separation of powers of federal systems, with the legislative function more the domain of the formal executive than the directly-elected legislature; the executive function more the purview of the Commission bureaucracy than the formal executive to which it reports (Hayes-Renshaw and Wallace 1995; Nugent 1995); and the judicial function encroaching on the executive and the legislative in its judiciary activism (Wincott 1995; Weiler 1991).

When scholars turn to the impact of the EU on member state institutions, moreover, they see a general loss of autonomy as EU institutions increasingly take precedence over national ones, and a change in the institutional balance of power within national governments as EU institutions reinforce the powers of some national institutions and undermine those of others. For example, scholars find that although the executive's autonomy is diminished as a result of EU collective decision-making (Hayes-Renshaw and Wallace 1995; Scharpf 1994), its power over other national-level institutions and civil society is enhanced (Moravscik 1993b), although not in all instances (see Schmidt 1997b). In addition, they note that although the expansion of the powers of the European Court of Justice (ECJ) has reduced the independence of the national judiciary, national judiciaries

155

generally have seen a concomitant rise in their powers and autonomy vis-à-vis the executive, while the lower courts have gained a measure of independence from higher ones (Burley and Mattli 1993). By contrast, most comment upon a decline in the powers of national parliaments, despite the reforms related to Maastricht (see Raworth 1994). Finally, many also see a growth in the powers of subnational units, yielding a new, emerging system of 'multi-level governance' (Marks, Hooghe and Blank 1995; Grande 1996a).

Although EU policy processes have also been a topic of research, these studies have tended to be more narrowly focused. Lobbying at the EU level has received the lion's share of attention (e.g. Mazey and Richardson 1993c; Greenwood and Ronit 1994). By comparison with the plethora of institutional profiles of the EU, there have been relatively few attempts to characterise the EU policy-making process as a whole: 'transnational pluralism' (Streeck and Schmitter 1991) is the most frequently cited, although the recent analysis of the EU as an emerging system of network governance (Kohler-Koch 1996) holds great promise. What is more, by contrast with the large number of studies of the impact of EU institutions on those of member states, there have been even fewer attempts to consider the impact of EU policy processes on member states. This is because it is hard enough trying to encapsulate policy-making processes at the EU or member state level, let alone trying to assess the impact of the former on the latter.

None the less, in what follows I make just such an attempt. First, I define the EU as a quasi-pluralist system of governance most akin to that of the United States, but somewhat less open to interest influence in policy formulation, equally regulatory in policy implementation by applying the rules without exception, and more co-operative than competitive in decision-making culture, with decisions that are more technical than political but equally bottom-up. Then, I contrast it with first, statist polities such as France, Great Britain, and Italy, which tend to be more closed to interest influence in policy formulation, more administrative than regulatory in policy implementation by being open to interest accommodation, and more conflictual in culture, with decisions often political and generally taken at the top (Schmidt 1996a); and second, corporatist polities such as Germany, which tend to be open only to certain privileged interests in policy formulation, more corporative than regulatory in implementation by applying the rules in conjunction with those self-same interests, and more consensual in culture, with decisions less clearly political and rarely taken at the top (Dyson 1977; Lehmbruch and Schmitter 1982).[1]

By exploring the contrasts among policy-making processes, I seek to elucidate the problems for member states that strike at the very heart of their democracies, namely, the ways in which the lack of fit between EU policy-making processes and those of member states serves to jeopardise the ability of member states to govern effectively. I find that the EU's quasi-pluralist process is in most ways more charitable to systems characterised by corporatist processes than those characterised by statist ones, mainly because the 'fit' is greater in such areas as societal actors' interest organisation and access, and governing bodies' decision-making culture and adaptability. I conclude that statist polities have had a harder time adjusting to EU level policy formulation, a more difficult task in implementing the policy changes engendered by the EU, and a greater challenge in adapting their national governance patterns to the new realities.

The pluralist model: the United States and the European Union

There is little doubt that the EU's policy-making process is closest to the pluralist model found in the United States, with its openness to interest group influence in policy formulation and its regulatory approach to implementation. But although the EU policy process may be more pluralist than anything else, its pluralism exhibits significant differences from that of the United States in the nature of interest group access and influence in policy formulation, as well as in the content and character of interrelationships among actors. Overall, the EU's pluralist policy formulation process is more co-operative and less competitive than that of the US as well as more insulated from the pressures of undue influence, given its lesser vulnerability to the politics of party or money and its greater emphasis on the technical rather than the political in decision-making. By contrast, the EU's regulatory approach to implementation bears great resemblance to that of the US even if the EU has much less control over the process than the US federal government.

To begin with, the EU rules of the game better insulate policy-makers against the pressures of special interests. The Commission is able to resist interest group pressure as a result of the 'paradox of weakness' that follows from the plethora of public actors at the EU level from the concerned directorates and member states for any given policy initiative. This puts European public actors in a more favourable position to refuse interest groups' unwanted or unrealisable claims (Grande 1996a). Moreover, the presence of a multitude of public and private actors not only protects the EU much more against agency capture of the kind found in the United States (Mazey and Richardson 1993a), it also helps it avoid the United States' traditional 'iron triangle' of legislators, lobbyists, and governmental agencies, in which only a small group of actors determines policy in any given area. The Commission itself ensures against this not only through its openness to interest representations, but also through its active recruiting of representations, where it sees the need to gain better sources of information or, more simply, to get its own way. In fact, EU level interest groups and lobbies are frequently created by the

Commission, as in the cases of information technology (Grande 1996a) and women's rights (Mazey 1995).

The Commission's use of interest groups to help it elaborate new legislation, however, can sometimes give undue influence to industry experts. Often the Eurocrats' lack of technical knowledge, combined with the need to make decisions quickly, means that they risk falling into quasi-clientelistic relationships (Mazey and Richardson 1993a: 21–3). But given the lack of any associated pecuniary interest on the part of EU policymakers within the Commission, any resulting clientelism can be nothing like it is in Italy or even the United States, where party funding and campaign needs make the politics of money almost inevitable.

The process of policy formulation in the EU avoids not only the politics of money increasingly evident in the United States but also to a large extent the politics of party. The EU is a good deal less affected by partisan politics than the US, given that apolitical EU civil servants, rather than partisan legislators and their staffs, are the primary drafters of legislation, and that the European Parliament, where parties are in any case not highly consolidated, plays a minor role as co-decision maker and consultative body. Moreover, the European Commission's decision-making culture, which puts the most value on decisions taken primarily on technical and economic arguments, enables the Commission to maintain its legitimacy while denying undue political influence to any individual country or its nationals (Donnelly 1993; Hull 1993). In the Council of Ministers, of course, politics do come into play, as national ministers seek to promote and/or protect the interests of their own national constituents : but this is the politics of interest rather than party; and even here, the arguments most likely to prevail are technical in basis, even if they sometimes serve merely as a cover for political decisions based on member state power and influence.

However, at the same time as the EU may therefore be less politicised in its pluralism than the US, it is also less 'pluralistic' in the kinds of interests represented as well as in their access and potential influence. While in the US any interest that organises itself is regarded as legitimate so long as it can make itself heard, in the EU it is the European Commission bureaucracy that has a primary role in legitimising interests, by choosing which interests it will consult with. Within this context, most business-related societal interests that knock at the door are allowed in, unlike many non-business-related societal interests. National government interests, as well as the interests of national groups which national governments choose to represent, are of course heard by definition, since they are officially represented in the Council of Ministers and in a wide variety of ways in the Commission, as are sub-national authorities to a lesser extent through the Committee of the Regions, through representation in national delegations (e.g. Belgium and Germany), and through regional policy and the structural funds. This differs from the United

States, where the states and sub-national authorities form and join lobbying associations like any other interest, and are in no way officially represented at the federal level.

Of all non-governmental interests, business has the greatest influence at the European level both through its direct access, unmediated by national governments, and its indirect access through national governments. In a large number of areas, including standard-setting and competition policy, businesses are major players alongside their national governments. And although the nature and extent of business influence vary greatly – owing not only to structural and cultural factors related to country of origin (see below) but also to differences in sector of industry, level of organisation, and degree of cohesiveness (McLaughlin and Jordan 1993; Greenwood and Ronit 1994) – there is no question that the influence of business is much greater than that of any other non-governmental interests. This influence has led some to characterise the general relationship between EU and business as 'elite pluralism' (Coen 1997), although there are a few sectors, such as social policy nowadays or steel and agriculture in the 1960s and 1970s, where a better description of the relationship would be corporatism.

Non-business, non-governmental interests, by comparison, have no such direct access and influence. They often find that they must go to the European Parliament first in order to gain access to decision-making in the Commission, or to their national governments in order to have an impact in the Council of Ministers: unless, that is, they are officially sanctioned consultation committees set up by the European Commission (Nentwich 1995). The low level of Europe-wide mobilisation and organisation of non-business interests, especially compared with the US and in comparison with business interests, is an added factor contributing to the comparative monopoly of business on access. Although the years since the Single European Act have witnessed an explosion of interest representation, this has primarily been of business interests, which represent 90 per cent of all lobbyists compared with only 2 per cent of non-commercial interests (Nentwich 1995). This ratio of business to non-business interest representation results primarily from the fact that, while business has a clearly perceived interest in lobbying at the EU level and has been organising itself to do so at an individual, national, and European level for a very long time now, non-business interests have had a much more difficult time organising themselves. In this they have been hindered by such factors as the differing levels of interest aggregation among member states and the difficulties in arriving at a consensus on the issues, given cultural and political differences.

Nevertheless, non-business interests such as the environment, labour, and women have been gaining increasing entry and influence at the EU level, despite national-level differences in organisation and influence. For example, although environmentalists have very different agendas, political affiliations, objects of concern, levels of organisation, and numbers of adherents in different member states, EU level environmental groups have nonetheless been relatively successful in recent years in building coalitions and setting the political agenda (Mazey and Richardson 1993b). Labour has been comparatively less successful, primarily because although it has been more present and better organised than the other non-business interests, it has been slow to organise, hampered by the lack of any pan-European labour movement, and handicapped in its support of the expansion of social regulation by strong resistance both on the part of member states such as Great Britain and from the business lobbies. Finally, the least successful have been individual citizens. Although citizen involvement in the EU has been slowly increasing in recent years, it remains mostly indirect and non-binding, with the European Parliament not very representative of European citizens or concerns, the Commission's relationship with citizens primarily one of information provision, and the ECJ's involvement with citizens taking the form of an exceptional tool aimed at enforcing decisions already taken by member states or the EU (Nentwich 1995).

In sum, the EU system of interest representation in policy formulation is less open than that of the US, with the overall number and variety of interests represented more restricted and more heavily weighted in favour of producer interests, and with comparatively few organised interests representing consumers, the elderly, immigrants, the public interest, and so on. Balancing this out somewhat, however, is the fact that the system is less subject to the abuses of undue influence and has itself been generating counterweights to what might be seen as narrow business interest. It has managed this either by creating more avenues for participation or by introducing considerations of the 'general interest' or the public good, of women's rights, of consumer protection, of environmental protection, and so forth, as by-products of European Commission policy initiatives, ECJ decisions, and the generalisation of prior member state legislation.

Thus, in American pluralism, where the public interest is generally defined as the outcome of the conflict among all 'interested' organised interests as mediated by the (in theory) 'impartial' elected servants of government, the resulting policies – given problems of unequal interest access, undue special interest influence, and easily influenced legislators – may be far from any public interest. In European pluralism, where the public good could be defined as the outcome of co-operation between representative interests, the (more truly) impartial, un-elected civil servants of the European Commission, and the more partial masters of the Council of Ministers, the end result may be much closer to the general good. And at the very least, there is more movement (especially since qualified majority voting), given that in the US the pluralist formulation process leads to paralysis on most important issues except in moments of perceived crisis, and sometimes not even then. (The health care reform fiasco of Hillary Clinton is a case in point.)

But while the EU's pluralist policy formulation process may avoid some of the worst problems of the US, even admitting its own problems with regard to access and representation, in its policy implementation process the EU courts many more problems than the US. Although at the implementation stage, the EU's pluralism greatly resembles that of the US given a regulatory approach in which the rules are to apply equally to all, with any exceptions seen as illegitimate, there is one significant difference. In the US for the most part federal civil servants implement the rules – albeit sometimes in tandem with or in addition to state-level civil servants – according to the same procedures, and therefore ensure great relative uniformity in application. (The major exception to this rule is the new welfare reform of 1996, which has for the first time in sixty years given back responsibility for social assistance programs to the states.) By contrast, in the EU the process is more complex, given that member states themselves implement regulations as well as transpose directives into national law, and then implement them according to national procedures. This has led to problems that are much greater than in the US with respect to enforcing the equal application of the rules, given that member states' implementation is often of necessity very different, with different regulatory cultures and practices (Dehousse 1992).

But whatever the differences between the EU's model and the traditional pluralist model, they are as nothing compared to those between the EU's quasi-pluralist model and corporatist or statist models. This has important consequences for those polities that conform to either of the alternative models: and that means most EU member states.

The clash between the EU's quasi-pluralist model and the statist and corporatist models of member states

Although the EU is most akin to the pluralist system of the United States, it none the less holds certain characteristics in common with statist and corporatist systems. Most importantly, the dominance of civil servants as gate-keepers in the policy formulation process, with their greater powers of policy initiation and their greater control over the interest articulation process, introduces a statist element into the system, even if the pluralist legitimation of lobbying has little in common with the statist. On the other hand, the more one-sided nature of interest access in EU policy formulation, where industry predominates and opposing societal interests have comparatively little impact, brings it closer to a corporatist polity such as Germany, albeit with only one of the two privileged interests in the corporatist equation: business, not labour. Moreover, the pluralist EU's more co-operative decision-making culture finds echoes in the corporatist concern with consensus, as compared to the more conflictual culture of statist polities.

These similarities are minor, however, compared to the differences between the EU's pluralist decision-making system (which has allowed an ever-expanding set of interests into the policy formulation process, even if business has the most access, while keeping them for the most part out of implementation, where the regulatory approach applies) and both statist systems (in which societal interests are little involved in policy formulation but are generally accommodated in the implementation) and corporatist systems (in which business and labour have privileged access to both policy formulation and implementation). These differences have ensured that the juxtaposition of EU and member state policy-making processes or, in some cases, the superimposition of EU processes on national ones, has served to alter policy-making processes in both kinds of systems. They have, however, produced greater disruption for the statist than the corporatist system in such areas as interest access and government autonomy in formulation, and citizen access and government flexibility in implementation.

The differences in policy formulation

For statist polities such as France and Great Britain, the resemblance with the pluralist EU stops at the elite status of civil servants and their predominant role in the interest articulation process, since societal interests are not formally involved in policy formulation; for Italy, it does not go even this far. For a corporatist polity such as Germany, the resemblance is somewhat greater, not so much with regard to the elite status of civil servants (although they, too, make up an elite) or their predominance (since they are co-equals in the interest articulation process rather than firmly in charge) as with the involvement of interest groups in policy formulation. However, whereas in the EU interest group access is unlimited at least in theory, even though business is the main interest represented, in Germany access is limited mainly to business and labour, which is an equal player, unlike the EU, where it is virtually absent.

While the EU bureaucracy, like the German bureaucracy in a more limited sphere, actively encourages organised interest representation, listens when it consults, and incorporates the recommendations of interest groups in its own recommendations, the bureaucracy in statist polities regards the influence of lobbies as illegitimate and traditionally employs its formal consultation process with the aim of informing rather than incorporating interest views. This attitude towards interest representation is most in evidence in France, since American-style or EU-style lobbying is seen as corruption (even though it is encouraged for French companies by French officials at the EU level). On the other hand, 'lobbying *à la française*,' which involves a more subtle, informal process of influencing one's *'camarades de promotion,'* or classmates from elite schools, in government (Schmidt 1996a), is perfectly legitimate. In Great Britain, by comparison, although lobbying is also viewed as illegitimate in formal policy-making, lobbies do find other ways in, particularly through the British Parliament (where MPs are often themselves recognised, paid lobbyists for large companies or for labour) and through more informal relations with the national bureaucracy, which, apart from in the Thatcher years (Richardson 1993), has tended to be more consensus-seeking and less 'heroic' than the French. Italy, of course, is a different case entirely, or at least it was until the collapse of its post-war system of *partitocrazia*, in which parties rather than civil servants (which also are not an elite comparable to that of France, Britain, or the EU) dominated the interest articulation process; where groups exercised influence as clients and/or patrons of political parties; and where corruption was endemic.

Thus, although statist polities may reject societal interests' active participation in policy formulation as illegitimate, societal interests do nevertheless manage to exert influence. Generally, however, this influence takes a more political route, and is often part of a more conflictual decision-making culture, unlike the EU. For while decision-making in the EU is generally co-operative and only minimally political for the vast majority of cases, with the most important level at the bottom (Hull 1993; Donnelly 1993), in statist polities decision-making is more often conflictual and tends to be much more political and top-down. France, for example, has a conflictual culture where decisions are ultimately political and the most important level of decision-making is at the top, such that any decision, however technically competent, can be reversed relatively easily for purely political reasons (Schmidt 1996a: ch. 7). The highly personalistic and political manner in which the French tend to exert influence internally makes it no wonder that, when Jacques Delors was head of the Commission, the French typically – and mistakenly – assumed that a simple telephone call to Delors would solve any problem. It also lends insight into the early lobbying failures of French business since, instead of providing technical arguments that might have swayed the Commission at a preliminary stage, as in the de Havilland case (Schmidt 1996b), they generally sought to apply political pressure late in the game. And even though French businesses have surely learned to do better over time, the French traditional reliance on government and informal relationships to influence decision-making, rather than on lobbies leaves them at a continuing disadvantage compared with those countries with long-standing, well developed lobbies, as in the case of the British, or with cohesive peak associations, as in the case of the Germans.

Although the British clearly do better than the French when it comes to lobbying, the clash of the United Kingdom's overall decision-making culture with that of the EU is no less significant than it is for the French. With the British, for whom decision-making is equally centralised at the top, the clash is most evident in the frequent British government demands for 'opt-outs' from EU directives. This reflects their unease at their inability to make a last-minute political decision when they do not control the process. For British business, by contrast, the clash of cultures is not as significant as it is for the French, not only because of their more extensive lobbying experience but also because of their closer collaboration with the national government on EC matters. This in turn has much to do with the different ways in which business-government collaboration is organised in Britain compared with France. Great Britain's larger, more fluid, more frag-mented, horizontally integrated policy networks tend to be better suited to representing domestic interests in the multi-polar, competitive decision-making structure of the EU than France's smaller, tighter, more cohesive, vertical, state-dominated networks (Josselin 1996).

The clash of decision-making cultures is also clear with the Italians, given that any political decisions, albeit also emanating from the top, have been much more clearly political in being party- and patronage-related. Like the French, moreover, Italian business has also had a hard time adapt-ing to the lobbying process, albeit for other reasons, given that business influence has typically been handled under-the-table, as recent scandals have borne out, or as part of the consociative process. And although one might have expected that Italian businesses, given their greater participa-tion in regionally-based economies with horizontally-linked networks, would be better prepared than the French to interact in EU-based net-works, there is evidence to suggest that this is not the case.

Only with corporatist Germany is there little clash with the EU in terms of decision-making cultures, given that decisions there are generally arrived at consensually, are much less clearly political, and are seldom arrived at quickly or taken at the top. In the complex process that is German decision-making, where most initiatives require agreement among all relevant actors, the top has little power to impose, given the requirement – depending upon the issue – that there have to be legislative compromises between the Bundestag and Bundesrat (where they are controlled by dif-ferent majorities); for regionally-negotiated collective bargaining agreements between the national peak associations of business and labour; and co-ordinated agreements between federal government and the Länder on fiscal and implementation policies. As such, Germany's consensus-generating experience is not so different from the EU's many-layered institutional process, or from its culture of co-operation. And it also makes lobbying the EU an easier task for German industry than for its French, Italian, or even British counterparts. For German business, the corporatist policy-making process is excellent training for exerting influence in EU policy-making, even though in Germany business is inside the formulation process as a co-equal rather than, as in the EU, outside it as a lobbyist. German firms have a leg up with regard to EU-level lobbying because they are used to influencing the policy formulation process from the ground up, with highly developed national networks that help form a springboard for EU lobbying as well as for participation in standard-setting. Germany's industrial organisation not only puts its firms at an advantage compared to France, which has lacked cohesive peak associations and co-operative relations among employers and between labour and industry, and which has therefore traditionally left it to the state to impose agreement and to construct strategies for growth. It also, through German firms' great cohesiveness, puts those firms in a better position than the British, mainly because German big businesses not only can act as effectively on their own as the British but also can act more – and better – in concert. The benefits are evident not just in German lobbying successes but in standard-setting as well, where German industry controls 39 per cent of the secretariats, compared with Great Britain's 20 per cent, France's 14 per cent, and Italy's 8 per cent (Egan 1994).

Superior organisation is not the only reason German firms do well. Their experience of a consensual style of negotiating with a multitude of actors in horizontal networks, without any clearly-recognised authorities, makes their adaptation to the EU model much easier than for the French, who are typically used to vertically-organised networks where clearly-defined governmental authorities generally make the decision. Moreover, although the British are better used to dealing in such horizontal networks, they may offend more, given a policy-making culture in which the signature British politeness is sometimes but a thin veneer barely hiding a combative and conflictual style. This is not to say, of course, that Germans compromise because they cannot deal with conflict. On the contrary, consensus even in Germany is often achieved only through conflict: but their style has less of the brinkmanship quality sometimes shown by the British, the 'mad cow disease' episode being a case in point. Germany's public actors have, out of necessity, learned as much as its private actors not only how to bargain very hard for what they want, but also when to give up and acquiesce, unlike the British who leave rancorous feelings in the EU when, time and again, after a long and arduous process of negotiation, they opt out in the face of defeat and depart, rather than agreeing to a compromise.

With compromise and consensus the *modus vivendi* then, Germany's policy-making style resembles the EU the most. In corporatist Germany, where, just as in the pluralist EU, societal interests are brought into policy formulation, the complex decision-making process ensures against the kinds of 'heroic' policies found in statist regimes such as France and Great Britain, where policies can be instituted without any societal input apart from electoral (Schmidt 1996a, ch. 2). Contrast the quick moves to privatise in France and Great Britain with the long, elaborate negotiations for the Single European Act, the Maastricht Treaty, and other major initiatives among member states. The problem for statist regimes today, however, is that these kinds of heroic initiatives taken without consultation are less and less possible because they are increasingly supplanted by EU initiatives and subject to EU rulings and reviews.

For statist France, this loss of governmental autonomy in policy formulation has been largely accepted in exchange for greater predominance in Europe. In this, however, the French have only been partially successful since, while they have managed to impose at the EU level where grand strategy is concerned (Ross 1995; Grant 1994), they have been unable to institute the kinds of 'heroic' policies at the EU level regarding industrial policy that they had to give up at the national level (Schmidt 1996a), and they have been at something of a disadvantage with regard to more everyday policy-making, as discussed above. Ironically, France's ability to predominate in the more everyday policy-making of the EC has been undermined by the very attributes that have ensured it a pre-eminent role in the initiation and negotiation of major EU treaties, namely the great autonomy and the grand style that are key elements in its heroic policy-making, plus the political and personalistic character of interaction at the top.

For statist Britain, the threat to governmental autonomy has been even more keenly felt than in France, and more successfully resisted, as the opt-outs from the Social Chapter of the Maastricht Treaty and from Economic and Monetary Union attest. Where the French response has been to seek a greater EU 'heroism' in exchange for its loss at the national level, the British response has been to resist 'heroically' what it sees as European incursions on national sovereignty. But while Britain's self-styled role as reluctant partner has undermined its ability to have significant influence over grand strategy, such a role has made it very effective not only in gaining opt-outs but also in pushing a more neo-liberal agenda in industry deregulation.

Italy, by contrast, has welcomed the loss of government autonomy as a gain in government capacity. Because Italy has for a long time suffered from a lack of 'heroism', given its inability to overcome state paralysis and parliamentary division, European imperatives to translate directives into national law or to pass an austerity budget in order to meet the Maastricht criteria have been seen as the necessary impetus for change, a *deus ex machina* saving Italy from itself.

Germany, needless to say, does not feel the threat to government autonomy as strongly as France or Great Britain, since it has never had the same kind of heroic policy-making. More importantly, however, it cannot feel the same kind of loss of government autonomy because Germany's 'semi-sovereign' state has never been autonomous in the manner of statist regimes, given the constitutionally-guaranteed powers of the *Länder*, the independence of the *Bundesbank*, the legally separate collective bargaining powers of the social partners, and so on. What is more, Germany has better protected its policy-making process from the kinds of changes that the EU has imposed on other member states, by ensuring that the Maastricht Treaty allowed the *Länder* to participate officially in policy formulation and that the social partners continued to have a role in policy implementation. By the same token, however, Germany's lack of autonomy and heroism, due in large measure to its federal institutions and corporatist processes, have made it very difficult for it to exercise leadership when it comes to grand strategy in the EU, where France excels, or forcefully to resist policy initiatives of which it disapproves, where Great Britain is past master.

In short, the quasi-pluralist policy formulation process of the EU affects each of the member states very differently, although it is more at odds with those following statist formulation processes than those with corporatist ones. The same is true with regard to the policy implementation process.

The differences in policy implementation

While there are certain resemblances between the EU's approach to policy formulation in both statist and corporatist models, there are none with regard to the policy implementation process, which follows a regulatory model. While the pluralist EU allows interest groups into policy formulation but not implementation, where the rules are to be applied without exceptions or adjustments, in statist polities interest groups that have no access to policy formulation tend to be accommodated in implementation, and in corporatist polities the privileged interests with access to policy formulation are also involved in implementation. Although the EU therefore differs greatly from both statist and corporatist regimes, its approach to implementation is more at odds with the former than the latter. And whereas corporatist regimes have not had to change much to meet the requirements of the EU's regulatory model of implementation, statist regimes risk a loss of administrative flexibility, a reduction in citizen access to decision-making, and thereby an increase in citizen disaffection and even confrontation.

In the administrative approach to implementation of statist polities such as France and Italy, civil servants have great flexibility in interpreting policy. In France, where Alexis de Tocqueville already noted years ago that 'the rule is rigid, the application flexible', implementation is characterised by the politics of accommodation or co-optation, or else there is confrontation. While in France, civil servants tend to allow derogations to the rule as often as not (Schmidt 1996a: ch. 7), in Italy, the same pattern is more extreme: exceptions to the rule seem to be in the offing most of the time (Lange and Regini 1989: 254-5); and confrontation is even more accepted when accommodation or co-optation is not available (Tarrow 1988). The pattern differs in Great Britain, given its greater emphasis on the rule of law, its less confrontational history, and its lack of the Napoleonic tradition of promulgating laws in order to ignore them, which may be why so much less is codified, allowing government and bureaucracy flexibility that they would not otherwise have.

The increasing purview of EU law, together with the institution of EU-like – if not EU-inspired – regulation in member states, has served to disrupt these traditional patterns. Deregulation in particular has led to the establishment of independent regulatory agencies which have ended the traditionally close, often informal relationships of the past where ministries and industries were free to work things out amongst themselves, either without the constraints of formal rules, as in Great Britain, or ignoring those rules that existed, as in France and even more so in Italy.

For Great Britain, where regulation of business was for the most part not formalised, deregulation has sometimes been experienced as re-regulation, with the creation of legal procedures and recourse where informal agreements generally held sway, and the establishment of independent regulatory bodies where there were none, where civil servants made administrative decisions and/or business associations constituted 'private governments' that resolved any matters of controversy. For France, by contrast, where the countless burdensome laws and regulations governing business were honoured as often as not in the breach, deregulation has served not only its expected purpose, by rationalising the rules, but also an unexpected one, by increasingly supplanting civil servants' administrative discretion with independent regulators who apply the law without discrimination or administrative discretion. For Italy, finally, where, rules or no, maximum flexibility was exercised, and where deregulation has only just begun, the French pattern is likely to be followed.

Although the differences between corporatist polities' 'corporative' approach to implementation and the EU's regulatory approach have an even greater potential for disruption for corporatist polities than the differences between the administrative approach of statist polities and the EU's regulatory approach, this has not occurred. Because the EU allows for directives to be translated into the national context and implemented according to national procedures, Germany's decentralised, corporative implementation process, where the *Länder* and/or the social partners have major responsibility for carrying out the law, has been able to remain more or less intact. Moreover, because of Germany's continued 'hidden flexibility within stable institutions' (Katzenstein 1989), any change related to deregulation has involved a slow and subtle process of shifting power and responsibilities without altering existing structures (Esser 1995). In addition, because Germany has not only always respected the law as much as the British have, but has also always codified it much more, the increasing legal formalisation coming from the EU does not cause the kind of consternation that it does in Great Britain: and need not, since the regulatory respect for applying the laws without exceptions has not brought with it quite the proliferation of independent regulatory agencies that it has for Britain, France, and Italy (although this might be coming as deregulation accelerates).

Finally, in corporatist Germany, because the *Länder* and/or the social partners responsible for policy implementation have participated in policy formulation at both national and European levels at the same time as Parliament is also actively involved in formulation (Bulmer 1992), there is much less potential than in statist regimes for non-business societal actors to feel disenfranchised by the increasing importance of European level decision-making. Nevertheless, problems with citizen access to decision-making do remain in Germany, given that whereas business and labour interests benefit from direct representation in the formulation and implementation of national policies, other citizen interests must rely more on political party representation. In some cases this ensures almost as much access and influence, as in the case of the environmentalists who have their own party, but in other cases it does not, as for example, with consumers, women, or immigrants. In fact, although German citizens' non-business interests in general are likely to have greater representation in supranational policy-making than those of their French, Italian, or even British counterparts, those citizens with less direct access to policy-making at the EU level are also for the most part those with less at the nation-state level in Germany.

The main problem for statist polities is that where EU law takes precedence over national law, or more simply where the regulatory approach substitutes itself for the administrative, the loss of government flexibility in implementation entails a diminution in citizen access to decision-making. Citizen and non-business interests in statist polities that already find themselves without much direct access at either the EU or national level in policy formulation, especially where it is most heroic, will now discover that they have less influence in policy implementation. Where EU laws or EU-instigated reforms apply, citizens, already denied entry at the front end, are likely to be cut out at the back end too and, lacking accommodation or co-optation, are likely to have recourse to confrontation. This was certainly the case with French farmers during the GATT negotiations, and it was equally true for the French public sector workers in late 1995. But French governments, faced with European negotiated agreements and/or economic imperatives, let alone European regulations, are no longer as free to bend, or not, in response to citizen protest (Schmidt 1997a).

Italian citizens, by contrast, have yet to feel deprived of decision-making access by the effects of the EU regulatory approach. This is not only because they ordinarily feel deprived by a government that has gone from unchanging paralysis to constant crisis, and have therefore normally found societal routes around blockages. It is also because the government has only begun to implement many of the directives and to submit to the pain of austerity budgets as completely as the French have done. As they increasingly implement such reforms and faithfully apply EU directives, however, the loss of flexibility is likely to be a source of as much if not more citizen disenfranchisement as in France: if, that is, they do not follow the old pattern of making exceptions to the rule.

The effect on British citizens is a bit more difficult to assess, given their lesser tradition of confrontation and Parliament's greater role in the vigorous debate of ideas, enabling it to give voice if not shape to public concerns. Moreover, governments have themselves been consistently protesting the encroachments of EU regulation which reduce the space left open to administrative discretion at the same time as they have been almost exclusively promoting national interest in the collective decision-making in the Council of Ministers (Hayes-Renshaw and Wallace 1995). All of this has given British citizens the appearance at least of their interests being represented, even as their access to decision-making diminishes. This is in contrast to the French, where Parliament has little voice and even less power, and where there was little debate on the EU until the debate on the ratification of the Maastricht Treaty.

The problems of citizen access to decision-making persist, in short, regardless of the model of policy-making, even if the EU's pluralist model is more charitable in its impact on member state democracies characterised by the corporatist model than the statist. And this is only compounded by the fact that the EU pluralist model has so far allowed greater access to business interests than any other interests, even if the effects are not nearly as one-sided as one might have supposed, given counterweights in the common notions of the public good promoted by EU institutional actors or by the generalisation of prior member state legislation.

Conclusion

Statist countries have had a markedly more difficult time adjusting to the impact of the pluralist EU than corporatist countries. In policy formulation, the EU-generated loss of government autonomy has had less of an effect on corporatist Germany, which never had much internal autonomy anyway, than on statist polities such as France, which accepted that loss in exchange for greater EU influence; Great Britain, which resisted it to gain EU opt-outs; and Italy, which embraced it to enhance national governmental capacity. Moreover, it has been easier for public and private actors from corporatist Germany, given the country's own similarly co-operative albeit less open interest-based process, to adapt to the EU's co-operative, open interest-based formulation process, than it has been for those from statist polities such as France, with its more conflictual and virtually closed, non-interest-based process which leaves public actors less adept in everyday negotiations and private actors less effective in lobbying; Great Britain, with its only marginally more open and interest-based process which nevertheless benefits its private actors in lobbying; and Italy, with its more open but essentially ineffective and corrupt traditional process.

In policy implementation, the EU's regulatory approach has similarly engendered less of a loss of flexibility in corporatist Germany, where sub-national authorities and social partners participate as they traditionally have in their areas of jurisdiction, than it has engendered in statist polities, where the regulatory model has altered traditional patterns of implementation, depriving civil servants of administrative discretion, increasing regulatory rigidity, reducing citizen access to decision-making, and increasing the possibilities of confrontation.

For all this, however, all is not lost for statist polities such as France, Great Britain, and Italy; and all is not halcyon for corporatist Germany. Although Germany has largely been less affected by the EU because of the particular structure of its institutions and the patterns of its policy-making processes, other factors have also been at play. Deregulation has been less disruptive primarily because Germany, given the strength of its economy, has been able to delay it much longer than the statist polities. With the erosion of German competitiveness and the acceleration of deregulation, one might question whether Germany can sustain the very institutions and processes that have enabled it to adapt so successfully to the EU, with solidarity among the Länder also under strain due to the costs of unification and the social partnership beginning to fray at the edges as unions protest at employer cuts in wages and benefits. The examples of countries such as the Netherlands, which had radically to readjust its corporatism in the early 1980s, and Sweden, which has had to do much the same in the early 1990s, suggest that the adaptation process may not be quite as easy as many Germans appear to believe.

While the ability of corporatist policy-making processes to adapt to the EU may thus be overstated, the lack of adaptability of statist policy-making processes may also be overstated, since the pressures of EU-level processes may very well have opened up new avenues for change and innovation at the national level. For although citizens in statist polities are indeed increasingly disenfranchised by the loss of flexibility at the implementation end, there is nothing to stop national governments introducing more pluralist elements into policy formulation by, for example, enhancing citizen access through real dialogue and concertation, although this has yet to materialise. In statist polities such new avenues must be the choice of state actors who have the political will and capacity to change, and societal actors with the political trust to agree to follow, both of which have been lacking of late (although the Jospin government may be changing this).

In the interim, however, citizens in statist polities are nevertheless gaining more direct access to European policy formulation through their participation in European governance networks, and more experience in influencing policy-making at the EU level that is also likely to affect their approaches to national policy-making. In other words, the more private actors are involved in quasi-pluralist processes at the EU level, the less likely they are to sit by as public actors make decisions without them at the national level. And by the same token, the more those self-same public actors are involved in EU level decision-making, the more likely they are to realise that other ways of making decisions are possible. The EU has in fact already done much to alter the role of state actors in positive ways by enabling them to overcome institutional hurdles and interest group resistance to change, and to move from a role as authoritative allocator and regulator into the role of partner, mediator, and central relay in a system of networks that contributes to the complex, multi-level governance system that is the European Union and its member states (Kohler-Koch 1995). The only problem is that those who already have the greatest access, business and subnational authorities, are those benefiting the most from the newly developing governance networks, whereas those with the least access, individual citizens, women, consumers, environmentalists, union members, immigrants, and so forth, still have a long way to go in most member states before they become part of national governance networks, let alone European ones.

In sum, although statist polities such as France, Great Britain, and Italy have had more difficulty up until now in adapting to the EU, given policy-making processes that are more at odds with the quasi-pluralist pattern of the EU than those of corporatist polities such as Germany, there is nothing to preclude easier adaptation in the future for statist polities, just as there is nothing to guarantee continued compatibility for corporatist polities. For whatever the pattern of policy-making, the EU has begun a process of change through the development of new governance networks that will demand increasing adjustment by its member states. And although for a very long time statist polities are likely to retain their statist characteristics and corporatist polities their corporatist characteristics, both kinds of polities may slowly gain enough pluralist elements – and adopt enough regulatory practices – for their policy-making models to become increasingly indistinguishable from one another or from the EU. But this is likely to take many, many years yet to come.

Notes

I would like to thank the members of the ECPR workshop in Oslo and the follow-up workshop in Mannheim for their comments, and in particular, Beate Kohler-Koch, Gerda Falkner, and Klaus Dieter Wolf. In addition, my thanks to Fritz W. Scharpf.

1   Although in recent years the literature has pointed to the increasing sectorisation of European and national-level systems, especially with the growing importance of policy networks in Europe, this in no way denies the fact that overall EU and national patterns of policy-making, as outlined herein, continue to predominate. This holds as much for Italy, which is the least ideal-typical of statist polities given that it lacks elite civil servants and has a weak executive, as for Germany, despite the fact that it is often cited as a lesser case of corporatism because its peak associations are less cohesive and the interactions of its social partners more conflictual than in more ideal-typically corporatist countries such as Austria.

10

BUSINESS, GOVERNANCE STRUCTURES AND THE EU

The case of Denmark

Niels Christian Sidenius

The issue and hypotheses

Policy-making in a number of Western European countries has for years been characterised by the integration and importance of organised interests (in general, Hayward 1995b). Whether these relations between state agencies and organised interests could be conceptualised as corporatism has been the subject matter of an intense debate. Some researchers assert that corporatism is dead (e.g. Lewin 1992, Schmitter 1989, Streeck and Schmitter 1991), and today most researchers seem to agree that the concept of policy-making networks is more useful in analysing policy-making processes in most Western European countries than is the concept of corporatism (e.g. Jordan and Schubert 1992). But whichever concept is chosen, organised interests still play an important role in Danish domestic and EU-related policy-making (Christiansen and Sidenius 1995, Bregnsbo and Sidenius 1993, Sidenius 1998).

The general issue addressed by this chapter is the role of Danish business in domestic as well as EU governance. This issue is twofold. How does Danish business perform politically in the perspective of the changing institutions and increasing competencies of the EU?[1] And what consequences does this have for governance at national and EU level? These questions are interrelated, because the changing political activity of Danish business is at the same time adaptation and part of the overall governance change.

This chapter focuses on the change of governance structures in two different ways. First, whether the development of the EU during the last ten years has increased the integration of Danish business into the policy-making institutions of Brussels. The point of departure on this issue is that EU institutions increasingly influence agenda-setting and politics at the supranational, national and subnational levels, and the hypothesis is that business has become more integrated in Brussels politics. Second, whether the formation of an EU polity has led to a disintegration of Danish policy-making. The point of departure on this question is that European integration as multi-level governance leads to a decline in the importance of the nation-state level 'as the exclusive seat of formal political power' (Marks and McAdam 1996: 96), and the second hypothesis is that national-level policy-making has become disintegrated. Before specifying these hypotheses and the research design, the underlying concepts of governance must be presented.

The governance concepts

Hollingsworth *et al.*, studying the performance and control of economic sectors, define a governance system as 'the totality of institutional arrangements – including rules and rule-making agents – that regulate transactions inside and across the boundaries of an economic system' (Hollingsworth *et al* 1994: 5). This definition reflects the premise that economic actions are social actions which need to be governed by institutional arrangements. Markets, hierarchies, states, networks, and associations are the five distinct modes of governance which to varying degrees are found in the economy or in economic sectors. It is the complex mix of these modes of governance, i.e. their relative importance, which determines the nature of a governance regime at a given time (ibid.: 8).

Within the same theoretical reasoning, Lindberg *et al.* deal with the transformation of governance of the American economy in a historical perspective. The structural characteristics of governance as a system of social control are elaborated along two theoretical dimensions. The first dimension concerns the degree of formal organisation among economic actors in co-ordinating economic activity; the second dimension relates to the number of actors participating in co-ordinating economic activity. A typology of six governance mechanisms is suggested: markets, obligational networks, hierarchies, and monitoring, promotional networks, and associations (Lindberg *et al* 1991: 12–14). The structural characteristics of governance mechanisms are supplemented by distinctive processes concerning rules or terms of exchange between economic actors and means of coercion and consent in order to obtain compliance with rules of exchange (ibid.: 16).

The aspect of governance transformation is very important to Lindberg *et al.* (ibid.: 32–3). They see the change from one dominant governance mechanism to another as caused by an initial pressure for change leading to a search for new strategies which can cope with the pressures and become institutionalised as a new governance regime (also Campbell and Lindberg 1991: 319).

The main difference between the two contributions seems to be the role ascribed to the state. Hollingsworth *et al.* conceptualise the state as a governance mechanism in its own right, while Lindberg *et al.* see the state as having a privileged position in its relations with governance mechanisms. This is owing to the fact that the state can have a decisive impact on governance mechanisms in at least three ways. First, the state can provide ways of participation in governance for new groups, the gatekeeper function. Second, the state can allocate resources and information in ways that facilitate or inhibit exchange between economic actors, thus influencing the development of governance mechanisms. And third, the state can influence and structure property rights, thereby altering the mix of governance mechanisms. Taken together, in this perspective the state can play a crucial role in the transformation of governance regimes (Lindberg *et al.* 1991: 30–1).

Kooiman conceptualises governance differently. His point of departure is that instead of making a rigid distinction between public and private tasks and responsibilities, and thus focusing on the transfer of tasks from the public sector to the private sector or vice versa, it is more productive to look upon the sharing of tasks and responsibilities, that is, doing things together (Kooiman 1993a: 1). Both theoretical strands suggest that steering and regulating activities cannot exclusively be explained from the point of view of 'official policies' (ibid.: 5).

To Kooiman, the concept of governance relates to the patterns emerging from the guiding, steering, controlling and managing efforts of social, political, and administrative actors which take place in a more or less continuous process of interaction (ibid.: 2–3). The process takes place in a framework of social, technological and scientific developments causing a growing societal complexity, which challenges governing activities and makes new concepts of governance necessary (ibid.: 6). In this way the aspect of transformation becomes part of the governance concept.

Kohler-Koch argues along the same line as Kooiman. Her emphasis on governance as 'co-ordinating multiple players in a complex setting of mutual dependence' (Kohler-Koch 1996: 16) abolishes the traditional model of the state, in which governing becomes what governments do due to their abundant amount of resources. Instead the concept of network is a fruitful way of theorising the complex interdependencies among autonomous societal actors. In this institutionalist perspective, the state becomes an actor among other actors, being a partner and a mediator (ibid.: 371), although not 'just another group among the multitude of pressure groups' (ibid.: 377 n. 20).

The two concepts of governance diverge, but they can be reconciled in an analytical approach. Hollingsworth *et al.* and Lindberg *et al.* point to the importance of path-dependency in understanding institutional change and the shift from one governance regime to another. This chapter therefore focuses on the persistence of institutions in periods of encompassing political change. The productivity of Kooiman's concept is its emphasis on the interplay between public and private actors within modes of governance, and its focus on the impact of economic, political, and institutional changes on governance. Accordingly, the focus here is on the integration of private interests in policy-making and their interplay with state actors.

Research design and data

'Europeanisation' is supposed to be the independent variable leading to changes of governance.[2] Europeanisation is here understood generally as extending the boundaries of the space of the polity (Kohler-Koch 1996) and specifically as 'an incremental process reorienting the direction and shape of politics to the degree that EC political and economic dynamics become part of the organisational logic of national politics and policy-making' (Ladrech 1994: 69; also Andersen and Eliassen 1993).

Europeanisation leads to a wider European polity, not only by including more member states but also by integrating more societal actors in European policy-making. Evidence is found in the analyses of lobbying and private actor participation in policy-making in Brussels (e.g. Van Schendelen 1993, Van Schendelen and Pedler 1994, Mazey and Richardson 1993c, Greenwood et al. 1992a). Europeanisation also impacts upon the ways in which national politics and policy-making are carried out – through the increased importance of EU aspects of policy and changes of public and private organisations in order to adapt to and influence EU institutions and policies. Europeanisation is seen as a gradual process, though the speed varies over time. Change of governance, as an outcome of Europeanisation, occurs only gradually at the EU level as well as at the national level where Europeanisation is moulded by existing political institutions varying across countries. The concepts of integration and disintegration of political institutions have to take this into account.

Danish membership of the EC as from January 1973 has had a number of characteristics. The fierce debate on membership, which continued until the referendum on the Single European Act, made most of the political parties reluctant to put forward an affirmative market programme, let alone an integrationist programme. Governments became more and more responsive to the Market Committee of *Folketing*, making it troublesome to engage in the wheeling and dealing of Brussels. Inter-ministerial co-ordination and the integration of interest associations were institutionalised from the very first day of membership, and successive changes of parliamentary procedures on the handling of EC matters have reinforced these characteristics. Finally, Denmark is usually said to have a very fine record concerning the implementation of Community policies, for example the implementation of Internal Market directives (Bregnsbo and Sidenius 1993, Nedergaard 1994, Sidenius 1997).

As pointed out in the hypotheses, the EU institutions' increased power and policy-making activity in ever more policy areas is supposed to change the relations between political actors, both in Brussels and in Denmark. Potentially, the impact of EU membership on member states – changing agendas, policies and institutions – is encompassing and diverse. The impact may relate to the domestic political setting, including policies and policy-making practices, as well as administrative structures and procedures, implying changed relationships between the legislative and executive power; eventually it may relate to principles of the constitution. Bearing in mind the concept of overlapping competencies, it seems reasonable to suspect that the impact depends very much on the national, sectoral or sub-sectoral regimes of governance. It is, in other words, contingent upon networks between varying societal actors. The impact may also relate to the EU political setting, in the sense that domestic actors may increase their direct EU political activity through lobbying or creation of liaisons and networks. This is proof of – and in itself increases – the independent action of the EU institutions and the international activity of domestic interests, emphasising the growth of multi-level governance (e.g. Andersen and Eliassen 1993, Rhodes and Mazey 1995: Part 2).

Increased integration of Danish business associations in EU policy-making in Brussels implies more intense contacts and more varied activity with public and private actors from other countries and from EU institutions. There are methodological problems in finding valid indicators of increased integration of interest associations in EU policy-making, and even more so in measuring the extent to which such integration is caused by changes in the EU(i.e. the Single European Act, the Internal Market Programme and the Maastricht Treaty). From the general notion that associations are very alert to changes in their environment, which they try to influence and adapt to (Meyer 1978), it can be asserted that business associations would not invest more resources in lobbying and EU associability if they did not find it worthwhile – that is, if they did not see it as a proper response to changes in the institutions, policies, and competencies of the EU having a potential impact upon the organisation and its members.

Europeanisation is a gradual process, and associations and business associations in particular have participated in EU associability before the time of Danish membership (Sidenius 1998). Integration of interest associations into the policy-making institutions of Brussels will be measured by their efforts to monitor and influence EU policies, be it directly or indirectly. This chapter therefore concentrates on participation in policy-making in Brussels, measured by contacts with EU institutions; on the establishing of own offices in Brussels; and, finally, on associational membership and activity in Euro-groups. If increasing activity is found over time on these parameters, it will be taken as evidence of a growing integration into and contribution of Danish associations to a European polity.

The second hypothesis about the disintegration of national policy-making implies the loosening of relations between state actors and private actors, a loosening that might eventually lead to the disappearance of this feature of Danish policy-making. Loosening of relations is measured by less intensive contacts, and the hypothesis will be regarded as confirmed if decreasing interaction is found between state institutions and business associations on general domestic policy issues and on EU-related issues. Likewise, the hypothesis will be viewed as confirmed, if business associations attach more importance to EU relationships than to domestic political relationships. The relationships concern policy-making in the EU, policy-making in the national context, as well as the reactions of societal actors to economic, political and institutional changes in the EU, or caused by the EU, and the impact of these reactions.

Business political activity, contacts and influence are often believed to be crucial in understanding national and EU policy-making (e.g. Van Schendelen and Pedler 1994; Greenwood 1995). Throughout the years, business–politics relations may have become so institutionalised that they are almost rendered immune to changing politics and political environments. On the other hand, business is very alert to changes in the EU (Sidenius 1995). In general, this alertness is a consequence not only of the Maastricht Treaty of European Union, but to a still larger extent of the Single European Act and the Internal Market Programme and its intention to revitalise market forces. For a number of business associations – though not agriculture, which was already mobilised by the common agricultural policy – these changes of politics and institutions have had an effect on the core activity of business association members. By focusing on business political activity, it is expected that profound changes of governance structures will be found, namely changed relationships between business and political-administrative institutions in policy-making.

The effect of focusing on the change of broad policy-making patterns and institutions at the European and national levels is that a state-centrist approach is gradually dropped. This approach concentrates on a two-level game, in which member state executives deal with each other at the EU level, and the domestic interest associations lobby indirectly via their respective governments. Instead, we move to a multi-level game, which leaves much more room for independent action of supranational institutions and – more important in this context – EU action directly by domestic interests. Consequently, we are talking about 'overlapping competencies among multiple levels of governments and the interaction of political actors across those levels' (Marks *et al.* 1996: 41).

The focus on Europeanisation as the generator of changing governance structures makes it obvious for two reasons to take the mid-1980s as the starting point. At that time the EC had gained a new momentum which, it was intended, would add new quality to the co-operation; and after the Danish referendum of February 1986 on the Single European Act,

178

membership of the EC was for all practical purposes no longer an issue in the Danish debate, where it was succeeded by a debate on integration. The implication of the gradual change of governance structures is that the empirical evidence is supposed to demonstrate higher or lower values of the chosen parameters, but not the total dominance of some parameters and the disappearance of others.

The data underlying this analysis are primarily quantitative. The basic fund of data is from a comprehensive survey of interest associations which were mainly asked about their organisational structure and political activity, whether in Denmark or in Brussels.[3] The responses of the associations relate to 1993, but on a number of issues the associations were also asked about their activity or attitudes in 1985, which allows for some systematic diachronic analysis. To strengthen this dimension of the argument, the analysis also utilises a database of Danish interest associations which was set up in 1981.[4] The final quantitative supplement stems from a survey of Danish business associations' membership of Euro-groups which was carried out in 1996.[5] In combination, these data systematically map the patterns of interrelations among interest associations and between interest associations and political-administrative institutions, domestically as well as abroad. This kind of data is chosen instead of more casuistic presentations of specific policy areas, acknowledging that both approaches have advantages as well as disadvantages.

The empirical evidence

This empirical analysis is intentionally short as its purpose is merely to test the hypotheses. More detailed analysis is partly to be found through the references.

Integration in EU policy-making

Business associations' fields of activity are increasingly influenced – 'very much' or to 'some extent' – by EU policies and policy-making. That applies to 65 per cent of all business associations. As a consequence, 38 per cent of business associations enlarge their contacts with the institutions of the European Union, and 48 per cent move into closer co-operation with associations at the European level. Many Danish business associations have had some kind of contact with EU institutions, *in toto* 39 per cent, but contacts are not very intensive. Only 12 per cent of business associations report that they communicate at least once a month with the DGs, the Council Secretariat, the ECOSOC, the European Parliament, or with the European Court of Justice. Compared to the situation in 1981, however, the growth is evident; at that time only 4 per cent of business associations performed this political activity with the same kind of regularity. This growth in interaction is further confirmed by the fact that in 1993 27 per cent of business associations had more frequent contacts with EU institutions compared to 1985.

We do not have complete data as to which year business associations set up their own offices in Brussels, but, from the 1993 and 1996 data it is clear that more and more business associations with a political presence in Brussels actually perform that activity by using an office of their own (Sidenius 1998). It can therefore be confidently asserted that the number of business association offices in Brussels has increased markedly during the last three to four years. The function of an office in Brussels is primarily to lobby and create liaisons in a broad sense. Although the setting up of an office in Brussels can be seen as the creation of a mere additional instrument, the presence in Brussels – the activity related to the EU, to Euro-groups and to other national associations – adds magnitude and nuances to the EU polity.

The third way of measuring integration in a larger European polity is to consider Danish business associations' membership of Euro-groups. Euro-groups can be conceptualised as an instrument of lobbying, but as collective units they perform functions of interest aggregation and formulation. It is disputed to what extent national associations' membership of transnational bodies like Euro-groups can be conceptualised within collective action theory, in other words, to what extent membership is motivated by selective material incentives or, rather, by political and solidarity considerations (McLaughlin and Jordan 1993, Sidenius 1998). In any case, membership and active participation in the affairs of Euro-groups add to the associations' political activity and representativeness which furthers their involvement in EU policy-making, and this, in turn, expands and diversifies the polity of the EU. In 1993, a total of 50 per cent of Danish business associations were affiliated to one or more Euro-groups. On the one hand, one may wonder why the proportion of affiliation is not even higher; on the other hand, however, in 1981 only 18 per cent of business associations were engaged in this international activity, making the increase significant.[6] Almost all member associations assign 'great importance' or 'some importance' to Euro-groups, and three out of four associations think that the importance of Euro-groups as of 1993 has increased compared to 1985.

This importance of Euro-groups in 1993 manifests itself in different ways. Most frequently (about 80 per cent of member associations), the provision of information on specific policy issues and decisions of the EU and the creation of contact with associations in other member states are said to have 'great importance' or 'some importance'. Following this comes influencing the decisions in the EU (75 per cent). Finally, the provision of information on general EU development is also deemed important (66 per cent of member associations).

The ranking of these functions was somewhat different as regards 1985. At that time, creation of contact with other associations was by far the most frequent activity (72 per cent of members), followed by provision of information on the general development of the EC (64 per cent). Very close to that came the provision of information about specific policy issues and decisions in the EU (63 per cent), and finally came efforts to influence the decisions of the EU (55 per cent). Although the creation of contact with associations in other member countries is still very important, it has given way in relative terms to Euro-group activity more focused on policy and politics, that is, focused on specific policy issues and policy-making. This leads to the assertion that Danish business associations through Euro-groups have become more integrated in the evolving polity and politics of the European Union. The variables found unequivocally confirm the hypothesis that Danish business has become more integrated into the EU system of governance, either directly or through Euro-groups. And there is also evidence to suggest that this development is due to policies and politics at the EU level. The next question to answer is whether this has had an impact on the domestic pattern of relationships between state and business actors.

Disintegration of national policy-making?

In 1981, 63 per cent of Danish business associations had some kind of contact with national political and administrative institutions, and 30 per cent had this contact on a regular basis, that is, at least monthly. Disintegration is occurring, then, if this magnitude of interrelations is decreasing, but there is no evidence of this. On the contrary, in 1993 69 per cent of business associations had contact with national authorities, and 42 per cent had contact at least monthly. In the early 1980s, interrelations between business associations and political and administrative institutions took place very frequently; but interrelations on a regular basis have developed even further since then, in particular those on a regular basis (Christiansen and Sidenius 1995: 441), during the revitalisation of the EC.

Decisions at EU level have a positive effect on contacts between Danish business associations and EU institutions, and on their co-operation with associations at the European level. EU decisions also lead to a higher level of contact between business associations and national political and administrative institutions, a fact stated by half of all business associations in 1993. And without doubt, EU decisions also lead to increased interaction among Danish associations, as stated by 44 per cent of business associations. It therefore seems that EU development does not disintegrate the national policy-making system but, on the contrary, integrates this feature of policy-making even further.

To qualify the argument, we move from the general political relationship between Danish business associations and political and administrative institutions to their relationship directly concerning EU matters. After Denmark became a member of the EC in 1973, it did not take long to set up the institutions and division of labour among the state and private actors in charge of the formulation, co-ordination and implementation of Danish policy-making and policies *vis-à-vis* the EC (Christensen 1978, 1981; Bregnsbo and Sidenius 1993). With the exception of the position of the parliamentary Europe Committee, previously the Common Market Committee, the changes to these institutions have been very small and incremental.

As a consequence, Danish business associations were used to dealing with domestic authorities on EC matters long before 1981, when one out of three business associations (35 per cent) had this kind of contact, including the associations acting via their peak association (7 per cent). However, only 11 per cent had contact on a regular basis, that is at least monthly. In 1993, 52 per cent of all business associations had become engaged in this activity, and one out of four on a regular basis. This development is probably due to the spreading and increased importance of EU policies, which seem to make it even more necessary for business associations to participate in EU policy-making via, and concurrently with, domestic authorities.

The previous section demonstrated that Danish business associations have become more active *vis-à-vis* the political and administrative institutions in Brussels. In 1993, 11 per cent of all business associations were in contact with EU institutions more often than with Danish political and administrative institutions. Another 11 per cent had as frequent contact with EU institutions as with domestic political and administrative institutions. However, four out of ten business associations were in contact with domestic authorities more often than with EU institutions. There are no comparable data on this issue for 1981, but it seems reasonable to suppose that the weight of EU relationships regarding EU policy-making has been growing in this respect, too. Nevertheless, the weight of domestic political relations is still dominant. The only minor indication that the cohesiveness of the domestic political and associational system might be decreasing concerns inter-associational relationships. In 1996, business associations found it more important to have contact with Danish associations than with foreign associations (30 per cent versus 16 per cent); but a little more than half of all business associations, as members of Euro-groups, were not able to state their opinion unequivocally (Sidenius 1998).

The analysis does not confirm the second hypothesis about disintegration of Danish policy-making. Business associations have not become less but, on the contrary, more active in domestic policy-making. In the next section this finding is placed in a broader context.

Conclusions and perspectives

Institutional persistence

The changed co-operation in Western Europe during the last ten years has had consequences for governance in the EU, where state centrist relationships have become increasingly supplemented by elements of multi-level governance. A new polity is evolving, and organised interests are an integrated part of it. This applies to Danish business associations, too, which have become increasingly involved in policy-making in Brussels. This growing international political activity is performed either directly *vis-à-vis* EU institutions or more indirectly via Euro-groups. The trend is to enhance the relative importance of influencing policy and to decrease that of monitoring affairs in Brussels.

Danish business associations' political activity in Brussels has become more similar to their domestic political action. The relationships between business associations and domestic political and administrative institutions have developed over decades, and they have functioned as the basic learning fora for the participation of business associations in international policy-making. A main finding of the analysis is that this domestic element of governance has not been disintegrated by the evolving European political system. On the contrary, relations between business associations and domestic political and administrative institutions have increased. The liberal declarations of the 1980s and their plans to reduce the regulation of business very often turned into much ado about nothing, because business itself demands regulation (Christensen 1991), and the integration of collective interest representations in policy-making remains important, whether it is initiated by associations or by public authorities (Christiansen and Sidenius 1995: 442–3). In terms of the network approach, one might say that the European network is not yet attractive enough for Danish business associations to diminish the importance of the domestic network (Daugbjerg 1994).

Danish business associations use the strategy of a domestic as well as an international route to the EU (Averyt 1977). The most proper conclusion to the analysis seems to be that business associations' increased political activity in Brussels augments their political action at home. And in this way multi-level governance, promoted by developments in Brussels, has had a direct impact on this domestic element of the overall governance system. Speaking in terms of governance transformation, increased employment of a European strategy in order to cope with the international pressures on business is found, but this strategy goes hand in hand with the well-known strategy of domestic involvement in policy-making. So, growing international integration does not lead to domestic disintegration; domestic governance features are supplemented, but not really substituted for, by international integration. The degree to which close relations between societal actors is embedded in Danish policy-making makes it an important structural feature of governance; 'it is the expression of an orientation towards institutionalised norms, principles, rationality criteria and their implied problem solving strategies' (Knodt 1996: 25). The integration into the existing national political order acts as a 'source of resistance' to a more

183

encompassing institutional adaptation (Marks and McAdam 1996: 103). An example of this path-dependency is the ongoing debate on the proper division of labour between the Europe Committee and other standing committees of the Danish parliament. This debate includes solutions which not only integrate interest associations further into the web of hearing institutions, but which may also have broader implications for the exchange between parliament and organised interests, as it potentially makes EU-related parliamentary procedures more similar to those of domestic issues (Sidenius 1997).

Changing the focus from integration versus disintegration to the relative importance of political processes adds more nuances to the conclusion. The expansion of EU politics and policies and the concomitant change of policy attention, agenda-setting and decision processes at all levels of the EU have had their consequences. The impact of multi-level governance has been to weaken the importance of domestic political institutions, and by implication also the importance of domestic governance features. So, governance transformation is occurring, but rather slowly it seems, and a new governance regime has not yet become dominant.

Europeanisation and globalisation

It may be asked whether the involvement of Danish business associations in the evolution of an EU polity and governance regime including private actors, i.e. multi-level governance, should be viewed as a result of Europeanisation. Is it not merely the result of the liberalisation of European markets or a consequence of economic globalisation? Business may reorient its activity due to economic liberalisation and globalisation, which increasingly infringe upon the capacity of the nation-state to create a profitable business environment (cf the discussion in Hollingsworth and Streeck 1994). In that case companies might substitute networking and market-oriented activity, 'governance mechanisms' in the terminology of Hollingsworth *et al.* (1994) and Lindberg *et al.* (1991), for political contacts, and associations might increase their political presence in other countries through lobbying. Analytically, the two independent variables – Europeanisation and globalisation – can be dealt with separately, but in real life they are interconnected. The economic policy and deregulatory initiatives of the EU are both a reaction to and an impetus for further economic globalisation – with the aim of promoting EU businesses. Very few, and certainly no Danish, business associations have the capacity to regulate or deregulate markets, which is left to the multi-national enterprises, to the international organisations and major economic powers and partly to Euro-groups as participants in EU political processes (Martinelli 1991, Greenwood *et al.* 1992b).

Outside the national space, business associations, and especially those from countries like Denmark with a very open economy, have little choice but to increasingly participate in Euro-groups and to carry out more lobbying activity in Brussels; this extension of the boundaries of the space of the polity (Kohler-Koch 1996) equals Europeanisation. Likewise EU politics and policy, though very often a reaction to economic globalisation and its expected impact on EU business, penetrate national politics and policy-making (Ladrech 1994), which in this case is found in the increased interaction between business associations and national political and administrative institutions, and this amounts to an incremental process of Europeanisation.

Other findings on multi-level governance

On a general level, the findings on governance in Denmark concur with those of Goetz on governance concerning intergovernmental relations in Germany (Goetz 1995). Again, the distinction between the impact on relations and change of governance is important in understanding the development. In Germany, the defining principles of the federal system have not been altered; in Denmark, the institutionalised integration of business associations in policy-making has not been weakened, but rather reinforced. Therefore, ' Europeanisation of national governance is compatible with the maintenance of very distinct national institutional arrangements' (ibid.: 93).

This position differentiates itself from another position, which points to more encompassing effects of the evolving EU polity on national governance. Eising and Kohler-Koch (1994: 176) assert probably more general consequences of increased complexity and fragmentation. Schmidt (1995) suggests major alterations concerning the relative position of important political actors in that business has become stronger and labour weaker. She rightly asserts that business is looking more to Europe than before, although her point on changes of national policy-making processes is far from unequivocally confirmed by Danish evidence. Ladrech, too, finds evidence of an impact of Europeanisation on relations between groups and the state and between different territorial actors (Ladrech 1994: 82, 85), implying the possibility of diverse effects on national governance of the evolving EU polity. This is further confirmed by Jachtenfuchs and Kohler-Koch, who underline that national changes of governance occur along national paths, and therefore, 'there is no increasing uniformity of national systems as a result of the Europeanization of politics' (Jachtenfuchs and Kohler-Koch 1995: 13). This concurs with the conclusion in Marks and McAdam (1996) on the differences between social movements in particular policy areas.

The position pointing to more thorough changes in national governance is also found in analyses focusing on policies and policy-making in a multi-level complex political system. Eichener (1996) makes it evident that EU policies and policy-making in specific areas may have a major impact on the relative positions and powers of political actors, increasing the opportunities of interests who at the national level have not had much clout. Another governance-changing consequence of EU policy-making is the enhanced room for manoeuvre of national ministers brought about by the externalisation of the costs of policy changes through '*Legitimationsentlastung*'. Fuchs (1994) points to the same kind of changes regarding the telecommunications sector.

Grande demonstrates that the multi-level European political system, '*europäische Politikverflechtung*', in the case of the Community research and development policy caused a 'substantial change in the logic of influence of public policy' ibid 1996b: 376). His point is that business influence has not increased, but on the contrary has decreased due to a very complex change of state autonomy *vis-à-vis* its societal interlocutors, designated as a 'paradox of weakness' (ibid.: 389). The conclusion is that the logic of influence between public and private actors has changed as a consequence of the Europeanisation of R and D policies (ibid.: 392).

Specifics of the Danish case

The persistent domestic relationship between business associations and political institutions has to be seen in the light of the continuing important role played by national governments in EU decision-making and the implementing powers of the member states. The Danish case of governance transformation can be understood more thoroughly if some of its particular features are outlined, pointing at the same time to limits of generalisation. Business associations have for decades been partners of the political and administrative institutions at the national level and thus become integrated into policy-making. More and more policy areas have been included, most prominently foreign trade policy, industrial policy, fiscal policy, environmental policy, educational policy and – where its impact upon policy has been important – EC Policy (Sidenius 1982, 1984, 1989). The focus on national associations neither implies that individual companies abstain from lobbying for specific interests, nor that collective business interest representation at the national level tells the whole story about government-business relations (from different viewpoints, Christiansen 1993 and Pedersen *et al.* 1992). But, owing to the high proportion of small businesses and the relatively small number of large companies, collective interest representation is very prominent in political matters compared to the activity of individual companies, especially so far as international political activity is concerned, where trade and peak associations compensate for the limited individual company activity (Sidenius 1994).

The persistent integration of business in domestic policy-making and its increasing activity in Brussels seem to support the notion that the EU is advantageous to business as compared to labour. Though correct in general, the Danish data on policy participation do not confirm the notion. Like business, labour associations have for decades been integrated into policy-making and, currently, even more so than business associations (Christiansen and Sidenius 1995). This holds true whether we focus in general terms on domestic political activity, EU-related political activity, political activity in Brussels or Euro-group membership (Sidenius 1998). The integration of labour into policy-making is partly explained by the frequency of governments led by the Social Democratic Party, which previously had very intimate relations with the Danish Trade Unions Congress (*LandsOrganisationen*) and most of the trade unions, and partly by the encompassing integration of interest associations in Danish policy-making, which is a very stable feature of the governance structure (Christiansen and Sidenius 1995, Sidenius 1998). Europeanisation has thus had an effect on the political activity of collective interest representations in general, reinforcing path-dependency and creating more international political activity.

The governance feature of close relations between business associations and political and administrative institutions has been influenced by the 'tradition' of minority governments in Denmark (Damgaard 1992). The desire for policy influence always makes business associations keen to participate, and this is reinforced in times of unstable political majorities where parties other than those in government become relevant interlocutors, not to mention the bureaucracy. At the same time, governing as well as non-governing parties see the advantage of including business associations – and very often other associations too – on their side of the political debate. The increase in contacts between business associations and public authorities is, therefore, the result of an increase in contact initiatives by both political partners (Christiansen and Sidenius 1995: 443), mirroring a dual necessity and advantage.

This analysis has not differentiated between policy areas. It is possible that there are variations across policy areas as to the integration of business associations in policy-making. Europeanisation has not yet, however, more than marginally included the traditional core of national business-government relations, i.e. industrial relations. The relative autonomy of national business and labour associations in negotiating wages, working conditions, etc., supplemented at times by regulations passed by parliament, is institutionalised at the national level and on special issues also at the regional level. It is presumed that a comprehensive transfer of policy-making competencies regarding this area from the national to the EU level will focus the attention of business associations more profoundly on the European scene, and reduce their attention on the national scene. In that case, the creation of an EU polity will take place to the detriment of the national polity.

Notes

1 To what extent the policy-making capacities of the EU have been strengthened less than those of the member states have been weakened is another question (Scharpf 1994, Hollingsworth and Streeck 1994).

2 The interplay between national actors and evolving Europeanisation making the latter the dependent variable, as it is hypothesised by neo-functionalist theory, is not discussed.

3 'Interest Associations' Resources, Structure, Tasks and Contact with Public Authorities' (ORGSPSS4). The survey was carried out from late 1992 until early 1994 by Niels Chr. Sidenius, Peter Munk Christiansen, and Jørgen Grønnegård Christensen of the Department of Political Science at the University of Aarhus. The unit of the survey was nation-wide interest associations, and the size of the group was about 1900 (our best estimate); 1316 associations responded to the questionaire, i.e. about 69 per cent of the group. Industrial associations are under-represented in the survey in comparison with the associations of workers and civil servants and academics, but it is not thought that this creates a systematic distortion of data. The responding number of business associations was N=358.

4 'Danish Interest Associations, 1981' (DDA-0510). The survey was carried out by Jacob A. Buksti, University of Aarhus, and Lars Nørby Johansen, University of Odense. Data and documentation of the survey were made available by Dansk Data Arkiv, Odense. The number of responding business associations in this survey was N=664. The use of data in this paper is the responsibility of the author.

5 'Membership of Euro-groups' (EUROORG). The survey was carried out by the author among those business associations who in the 1993 survey stated that they were members of Euro-groups (N=179), irrespective of the time of entry; 137 associations responded to the questionaire, of which 25 per cent had joined a Euro-group prior to 1973, 39 per cent joined from 1973 to 1985 and 33 per cent joined from 1986 onwards (four associations did not respond to this particular question), e.g. Sidenius 1998.

6 Part of the relative growth from 1981 to 1993 is explained by changed population size (notes 4 and 5) due to heavy centralisation among business associations. But the result – that a higher proportion of Danish business associations participate in Euro-groups – mirrors a change on the part of this societal actor which has a bearing on political activity and networks.

11

PERCEPTIONS OF GOVERNANCE IN GREEK STATE RETREAT

Implementing policy change against policy-making persistence

George Pagoulatos

In its most generic depiction, European governance is a multi-level process (or game), beginning at what is symbolically perceived as 'Brussels', and ending at the street implementation level of every member state, before turning back again to policy-makers for evaluation and reformulation. Thus, while the formulation stage of European policy is shaped predominantly by the institutional and political forces acting at the supranational level, the implementation stage is crucially defined by those operating in the national policy arenas. The unique constitution of each one of those national policy arenas accounts for considerable cross-country dissimilarity of both policy outcomes and domestic governance patterns (Hall 1995: 22–26). Though trivial, the above remark is useful in refocusing well-deserved attention on the implementation stage of European policy, where national politico-institutional dynamics are prominent (e.g. Unger and van Waarden 1995: 28). Implementation of European policy at the member state level constitutes a distinct procedural unity subject to the traditional 'stages' breakdown into agenda setting, formulation and implementation (Anderson 1979; Hogwood and Gunn 1984; Peters 1986).

This chapter will explore the question of a transformation of European governance within the above described conceptual framework by drawing on the twin policy cases of Greek privatisation (an ongoing process initially launched in 1990) and banking deregulation (which began in the second half of the 1980s and was concluded in the early 1990s). From a comparativist's perspective, Greece offers a telling case of generalisability through extremity; tailing the Southern European block in terms of economic development, it lies at the end-point of the EU continuum in a number of institutional, economic and policy aspects (see Maravall 1993; Diamandouros 1994; Pagoulatos and Wright 1999). In that sense, from a purely analytical but no less ironical viewpoint, Greece's comparative interest is directly proportional to its degree of divergence. On the other hand, the chosen twin case study lends itself to the intriguing paradox inherently entailed in the practice of making state policy for state reduction.

Four principal questions will be addressed. First, which factors accounted for policy convergence in the EU and how did Greece respond to those factors? Second, taking as given that governance (i.e. policy-making) at the EU level has been evolving toward the 'network' type, was any such governance transformation visible at the national level: in other words, was policy convergence followed by convergence in policy-making, and, if not, why not? Third, what are the particular implications of deregulation and privatisation, i.e. state retreat policy, for network-type policy-making? And fourth, what specific patterns of governance and interest organisation encourage or discourage a transformation of policy-making towards a 'network' mode?

'Network governance' throughout the chapter denotes all the policy-making arrangements that the literature identifies with the concept or metaphor of policy networks, such as autonomous interaction of multiple interdependent action units of organisations or individuals, horizontal, informal, decentralised relations, and lack of central steering by the state (see e.g. Kenis and Schneider 1991; Dowding 1995). Thus, the network notion is used here in its *substantive* meaning, as opposed to where the policy network is explicitly employed in its *formal* sense, i.e. to refer not to a specific structural configuration but to any set of links between actors and *any* pattern of interrelationships, be they of a pluralist, corporatist or statist type (Schneider 1992: 109–13).

Pressures, convergence, transmission belts and Europeanisation of policy

Privatisation and banking deregulation can be perceived as parts of the same broader national agenda of reducing government control over the economy.[1] The pressures behind this twin devolution were neither entirely similar nor of equal relative importance. Both programmes, none the less, can be viewed as integral national parts of a wider EC/EU dynamic of policies converging toward a lesser or redefined state role (Müller and Wright 1994). Thus, in both programmes discussed, the notion of policy convergence stands out as central and prominent.

But what exactly makes policy convergence come about? In addressing the question, Colin Bennett (1991) distinguishes the notion into five possible meanings: first, convergence in policy goals; second, policy content (the more formal manifestations of government policy such as statutes and regulations); third, policy instruments (the institutional tools available to administer policy); fourth, policy outcomes; and fifth, policy styles (signifying the process by which policy responses are formulated). Bennett then goes on to identify a fourfold framework of (highly interrelated and often difficult to separate) processes through which convergence might arise: *emulation*, where state actors copy action taken elsewhere; *elite networking*, where convergence is brought about by transnational policy communities; *harmonisation* through the international regimes and the recognition of interdependence resulting from the transnationalisation of economies; and *penetration* by external actors and interests, where states are forced to conform to actions taken elsewhere by external actors.

These processes transmit international systemic pressures onto national policy-making systems. Across the EC/EU since the 1980s parallel programmes have been initiated by national governments whose prominent feature, among others, was a bold redrawing of the public-private boundary to the benefit of the latter. The project of 'rolling back the state' was prompted as Europe's response to the anticipated erosion of its competitiveness under conditions of post-Keynesian market globalisation and liberalisation. Corresponding to the process of harmonisation mentioned above, the European response consisted in a strategy of enhancing EC economic competitiveness through strengthening the efficiency of national economies via 'structural adjustment' policies of market integration and liberalisation (Tsoukalis 1993: 34–45). The redefinition of the state's role, among others, was implemented through, first, the abolition of nationally specific postwar regulatory structures (deregulation) followed by the establishment of new regulatory frameworks usually aimed at stability and consumer protection (prudential reregulation), then second, extensive privatisation.

A common enhancing factor of both programmes was the monetarist and supply-side economic ideology of the 1980s, in the ascendant in Greece particularly from the second half of the 1980s. Economic neo-liberalism was internationally championed by major business interests, both industrial and financial, anxious to gain competitiveness on a global scale (Strange 1985). It had a crucial impact in structuring the perceptions of international and domestic actors, offering them a convincing legitimising discourse for implementing market-oriented reform (Haggard and Kaufman 1992: 12–15; Hall 1995).

EC financial reform relied extensively on competition policy. One EC country after another proceeded to stimulate internal banking competition through deregulating interest rates, removing domestic and cross-border obstacles, phasing out direct lending controls and investment requirements, and encouraging the creation of new financial instruments (Bröker 1989). Arguably the single financial market programme, combined with EMU, represented an affirmation of the rising importance of the financial sector and central bankers (Dyson *et al.* 1995). Moreover, the new strict 'sound finance' orientation contented the typically inflation-averse European bankers. Thus, the implementation by national systems of EC-sponsored financial reform programmes (itself an offspring of internationalisation and interdependence) signified an erosion of the impact and sovereignty of domestic politico-institutional factors. At the same time, it indicated a dimension of effective transnationalisation of policy communities serving as a force for convergence.

With regard to privatisation, convergence via policy harmonisation related mainly to competition policy and EMU objectives. As financial liberalisation deprived European governments of the ability to influence real interest rates, the cost of servicing large public debts rose dramatically (Wyplosz 1993: 441). As a result, governments were compelled to offset public debt by generating consecutive primary budget surpluses (i.e. net of interest payments). For countries with high public debt and deficits, the policy mix of fiscal discipline was completed with the need to maximise budget revenue through privatisation. The overall importance of domestic conditions was crucial (to a much greater extent than with banking deregulation) in making privatisation part of Greek economic reform policy. Indeed, the EC impact on Greek privatisation, if compared to that in banking deregulation and liberalisation, was considerably less powerful and direct, the Treaty of Rome being tolerant of public entrepreneurial activity. None the less, EC competition policy (applicable in a number of Greek companies thus forced into privatisation) demanded the termination of a range of illegal (under EC law) state subsidies and the operation of public enterprises in full adherence to market competition rules (Commission 1994c: 34-8). On the whole, EC competition policy incorporated, first, the outcomes of national governments' efforts to protect their industrial sectors; second, the mobilisation at Community level of transnational private businesses to ensure access to cross-border markets; and third, the formidable policy control of the European Commission (Hayward 1995a; Allen 1996: 178–9; Schmidt 1997).

In financial liberalisation, policy emulation served as a crucial convergence mechanism. A small, open EU economy, Greece is a 'policy receiver' not only as regards external positive pressures, but also in its susceptibility to influential policy models from abroad. Just as postwar credit regulation across Europe had served as the model for the Greek regulatory system, so too did the dismantling of those same European systems offer a blueprint for Greek banking deregulation (see OECD, 1992: 27; Dermine 1993). Equally, neo-liberal privatisers in the ruling conservative *Néa Demokratía* (ND) party were particularly inspired by privatisation under the governments of Thatcher, Gonzales, and Cavaco Silva.

That shift of policy direction incorporated the additional dimension of elite networking and peer pressure within the European expert community. During the second half of the 1970s, and in view of Greece's prospective entry into the EEC in 1980, expert contacts and exchanges between Greek central bank officials, academics and technocrats and their European counterparts intensified. The domestic banking expert community became increasingly subject not only to the fashionable monetarist ideas of the time but also to the personal influence of their peers. 'When a small number of like-minded people constantly communicate privately and informally, and read the same reports and journals' (Moran 1984: 35), they 'then go forth to "spread the word" to their respective societies and governments' (Bennett 1991: 225). In banking deregulation, the formalised relations with the EC competent bodies and committees were highly significant, from the Committee of the Central Bank Governors and Directorate General (DG) XV (Internal Market and Financial Services) downward to specialised committees at the lower levels. Similar peer pressure, though of a shorter time span and less institutionalised, was exercised upon Greek privatisers throughout the programme's implementation. At the top level the ECOFIN, the Internal Market Council and the Monetary Committee, and notably the Commission services, served as powerful transmission mechanisms of policy directions. The Inter-ministerial Privatisation Committee (IPC), which was established in 1990 and handled the Greek government programme, regularly informed Commission representatives from DG II (Economic and Financial Affairs) of the progress in privatisation. Tighter EC control was required under the terms of the 1991 EC balance of payments support loan, which activated a more rigorous surveillance mechanism.

Convergence of policy, yes: but what about governance?

There is no compelling reason to dispute the remark that the same mechanisms which diffuse policy ideas also transmit normative perceptions of governance (Kohler-Koch 1996: 373–5; Bennett 1991: 218). Ideas of governance 'efficiency' or 'fairness' are equally communicated to national policy milieus via the same transmission belts of harmonisation, peer pressure, and so on, like equivalent perceptions about policy. Moreover, it has been convincingly argued that a network model of governance is actively propagated by the European Commission (encouraged by the EC tendency to pursue governance strategies minimising opposition) and facilitated by the EC activity in policy areas where network governance is more plausible, such as regional and R and D policies (Kohler-Koch 1996: 372–5).

However, breaking down the exact process of policy Europeanisation reveals that the transmission belts of European policies into the domestic policy structure do not also necessarily operate with the same effectiveness as transmission belts of governance (Coleman 1994: 275). A preliminary argument would draw attention to the different adjustment function of policy and governance. Policy convergence operates by forcing the weaker *part* (the economy and institutions of a small and divergent member state) to adapt towards the stronger *whole*. None the less, with governance the convergence process works in the opposite direction. As European policy in its implementation stage enters the national governance milieu it becomes *part* of the broader *whole* of the domestic macro-level and sectoral governance and interest organisation structure, and thus tends to adjust by acquiring the latter's features. This question will be further elaborated in the next section discussing advocacy coalitions.

In the previous section, the process of policy convergence was examined. The analytical framework pursued is summarised in Figure 11.1. Thus, systemic pressures were transmitted into the national policy system through the convergence processes described, and structured into ideologically consistent policy programmes through the mediating technocratic and political discourse of monetarist and supply-side economics contained in European integration rhetoric. Consequently, both the normative and the positive premises underlying the ideology of state retreat from the economy were to be conceptually or explicitly invoked. Indeed, interviews with state actors of the Greek privatisation and banking deregulation programmes have confirmed that their reform zeal towards rolling back the state was grounded on universal empirical assumptions projected onto and confirmed by the domestic reality. These included the common belief, indeed one transcending the pro-privatisation coalition, that the public sector throughout the preceding decades, culminating in the 1980s, was being used by governments as a mechanism for the extraction of clientelistic support, and that the dynamic of the electoral cycle was leading to grave fiscal deterioration.

The concept of the subjugation of government-controlled financial resources to party-political purposes underlay the reformist intentions of both Bank of Greece (BoG) deregulators and *Néa Demokratía* (ND) privatisers, as well as the privatisers of the post-1993 socialist governments of PASOK. In the case of deregulators, it fed on the electorally motivated increase of state-controlled bank subsidies to various protected societal groups, as well as the employment of the state-controlled banking sector for the monetisation of public deficits – both at the expense of banking system competitiveness – and the apparent functioning of an electoral- monetary cycle throughout the 1980s. In the case of privatisers, it drew on the notoriously extensive utilisation of the public enterprise sector as a repository for patronage appointees of the governing party (Commission of the European Communities 1992). On a more profound level, and in both cases, reformist intentions were well founded on a 'cyclical' disappointment

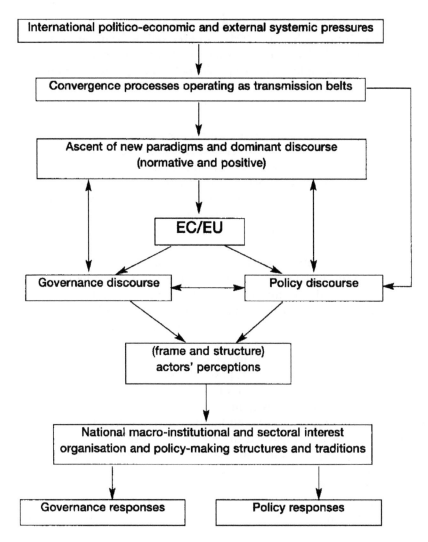

Figure 11.1 A governance framework for European policy implementation

with the perceived side effects of state expansion throughout the postwar period (Hirschman 1982).

Advocacy coalitions and the paradox of state retreat

The impact of the pressures and ideas enumerated in the previous section can be conceptualised in the ascendancy of domestic pro-deregulation and pro-privatisation advocacy coalitions, and the inclusion of their respective programmes in the policy agenda. An advocacy coalition, along the lines of Jenkins-Smith and Sabatier (1994), is perceived as being more than the makers of a particular policy programme, that is, the totality of organisational actors seeking to influence public policy in a particular domain and exercising an important role in the generation and dissemination of the policy ideas underlying the programme.

Employing the notion of advocacy coalitions helps to discern the particular concept of the state and governance held by deregulation and privatisation policy-makers. The closest and most frequent interaction of national policy-makers took place within their domestic advocacy coalitions, to whose direct influence they were constantly subjected, while they were also exposed to the European ascendancy of ideas and practices of state withdrawal not only from the economy but, to a certain extent, from the governance process as well. (The latter was for the sake of leaving room for network interaction of transnational private and institutional actors.) These advocacy coalitions pursued the withdrawal of government from the banking and industrial markets. However, there was no evidence of a similar view *vis-à-vis* the terms of tight state control over the governance process, particularly at a time when favoured public policies were being implemented. On the contrary, domestic advocacy coalitions embedded in the national politico-institutional scene, with its notorious adversarial traditions (see below), were inducing reformist state policy-makers to defend and further enhance their control over the policy arena in order to effectively resist interest opposition to reform.

A plausible disjunction is hence observable: while state policy-makers held strong normative views about limiting state involvement in the economy and society, they regarded the maximisation of their own control of policy as vitally important in bringing about the desired contraction of the public boundary. Being of an economically conservative disposition, the government and BoG actors perceived their own role in a rather voluntaristic way. They excluded themselves from the stereotypical public-choice depiction of clientelistically-driven state actors, and proceeded to minimise state involvement in the economy as an institutionally binding arrangement against politically driven excesses by other – less trusted – colleagues or future governments. State policy-makers, subscribing largely to an ideology of rational economic efficiency, pursued a policy of instrumental employment of any available state resources in the service of the ultimate objective of rolling back the state, and found no particular contradiction in doing so.

Thus, as in the privatisation experiences in Britain (Richardson 1994; V. Wright 1994a: 41) and France (Bauer 1989: 57) – though rather unlike that in Italy (Cassese 1993: 168) – state withdrawal in Greece was implemented in a crescendo of government effort to maximise control over the policy arena. Ministers handling privatisation tried to appoint their own allies to crucial positions instead of, for example, relying mostly on meritocratic non-political appointments. State bankers privatising subsidiaries attempted to concentrate authority away from all potential sources of opposition by keeping the latter at arm's length from the process. The 1991 privatisation law (upon which – with minor amendments – all privatising governments in the 1990s operated) was a statist's wildest dream, concentrating increased authority in the hands of government ministers. The government exhibited traits of feudalism, with ministers trying to extract control over a privatisation-related issue from their colleagues even at the expense of ultimate policy efficiency.

Equally, the implementation of deregulation by the Central Bank bore all the traits of unilateralism: secrecy, exclusion of societal outsiders and so on. Policy formulation took place almost exclusively inside the Central Bank, within the general policy framework decided between the BoG governor and the economic ministers, whose consent was necessary for the implementation of any BoG measure. Consultation with affected societal groups (such as small-scale enterprises whose special finance regime was to be abolished, or farmers whose main funding source, the Agricultural Bank, was to be stripped of most of its privileges) was largely cosmetic, carrying very limited practical impact on the final policy outputs. (See Table 11.1).

Europeanisation, strength of weakness, and the content of reform

All this is not to say that policy networks (in the formal sense) remained impermeable to Europeanisation at the national implementation stage. Indeed, in both privatisation and deregulation, instances of governance transnationalisation were clearly visible. In the EC bodies described above, national policy-makers participated in the formulation of European policy and subjected themselves to the reality of regime and politico-economic interdependence. In designing and selecting the exact timing and scope of deregulation measures, BoG policy-makers were fully enmeshed in the day-to-day adjustment of their monetary policy *vis-à-vis* those of other EC central banks, with a constant eye on the fluctuations of world financial markets. As far as privatisation was concerned, transnational actors were very close to, and in some cases part of, the decision-making core: for privatisation-related advice, the government relied predominantly on international firms; for its largest projects it systematically targeted and negotiated with international investors.

The duality of 'allegiance' of certain key policy actors also added a considerable element of transnationalisation. For example, the legislation which enacted the Second EC Banking Directive into Greek law in 1992 was formulated by a government-appointed committee led by a Greek official of the European Commission, who was one of the chief drafters of the

Table 11.1 Policy-making in Greek privatisation and banking deregulation

	Greek banking deregulation	Greek privatisation
Policy network actors	Main: BoG, economic ministers, (largest state-controlled commercial bank) Secondary: HBA, banks, other societal interests affected by deregulation	Main: IPC, non-IPC supervising ministers, holder institutions Secondary: various intervening private, societal and political interests
Function of main policy network actors	Closed, insulated, stable, civil service continuity, ideological cohesion of BoG apparatus, technocratic focus, vertical hierarchical, concentrated (BoG), resource self-reliance	Concentrated formal authority but dispersed policy control, hierarchical relations, blurred boundaries, penetration of non-governmental actors, discontinuity, unstable ideological cohesion, politically-minded, personalised, internally divided, inadequate resources
Relation of main with secondary policy network actors	Exclusion but open for consultation; pressure exercised by interests; close informal contact with banks; contact less close and formalised with other interests; low dissension; no politicisation	Exclusion but open for consultation; forceful pressures and networking with government; contact both formal and informal; strong dissension and conflict; high politicisation
Pattern of policy-making	Statist	Statist
Europeanisation of network / Presence of EC actors	Pressure at agenda-setting stage; feedback during formulation stage; loose supervision at implementation stage	Pressure at agenda-setting stage; loose monitoring of formulation and implementation; strong pressure when EC competition rules are at stake
Identification of prior regime as problem	Prior regulatory regime identified as problem since late 1970s (by BoG officials)	Prior state-control regime identified as problem since mid-1980s (by ND opposition party)
Advocacy coalition in power	Deregulation advocates since 1980 in BoG apparatus and 1986 in PASOK government	Advocacy coalition since 1990
Legitimising discourse	Increase market competition, strengthen competitiveness of national banking sector to cope with conditions of European financial integration	Limit state business involvement, maximise budget revenue and reduce deficits, rationalise and improve business efficiency and market competition

BoG: Bank of Greece (the Greek Central Bank)   IPC: Interministerial Privatisation Committee
HBA: Hellenic Bank Association
PASOK: Socialist party (in government between 1981–89 and 1993–present)
ND: Conservative party (in government between 1974–81 and 1990–93).
Note: The term policy network in the table is used in the *formal* sense, as opposed to the *substantive* one employed in most other parts of the chapter.

Directive. In a number of aspects, the committee's chairman held a Commission perspective, which could be claimed to differ from that of the government. In privatisation, at least two of the principal Greek advisers of the government were career officials with international organisations such as investment bankers and the International Monetary Fund (IMF), to which – after the ND government's fall – they returned. The considerable impact of such 'imported' technocrats (who filled lacunae of government indecision or specialised ignorance) was largely a function of the scarcity of expert *and* trusted human resources within upper and inner government circles, combined with the lack of a reliable public bureaucracy. However, as the central role and final word of government actors was never disputed, much of the input of not-strictly-state policy-makers was perceived by state actors as an influential part of the surrounding context of pressures, rather than as a form of joint decision-making. The interaction was thereby prevented from acquiring the form of network governance.

A further important insight confirmed by the cases mentioned is the so-called *paradox of weakness:* the state loses part of its autonomy to the supranational level (as a result of interdependence, harmonisation, etc.) but gains power to pursue its own (public) interest against strong pressures from societal actors (Kohler-Koch 1995). Along the same lines, it has been argued that policy convergence may occur through the autonomous preference of policy-makers to fashion convergent policies (Bennett 1991: 232). Indeed, externally induced policy convergence enables democratic governments concerned with the political cost to put policy before politics by shifting the blame for their policies on to forces external to and beyond their control.

In Greek banking deregulation, a double process of scapegoating took place. In the face of pressure from disaffected and previously state-protected groups such as farmers and small-scale enterprises, the government blamed the EC and the central bank, which in turn invoked the binding nature of EC requirements. Equally, in privatisation, the downsizing of public enterprise employment was attributed to the terms imposed by the EC balance of payments support loan, while EC coercion was also extensively blamed for the sale of major industries such as shipyards. In such ways, the Europeanisation of policy made it possible for governments to eschew societal and interest group pressure, thereby helping them to pursue their statist and exclusive policy-making patterns. Facilitated by the invocation of an external force, the statist components of domestic governance were intensified in the application of adjustment policies, which themselves largely relied on the project of rolling back the state from the economy.

A final explanatory dimension concerns the qualitative content of reform policy and previous state control. Policy-making in the process of state retreat remained nationalised and state-centric because of the very objectives of deregulation and privatisation, combined with the nature of state intervention exercised up to that point. Both policies aimed to uproot the system of credit regulation or state ownership control through which certain domestic resources were distributed to a specific matrix of recipients. Subsidised credit was extended to preferred categories at the expense of unfavoured borrowers and the financial sector. State protection was offered to ailing state-controlled companies, entailing easier finance and the capacity to operate below cost to the benefit of privileged procurers, clients and company employees but at the expense of private market competitors.

Thus, the object of both banking deregulation and privatisation was highly pertinent to the domestic configuration of societal interests and redistributive in its function. Antagonism among domestic interests was not about maximising common resources through a joint cooperative effort, nor about opening channels to external funds (which would have shifted the balance toward the transnational level, encouraging a network-type governance) but about zero-sum access to state-controlled resources. The role of the state in that process was not one of co-ordinating or bringing together relevant actors, but about achieving the successful transition from a distributive to a limited regulatory state function through institutionalising a new framework of resource allocation according to market forces instead of government decree (Lowi 1964). Given the intensity of group pressure (on the part of both the expected winners and losers from the reforms), state actors sought maximum control over the policy process (in a manner framed by the existing statist policy traditions, perceptions and operating patterns) in order to ensure its implementation.

Propensity to network governance and perceptions of the state

An argument has now been sketched linking the transformation of governance with perceptions about ongoing governance patterns (Jachtenfuchs 1995). Perceptions about the *new* role of the state are contingent upon already existing perceptions about the state's *established* role, in the economy as much as in the governance process. Such perceptions are themselves intertwined with national-level institutional and politico-cultural structures. Established policy styles serve as normative guides to policymakers, and structure beliefs and expectations of how policy will, rather than should, be enacted (Freeman 1985: 473). In the words of March and Olsen (1989: 34), '[a] repertoire of routines is also the basis for an institutional approach to novel situations; the most standard organisational response to novelty is to find a set of routines that can be used'. Such routines, embedded in governance milieus, structure the policy actors' responses to reform challenges, operating as pathways created under past (random or causally determined) conditions and perpetuated through repeated usage. Thus policy responses to matured pressures for institutional reform are still being defined, often *in extremis,* by the existing institutional arrangements, a part of which they are attempting to upset. Policy-making in such moments carries both the constraints of the conditions it is venturing to overthrow and the dynamics of their dismissal (Pagoulatos 1996: 759).

To illuminate the above, it would be worth hypothesising and comparing how perceptions of the state would operate in different contextual settings of interest organisation. In a pluralist context, where opposite interests compete for the extraction of public resources, the state might be viewed as a 'neutral' arbiter state (old-pluralism) or as a 'special interest state' skewed in favour of big business (neo-pluralism), but in any case as a state with a limited role of ensuring the procedural framework for 'equal' representation of interests, and setting and policing the rules of the game. The societal normative premises underlying pluralism tend to rest upon, or value, liberal individualism, market competition, adversarial traditions and free contractual negotiation, and to disfavour collusive behaviour, co-ordinated, planned or state-directed economic policy-making and the regulation of prices and wages suggested by statist or corporatist systems (McFarland 1992: 78–9). On the contrary, corporatist-leaning traditions and cultures tend to be based on and promote normative notions of concerted action towards collective goals, a 'stakeholder' capitalist culture, consensus-seeking, a positive-sum long-term sense of gain for the social partners and, on top of all that, an activist role of the state both in the economy and industrial relations, endowing peak private economic associations with quasi-public authority (Maier 1984; Offe 1981).

In its emphasis on sectoral governance, the network model of policy-making displays a high degree of compatibility with corporatist governance and surrounding perceptions, appearing as an 'evolved' state of meso-corporatism (Cawson 1985). Distinct differences from corporatism probably pertain to the horizontal structure of network governance, its emphasis on informal and personalised interaction, its inclusion of trans-national EC actors, the likelihood of non-participation of peak associations, and the relatively weaker bargaining strength of the latter. The stability and high degree of interaction between state and private actors, the cooperative, consensus-seeking, positive-sum orientation, the recognition by state actors of societal interests as legitimate social partners and respected interlocutors: all these typical traits of corporatist governance 'culture' form the probably optimal basis for an evolution of governance toward a network mode. The prerequisites of trust and duration, the perceived long-term horizon of the interaction enabling actors to see their relationship in terms of an iterated positive-sum game (Axelrod 1990) would enable the strengthening of close and informal personal relations indicative of a network type. Thus, network governance can be perceived metaphorically as the next evolutionary stage following the demise of corporatist arrangements, or as a type of post-corporatism in which both the state and the peak social partners have lost power to new actors brought about as a result of the multiplicity and fragmentation of governance units.

At the opposite end of the spectrum in terms of negative propensity to network governance lie statism and pressure pluralism. Both are connected by their tendency (stronger in statism, relatively weaker in pluralism) to exclude societal interests from policy-making. While in pressure pluralism the state is subject to the competition of interest groups for channelling access, and might accept some for consultation, no joint negotiation, co-ordination, or any co-operation of societal interests in policy formulation or implementation takes place in either statist or pressure pluralist structures (van Waarden 1992: 39). Both statism and pluralism are defined by an adversarial culture of interaction between state and societal interests, which enhances politicisation and discourages mutual trust and co-operation.

Where are Greek policy-making traditions located in this framework? From the postwar period to the end of the 1980s Greek economic governance has been statist overall, characterised by extensive and particularistic government interventionism and regulation. Public policy making has been essentially unilateral, varied at times (particularly since the 1981 advent of the socialist PASOK) by processes of interest group consultation. The latter, however, far from constituting co-decision or actual multilateral policy deliberation, were more of a government effort to invest its policies with societal democratic legitimisation, or simply to pre-empt anticipated opposition in a highly adversarial political context. Notably, that Greek version of statism did not correspond to the features typically identified with a 'strong state', such as high state autonomy, a powerful and resourced public bureaucracy, real state capacity to implement policy over the objections of key social groups, or a recognised ability to speak for the public interest (Atkinson and Coleman 1989; Sotiropoulos 1995). It was not statism *as a structure of state-society relations* but statism as an adopted *policy-making strategy* of unilateralism and exclusion, geared towards what government actors regarded as greater policy efficiency.

Government unilateralism was encouraged by the limited autonomy of civil society, a wide range of interest organisations being dependent on party paternalistic control or government funding. With regard to patterns of interest organisation, the prevailing overall tradition has been one of pluralism (Kazakos 1991), albeit characterised by interest fragmentation of a *corporatist* equality: in the sense of the French word *corporatisme*, signifying 'the myopic and exclusive pursuit of short-term, sectional interests' (Hayward 1991: 383). Interestingly, in a continuum of national policy-making traditions across EC states, if one places a Scandinavian model represented by Sweden at one end of the continuum, defined by deliberative, rationalistic, open and consensual policy-making (Freeman 1985: 475), then Greece should lie exactly at the opposite end, being characterised by a tradition of state-unilateral, discontinuous or incremental (depending on the policy sector: see below), closed and dissensual policy-making.

In view of the above argument, focusing on the normative premises and implications surrounding interest organisation and state operational patterns, it appears that the combination of statist economic governance and fragmented pluralist interest organisation provides the most adverse mix as regards a 'network' mode of governance. Economic statism is associated with a deeply-held suspicion of state policy-makers towards interest groups, which, in the specific case of Greece, are considered to be narrowly self-interested, rent-seeking and politically motivated. Pressure pluralism, of a strong Southern European clientelistic hue, rests on a dissensual culture, whereby each particular interest group seeks to extract public resources at the expense of another. Notice that the combination has a vicious self-feeding, self-enforcing quality: state actors distrust societal interests, and keep them at arm's length from the policy process; being locked out, organised interests try to attract attention to their demands by mobilising in a vociferous and confrontational manner, which further strengthens the government's resolution to keep them out.

Chances of corporatism and the relevance of time horizon

A neocorporatist organisation of interests has not yet quite flourished in Greece.[2] Adversarial pressure politics have been predominant in the postauthoritarian decades, with trade unions being practically excluded from, or with a very low degree of participation in, policy-making. This is despite external signs resembling corporatist network structures, such as the vertical networks linking trade unions with ideologically similar political parties (Peters 1995), exemplified in the frequent election of former or acting trade union leaders in the higher echelons of the main party mechanisms and parliamentary groups. The important missing element differentiating the above pseudo-corporatism from a corporatist or, even more, a network type of governance, is the *animus* or culture of corporatism. Even in the banking sector where, on a cross-national European and EC scale, corporatism is widespread (Coleman 1994) and employee peak organisations are quite influential in sectoral policy-making, the Greek banking employee federation (OTOE) was largely excluded from the deliberation processes of banking policy. While the EC umbrella-organisation of national banking employee associations participated in the European Commission processes of banking legislation, the OTOE was excluded from both Greek expert committees on banking reform (in 1987 and 1992).

However, again in line with the alleged ascendancy of post-corporatist governance in Europe, varying nuances are now observable, and a dynamic of motion can be discerned. Since its liberalisation, the Greek banking sector has exhibited signs of a move in a sectoral corporatist direction, which given both time and the high degree of internationalisation of the financial industry, may form the precursor of a network type of sectoral governance. For instance, the Hellenic Bank Association took steps to upgrade its status into that of a representative peak organisation, institutionalising contacts among its members. In addition, the intense zero-sum politicisation formerly characterising the OTOE of the 1980s was relaxed in the 1990s in favour of a technocratically informed 'realistic' strategy of encompassing sectoral interest representation, and the institutionalisation of communication channels between bankers and employees was undertaken. No such progress was observable in the various industrial sectors affected by privatisation, where the militant strategy of party-incited 'total conflict' tended to prevail against compromise alternatives.

The latter comparison points to an additional parameter underlying governance evolution toward consensual and inclusive policy-making of a network type, namely the elapsed time length from the beginning of the application of a new policy paradigm. As reforms settle in sectors exposed to high transnational economic and policy interdependence, operational patterns tend to become established, leading to a less 'anxious' and 'insecure' attitude on the part of state policy-makers. The latter are faced with gradually less militant policy opponents as the broader issue network becomes exposed to the settling experience of a particular policy which initially represented radical change but slowly after some time acquires the features of a consolidated inevitability. Thus privatisers of the post-1993 PASOK governments faced considerably less reaction by opponent coalitions, in the same way that BoG deregulation policy was implemented in a more consensual policy arena at its later mature phase of implementation. This gradual soothing of intra-sectoral dissent forms an important structural prerequisite for a piecemeal transition towards network governance.

Incrementalism, paradigm shift and policy learning

The issue of acclimatisation to the application of a new policy paradigm refers to the question of an incrementalist style of policy-making (Lindblom 1979; Richardson and Jordan 1979: 18-24; Wildavsky 1975), an intriguing question indeed. Step by step policy change (where policies differ only marginally from the *status quo*) as a strategy of simplifying the analysis of possible options, results from the limited capacity of policy-makers to theoretically understand and evaluate relationships among relevant policy variables. This leads policy-makers to confine themselves considering only those variables (including values and consequences) that are of immediate concern (Gregory 1989: 140): or, in rational choice terms, to content themselves with a limited rationality of 'satisficing' rather than maximising solutions (Simon 1954). In Greece in the 1980s, two strong external indicators of a proclivity towards incrementalism could be discerned. One was the reluctance of Greek monetary authorities, until well into the 1980s, to completely abandon credit interventionism (despite its already visible perverse effects), instead of pursuing only marginal adjustments. The other was the governments' disinclination, until the end of the 1980s, to shift direction and begin contracting the large scope of the public enterprise sector (despite the obviously detrimental effect on budget deficits). But how can the above observation be reconciled with the radical break with the policy *status quo* represented by deregulation and privatisation? These lie quite clearly at the opposite end of the public policy-making continuum, forming a case of economic instead of incrementalist rationality.

The question is best dealt with by focusing again on the concept of policy paradigm (Hall 1993). Thus, the observation should be modified by asserting the existence of an incrementalist policy-making pattern, operating however *within the conceptual realm of the already established specific policy paradigm.* When various systemic pressures, such as the ones described earlier in the chapter, and including an adequate period of exposure to policy learning (Hall 1993: 278, 289), lead to a paradigm shift in the domestic policy system, then incrementalism is abandoned in favour of the new policy 'orthodoxy', implemented initially, in an adjustment phase, in a rationalist manner. However, when that new paradigm also becomes established, policy makers tend to return to the satisficing rationality of incrementalism, and refrain from analytically challenging the entire range of policy variables for the sake of marginal adjustments to environmental change (as all indications suggest for the BoG's monetary policies into the 1990s, but also for the limited privatisation of the post-1993 period).

In the conceptual framework of policy learning and acclimatisation to paradigm shift, the aforementioned notion of a time horizon has a significant impact upon the practice of governance and policy-making styles. Of the two cases discussed above, banking deregulation had a generous time horizon ahead, enjoying considerable policy stability and continuity. It was thus enacted by means of a gradualist strategy of piecemeal reform with predefined targets and, after a certain point, preordained deadlines. In a reform programme planned by BoG officials from as early as the beginning of the 1980s, objectives had been crystallised and policy experience had settled. Having had to cope with government reluctance for, if not outright opposition to, banking liberalisation for the entire first PASOK term, and being aware of its political subjection to government control, the BoG apparatus had been accustomed to operating cautiously, exploiting windows of opportunity created by government inertia, internal disagreement or lack of adequate technical control over deregulation policy specifics, and moving ahead. On the contrary, privatisation was drawing neither on a similar policy precedent nor on prior technical preparation. Operating in a time horizon of indeterminacy and a political context of high uncertainty, insecurity and conflict, being forced to rely on weak and internally fragmented organisational infrastructure for policy implementation, government privatisers felt compelled to act in a unilateral, exclusive and hasty manner, treating privatisation issues in a largely *ad hoc* fashion.

Conclusions

At one level, our discussion has offered a framework for understanding why Greek banking deregulation and privatisation policy-making did not evolve into network-type governance despite the Europeanisation of policy, the dynamics of transnationalisation of European policy communities and all similar processes already described, and notwithstanding the presence of EC/EU actors.

On a broader level, we have attempted to approach the question of governance transformation by paying particular attention to policy cultures and traditions operating as conceptual factors in structuring the perceptions, expectations and, finally, the behaviour of policy actors. Our cases have shown that in national settings or sectors with a traditionally dominant role of state actors in policy-making, those actors are highly reluctant to relinquish even part of their role to private interests. Even if the nature and scope of policy invites the involvement of diverse non-state domestic and international actors at various levels, national state actors will safeguard their sovereignty over the policy process in order to ensure the effectiveness of implementation, perceiving that notion of effectiveness in a manner highly conditioned by their surrounding governance traditions at the national level.

We have seen that the Europeanisation and convergence of policies was realised and transmitted to the national policy-making milieus through processes such as harmonisation, elite networking within transnationalised policy communities, peer pressure and policy emulation. However, while the formulation of such policies at the Community level is highly Europeanised, their implementation at the domestic level (i.e. their formulation and implementation into national policies) remains 'nationalised' and subject to the institutional and politico-economic particularities of the national policy arena. Rather than viewing national policy arenas as simply complementary to EU decision-making, or disregarding their dynamics as a mere implementation stage of European governance, we have offered evidence to substantiate the argument that national politics retains its predominant role, even if to a lesser degree, when it comes to making or constraining policy.

Thus, the spill-over of network-type policy-making to the national level is highly dependent upon domestically existing structures of governance, interest organisation, and their attendant normative conceptions. It is considerably enhanced by neocorporatist arrangements on the national or sectoral scene and discouraged, if not obstructed, by statist and pressure pluralist ones. Moreover, a transformation of governance into a network mode seems to be further discouraged – at least in the structural contexts of traditional exclusion of societal interests from policy-making – when the object of public policy is the reduction of the state, in the form of either deregulation or privatisation. However, viewed in its dynamic form, the evolution of a policy attitude towards further deliberation, more consensus, and greater inclusion of non-state actors, seems to be contingent upon the degree of development and maturity within the broader policy network (in the formal sense) of a new perception about the role of the state with regard not only to the economic but also to the policy process.

Notes

1 This is not to dismiss the argument that deregulation can signify 're-regulation' rather than a direct reduction of government control (e.g. Majone 1996). However, even if one agrees that deregulation may be followed by an increase rather than a decrease of regulatory authority, one should still have to concede that it is usually independent or semi-independent regulatory bodies that will carry this increased authority rather than government *per se*. In any case, the emergence of any such regulatory authorities in Greek privatisation was very limited; as for banking deregulation it offered a clear case of loss of government control over the banking system, followed by the gradual vesting of the Bank of Greece with institutional independence from government.

2 With the exception of agricultural cooperatives, where structures of state corporatism (Schmitter 1979) – or sectoral corporatism, in Lehmbruch's (1984: 60–4) taxonomy – were developed in the 1980s. See Mavrogordatos (1988). However, the question of classifying interest intermediation in postauthoritarian Greece is still debated, the dominant view holding that it should be characterised as state-corporatism (as opposed to societal corporatism / neocorporatism) due to the authoritarian historical roots of state–society relations (see Mavrogordatos 1988; Sotiropoulos 1995). Though such cursory reference here does not do justice to either of the two positions, I would counterargue that the term state-corporatism should be confined only to authoritarian regimes, and that the state-corporatist argument overestimates the degree of state control over organised interests and underestimates the latter's rent-seeking, *corporatiste* character. However, both positions agree that (especially since the mid-1990s) there are increasing instances of a neocorporatist type of intermediation.

12

RESHUFFLING POWER

The liberalisation of the EU electricity markets and its impact on the German governance regime

Rainer Eising

Reshuffling sectoral governance

In the second half of the 1990s, after years of controversial debates, both the European Community (EC) and Germany decided to liberalise their electricity markets.[1] These regulatory reforms fundamentally alter the established sectoral governance regimes. Such regimes can be defined as the 'totality of institutional arrangements – including rules and rule-making agents – that regulate transactions within and across the sector's boundaries' (Hollingsworth *et al.* 1994: 5). Compared to other sectors, the electricity supply regimes have been characterised by a high degree of state regulation, a strong presence of public enterprises, the exclusion of competition, the national character of the markets, and closed policy networks between sectoral and state actors. The utilities have displayed co-operative relations and long-term investment strategies based on the exclusion of competition.

This chapter analyses how these regimes are now reshuffled by the EC and the national regulatory reforms. It argues that the twin processes of liberalisation and Europeanisation fundamentally alter the institutionalised patterns of governance. *Liberalisation* is a type of policy which aims directly at the transformation of the governance regimes of the electricity supply industry (ESI). By introducing competition, it fundamentally changes the market relations and the investment criteria of the utilities. The regulatory reforms also reduce the range of energy policy options open to the member states and affect vital interests of the utilities in a sector which has long been able to resist major reforms.

The *Europeanisation* of policies affects different elements of the national governance regimes and transforms the institutional set-up of the member states to create a multi-level system. The competencies for the political governance of the sector are now distributed among the EC, national, and sub-national territorial levels. This means that the sectoral actors now have to be present at both the EC and the national level in order to represent their interests. Several analyses have already demonstrated that institutional structures shape the weight, preferences and strategies of actors (e.g. Thelen and Steinmo 1992: 8–9). Accordingly, these institutional changes are particularly relevant for a sector which has been deeply embedded in national economic structures and politico-administrative institutions. Therefore, this chapter analyses how the EC's liberalisation process and institutional structure impinge upon the preferences, power and decision-making routines of both sectoral and political actors.

On the basis of the case study, three generalisations about the impact of the Europeanisation and liberalisation processes can be formulated. First, the Europeanisation processes transform the relative weight of national actors. On the one hand, the leading national ministries play two-level games and have to compromise in EC negotiations. On the other, their autonomy *vis-à-vis* national interest groups and other ministries can be enhanced by the integration process (Grande 1994). However, the strengthening of the leading departments is contingent upon a number of additional factors, the most important being the legitimacy of the policy concept at stake and the effect of the proposal on the competitiveness of the member state and its industry.

Second, the European policy debates can gradually transform the preferences of member state and sectoral actors. On the EC level, the European Commission acts as a catalyst for the reassessment of national concepts of sectoral governance, even in the face of strong resistance from private and public actors. Third, within the sector, the Europeanisation and the liberalisation processes have contrary effects: on the one hand, the introduction of competition enhances the role of formal governance mechanisms (contracts as well as mergers and acquisitions) on product markets; on the other, increased involvement in EC associations strengthens the importance of informal elements (such as trust, fairness and self-restraint) in the sectoral co-ordination processes.

In the following sections of the chapter, first, a typology of sectoral governance regimes is developed, then the German governance regime is outlined. This is followed by an analysis of the development of EC liberalisation, and then, finally, an explanation of its repercussions on the German sector.

The sectoral governance regime of the German electricity supply industry

Sectoral governance regimes in the European Community

Compared to other sectors, the electricity supply industry has some particular technological and economic features: electricity cannot be stored and must be generated in parallel with consumption; its supply is highly capital intensive and based on networks regarded as natural monopolies; and generation, transmission and distribution require a high degree of technical and organisational co-ordination. These factors mean that the supplying of electricity has largely been exempted from competition. From early on, the main principles underlying its governance regimes were the provision of a secure and an economic supply. During the last twenty years these principles have also included environmental protection. Significant differences among the member states affect the relevance of the different principles, the role of different primary energy sources, the size of markets and the extent of foreign trade (McGowan 1993). Along with geographic and geological factors, the main origin of these differences can be traced to the role of the state. Because of its economic weight, its network characteristics and its relevance for primary energy sectors, the ESI has been heavily regulated by state actors. Political regulation not only applied to the natural monopoly parts of the sector, but also to the use of primary energy sources and environmental protection.

In the EU member states, two types of governance regimes emerged before the regulatory reforms were launched from the late 1980s. In some countries the supply of electricity was co-ordinated by a vertically integrated public utility (France, Greece, Ireland, Italy, Portugal and the United Kingdom (until 1990)). These countries also displayed a strong preference for state activities in the economy. In the other member states, the ESI has been made up of a multitude of public, private or mixed companies, whose activities are co-ordinated by contracts and associations. Within these countries, public law has been much more important for political governance than in the vertically integrated sector countries. But in both regime types competition was restricted and foreign trade rather limited, with prices varying greatly between the member states.

The institutional structure of political governance in Germany

The international variations in the electricity industry indicate that technical, geographical and economic factors do not determine the patterns of sectoral governance. In Germany, the main mechanisms of sectoral governance evolved decentrally. Due to the local start of the technology in the late nineteenth century and because of the federal structure of the German state, they emerged through the economic activities of firms and through negotiations among the utilities, the states and the municipalities (Evers 1983; Gröner 1975). Even the energy law (*Energiewirtschaftsgesetz*, EnWG), formulated in 1935 under National Socialist rule, must be regarded as a compromise among the large utilities, the political actors, and the municipalities. Nevertheless, it introduced the *central* economic regulation of the sector.

Within the Federal Republic, the patterns of sectoral governance were adjusted to the 'semi-sovereignty' (Katzenstein 1987) of the new political system, and changed only incrementally. The energy law was scarcely modified, and the sector's established contractual arrangements were exempted from German competition law (*Gesetz gegen Wettbewerbsbeschränkungen*, GWB). The system of concession and demarcation contracts provided for closed franchise and bulk supply areas. In the 1980s, the fourth and fifth amendments to the GWB changed the legal framework only slightly, strengthening the position of the industrial consumers and of the municipalities *vis-à-vis* the regional and interconnected utilities.

Within the Federal Government (*Bundesregierung*), a high degree of ministerial autonomy (*Ressortprinzip*) makes horizontal co-ordination among ministries difficult. In the Federal Economics Ministry (*Bundesministerium für Wirtschaft*, BMWi), the energy policy division is responsible for the sector. The high degree of economic regulation means that the division maintains close relations with the sectoral actors. In contrast, the basic policy division (*Grundsatzabteilung*) is characterised by its strong economic liberalism. It is responsible for overall economic policy, the '*Ordnungspolitik*'.[2] In addition, the Federal Cartel Office (*Bundeskartellamt*) has powers to enforce the GWB. The implementation of the energy law and of some aspects of the competition law rest with the *Länder* ministries. The provisions for the review of political and regulatory decisions by the various lower and higher courts limit the autonomy of the political actors and may transform political conflicts into legal ones.

The decentralised and interlocked character of the institutional set-up has immediate consequences for the sector. It not only constrains the capacity for action of the various political actors, it also introduces different decision logics and cleavage lines into the political governance of the sector: party competition, administrative and territorial interest mediation, and judicial decision logics. The impact of these decision logics varies depending on the issue. This institutional segmentation is often regarded as an important cause of an ineffective regulatory review (Evers 1983).

In other policy areas, previous studies have shown that the continuous vertical interaction among the federal, state and local levels led to a harmonisation of perceptions and a common policy understanding (Scharpf, Reissert and Schnabel 1978: 102). In general, this also holds good for the interaction among the regulatory authorities. However, deeply rooted value conflicts about nuclear energy, and the strengthening of the environmental dimension within the German party competition, brought to light the limits of consensual decision-making in the federal system. At the federal level, the governing coalition made up of the Christian Democrats (CDU/CSU) and the Liberal Party (FDP) favoured the use of nuclear energy, while the Social Democrats (SPD) and *Bündnis 90/Die Grünen* (the Greens) preferred a phasing-out of nuclear plants. In their *Länder* governments and at the federal level, the opposition parties also emphasised the significance of energy efficiency and renewable energies.

The institutional structure of the sector

For the self-regulation of the sector, four governance mechanisms are of prime importance: firms, ownership linkages, associations, and the contracts which perpetuate the exclusion of competition. To a large extent, the development of the sector was path dependent. The configuration of the governance mechanisms emerged through the interaction of the network characteristics with the segmented structure of the German state and the interventionist philosophy of the state actors. As a result of this pattern, the German governance regime is still marked by a strong presence of municipal and state owned companies and extensive ownership linkages among the utilities. After the Second World War, the foundation of sub-sectoral associations institutionalised specific cleavages in the sectoral regime: the regional utilities, the municipal utilities and the large integrated generators and transmission companies (*Verbundunternehmen*) all founded their own associations which perpetuated sub sectoral orientations.

The development of the sectoral associations modified the pre-war structure to a limited degree. The Association of German Electricity Supply Companies (*Vereinigung Deutscher Elektrizitätswerke*, VDEW), already founded in 1892, was re-institutionalised in 1950. The sectoral association is very comprehensive. In 1993, it had 658 member companies responsible for about 99 per cent of all electricity generation, transmission and distribution.

The nine large utilities which make up the Association of Grid Companies (*Deutsche Verbundgesellschaft*, DVG) own the high-voltage transmission grids and control inter-regional and foreign trade. In 1993, the eight utilities of the old Länder accounted for 81 per cent of electricity generation, and 34 per cent of the distribution to the final consumer (Schiffer 1995: 166). This means that, despite the large number of firms, the sector is highly concentrated in generation and transmission. The size of the *Verbundunternehmen* varies from large municipal firms, such as HEW Hamburg, Bewag Berlin to the largest German utility, the RWE Energie AG. Only PreussenElektra is fully privatised. The states and the municipalities hold shares in the other firms, even if the states gradually withdraw from public ownership.

A network of interlocking ownership links the large utilities and the regional utilities (Klöcker 1985) and extends vertically into the coal and nuclear industries.[3] In 1993, the fifty-six regional companies of the Association of Regional Energy Utilities (*Arbeitsgemeinschaft Regionaler Energieversorgungsunternehmen*, ARE) accounted for 9 per cent of electricity generation, and 39 per cent of distribution. They depend heavily for their electricity deliveries on the large utilities. Ownership linkages also result in close co-operation between the ARE and the DVG. The almost 800 members of the Association of Municipal Utilities (*Verband Kommunaler Unternehmen*, VKU) accounted for 10 per cent of generation and 27 per cent of distribution in 1993. The VKU maintains interlocking directorates with the other municipal federations, for example, the Association of Local Authorities of Cities (*Deutscher Städtetag*). It also has close relations with the gas and water association (*Bundesverband Gas und Wasser*) which organises a multitude of municipal utilities. Compared to the ARE, which has roughly the same economic weight, the VKU is highly influential. First, its political weight rests on the position of the local authorities in the German public administration, 'local self-administration' (*kommu-*

nale Selbstverwaltung) being constitutionally guaranteed. Second, and most importantly, owing to the local party governments the local public enterprises have close ties with the different parties. This is particularly true for the CDU/CSU and the SPD, while it applies less to the FDP and *Bündnis 90/Die Grünen* who are not as strongly represented on the local level.

Among the different associations, there are well established 'channels of communication and conflict resolution' (Padgett 1990: 183). Sectoral co-ordination is facilitated by three factors: ownership linkages, the exclusion of competition, and the high degree of personal continuity in the sectoral association work of the utilities. In general, the VDEW represents the whole sector. The sub-sectoral associations and the large utilities emphasise that they act only when the VDEW does not or cannot. But the high degree of interest differentiation across several dimensions – ownership, sub-sector group, size, function, primary energy base – renders the formulation of common positions on various issues difficult (interviews ARE, VDEW, VKU, DVG, RWE Energie AG). The representative status of the VDEW is under-mined by sub-sectoral associations as well as by the large utilities. Their investment power gives them considerable political weight and allows them to shape discussions which affect the whole sector. Thus, the three largest utilities in the old Länder, RWE Energie, VEBA/PreussenElektra and the Bayernwerk, were the central sectoral actors when the governance regime in the former GDR was transformed. By now, they are the main owners of the VEAG which generates most of the electricity in the new *Länder*. The municipalities could only enter the field after they had provoked a recom-mendation from the German Constitutional Court (Richter 1995).

The large industrial consumers are represented by the Association of Industrial Energy Consumers and Generators (*Verband Industrielle Energie- und Kraftwirtschaft*, VIK). It organises about 70 to 80 per cent of industrial energy consumption and about 90 per cent of industrial energy genera-tion. The most important sectors are the chemical and hard coal industries. Through their sectoral peak associations, many VIK members are repre-sented in the Confederation of German Industry (*Bundesverband der Deutschen Industrie*, BDI), which provides a forum for communication because it also includes the members of the DVG. In 1979, under pressure from the Federal Economics Ministry and the Federal Cartel Office, the VDEW negotiated a sectoral association agreement with the VIK and the BDI. It lays down the principles governing the trade of electricity between utilities and industrial firms, and has been amended four times.

The liberalisation of the EC electricity markets

The Commission's first steps

The previous section has shown that the ESI is heavily regulated and that the sectoral actors have developed close ties with the national political actors. In great contrast, despite its legal powers, the EC hardly played a role in the governance of the sector until the mid 1980s (Andersen 1993: 138). The legal bases of the EC's energy policy are spread over the three treaties: EURATOM, ECSC and EC. So far, there is no legal provision for a Community energy policy in the EC treaty. Due to the emphasis of the member states on their national autonomy, the role of the Commission's Energy Directorate General (DG XVII) was mostly restricted to the formulation of studies and forecasts.

Only the Internal Market Programme encouraged the extension of the liberalisation rationale to those economic sectors which had previously been exempted from competition, such as transport, telecommunications and electricity (Aspinwall, in this volume). In 1988, the Commission identified the most obstacles to an Internal Energy Market as being in electricity and gas. It therefore envisaged the comprehensive application of Community law to these sectors, and set as its goal free trade between member states (Kommission 1988: 20). Just one year later, DG XVII presented four draft proposals which already introduced a few competitive elements into the sector, namely, directives on the transit of electricity and gas and on price transparency throughout the Community. Of these proposals, the member states only objected to a regulation on investment notification, their reason being the interference with private investment decisions (*Agence Europe* 19 May 1990: 12).

The restructuring of the associational arrangements

Until these Commission initiatives the utilities were deeply embedded in the national institutional configurations, and had developed close ties with the national political actors. To them, the Commission proposals signalled the beginnings of a new mode of political governance and completely transformed their relevant political arenas. The proposals formed a new policy sharply diverging from their national regimes and triggered a major restructuring of the associational arrangements. The overwhelming majority of the utilities wanted to preserve their national regimes and feared further initiatives by the Commission which were associated with substantial costs and the reshuffling of the established governance regimes. Accordingly, high-ranking representatives of major utilities, who already co-operated in rather technical international and European associations, developed plans for an EC association.

In 1989, the European Grouping of the Electricity Supply Industry (EURELECTRIC) was set up, to organise national associations as well as utilities. In addition, in 1992 local public energy suppliers from five member states formed the *Conféderation Européenne des Distributeurs d'Energie Public Communaux* (CEDEC) under the strong leadership of the German VKU. It vehemently opposed the Commission's proposals and emphasised the public service duties of utilities because of its members' linkages with the localities (CEDEC interview). Unlike most of the EURELECTRIC and CEDEC members, some utilities perceived the Commission initiative as an opportunity to reform their old regimes, while a few distributing companies hoped to benefit from the EC regulatory reform and improve their market position by reducing their dependence on monopoly suppliers. In 1991, the *Groupement Européen de Sociétés et Organismes de Distribution d'Energie* (GEODE) was formed predominantly by Spanish and French distribution companies. The GEODE members wanted to obtain rights to generate electricity themselves and to purchase it from generators of their own choice. In a similar move, Dutch distributors had already initiated legal cases against the trade monopoly of the Dutch transmission company in the 1980s.

Of these three associations, EURELECTRIC has the advantage of being highly comprehensive. It represents about 95 per cent of the EC's electricity utilities. But as in many other EC associations, this goes hand in hand with a disadvantage in that its membership is very heterogeneous. The national differences rendered the formulation of a common position and an active representation of interests difficult. Therefore some large utilities, such as Electricité de France, RWE AG and VEBA/Preussen Elektra AG, and some national associations such as the VDEW and the British Electricity Association, set up their own offices in Brussels. Because of the cleavage lines within the association EURELECTRIC was restricted to a defensive position throughout the liberalisation process. The large majority of its continental members initially advocated the value of the *status quo* (EURELECTRIC 1991). But its British members supported the Commission proposals from the outset because the British sector had already been liberalised in a national reform in 1990. Some continental utilities also expected advantages from liberalisation, with the Dutch distributors anxious to loosen their dependence on their suppliers. Finally, the ongoing debate on the EC level gradually raised the awareness of an uneven distribution of costs and benefits of the regulatory reform among the EURELECTRIC members. Genuine economic interests therefore came to the forefront of the debate within the association and forestalled the formulation of joint position papers.

Techniques of consensus formation in the European Community

As it had indicated in its previous initiatives, the Commission developed a major proposal for the liberalisation of the EC electricity and gas markets. After an extended debate covering both procedures and content, it presented a far-reaching proposal for a directive on the basis of Article 100a (EC) to create an Internal Energy Market (Kommission 1991). It emphasised a step-by-step approach and the use of the co-decision procedure. The choice of this procedure was a signal that the Commission did not wish to proceed unilaterally on the basis of Article 90 III (EC) without consulting either the European Parliament or the member states. Taking as a precedent its opening up of the telecommunications market, DG IV (Competition) had suggested this strategy. But the other institutions and also parts of the Commission regarded it as illegitimate.

The three core elements of the proposal mainly introduced competition into the generation of electricity, which has a 50–70 per cent share in the total cost of supply.[4] The first of these elements, subject to some restrictions, was that large industrial consumers and distribution companies would be given statutory access to the networks and enabled to purchase electricity from a generator of their choice: in other words, third party access (TPA). Second, exclusive rights for the construction of power stations and networks would be abolished and replaced by a non-discriminatory authorisation procedure. Finally, to prevent cross-subsidies between different activities, the management and accounting procedures of vertically integrated utilities would be separated, a process known as unbundling.

The directive proposals provoked widespread opposition from the utilities and the member states. The member states' orientations were shaped by the long stability of their national regimes which had excluded competition. In their opinion, the radical Commission proposals were incompatible with their established regimes and long-standing orientations. Most of them refused to allow the introduction of TPA in particular. Only the United Kingdom and Ireland were clearly supportive because they had already liberalised their sectors or planned to do so. Various member states also feared a negative economic impact on their national sectors arising from the opening of the markets. Due to the heterogeneity of the national sectors with state monopolies on the one hand and more segmented sectors on the other, the reciprocity of the market opening in all of the member states became a major issue in the liberalisation debate.

Even though they were heavily disputed, the Commission proposals at the same time forced a European debate upon the member states and an intense exchange of information. The protracted discussion covered every single aspect of electricity supply in any member state. This caused some member states to reassess their established governance regimes and gradually opt for the liberalisation. Throughout this debate, DG IV stressed its competition policy mandate so as to maintain a high degree of pressure on the member states and the European Parliament (*Financial Times Energy Monthly* 53/15 (May 1993)). But in order to allow for a political compromise in the Council, it refrained from starting legal procedures against the export and import monopolies in some member states until 1994. In addition, it needed the support of the European Court of Justice (ECJ) for such a proceeding and could not predict the content of a Court decision on the internal energy market. In two earlier key judgements on utilities – Corbeau and Almelo – the ECJ had argued that utilities could be exempted from competition in order to maintain 'sufficient financial equilibrium to guarantee the provision of public services' (Hancher 1994: 4). But the Court had passed the burden of proof back to the national courts without specifying in detail the criteria for sufficient financial equilibrium. The interpretations of these judgements differed widely across the economic actors, the member states and the Commission (Hancher 1994; Le Nestour and Zinow 1994). Legal strategies to open up the market or to maintain the *status quo* therefore did not appear entirely credible.[5] For all of the actors, political negotiations among the Community institutions promised a higher degree of control over the outcome than a legal strategy.

In this highly controversial debate among the Commission, the member states and the utilities, the European Parliament (EP) stressed the traditional orientations of the national governance regimes. In the Parliament's first reading of the Commission proposal, its largest group, the Socialists, emphasised the value of the established regimes and the public service aspects of the electricity sector (EP 1993a, 1993b). The European People's Party, which favoured more competition, mainly abstained from the vote in order to allow a position to be taken by the EP. As a result the EP strengthened the position of the utilities and of those member states with a high degree of state control over the sector. But it was evident from the parliamentary parties' voting behaviour that the EP was unlikely on its second reading to reach the absolute majority required to amend or to reject the Council's common position. As a consequence, the Commission included in its own amended proposal only those elements of the EP's proposal which would not run against the spirit of market integration (Kommission 1993).

Following the production of the amended Commission proposals, the highly controversial discussion was continued in the Council of Ministers. In general, the major cleavage was between those member states with vertically integrated utilities and a preference for central planning, and those with more decentralised regimes who emphasised the introduction of competition more strongly. The first group consisted mainly of France, Greece, Italy, Spain and Belgium. In the beginning, the second group consisted only of the United Kingdom, but they were later joined by Germany, the Netherlands, Sweden and Finland.

France and Germany were the main antagonists. While France feared the repercussions of liberalisation on its nationalised regime, Germany dwelt on the economic consequences arising from a market opening in the context of heterogeneous national regimes. The German utilities feared an inflow of French electricity because of the high excess capacity and price advantages of the French state monopoly Electricité de France (EdF) (Harms 1987) on the one hand, and the closure of the French market on the other, because of the high degree of vertical integration in the French sector. The French government and EdF perceived liberalisation as a threat to the fundamental principles of the French governance regime (*Agence Europe* 24 March 1995), namely the ability to conduct long-term planning, energy autonomy based on nuclear power, long-term security of supply and equal treatment of the same customer categories throughout the country.

Nevertheless, even in France the EC debate and also the advent of the new conservative government led to a reconsideration of the national governance regime. In late 1993 the French industry ministry published the outcome of its deliberations, the *Rapport Mandil,* which concluded that the major principles of the French governance regime should be preserved. It also proposed, however, to abolish the foreign trade monopoly of EdF and to improve the market access of some independent generators (Mathis 1995). On the basis of this report, France proposed an alternative to the Commission model, calling it the 'Single Buyer' model. According to a study it had ordered the Commission's own model led to a far higher degree of competition than the 'Single Buyer' (EWI 1995). The Commission was now afraid that the debate might be further delayed. At this point, in order to increase pressure on the Council, DG IV commenced infringement procedures against import and export monopolies in France, Spain, Ireland, Italy and the Netherlands.

After the French proposal, the need for the reciprocity of the market opening in all member states was strongly emphasised by some Council members and by the Commission. Both competition models, it was claimed, should guarantee a similar degree of market access, market results and customer choice. The successive solutions to many detailed problems in the directive and further compromise proposals progressively enhanced the willingness of the member states to agree to a settlement. Due to the problem-solving and moderation strategies in the Council debate, at the end of 1995 some member states, namely the United Kingdom, Sweden, Finland and Denmark were willing to compromise (*Agence Europe* 21 December 1995). Franco-German disagreements over the compromise position still threatened to forestall agreement, which was only achieved after bilateral consultations between the French and German heads of state. These two actors were not bound by sectoral considerations; their agreement to the liberalisation was motivated by broader considerations of Franco-German relations and the integration process. They did not change the content of the Council debate however. The Council of Ministers managed to agree on a directive based on the prior compromise proposals and the new bilateral understanding.

The directive provides for a minimum market opening and allows the member states to choose between alternative competition models. From 1999, they have to accept industrial consumers with a consumption of 100 GWh per year as eligible consumers. Moreover, between 1999 and 2003 they must gradually open their markets from 25 per cent to 33 per cent of national consumption. This degree of market opening is based on the share of aggregate EC consumption held by industrial consumers above certain thresholds (40 GWh, 20 GWh, 9 GWh). The member states themselves decide whether industrial consumers below the 100 GWh threshold and distributing companies are to be treated as eligible consumers. To regulate the network access, a strongly modified Single Buyer model and a form of Negotiated Third Party Access (NTPA) were established as alternatives to the regulated TPA. In the NTPA model, the conditions for network access are not statutory but are instead negotiated between the eligible consumers and the utilities. As an element of 'negative reciprocity', a member state can refuse to allow delivery contracts between a supplier from another member state and a national consumer if the latter would not be eligible as a consumer in the other member state (European Parliament and Council 1996).

The formulation of the directive on the internal electricity market after a protracted and highly controversial debate provides important evidence that involvement in the EC negotiations can gradually alter the preferences of the member states, and transform fierce national resistance against Commission proposals into support for an EC solution. The EC compromise has been aided by the routine problem-solving and consensus mechanisms in the EC institutions, and the great legitimacy of market integration and the liberalisation doctrine. Even if the directive allows the member states to choose between several alternatives and provides only for a partial market opening, it introduces competition into the sector and thereby fundamentally alters the established sectoral regimes. The strong modification of the original French 'Single-Buyer' indicates that member states opting for this concept will not be able to evade the aim of market integration which the directive implies.

The repercussions of EC liberalisation on the German regime

The EC's liberalisation programme has had important repercussions on the governance regime of the German electricity sector: Their involvement in the regulatory reform process has gradually changed the preferences of the political and sectoral actors for the governing principles of the sector. Due to the Europeanisation processes, the autonomy of the leading ministries *vis-à-vis* other ministries and sectoral actors was strengthened to a limited degree, and within the sectoral associations' decision processes, fairness and trust became more relevant.

The changes in political governance

Until the EC initiative, the attitude of the Federal Government towards the German ESI was shaped by the traditional patterns of political governance, and the established governance regime was extended to the new *Länder*, even though major reforms were already under way in the UK. In a mainly symbolic reform, the Federal Economics Ministry wanted to integrate environmental protection into the Energy Law in the early 1990s. It was felt that it should complement the established principles – the security and affordability of supply – but the inclusion of this new principle should not allow environmental considerations to enter into the implementation process, and nor should new environmental legislation be introduced. And lastly, according to the Federal Economics Ministry, the competition law already warranted a sufficient degree of competition and additional amendments to it were not envisaged (Cronenberg 1991: 45).

Therefore, all of the political actors in the Federal Government, the parties, and the *Länder* were very hesitant with regard to the EC proposals on the Internal Energy Market. They welcomed the procedural principles outlined by the Commission, but as regards the core elements of the proposal, they emphasised the heterogeneity of the national governance regimes and the need to maintain the long-standing sectoral principles. In accordance with the position of the German sectoral actors, they insisted on the reciprocal aspect of liberalisation:

> the Federal Government welcomes the fact that the EC Commission wants to discuss its plans for the introduction of more competition in the network-bound energies with the member states. The proposals require careful examination. The Federal Government assumes that the path towards greater competition in the Internal Energy Market will be pursued reciprocally in the different member states. Equal opportunities for the different utilities must be guaranteed, and the attainment of security of supply, environmental protection and affordability must be ensured.
>
> (Bundesministerium für Wirtschaft 1991: 97)

Nevertheless, some state actors gradually changed their preferences and regarded the EC debate increasingly as a chance to reform the German regime. The close interaction at EC level, ranging from the energy group (consisting of officials from the national ministries) to the Energy Council itself, had led to a review of the established practice of political governance. As a result of the liberalisation programme, the frequency of the energy group meetings increased from three or four times a year to once or even twice a week (BMWi interview). The political actors' awareness of alternative governance regimes and their economic potential was greatly increased. The attitude of the energy division, which had been characterised by its close interaction with the sectoral actors, shifted towards a more positive evaluation of a competitive regime. Within the ministry, an overall consensus for the introduction of competition emerged.

The acceptance of the concept of liberalisation was greatly aided by three other conceptual factors. First, British privatisation from 1990 onwards had an important demonstration effect: it showed that competition could be introduced into the electricity sector without endangering a secure supply, and was greatly esteemed by the BMWi officials. The British reform completely undermined the general argument that competition could not really work in the sector due to its economic and technical features. Second, in Germany the deregulation commission, consisting of economic experts, presented a report on the network-bound energies in March 1991. It also suggested the liberalisation of these sectors. Four of its proposals were accepted by the Federal Government and officially represented in the EC debate. Formally, the German position was based on the deregulation commission's proposals, but independent experts had been putting forward these proposals in part since the 1960s and 1970s (e.g. Emmerich 1978; Gröner 1975).

The input by the deregulation commission provided additional legitimacy for national reform, as did further reports by the *Monopolkommission* arguing in a similar vein. Finally, electricity liberalisation was linked to the broader debate about the competitiveness of German industry and the 'production site Germany' (*Standort Deutschland*) which had been launched by the national producers' association, BDI, in the late 1980s. This debate had gained strong momentum in the 1990s due both to the economic structural crisis in the new German *Länder* and the perception of growing pressure from economic globalisation. The acceptance of the liberalisation proposals was greatly facilitated by this climate of debate.

Furthermore, the new position of the BMWi was supported by important state and economic actors. The Federal Cartel Office also developed an active liberalisation policy and, on the basis of German and EC competition law and in line with the Federal Economics Ministry, it brought test cases on the contractual arrangements and on third party access (Markert 1996). But to date the courts have not agreed with the Federal Cartel Office's changed opinion. Important interest groups also supported the move towards liberalisation and pressed for change. Large industrial consumers in the VIK, the BDI and smaller economic consumers in the German Federation of Chambers of Commerce (*Deutscher Industrie-und Handelstag, DIHT*) demanded reductions in their energy prices.

In January 1994, in parallel with the EC debate, the Federal Economics Ministry put forward a draft proposal for a new energy law and amendments to competition law which would liberalise the German sector. In so doing it was deliberately playing a two-level game (see Putnam 1988) and intended to advance the EC discussion, which was stagnant at the time. The content of the proposal was heavily influenced by its involvement in the EC debate, and by the proposals of the deregulation commission (BMU and BMWi interviews).

However, despite the institutional transformation the further decision process was marked by the interlocked and decentralised character of the 'semi-sovereign' German state (Katzenstein 1987). First, the anticipated consequences of the reform forestalled an agreement within the Federal Government where it was generally expected that liberalisation would lead to a higher degree of concentration and vertical integration. The planning horizons of the utilities would shift from capital intensive and long-term considerations to cost-oriented short and medium-term calculations. In addition, the ability of political actors to regulate the use of primary energy sources such as renewables, coal, or nuclear energy would be more limited. But most important was the impact on the municipalities, which voiced public-interest arguments against the reform. Localities who generated electricity themselves feared 'cherry-picking' of large consumers in their supply areas by the regional and inter-connected utilities. As a consequence, their energy-efficient combined heat and power schemes might be endangered. There might also be a rise in the prices to captive household and small economic consumers. The abolition of exclusive rights in concession contracts might also result in a loss of income from concession fees which in 1995 amounted to 6 billion DM. Altogether, the loss of earnings from their energy supply activities would endanger the usual cross-subsidies to other activities such as the local public transport system (VKU 1994).

Due to the political status of the municipalities and their associations, these considerations were accepted by the political parties, the Federal Council, and the Federal Ministries. The Federal Ministry of Finance (*Bundesministerium für Finanzen*, BMF) and the Federal Ministry of the Interior (*Bundesministerium des Inneren*, BMI) were concerned because of the financial consequences. The Federal Ministry of Urban Planning and Construction (*Bundesministerium für Raumordnung, Bauwesen und Städtebau*, BMBau) feared the introduction of inter-regional price differences. The Federal Ministry for the Environment (*Bundesministerium für Umwelt, Naturschutz und Reaktorsicherheit*, BMU) even took advantage of the EC debate to put forward its own model of ecological liberalisation. Because of the resistance from the other ministries, the Federal Economics Ministry could not pursue its national reform plans and had them included in the Cabinet debate in 1994. Its efforts to submit a compromise proposal at EC level during the German Council presidency in 1994 were also thwarted by the other ministries (BMF, BMI, BMU and BMWi interviews).

Only the backing of the compromise at EC level by the Federal Chancellor allowed for an agreement within the Federal Government. The EC compromise had transformed the national debate into an implementation process. But as the EC directive included multiple alternatives and formed a framework directive rather than a detailed prescription, the 'semi-sovereignty' of the German political system (Katzenstein 1987) also shaped the further debate. After a series of negotiations with the other ministries and the sectoral interest groups, the BMWi presented a modified reform proposal in 1996 (*Bundesministerium für Wirtschaft* 1996a, b) which was acceptable to the other departments. Nevertheless, at that stage the reform still required the consent of the Federal Council because it was related to the administrative powers of the German states.

The SPD majority and the Green Party in the Federal Council strongly supported environmentally-friendly ways of generation and the decentralised energy supply concepts put forward by the municipalities. The Federal Council therefore demanded major changes in the government proposal (*Bundesrat* 1996) which included a much stronger role for the localities and priorities for renewable energies and combined heat and power. In order to avoid negotiations with the *Länder* governments which would be marked by the impact of party competition, the Federal Government further modified its proposal. It dropped provisions, *inter alia,* for the detailed legal regulation of network access, and opted for self regulation by the economic actors instead. Economic self-regulation by the sectoral actors and the industrial generators and consumers would, it believed, free it from pressures to negotiate with the Federal Council. According to the Federal Government, the proposal no longer required the consent of the *Bundesrat* which vehemently opposed this proceeding. The recourse to self-regulation strengthened the position of the Federal Government *vis-à-vis* the Federal Council and the opposition parties. The European linkage and the national de-coupling were the main institutional conditions of the reform. Both of them reduced the relevance of traditional veto points in the state system (Immergut 1990).

Nevertheless, the parliamentary parties in the coalition government added important changes to the proposal, thus reflecting the negotiation pressures within coalition governments. It was mainly the CDU/CSU fraction in the *Bundestag*, which to some degree changed the 'industrial' character of the proposal. Because of the ties with their local constituencies and their close relations with party members in the municipalities, they strengthened public interest provisions and secured greater consideration for the localities' interests. First, they ensured the further subsidisation of renewable energies. Second, they provided for the preservation of municipal income from concession contracts and also included the single buyer option in the proposal, thus allowing municipalities greater control over their supply areas. Third, they ensured that inter-regional price differentiation would be limited (*Deutscher Bundestag* 1997).

The German reform abolishes the long-standing contractual arrangements which ensured the territorial monopolies of the utilities. It also goes far beyond the minimum provisions of the EC directive. First, it does not restrict the range of eligible consumers. This means that, in general, household customers as well as industrial consumers and distributors are now eligible to choose their supplier. However, as the municipalities still maintain a large degree of control over their local supply areas and no provisions are included that ensure the market access of domestic customers, competition will for some time be limited to industrial consumers and distributors. Second, it covers both the electricity and the gas sector. The reform did not, however, formulate explicit rules for network access in the gas sector. This was left open until the content of an EC directive on the gas sector would be known. So far as the general regulation of network access in the electricity sector is concerned, the reform law allows both negotiated third party access and the single buyer model. The detailed rules for network access have been formulated in a VDEW, VIK and BDI agreement, thereby greatly enhancing the functional scope of their previous agreements.

To sum up, being embedded in the EC has gradually changed the established orientations of the German state actors. The EC negotiations triggered learning processes within the Federal Economic Ministry: the institutional transformation and its central position in the EC and in the national debate also increased its autonomy *vis-à-vis* these actors. Without the

EC liberalisation, the German reform would not have come about. However, it was not the institutional transformation alone which allowed the Ministry to pursue its reform path. First, the market integration project and the liberalisation doctrine enjoyed a high degree of legitimacy among all the political actors, and, second, if there had been no disempowerment of the Federal Council, the Federal Government would have had to make major concessions to the Social Democratic Party and to *Bündnis 90/Die Grünen*.

The impact on sectoral interest intermediation

The EC liberalisation not only had important effects on the co-ordination processes and the preferences of political actors; it also impinged deeply on sectoral co-ordination and the preferences of the sectoral actors. To a limited degree, the integration process and the foundation of EC interest organisations modified the formal organisation of the German sectoral associations and firms, and specific EC divisions, committees and working groups were established in each of the sectoral associations. Unlike most of the other sections, the EC divisions only focus on public affairs. As in the state system, the involvement in multi-level negotiations has changed the logic of opinion formation much more profoundly than the minor organisational changes indicate.

The German sectoral actors are now both represented in the EC association and present in Brussels themselves. The political strategies and access points of the sub-sectoral groups in the EC resulted from their embedded positions in the national regimes, and from the new EC sectoral association structure. EURELECTRIC focuses on contacts with the European Commission and with the committees of the European Parliament, while contacts with individual members of the EP are mainly dealt with by national associations and utilities (EURELECTRIC and VDEW interviews). In addition, the sub-sectoral organisations are present in Brussels as well: the VKU, for example, was not just a founding member of CEDEC but also extended its practice of party-political mobilisation to EC level, and maintains very good contacts with the different German MEPs. Some large utilities (e.g. RWE AG, VEBA/PreussenElektra AG) are physically present in Brussels, and have regular contact with the Commission. Their offices function as listening posts and process a large amount of information. But the changes in the institutional structure have not meant that national political actors have become less important for the sectoral actors, and the Federal Economics Ministry is still their main contact partner in the EC debate (VDEW, VKU, RWE Energie AG and DVG interviews).

At the national level, Europeanisation changed the logic of sectoral opinion formation to some degree. An interdisciplinary European division was already established within the sectoral association, VDEW, in 1978. Its proposals form the basis for the debate on EC measures and are highly significant for the formation of the sectoral position. In general, the association opinion is then formed through committee work. Until 1992 the work on EC policy was dispersed among various standing committees, then because of the relevance of the liberalisation proposals, a special committee on the 'Internal Energy Market' was established, along with a subordinate task force on 'electricity directives' (VDEW interviews).

The extension of the patterns of interest representation to the EC level has altered the processes of opinion formation in two ways. First, the national representative in the EC association has to have room for manoeuvre during negotiations in order not to preclude conceivable compromises. Second, due to the dynamic development of the EC debate, position papers must often be provided in a hurry. The VDEW staff in the European division and the leading executives in the relevant committees therefore often work directly with the EC institutions and associations without further consultation.

These two factors entail a loss of control for the other members, and the heads of committees and working groups gain a hegemonic position *vis-à-vis* the other committee members. In part, this development has been restricted by the extension of organisational routines to the European affairs of the association. In the first place, the sectoral cleavages are embedded in long-standing practices of co-operation. The emphasis of the Federal Government on the consultation of umbrella organisations has provided an incentive to search for common positions – even if they are on a least common denominator basis – and these positions form a binding framework for the representation of interests at EC level. Second, in controversial questions, the neutral behaviour of the sectoral association's staff *vis-à-vis* the different sectoral groups is regarded as highly important. Third, each of the sub-sectoral groups has representatives in different sections of the EC association. Finally, the heads of the committees must act and speak for the overall interests of the sector and not privilege their sub-group.

In addition to these changes in the decision processes, liberalisation also impinges to a large extent on sectoral cleavage lines and has changed the preferences of the sectoral actors as well. Early in the liberalisation debate, the VDEW managed to develop a unifying concept for all of its members, namely, reciprocity of the market opening in the Community. According to the association, liberalisation was aimed mainly at the decentralised regimes and excluded state monopolies (VDEW 1993). The German sector adopted the reciprocity argument as a defensive posture with three important functions.

First, the concept had an important internal function. Despite the latent differences among the sub-sectoral groups, each of the utilities was able to agree on reciprocity as a condition of 'fairness'. The concept therefore helped to maintain the unity of the VDEW. Second, externally it demonstrated this unity *vis-à-vis* the political actors. Even if not all of them agreed with the anti-liberalisation stance of the association, the political actors accepted the quest for reciprocity and the Federal Economics Ministry represented this position in the Council negotiations. Finally, the concept linked the success of the national reform to the outcome of the EC negotiations. Without an agreement at EC level, a process of national reform would not have been pursued by most of the political actors because it meant a unilateral opening of the German market.

However, the interlocked pressure for reform at two political levels led to the erosion of the sectoral consensus. The position of the VDEW was undermined by the different sub-sectoral groupings. While the VKU still opposed any kind of liberalisation, the regional and large interconnected utilities opted for the introduction of competition. Given the positions of the Federal Ministries and of the Social Democrats, the regional and inter connected utilities were afraid that the municipalities would also be exempted from the competitive elements of the new regime (DVG interview). They regarded the EC liberalisation as an opportunity to attack the control of the municipalities over the local supply areas and get direct access to industrial customers. Such an opening of the municipal areas of supply was unlikely to come about in a national reform. Consequently, both ARE and DVG demanded that the municipalities be included in the liberalisation process. An explicit fairness criterion was introduced to increase the credibility and legitimacy of their specific position. Thus, at both EC and national levels, the sectoral actors tried to transform the arguments about liberalisation into a debate about equity and fairness in order to legitimise their positions. The regional and interconnected utilities demanded a system of:

> undivided and fair competition in all EU countries and at all levels of generation and supply. A selective, one way pseudo-competition, where state monopolies – whether at a national, regional or municipal level – are justified by the 'public service' philosophy, is not acceptable in any case.
>
> (Esser 1994: 1–2)

As a consequence of their strategic move, the credibility of arguments denying the potential of competition in the electricity sector was even more impaired. The new opportunities the EC reform offered and the strong support of the municipalities within the Federal Government and the Federal Council paved the way for an interest coalition between interconnected and regional utilities on the one hand and the Federal Economics Ministry and major economic interest groups on the other, thereby forcing the localities into a defensive posture.

Conclusion

The Europeanisation and liberalisation of the electricity supply industry caused a major reshuffling of the sectoral governance regimes in all the member states. During the EC negotiations the programme for the Internal Energy

Market had already triggered a debate on national reforms in almost all of the member states. In some cases this resulted in sweeping reform plans, as in Germany, while in others, such as Belgium and France, the reform plans were more modest. These developments show that involvement in EC debates can change member state preferences for concepts of sectoral governance. Compared with other concepts in the EC – such as the network concept in research and technology policy – the success of the Internal Energy Market initiative was greatly aided by the legitimacy of the liberalisation doctrine as both the backbone of European integration and the dominant economic policy doctrine since the early 1980s. Because of the EC directive the member states now have to introduce major changes in their national regimes.

The Europeanisation of policies transforms the national institutional configurations and actor constellations into a multi-level system. In the vertical and horizontal negotiations, the leading national ministries are central actors and their scope for action is enhanced. The Federal Economics Ministry was able to transform the plans for a limited reform of the German energy law into a comprehensive reform of the German governance regime. But this argument must be qualified: first, a consensus must be achieved at the EC level as a pre-condition for an agreement at the national level. A significant strengthening of a constrained national ministry can only result from an agreement at EC level. If it cannot be attained, the leading ministry is also blocked at national level. The national actors negatively affected by the policy proposals therefore try to develop arguments which forestall an EC agreement. Such arguments relate not only to the substantive policy on hand but also to the very context in which it is situated, and the patterns of national political discourse change as a result: the heterogeneity of the EC member states and the related questions of subsidiarity, fairness and reciprocity then become central topics.

With their quest for reciprocity, the German sectoral actors were able to develop a position which was accepted by all the political actors, even if they did not share the sectoral opposition to liberalisation. The leading German ministry was obliged to accept this fairness criterion for the opening up of the EC market, and was unable to pursue a unilateral programme of national reform. To sum up: the agreement at EC level and the national reform were not solely based on the institutional strengthening of the Federal Economics Ministry in multi-level negotiations; they also hinged to a similar extent on the legitimacy of the liberalisation doctrine and the de-coupling of the reform from the consent of the Federal Council (and the opposition parties).

Owing to the Europeanisation of policies, the capacity for action of national interest groups is no longer limited to the national level but extends to the EC as well. The perceived costs of the liberalisation proposals and their clash with the national governance regimes led to a major restructuring of the sectoral association set-up. The utilities and the national sectoral associations influenced the content of the EC debate, and built both permanent and temporary coalitions with the various political actors at the EC and national levels.

The organisational domains and policy orientations of the political actors formed the basis of these coalitions. The interest groups introduced important principles and concepts into the debate, such as Negotiated Third Party Access, reciprocity and Single Buyer. Moreover, national interest groups can introduce elements of the EC debate into the national context, in order to improve their standing. Thus, for example, the 'French' Single Buyer model has been included in the German reform law because of the demands of the German municipalities.

Finally, the Europeanisation processes also impinge upon the patterns of sectoral co-ordination. In the national associations, the position of the company representatives in the committees is strengthened by their presence and their negotiating mandate in the European associations. So far as policies on which sub-sectoral groups hold divergent opinions are concerned, representation of the national sector in the EC becomes difficult. In order to prevent the German representative from undermining the sectoral position in the EC association, the VDEW relies on established practices of co-ordination and mechanisms of personal reputation. In sum, involvement in EC policy increases the importance of informal and personal factors in the sectoral association, and equity, trust, and fairness are strengthened as integrative mechanisms. But at the same time they are put under a greater strain because of the greater demands that are made on them.

Notes

This chapter presents the results of a research project on the 'Europeanisation of Economic Interests', which has been sponsored by the Fritz-Thyssen Foundation. I would like to thank the contributors to this volume for valuable comments, in particular Niels Sidenius, Mark Aspinwall and Beate Kohler-Koch.

1 The chapter focuses on the first pillar of the European Union.
2 The term '*Ordnungspolitik*' cannot be translated. The normative concept refers to the general relationship between the state and the economy. In the German understanding, it emphasises the predominance of market relations and self-regulation of economic actors in a general framework of state regulation which has to ensure the functioning of competitive mechanisms.
3 Until reunification, the RWE AG controlled about 80 per cent of German light coal production.
4 The share of generation in the total cost of supply varies mainly with the type of customer. For large consumers its share is larger, while for small consumers it is smaller, owing to the higher network costs.
5 This is also confirmed by the judgements of the ECJ on these export and import monopolies: the ECJ argued that these monopolies do not confirm to the rules on the free movement of goods and services. Nevertheless, they may be maintained because of the utilities' public service obligations.

Part IV

THEORETICAL, NORMATIVE AND COMPARATIVE PERSPECTIVES ON EUROPEAN GOVERNANCE

13

DEFENDING STATE AUTONOMY

Intergovernmental governance in the European Union

Klaus Dieter Wolf

Introduction: the theoretical puzzle

In the following article a conceptual framework will be offered for the explanation of two characteristic features of intergovernmental governance. The argument to be developed raises doubts as to whether European integration can really be expected to be heading towards a more horizontal or network type of governance. It starts out from the theoretical puzzle which is posed by the concurrence of the following two elements of intergovernmental governance structures: the high degree of self-commitment among national governments ('self-binding'), and the lack of participatory rights granted to non-governmental actors ('democratic deficit').

In order to solve this puzzle, one has to conceptualise national governments as strategic actors with an interest in themselves, rather than as neutral partners or mediators of social groups and their demands. From a two-level game perspective, linking intergovernmental and domestic interactions with each other, the willingness of governments to bind themselves in intergovernmental governance structures can be interpreted as a response to the domestic and transnational pressures exerted on them.[1] Taking into account the challenge these pressures pose to internal autonomy, self-binding intergovernmental co-operation, which conventional wisdom associates with a loss of state autonomy, may contribute to an overall gain in the autonomy of national governments. Applied to European integration, this approach claims to account for the extraordinary degree of self-binding among the European governments, as well as for the lack of democratic participation in the European Union (EU). Following the assumption that the system of governance in the EU serves as an institutional setting to maintain governmental autonomy *vis-à-vis* societal actors, including

KLAUS DIETER WOLF

the control over which other actors will be granted access in given functional contexts, there would obviously be limitations to more horizontal modes of governance in the EU.

The theoretical challenge inherent in the 'self-binding/democratic-deficit' puzzle of intergovernmental governance in the EU is that its two components cannot easily be accounted for on the basis of the same set of assumptions, no matter which theoretical perspective is applied. For realists, the loss of sovereignty consented to by national governments in the course of European integration poses severe difficulties. How can a process be explained in which nation states threaten their very existence by sacrificing more and more of their sovereignty, if it is to be believed that the struggle for self-preservation and independence is what foreign policy is all about? The democratic deficit causes less problems for the realist interpretation. National governments are not likely to be interested in non-governmental actors' interference in foreign policy-making, which is after all still the business of diplomats. From this perspective the dominant role of the European Council (or the Councils of Ministers) within the governance structures of the EU comes as no great surprise, and the national governments' lack of interest in further democratisation of the EU appears quite logical.

From a liberal point of view European integration makes much more sense. Under the conditions of globalisation and growing economic interdependence, individual states lose their problem-solving capacity, which they try to redress, on a higher level of aggregation, by establishing new forms of joint governance in the form of integrated policy-making structures. From this society-centred perspective, however, which regards national governments primarily as problem-solvers geared to meet societal demands as effectively as possible, the democratic deficit in the sense of weakening domestic democratic participation without re-establishing it on the community level is puzzling.[2] Why should the problem-solvers be interested in evading the demands of societal actors? If one prominent feature of this democratic deficit lies in 'the gap between the powers transferred to the Community and the efficacy of European Parliamentary oversight and control' (Williams 1991: 155), why are the governments of these democracies so reluctant to provide the European Parliament (EP) with the fundamental prerogatives of parliaments in a democracy? Instead, we observe a 'process of de-democratisation' (Czempiel 1991: 108), which is even more puzzling if we regard the idea of democratic participation and control as a dynamic driving force in its own right, and if we take into account the fact that the member states of the EU are a selection of nations who take pride in their particularly high standards of guaranteed domestic societal participation.

Contrary to the solutions which a liberal perspective can offer to this puzzle – that is, either to deny that there are any societal demands for participation at all, or to interpret the loss of democratic participation as an

232

unanticipated consequence of international governance – I will try to account for both sides of the puzzle as *intended* results of rational behaviour and as two sides of the same coin. This requires a theoretical framework in which the realist understanding of states as rational actors who want to survive in a world of states and therefore strive for autonomy is transferred to a liberal model of international relations, which takes into consideration the emergence and growing influence of a domestic and transnational civil society.

From this widened perspective, the changing relationships between governments and non-governmental actors due to processes of transnationalisation and democratisation lead to inter-state co-operation as a new form of strategic interaction. In the context of an emerging world society the state's sphere of autonomous action is endangered not only by other states, but increasingly by these very societal and sub-state actors.[3] Challenged by the emancipation of their societal and sub-state environments, governments develop a 'new *raison d'état*' (see Wolf 1995: 261), a common interest in instrumentalising intergovernmental governance structures for the maintenance of their internal autonomy. After some short references to the empirical phenomenon to be explained, the problems of a state-centred approach and a society-centred approach to cope with the self-binding/democratic-deficit puzzle are described. Finally, an integrated conceptual framework will be developed.

Governance in the European Union: the empirical starting-point for the solution of an analytical puzzle

The EU serves particularly well as an empirical illustration of the self-binding/democratic-deficit puzzle. On the one hand, there is little doubt that all its member states are characterised by a relatively high degree of societal participation in domestic policy-making processes. On the other however, the EU represents an unrivalled, highly integrated multi-level system of governance which has developed differently from ordinary international institutions 'by *pooling* national sovereignty through qualified majority voting rules and by *delegating* sovereign powers to semi-autonomous central institutions' (Moravcsik 1993b: 509). With the extremely high level of commitment from its member states, the EU seems to come closer than any other example to the ideal type of a supranational organisation. It has, however, been suggested with some justification that we should interpret this commitment as 'the pooling and sharing of sovereignty rather than the transfer of sovereignty to a higher level' (Keohane and Hofmann 1991: 13).

At the same time, the establishment of this multi-level governance system has led to a substantial shift of weight in favour of governmental and executive actors at the intergovernmental and supranational levels, negatively affecting the influence of non-governmental actors. The first problem is that the growing complexity has substantially reduced the *transparency* of decision-making processes, which is after all a *conditio sine qua non* for effective democratic participation. There is no Europe-wide public debate. Information is monopolised by governments. The dominance of executive and governmental actors is strongly reinforced by the 'comitology' structures of 'advisory, regulatory, and management committees staffed by national civil servants, . . . answerable to national governments, not to the Community institutions: European Parliamentary scrutiny is largely excluded from both policy-making and implementation' (Williams 1991: 155). Europeanisation has weakened parliamentary participation and control on the national level without re-establishing it at the Community level.

Perhaps most relevant in terms of the loss and recovery of internal autonomy, the Europeanisation of governmental politics has strengthened the position of national governments *vis-à-vis* societal demands. Even special interest groups have lost much of their impact. Due to the multiplication of bodies, channels and levels of decision-making, the target structure for external influences has changed. The number of important points of access has increased, and special interest groups have to address a complex administration with fragmented competencies (Grande 1996b: 383–6, Jachtenfuchs and Kohler-Koch 1996b: 25). The relationship between government and big companies, which used to be clientelistic and comprehensible on the national level, has become difficult to keep track of, and even more difficult to exploit. Since they are no longer the only decisive addressees for special interests, national governments can evade domestic pressure with reference to international and European commitments. Grande (Grande 1996b: 392) has labelled the 'gain of autonomy of governmental actors *vis-à-vis* societal interests, which results from governments' loss of autonomy in interdependent decision-making structures' the *paradox of weakness*.[4] Regardless of whether we look at it as unintended, or as the result of a new and sophisticated *divide et impera* strategy, which also includes a deliberate dispersion of responsibility in order to secure support by the transfer of protest, the observed fragmentation of competencies proves successful even against the most powerful societal pressures.

Taking these observations together, the Europeanisation of governance goes along with a process of de-democratisation. Only national governments and executive bodies at Community level take advantage of what looks like an unintended institutional maze. With the key to legislative power in the hands of the Council of Ministers, assisted by a Commission which holds a monopoly on new initiatives, a substantial part of European political power has been removed from the electorate. Of course the representatives of the national governments have been elected, but not in European elections about European issues:

As state actors pool their de facto authority over transnational space, they remove it from direct democratic control. Territorial electorates may still retain the formal right to 'unelect' their leaders, but the ability to translate this right into tangible policy change . . . is constrained by the commitments that states have made to each other.

(Wendt 1994: 393)

By this mechanism, legitimacy cannot just be transferred from the national to the European level. Of course the treaties have also been ratified, but political action in the EU is far more than the execution of programmes which emanate from ratified agreements. Of course there is the EP, but its influence on European legislation is still insignificant. In sum, basic democratic principles do not apply to the political system of the EU (Kielmansegg 1996: 53–4)

'State' and 'autonomy': terminological clarifications

Before different theoretical approaches to the self-binding/democratic-deficit problem are discussed, some terminological clarifications are necessary. The first one refers to the different notions of the 'state' referred to later in this article. A simple but fruitful distinction which has already been employed above is to conceptualise states either as *strategic* actors or as *functional* problem-solvers. This distinction helps to differentiate between the realist understanding on the one hand, according to which states are unitary rational actors trying to maximise their autonomy (or, to the same effect, striving for relative gains), and the liberal perspective on the other hand.

According to the liberal view 'the state' is not an appropriate unit of analysis, but is substituted by the functional concept of the political-administrative system. Interpreted as a functional sub-system of society, the state (or, to be more precise, the national government consisting of various elected and non-elected executive and bureaucratic bodies) has to provide public goods.[5] Governmental policies solely reflect societal needs. If the term 'state' is used in what follows, the different meanings realists and liberals ascribe to it have to be kept in mind. The integrated conceptual framework to be developed in the concluding section of this chapter will, to some extent, follow the liberal understanding of the state as a sub-system of society, but we will attribute to the political-administrative system a logic and interest of its own, an assumption which differs fundamentally from the liberal perspective.

The second clarification refers to the term 'autonomy', which will not be described as a property of a given entity, but as a specific pattern of entity–

environment interaction. Implying administrative discretion and self-assertion, political autonomy is the capability of an entity to translate its own policy preferences into authoritative actions (see Nordlinger 1981: 19; Simonis 1972: 293). It is assumed to rest on:

- the existence of preferences: an entity is autonomous to the extent that it can choose its own preferences
- the ability to translate one's preferences into collective actions: an entity is autonomous to the extent that political action in which it participates conforms to its preferences
- the ability to organise one's environment according to one's own preferences: an entity is autonomous to the extent that it can reduce the discrepancy ('*Spannungszustand*') between the preferred and the existing structures of the environment, or to the extent that it can maintain an existing harmony between the two.

Adaptation to the preferences of other entities and to the constraints of existing structures of the environment would be the opposite of autonomy, while *autarky* differs from autonomy because it pre-supposes the functional independence of an entity from its environment when it comes to satisfying needs or translating preferences into actions.

Raison d'état as the striving of rational states to maintain external autonomy in a world of states

As already indicated, according to the realist understanding, states act rationally in the sense of striving to maintain their autonomy in competition *with each other* in an international environment, conceived as an anarchic world of states (Waltz 1979: 204). From their systemic perspective, structural realists, in particular, do not address the *internal* autonomy of states as a factor by which the foreign policy preferences of governments are (in the sense of a significant causal relationship), or even should be (in the normative sense) influenced. Rather, foreign policy objectives are derived from given, objective constraints such as international anarchy, and described in terms such as 'national interest' or '*raison d'état*'. The law, dictated by its *raison d'état*, necessarily directs each state towards self-preservation and growth (Meinecke 1963: 2), or forces it into the role of a defensive positionalist (Waltz 1959: 198; Grieco 1990: 10). National interest and *raison d'état* are therefore not a sum of changing preferences at the disposal of societal decision-making, but are either 'naturally' given, for example by geographic conditions, or historically or culturally rooted variations of the same objective necessities of security and survival (Wolf 1995: 250–3). For more traditional realists, societal interference in the pursuit of the national interest can only be detrimental. For structural realists it is irrelevant.

Domestic factors have not been eliminated completely from the realist perspective.[6] In Mastanduno, Lake and Ikenberry's 'Realist theory of the state', 'international and domestic politics are interactive' (Mastanduno *et al.* 1989: 458), and the strategies states employ for their survival as states have internal and external addressees. In analytical terms, 'the state serves as an important independent or intervening variable between social and international forces on the one hand, and foreign economic policy on the other' (Ikenberry, Lake and Mastanduno 1988: 2). This realist, state-centred approach assumes that 'state officials have both international and domestic goals' which must be defined in terms of the pursuit of wealth and power under conditions of international anarchy (Mastanduno, Lake and Ikenberry 1989: 459). Although both the domestic and international constraints on the state are taken into account, external threats to survival can easily be derived and integrated into this framework, whereas problems of 'domestic stability' appear under-conceptualised. In any case, this is not an appropriate model to interpret state-society relations within the EU, because this relationship can hardly be conceived as being dominated by the conditions of international anarchy.

The puzzle of intergovernmental self-binding

When states are treated as integrated, unitary and the only relevant actors in international politics, autonomy needs to be addressed only as external autonomy, i.e. with regard to the sphere of inter-state relations. As a consequence, international governance is a phenomenon which has to be explained without leaving the '*Staatenwelt*' model of international politics. Remaining within these analytical boundaries, the transfer of national competencies to international governance structures can be analysed, for instance, as a preference of autonomy-seeking states in terms of alliance-building, through which one group of states may wish to increase its leverage in order to achieve relative gains *vis-à-vis* other states or alliances. The pursuit of the national interest does not preclude the possibility of co-operation in general. Realists would concede that self-binding is more likely in issue areas which are less relevant to external security ('low politics'), or for small states who can achieve relative gains *vis-à-vis* more powerful ones. But the puzzle increases with the degree of commitment involved in a given governance structure. The more binding international agreements are, the less likely they are to be implemented. Realists doubt that states ascribe much importance to international institutions. Playing a definitely prominent role in European affairs by even obstructing the exit option, European integration remains one of the biggest unsolved challenges for any realist research programme (see Grieco 1995: 26–30).

Looking at the EU as a traditional alliance has been one reasonable attempt to cope with this problem (see Waltz 1979 or Mearsheimer 1990). However, deriving European integration from U.S.-Soviet competition, or, after this variant of the 'balancing'-hypothesis had to be withdrawn due to the end of the Cold War, from transatlantic or European-Asian antagonisms, seems to overstress the *external* dimension of European integration ('strengthening the West in the context of the Cold War', or 'strengthening Europe in the context of transatlantic rivalry'). Concentrating on the more interesting *internal* dimension of the dynamics of European integration realists are at a loss: as Gehring (1994) has convincingly shown, living in the shadow of the political system of the EU provides an institutional environment within which it is not very plausible to derive the goals of state officials from the conditions of international anarchy. But realists have to deny the role of international institutions.

Grieco's (1995: 34–8) efforts to save realism by introducing a 'voice opportunity' hypothesis does not lead very far either. If integration takes place because it provides weaker states with the opportunity to escape stronger partners' domination, the puzzle remains why the stronger states should go along with it. Whereas self-binding remains a problematic phenomenon for realism (see Hellmann 1994), this paradigm can cope well with the other part of our puzzle: the democratic deficit. Although realism, with its assumption of states striving for autonomy, holds the key to understanding the other part as well, it fails to do so because it is not applied beyond the world of states. Therefore it must consider self-binding, the pooling or even transfer of sovereign powers as a *loss* (see Williams 1991: 155). Table 13.1 identifies the scope of the state-centred realist actor/context-of-interaction model.

International governance as a response of problem-solvers to globalisation and interdependence

The liberal conceptualisation of state-actors in international politics is guided by the ideal type of the problem-solver. This perspective is society-centred in two senses: on the one hand, the dynamics which are inducing an ever-increasing level of institutionalised co-operation in international relations are not primarily produced by states, but have their origin in societal (i.e. economic, technological) developments. On the other, this view subscribes to a pluralist theory of state-society relations, in which governments aggregate and satisfy societal demands for welfare, security etc. These needs are not objectively given, but result from a continuous struggle among competing societal groups.

In this approach the state as government is just one among other functional sub-systems of society, the specific function of which is to take care of

Table 13.1 Focus of a systemic, state-centred perspective

	interaction among states	*interaction among governmental and non-governmental actors*
states as strategic actors striving for autonomy	self-binding unlikely democratic deficit likely	self-binding likely democratic deficit likely
governments as problem solvers satisfying societal demands	self-binding likely democratic deficit unlikely	self-binding likely democratic deficit unlikely

general welfare and to provide public goods, and the specific feature of which is its society-wide decision-making authority. In an ideal-typical society-centrism, however, the political-administrative system serves societal needs without any interests of its own. Like transmission belts, national governments have to accommodate whatever societal demands are entrusted to them within the constraints of the international environment. In this liberal perspective, and in sharp contrast to the realist 'national interest' or '*raison d'état*', there can be no such thing as a natural pre-existing, objectively given 'national' or 'public interest'. In liberal democracies, any 'different groups within the polity [may] claim it as a legitimising symbol for their interests and aspirations' (George and Keohane 1980: 220), but the question of which societal preferences will be selected and translated into authoritative actions by governments is left open to domestic decision-making processes. Governments' public policies are understood 'primarily as a response to the expectations, demands, and pressures of those [societal groups] who control the largest proportion of especially effective resources' (Nordlinger 1981: 3).

From a radically society-centred perspective, the state is a 'handmaiden' (Krasner 1978: 6, see also Moravcsik 1993b: 481, or Wolf 1995: 257). If any self-interest is attributed to governments at all, it lies in the assumption that they seek to be efficient problem-solvers and providers of the common good, because this secures them support. Being familiar with the conceptual inclusion of societal actors in foreign policy, and with different types of actors and spheres of interaction, liberals identify globalisation, transnationalisation and democratisation as the main features in respect of which the contemporary milieu in which international relations take place differs from the primitive notion of an anarchical international system of states.[7] Adding this assumption to the notion of the government as a problem-solving sub-system of society, they have few problems explaining the emergence of governance structures. A *leitmotiv* of the liberal paradigm of international relations is that globalisation has reduced the problem-solving capacity of each individual state (government), and has become a major incentive for pooling problem-solving potentials in international institutions.

Interdependence creates problematic social situations, in which the unilateral pursuit of individual interests may lead to unintended and inferior results. The interplay between interactions on the intergovernmental and the government-society level can be interpreted as two parts of a specific two-level game: international co-operation is organised in response to economic globalisation and interdependence, which challenge the problemsolving capacities of individual governments. International governance offers these governments a chance to maintain or redress their ability to satisfy societal demands (see for example Zürn 1996 and 1995, Junne 1996).

The democratic deficit puzzle

For liberals, the theoretical puzzle lies in explaining why governments are ready for self-binding in the international but not the domestic context. Obviously, the liberal approach can cope well with intergovernmental selfbinding within structures of multilateral co-operation intended to cope with the challenges of economic globalisation. Societal demands can be met more efficiently by collective action on the part of governments. But why do the same societal actors not succeed with their demands for democratising the governance structures of the EU? Liberals could bring forward two answers. De-democratisation may be attributed to a lack of interest on the part of the non-governmental actors. Societal demands for democratisation of the EU are indeed unevenly distributed among the member states, but they do exist, as the continuous claim to strengthen the EP, or the critique of the German *Länder* and *Bundestag* of being deprived of traditional competencies show. Or, the 'weakening of national parliaments *vis-à-vis* their own executives' may be treated as an accidental *unforeseen* consequence of the Community' (Williams 1991: 162; my italics).

In his modified liberal approach ('liberal intergovernmentalism'), Moravcsik deals with the democratic deficit in the EU. His impression that 'the unique institutional structure of the EC is acceptable to national governments only insofar as it strengthens, rather than weakens, their control over domestic affairs' (Moravcsik 1993b: 507) may be correct from our point of view, but is incompatible with his liberal notion of state-society relations. If the government is conceptualised as a neutral, uninterested transmission belt for preferences which are formed among competing social groups, there is no room for identifying any general logic according to which interests of governments and their domestic environments can diverge. Why should governments be interested in overcoming domestic opposition in the first place? The observation that '[n]ational governments employ EC institutions as part of a 'two-level' strategy with the aim of permitting them to overcome domestic opposition more successfully' (Moravcsik 1993b: 515) contradicts two basic liberal assumptions: the notion of the state as a political institution representing aggregated societal

- Liberal approach: analysed in the context of the decreasing problem-solving capacities of individual states (governments) brought about by globalisation, international governance is a form of *collective* self-organisation developed in order to satisfy societal demands more efficiently.
- Integrated approach: analysed as the result of strategic interaction among governments under the pressure of an emerging civil society, intergovernmental governance becomes a matter of *exclusive* self-organisation; its subjects are governments, but its addressees are non-governmental actors.

International governance as strategic interaction among governments vis-à-vis non-governmental actors in a complex environment

The notion of the state which underlies this integrated approach combines the realist understanding of a strategic actor with the liberal one, whereby governments represent just one segment of domestic society. This means that we have to ascribe to a government 'a logic and interest of its own not necessarily equivalent to, or fused with, the interests of the dominant class in society or the full set of member groups in the polity' (Skocpol 1979: 27). But how can we identify this 'interest of its own'? On the one hand, it must differ from the interests of other, non-governmental actors. On the other, it should neither be treated as objectively given, as the traditional understanding of the national interest would suggest, nor should it imply the pre-determination of certain *substantial* policy preferences. At least an *abstract* goal may be identified: the striving for autonomy as a kind of meta-strategy, no matter what substantial purposes this autonomy may be used for.[9]

Why should the state be interested in having autonomy? May there not also be incentives to give up autonomy? Contrary to the theoretical lines of argument discussed so far, the following view will be taken: whatever preferences a government may have, from seeking general welfare to just staying in office, the degree of internal and external autonomy – as defined above – will decide whether or not these preferences can be realised. Autonomy is an instrument to be employed for very different reasons, but the self-assertion it implies and the discretion it creates are pre-conditions for successfully pursuing any substantial preferences. Autonomy provides the room to make other, more concrete choices under more specific circumstances. These situational choices occur in concrete functional contexts, and may also include the enhancement of problem-solving capability by granting access to selected societal resource providers, a strategy which may at the same time increase societal acceptance and which is likely to be pursued as long as the gate keeper function itself is not irreversibly affected. The wish of governments 'to somehow forestall, neutralise, transform, resist, or overcome the societal constraints imposed upon them' (Nordlinger 1981: 30) will, however, make them hesitant to guarantee participatory rights to non-governmental actors.

There is obviously a *generic* and a *situational* element in intergovernmental self-binding as a strategy enhancing autonomy. The generic element refers to the general and instrumental interest of governments to create institutional settings which allow intergovernmental self-commitment. The situational aspect may come in whenever a specific political constellation leads to a consensus among governments about substantial policies. Only then can the instrument of a polity framework, which enables them to withdraw decision-making from societal control, actually be utilised. The politics of a stabilisation programme such as the EMU may serve as an example (see Sandholtz 1993) to illustrate this distinction. In order 'to achieve internal reform in situations where constituency pressures would otherwise prevent action without the pressure . . . that an external partner could provide' (Putnam 1988: 447–8), there has to be a consensus in substance among governments about neo-liberal economic policies. But these governments must also have governance structures at hand, which enable them to commit themselves and their successors to the substantial decisions on stabilisation measures.

If, at least in abstract terms, governments have strategic interests of their own, it is not plausible to assume that they should behave as strategists in one sphere of interaction and as problem-solvers in another (see Moravcsik 1993b). Rather, their strategic interests will result in varying policies which respond to different kinds of challenges to their autonomy. To the extent that foreign policy never was *foreign* policy alone, these interests have always been domestically oriented as well. After all, the historical emergence of the state cannot be separated from its interest in monopolising authority in order to control violence within its jurisdiction. Accordingly state sovereignty, perceived as the internally and externally recognized claim to make authoritative decisions and to intervene coercively in activities within a given territory, has traditionally consisted of an internal and an external dimension, and so too have strategic interests. However, the changing structure of the international political environment may be expected to have its own impact on how government-society relations are reflected in international institutions: 'What is conventionally called foreign policy will look substantially different in the societal world in comparison with the world of states' (Czempiel 1994: 2).

In the pre-democratic era, the security dilemma promoted the pooling of domestic resources in the hands of the government in order to maintain internal and external security. Under the dominance of '*Primat der Außenpolitik*', internal autonomy was not questioned. External autonomy became the main concern of 'national interest'. But the interplay between the international and the domestic/transnational realm has changed dramatically. At the *domestic* level, non-governmental actors insist on their right to participate ('democratisation of foreign policy'). At the *transnational* level, non-governmental actors build interaction networks of their own, emancipating the pursuit of their interests from governmental regulation and control ('emergence of a "*Gesellschaftswelt*"'). In response to these changes, mutual agreement on self-binding, not security against threats, has become an effective mechanism by which democratic governments support each other in their striving for internal autonomy: '[t]he international system lends domestic autonomy to the state through institutions such as international law and diplomacy, which empower the state to overcome societal resistance to its policing practices' (Thomson 1995: 226).

Going beyond the realm of the world of the states as unitary actors, the 'analytical distinction between state and society opens up the possibility for a distinctive form of interstate co-operation, one based on states' common interest in controlling non-state actors' (Thomson 1995: 222). The realisation of the domestic/transnational challenge to autonomy links *internal* and *external* autonomy with each other and paves the way for analysing trade-offs between the two: the striving for freedom from such constraints may become one strong motive for strategic interaction among governments. The state's involvement in an intergovernmental institutional network is instrumentalised as a basis for potential autonomy of action and against groups and economic arrangements within its jurisdiction (see Nordlinger 1981: 23). A 'new *raison d'état*' is expressed in the parallel application of this striving at two different levels of interaction. What must puzzle realist state-centrism when viewed as *inclusive* self-binding behaviour of states regulating their behaviour towards each other, appears rational as an *exclusive* self-binding strategy of national governments *vis-à-vis* the growing demands of non-governmental actors. Table 13.3 identifies the focus of a conceptual framework which combines the idea of strategic interaction with a two-level perspective.

Hypotheses

If we combine the realist assumption of the state as a strategic actor trying to improve its autonomy-enhancing capacities, with the liberal focus on the domestic realm of the complex two-level game of 'foreign' policy, two hypotheses could explain according to which general logic 'states can cooperate against societies' (Thomson 1995: 221).

First, there is the hypothesis that governments' willingness to bind themselves in intergovernmental governance structures is a function of the domestic and transnational pressures exerted by non-governmental actors, which not only challenge the competencies of national governments as problem-solvers but also the autonomy of the world of states *vis-à-vis* civil society.

The EU looks like a particularly suitable case for investigation for three reasons. It is characterised by, first, an extraordinarily high degree of societal

Table 13.3 Focus of an integrated perspective

	interaction among states	*interaction among governmental and non-governmental actors*
states as strategic actors striving for autonomy	self-binding unlikely democratic deficit likely	**self-binding likely** **democratic deficit likely**
governments as problem solvers satisfying societal demands	self-binding likely democratic deficit unlikely	self-binding likely democratic deficit unlikely

permeation, under which the national governments 'suffer'; second, an equally extraordinary level of self-binding; and, third, continuous complaints about the democratic deficit. Taken as a plausibility probe, it is an illuminating instance of states pooling their problem-solving capacities in the name of more efficient problem-solving, and at the same time exploiting these governance structures for their own strategic purposes.

Governments whose internal autonomy is affected most by their vulnerability to 'societal resistance' can be expected to be more willing than others to follow this *new raison d'état* and to initiate, accept and submit themselves to the constraints of international self-regulation. The costs of self-binding structures are traded off against the extent to which autonomy is threatened by non-governmental actors in the course of globalisation and democratisation. The transfer of regulatory competencies to international or even supranational institutions, to which national governments but not parliaments, sub-national or non-state actors have access, reflects the common strategic interests of governments in withdrawing their policies from the control of societal or sub-national actors. Governments may even transfer part of their sovereignty to the multilateral level in order to enhance their autonomy capacity *vis-à-vis* non-governmental interference. If this hypothesis is correct, there will be progress in policy integration on the European level to the extent that the weight of domestic '*Vergesellschaftung*' of foreign policy and of the transnational '*Gesellschaftswelt*' increases. Looking beyond the EU, this hypothesis could provide an explanation for the observation whereby developed liberal democracies, more than any other type of state, are inclined to initiate and submit themselves to the constraints of intergovernmental governance. It would also predict a reluctance on the part of domestically stable non-democratic states to participate in self-binding governance. In terms of a trade-off between internal and external autonomy, they have nothing to gain from submitting themselves to the rules of international regimes and international law. But this strategic function of intergovernmental governance will become more important in the course of the further societisation of foreign policy.

Second, there is the hypothesis that intergovernmental governance structures leave little room for democratisation in the sense of more transparency, guaranteed participation and control for non-governmental actors. The instrumental interests of national governments in using intergovernmental governance structures to maximise the sum of their *overall* autonomy (i.e. internal *and* external) will determine the degree to which international governance structures can be democratised. This hypothesis implies a preference for less formalised forms of selective societal participation within which the gatekeeper role of national governments can be secured. A transfer and sharing of competencies at the European level, a 'derogation of democratic control that is commonly mistaken for the erosion of sovereignty' (Thomson 1995: 230), will only take place as long and so far as the national governments perceive it as a way of enhancing their *overall* autonomy. If this is how we have to conceptualise the state, there are obvious limitations to more horizontal and network-type governance structures in the EU.

Conclusion

Rather than attempting a fundamental re-interpretation of the phenomenon of international governance, this paper suggests a conceptual framework to explain a specific feature of it, namely the self-binding/democratic-deficit puzzle. The aim was to conceptualise a possible *deep structure* underlying strategic interaction among governments. The logic derived from this ideal-typical argument, deliberately reducing actors' preferences to a kind of 'motivational monism', nevertheless helps to identify potential limitations to the transformation of governance. In particular, it renders any mode of governance unlikely within which the role of the state would be reduced to one of a mere partner or neutral mediator. Objections to the interpretation offered in this article are invited and may be raised, of course. While the puzzle itself may be widely observed, it need not be the result of the conscious strategising of governments to defend themselves against domestic incursions of their prerogatives. While the assumed strategy may be employed, the impact of the deep structural factor may be obscured and even be made unobservable by intervening factors when other layers come into play. After all, only a systematic analysis of different governance projects can ascertain to what extent intergovernmental governance may be regarded as part of 'an international institutional structure reflecting states' common interests in building power and exerting control *vis-à-vis* non-state actors' (Thomson 1995: 226).

Notes

The author wishes to thank the participants of the ECPR-workshop on the 'Transformation of Governance in the European Union' for their comments. Gunther Hellmann, Peter J. Katzenstein, Andrew Moravcsik, Ingo Take, Christoph Weller and Michael Zürn helped me to improve earlier versions of this article.

1 For the general elaboration of this concept see Putnam 1988; Evans, Jacobson and Putnam 1993 and Zangl 1994.

2 There is, of course, a reductionism involved by equating democracy with the guarantee of participation. By focusing on this dimension of the 'democratic deficit' in intergovernmental governance structures, I do not want to deny other sources of democratic legitimacy, such as identity or output, which will not be dealt with in this context.

3 The concept developed in this paper is based on a notion of world society which has been elaborated elsewhere (see World Society Research Group 1996), and which stresses the relationship between the regulation of international relations on the one hand and trans-border-oriented activities of domestic and transnational actors on the other.

4 The original German quotation is '*Autonomiegewinn staatlicher Akteure gegenüber gesellschaftlichen Interessen, der aus ihrem Autonomieverlust in verflochtenen Entscheidungsstrukturen besteht*'. Grande has elaborated this argument, which runs contrary to traditional theories about strong and weak states, in an empirical study about the Europeanisation of research and technology policy (Grande 1994). A similar conclusion can be drawn from Sandholtz (1993: 34–6) with respect to the Economic and Monetary Union.

5 This disaggregation could help to develop further the basic argument of this article by applying the notion of self-interest to the different parts of the executive and the bureaucracy in order adequately also to reflect the fragmentation of national policy-making. For the sake of clarity, however, I will 'unpack' the state only partially and not take this step here.

6 For different approaches to state-society relations within the realist paradigm, see Mastanduno, Lake and Ikenberry (1989: 459ff). In traditional realism, the statesman is in charge of the pursuit of the 'national interest' or '*raison d'état*', which is '*den geschichtlichen Wandelungen in hohem Grade entrückt*' (Meinecke 1963: 19), and which must be defended against any particularist desires of individuals or societal groups. This notion is related to the needs of society only in so far as 'a satisfied people' has to be considered as an important source of power.

7 Rosenau (1988) has used the metaphor of the 'two worlds' in order to distinguish analytically between two spheres in an increasingly complex international system. In a similar attempt, Czempiel (1991: 86–8) has added to the world of states ('*Staatenwelt*') a new sphere of interaction which he calls '*Gesellschaftswelt*'. The model serves to identify ways in which governmental and non-governmental actors interact on different levels. For a review of literature on domestic and international linkages, see Mingst (1995).

8 As Moon points out, more recent neo-Marxist theories of the state have at least partially given up a strict instrumentalist view and 'ascribe markedly greater autonomy to the state'. It is conceded that any 'slavish devotion to the interests of particular élites may well undermine the interests of the class as a whole. That is, the state must be partially *autonomous* of the very class it most represents' (Moon 1995: 191, 190).

9 The notion of a general instrumental preference that can be attributed to any actor has an undeniable smell of objectivism itself. This generic preference is, however, not assumed to be objectively given, but relies on a strand of literature which develops it from a historical-empirical argument (Skocpol 1979; Tilly 1975). The existence of such a preference may therefore be empirically falsified. Its assumption and inclusion in the conceptual framework of this article does, however, provide a theoretical account for the self-binding/democratic-deficit puzzle.

14

GOVERNMENT, GOVERNANCE, GOVERNMENTALITY

Understanding the EU as a project of universalism

Thomas O. Hueglin

The paradigmatic shift from European government(s) to European governance has a venerable if neglected tradition in modern state theory: 'Much would be gained if it was admitted that the problem of real unity within the plurality of acting human beings not only lies with the state but without exception includes all organisations' (Heller 1934: 229). Such an acknowledgement still seems to come more easily in a case such as the European Union because it is a transnational political system defying conventional statist classification.

The new focus acknowledges a plurality of governing processes in 'policy communities' engaging in specific 'policy networks' (Kohler-Koch 1995: 18). In doing so, however, it may overlook that such 'plurality of actions' might nevertheless result in 'unity of action' (see Heller 1934: 29). This is a question of methodological perspective. Rightly rejecting the universalist reductionism inherent in statist explanations of European government, analyses of policy networks often resort to a kind of deconstructed relativism. The story of European integration then no longer unfolds as a drama of good and evil, but as a comedy of errors in which nobody can, or needs to, assume ultimate responsibility (see Alexander, J. C. 1995: 27).

A balance needs to be struck between these two perspectives. On the one hand, any assertion of monocausal universality must be avoided. The processes of European governance neither follow a neo-realist or neo-functionalist master plan, nor can they be understood in their entirety as a conspiracy conducted from the commanding heights of Europe's large corporations. On the other hand, they can nevertheless be conceptualised as pieces of a puzzle adding up to a project with an, at least potentially, universalising outcome. That project can be described as:

- the *re-articulation of political space* beyond the state, whereby the conventional borderlines between domestic and international politics, but also between state and society, appear redrawn in a complex relationship of mutual interdependence among regions, organised interests, member states and the Union itself
- a *new constitutionalism* redefining the rules by which governments and societies are to operate within this redrawn space, and aiming at the removal of these rules from further political deliberation, thus giving universal cohesion to the emerging European order
- and, perhaps most importantly, a *new governmentality* providing a new ideological frame for collective action. The choice of term here is meant to imply that ideological cohesion only extends to Europe's governing élites or top decision-makers, but does not necessarily include the European populations at large.

The comedy of errors, in other words, appears recast as a plurality of subplots whose happy or not so happy endings may be predetermined by an encompassing larger drama.

Understanding this drama requires a new conceptual language precisely because, on the one hand, statist formulations of integration theory 'do not possess even the necessary notions to conceptualise governance beyond the state,' (Jachtenfuchs and Kohler-Koch 1995: 14), and, on the other, postmodern deconstructions of European reality, in their efforts to develop such notions for at least partial frames of that reality, may not even want to see the forest for the trees. What is needed is a synoptic reconstruction of unity and diversity.

Again, this is not so new. More than half a century ago, Hermann Heller conceptualised a dialectical relationship between state unity and the plurality of its actors and actions: while both exist and act autonomously in their own right, neither can be understood without comprising something of the other (Heller 1934: 63–4). The same idea reappears more recently in Anthony Giddens' theory of structuration: plural social actors 'fashion' structural properties (like the state) and are at the same time recursively 'fashioned' by them (Giddens 1984: 25, 220). This recursive relationship obviously extends beyond the classical liberal juxtaposition of individual and state. Giddens mentions sectoral and regional structures within the state as essential parts for the universal process of social reproduction (ibid.: 24). In the context of European integration, however, states themselves become actors who fashion the process of integration and are recursively fashioned by it. A complex picture of multi-level interdependence emerges, which might well be conceptualised as a 'cosmopolitan' or 'federal' model of politics (Held 1992: 33).[1]

For several reasons, the conceptual language of federalism appears particularly appropriate for the suggested synoptic reconstruction of unity and diversity in the European Union. First of all, the *pluralisation of governance* has been a central theme in the long history of federalism in theory and practice (Friedrich 1968; King 1982; Elazar 1987). Second, the *concept of federalism* contains a contractual consent requirement (Lijphart 1985; Abromeit 1996) which also constitutes one of the essential modes of European governance. And third, this consent requirement is in turn embedded in a normative commitment to *mutual solidarity* (Hueglin 1994), which may well turn out to be the most critical yardstick for European socio-economic and political union as well. As in the case of state theory, 'real analysis and normative deliberation belong together' (Ellwein 1990: 109).

In this chapter, an attempt will be made to reconstruct the form and content of European governance as a 'project of universalism' (Alexander 1995: 5), as an encompassing larger drama of transformation that is more, and is intended to be more by those giving it direction, than just the sum of pluralised governance. To this end, some evidence about the re-articulation of political space, its constitutionalisation and ideological framing will first be summarised from recent literature. Pluralisation of governance, consent requirement and mutual solidarity will then be introduced as components of a conceptual language of federalism which can finally serve for a critical evaluation of European governance as a universalist project.

Transformation of governance: some diagnostic evidence

Few will deny any longer that the EU has moved beyond the dichotomy of neo-realist intergovernmentalism and/or neo-functionalist supranationality. A growing body of literature suggests, at least, that significant shifts are taking place, according to which EU reality increasingly resembles, in analogy to the globalising system of international politics, a 'complex multidimensional process' anchored in 'transnational networks, social movements and relationships [that] are extensive in virtually all areas of human activity'. There is at least partial evidence, in other words, for a 're-articulation of . . . political space in which the notions of sovereignty and democracy are being prised away from their traditional rootedness in the national community and the territorially bounded nation state' (Held and McGrew 1993: 262–4).

This re-articulation of political space manifests itself through the emergence of new actors and processes. In territorial terms, according to this view, the European member states are becoming sandwiched between regional actors and the regulatory powers of the EU. At the same time, transnational interest organisations are moving flexibly between all three levels. Most important, perhaps, is the observation of a tendency for politics to become disaggregated into functionally differentiated policy communities or networks, in which territorial and social actors at all levels are engaged in professionalised processes of lobbying, policy formulation and regulation.

Particularly noteworthy are attempts to regionalise the European political space. This should not come as a surprise, as regionalist movements have contested, at least since the mid-1960s, both the centralism of unitary nation state action, and the misrepresentation of socio-economic regional interests resulting from it (Hueglin 1986). What is surprising, however, is the growth of transnationally active networks among European regions, and their focus on the European Commission as a supranational regulatory actor, creating a structurally balanced 'triangular relationship' with the nation state governments (Ansell *et al.* 1995). No fewer than seventy-six regional offices were lobbying in Brussels by 1994. Most Commission departments have established regular consultative contacts with this regional lobby. Regional associations, alliances and networks have found support even when their objectives fall outside the Commission's specific policy programs. Given this dramatically increased regional focus, the Committee of the Regions, only recently established under the Maastricht Treaty, may already possess a degree of legitimacy 'unique among Brussels institutions'.

How can this new activism be explained? A combination of answers appears plausible. First, the Commission is an important and autonomous regulatory actor in policy fields central to regional interests. Second, because the internationalisation of politics has undermined both the ability and the credibility of nation state governments as impartial agents of a common national interest, regions will increasingly want to look after their own interests. Conversely, confronted with an increasingly diverse Community space, the Commission simply may have to rely on direct regional input into its administration of structural policy. Third, regionalist activism may be driven by powerful sectoral interests playing the networking game at two or more levels. And fourth, earlier rounds of intra-national decentralisation, resulting in a transfer of professional-administrative know-how in at least some member states, may have triggered a mobilisation of regional élites against what they perceived as central domination of their career aspirations.[2] Common interests, then, may bring forth common transnational strategies.

The other main factor suggesting a re-articulation of political space in the EU is the 'explosive growth' of transnationally organised interests and their professionalised representatives (Kohler-Koch 1994). The Commission alone registered some 525 interest groups in 1990, and there may be as many as 10,000 interest representatives active Community-wide. While endowed with uneven organisational powers, these interest groups all depend on the efficient use of information networks in order to exercise influence upon the complex processes of EU governance. Typically, they have in the past employed a 'dual strategy', exercising influence upon the agenda-setting Commission via their transnational federations, and using their national organisations during the subsequent phase of decision-making among governments in the Council. Since the Single European Act and Maastricht, the 'logic of influence' seems to have shifted more onto the European level, because the greater use of qualified majority voting in the Council and the extension of co-decision powers to the European Parliament now require transnational interest coalitions at the decision-taking stage of the policy process as well. Overall, one can observe a growth in 'issue specific coalitions'. The result is a trend towards the 'fragmentation of public policy' as well as a certain diffusion of private and public at all stages of the policy-making process.

Again, an explanation for this explosion of interest group activism must be sought, and two inter-related answers appear plausible here. First, although organised private interests obviously also play a significant role in national governing processes, that role is contained by processes of democratic accountability on the basis of parliamentary party governance and representation of individual citizenship. Given the relative absence of both at the European level, organised interests can more easily occupy that void. Second, it seems that the pluralisation of access levels, the regulatory character of European governance, and the fragmented channelling of policy-making in specialised and professionalised policy communities facilitate and even encourage disjointed private interest aggregation.

In other words, the re-articulation of political space in the process of European governance has taken two directions. On the one hand, there is a tendency for territorial pluralisation above and below the traditional realm of nation state governance. Nation states may still play the central role, but no longer the only one. On the other hand, transnationally organised interests appear to have succeeded, to a certain extent, in displacing parties as the dominant transmission belt for opinion and policy formation.

It is within this changing picture of European governance that elements of a new constitutionalism beyond intergovernmentally established treaty relations among sovereign member states can be detected. Its beginnings may date back to the early 1960s, when the European Court of Justice ruled that the member states had agreed on a real power transfer to the Community and therefore agreed to a lasting limitation of their own sovereignty. This judicial assumption of an existing 'supremacy clause in the Community framework' which is not found in the original Rome Treaties, appears undisputed today by both original and new Community members (Mancini 1991: 180). This is the constitutional language of the federal state: *European law breaks member state law.* However, since the new supremacy is contractually established as a limited power transfer, the EU would appear as a partial supranational regulatory regime rather than a federal state.

One can speak of a new constitutionalism nevertheless. It is not so much grounded in Community law as resulting from a complex matrix of autonomised governance. Particularly since the increased adherence to majority voting in the Council, European regulatory powers have become at least partially independent of treaty consent. And at least in some significant instances, such as setting price limits and production quotas for the ECSC, imposing temporary tariff protection against third country dumping practices, and shielding Community competition from member states' protectionism, these powers amount to autonomous policy-making rather than implementation (Nugent 1991: 78–9).

The establishment of a European Central Bank (ECB) must be considered as the decisive turning point in this respect. Once institutionalised, the ECB will be entirely 'independent of instructions from other European institutions', a development 'unprecedented in the modern history of central banking', because the establishment of independent monetary governance would precede those political institutions that normally create such statutory independence (Woolley 1992: 176–82). As a consequence, the ECB would constitutionalise 'a substantive policy commitment' to monetary efficiency which means, in conjunction with the 'freeing of European capital markets', a commitment to 'inflation fighting' as a priority over all other political goals (ibid.).

The overall quality of the emerging European political order can thus be described as a somewhat disjointed mix of three different models or types (see Jachtenfuchs and Kohler-Koch 1995: 20–2).

- Treaty-based policy-making, primarily among member state governments, but increasingly taking into account the 'action capacity' of intermediate actors, such as regions and organised interests, resembles the model of a 'negotiating state'.[3] Its constitutionalism is framed in procedural agreements.
- The administrative autonomy of the Commission on the other hand, again increasingly embedded in plural networks of interest intermediation, can be interpreted as the nucleus of an emerging 'regulatory regime'. Its constitutional logic is rooted in the separation of 'efficiency-oriented' policy-making from the liabilities of political expediency and partisanship.
- In the case of the ECB, finally, one can detect the making of an entirely new European 'economic constitution', guaranteeing a 'functioning market' and rejecting 'demands for the correction of market failures, social welfare systems and the creation of a more just society'.

Despite the fragmented re-articulation of political space and its embeddedness in a disjointed new constitutionalism, the EU does function as a political community. This can be taken as evidence that EU governance is in turn embedded in at least a 'minimum of a common political culture' mediated through a 'common language' (Jachtenfuchs and Kohler-Koch

1995: 22). But even this minimum of commonality appears further limited in two ways: the common language only extends to the sphere of the market, and even there the common political culture only comprises the decision-makers and regulators themselves.

The first limitation can be discerned in institutional mechanisms which constitute 'conditioning frameworks' for common behaviours (Grinspun and Kreklewich 1994: 35–8). Regulatory institutions of the ECB type are not only removed from democratic control, they also tend to limit the general political discourse to the requirements of a 'functioning market'. The common language they disseminate is couched in technical neutrality which renders ideological opposition ineffective: One can hardly be against macro-economic and monetary stability. In other words, the institutionalisation of independent regulatory agencies such as the ECB has far-reaching ideological consequences, because it predetermines the boundaries of the political discourse within which governance can take place.

Indications for the second limitation arise from the attitudinal gap which exists between the general public and top decision-makers in the EU. According to a recent survey (Commission 1996c: 4–5), a 'sharp contrast' exists between the two groups with regard to both the question whether EU membership is a 'good thing' generally (48 per cent to 94 per cent), and the further question of whether individual countries have benefited from this membership (45 per cent to 90 per cent). Such findings support the suspicion that a common political culture at the European citizenship level exists at best as a 'permissive consensus' (Kreile 1992: vii), and that common behaviours can be expected to be largely confined to a new breed of European policy-makers sharing an ideologically framed new governmentality.

Such a governmentality is required because 'common markets demand a common language, as well as a common currency', in order to produce the kind of 'common behaviours' a functioning market requires (Barber 1992: 54). However, considerable caution remains warranted. Even among Europe's top decision-makers, the formation of a universally shared European governmentality finds its obvious limits in a wide range of leading ideas and conceptual frames among member state governments and across policy communities. It may indeed be the ideological hallmark of the integration process that it remains embedded in an open-ended conceptual discourse meant to conceal persistent dissent about goals and means rather than representing consent. The subsidiarity principle, for instance, may have found its way into the Maastricht Treaty for precisely this reason (Neunreither 1993). It is far more a guiding principle for the further deliberation of 'colliding values' in a multi-level system of governance than a constitutional principle establishing 'justiciability' in the allocation of powers (Bruha 1994: 399).

Nevertheless, the question remains: 'Who can give the conceptual discourse within the Community . . . direction and therefore shape ideological hegemony?' Some evidence suggests that the most probable answer points to a 'modernising coalition between European leading industries and the Commission'. At the same time, the pace-setting ideas of such a coalition may be contested by those 'who have to bear the costs', and by the governments from whom they demand protection (Kohler-Koch 1996). In other words, the governmentality of an efficiency-oriented regulatory regime finds its limits in the electoral liabilities of the negotiating state.

European governance as a project of universalism: federalism as a critical yardstick

It was suggested at the outset that the European Union can and must be understood as a project of universalism, and that comparative federalism provides both an adequate conceptual language for doing so, and a critical yardstick for real analysis as well as normative deliberation.

Federalism in this conceptual sense must not be confused with the architecture of existing federal states. The two- or three-storey federal state with its vertical separation of powers is only one possible model, and a rather simplistic one at that. Instead, federalism denotes a general principle of adequate societal structuration aiming at the recursively balanced organisation of unity and diversity (Laski 1925; Davis 1978; King 1982; Elazar 1987). It is in this latter sense that federalism can offer guideposts for the critical evaluation of the EU as a pluralised system of multi-level governance even if it will not in the end develop into a federal state (Sbragia 1992b).

For this limited purpose, and without any intention to construct a fully-fledged theory of federalism, the following three elements of federal structuration, which also appear to play a central role in the European discussion, can be introduced: pluralisation of governance, consent requirement and mutual solidarity.

- *Pluralisation of governance* in a federalist sense means more than divided government or plural access to one government. It implies a plural process of multi-level governance on the basis of pluralised choice among autonomous collectivities within a political community. Typically, the main actors will be spatial collectivities such as provinces, regions, states and, as in the EU, the overarching universal community. However, the inclusion of social collectivities such as organised interests is by no means without precedent (Hueglin 1991).
- The *consent requirement* is nothing other than the procedural acknowledgement and organisation of pluralised governance among autonomous collectivities. Autonomy in the context of a complex and interdependent community cannot amount to complete independence. Governance has to rely on mutual compromise preventing the

256

tyranny of both majorities and minorities. In federalist terms, this typically implies the over-representation of smaller collectivities in legislative and executive governing bodies, as well as a non-majoritarian governing style based on executive bargaining.[4]

- The normative commitment to *mutual solidarity*, finally, refers to the procedural as well as material basis required for a federally organised system of governance. Compromise as a non-competitive pattern of decision-making requires a pre-emptive disposition towards the needs and concerns of others, and consent can only be reached, at least in the long run, if the socio-economic results of community policy are acceptable to all as fair and equitable.[5] Form and content of governance cannot be separated. In federalist terms again, this is typically a matter of fiscal federalism and regional equalisation.

This reconceptualisation of federalism obviously differs from conventional definitions which are extended in two ways. First, the inclusion of non-territorial (social) as well as territorial (spatial) collective actors suggests a kind of 'societal federalism' (Hueglin 1991) corresponding to the new focus on 'governance beyond the state'. Second, the insistence on a commitment to mutual solidarity leads from technical definitions of federalism in a constitutional sense to what might be called a 'political economy of federalism' (Hueglin 1990). Its critical focus is not so much directed at the investigation of formal democratic deficits as it is concerned with the underlying social forces producing them. This shift in focus includes the assumption that democratic deficit and social/spatial inequality are correlated. The linkage between democracy and material equality closely corresponds to a fundamental tension between pluralised self-governance (*subsidiarity*) and universal socio-economic commitment (*solidarity*).[6] This linkage lies at the heart of the federalist bargain because, in the language of political economy, the actors in a pluralised process of governance can only make use of their self-governing and participatory rights under conditions of relative material equality (Cunningham 1987: 127).

The constitutionalist expression of this fundamental tension is only 'epiphenomenon' (Rocher and Smith 1995: 8). Federal constitutions are codifications of a federal bargain bounded in time. They are based on a compact or treaty among the member collectivities of a political community. Compact theories of federalism are based on the assumption that constitutional changes amount to a change of the original treaty that established a federal community, and that such changes therefore require the renewed consent of all participants.[7] While compact theories of federalism are usually dismissed as lacking legal foundation in modern federal states, they have nevertheless found general expression in bicameral legislative processes, and more importantly in qualified majority requirements for constitutional change. In this sense, the distinction of constitutional and treaty federalism

(Sbragia 1992b: 271–4) is as misleading as the dichotomy of supranational-ity and intergovernmentalism in the case of the EU.

With these yardsticks or guideposts borrowed from the conceptual lan-guage of federalism, a critical evaluation of the EU as a project of universalism can now be undertaken. The central questions are: does the re-articulation of political space lead to political and socio-economic soli-darity? Will the new constitutionalism enhance or restrict pluralised choice? And is the new European governmentality based on consent?

Transformation of governance: critical evaluation

The conceptual language suggested by a political economy of federalism is particularly adequate for a critical evaluation of the transformation of gov-ernance in the EU, because its functional economic bias can hardly be denied.[8] Not least because there has been a direct transfer of power from the state to the market (Tsoukalis 1994), 'economic-technical action' constitutes the 'decisive momentum' (Heller 1934: 106) in this transfor-mation. European governance is not only characterised, in federalist language, by the tension between subsidiarity and solidarity built into the overall political order, but also by a fundamental tension between this political order and autonomous economic forces.

This is the 'conditioning framework' for the ongoing *re-articulation of political space* in the EU. It redefines the way in which regions, organised interests, nation states, and the overall Union itself can pursue their inter-ests by generating influence within the pluralised system of governance, and it predetermines the spatial and social allocation of resources resulting from it. To speak of pluralised governance in this context may be misleading, because the cards in this multi-level game of allocation and regulation appear stacked in favour of a few powerful actors. The universal outcome will more likely resemble a European society of winners and losers, for which the open question is only whether it will be a two-thirds society or 'merely' a four-fifths society.

Despite the impressive growth of network relationships between regional actors and the European Commission, it has been pointed out that regional network influence over EU regulation is 'rarely powerful' on its own in Brussels. It typically requires linkages with national government agendas and/or regional alliances with powerful corporate interests (Keating and Hooghe 1996). This favours economic core countries like Germany (Graf 1992), and a few dominant regions in other countries which hold the balance of economic and political power as, for instance, Catalonia in the case of Spain (Keating 1994). Generally speaking, the interests of European regions appear divided. On the one hand, there exists a common interest in structural policy, the material basis for which has remained embarrassingly narrow, despite a recent quadrupling of the

Structural Funds.[9] On the other hand, inter-regional competition intensifies, because economically advanced regions tend to abandon regional solidarity, linking up instead with corporate interests as well as market-driven policies of national governments and the Commission. Obvious contradictions resulting from the pursuit of structural *and* market-driven policy preferences across (and within!) regions make it further unlikely that the regions of Europe (or even of one member state) will be able to bring their influence to bear on Brussels with one voice.

Overall, the prospects of regionally balanced federalism in Europe seem distant at best. More likely is the formation of a multi-level system of governance characterised by centre-periphery relations in overlapping concentric circles of power and influence: among dominant and dependent member states, among strong and weak regions within member states, and among newly established industrial parks and neglected hinterlands within regions (Nugent 1992: 327; Campanella 1995).

The dynamic leading to this transformation is both market- and policy-led. Mobilised transnational capital will re-draw a regionalised map of European capital valorisation, and it will find its political allies in the European single market regulators, national union busters and regional providers of infrastructural and tax concessions at public expense.

> The danger is that a 'Europe of the regions' will emerge not as a result of an equitable balance of power between federal, national and regional levels, but from the reverse. Europe will be divided into successful and failing regions, in conflict with their nation states and the Union over the direction of policy and the distribution of resources.
>
> (Hirst and Thompson 1996: 168–9)[10]

The proliferation of specialised organised interests in the European arena does not necessarily amount to pluralised balance either. If generating influence through networking is the name of the game, the bottom line is that 'only transnational corporations with a considerable economic and political weight are strong enough to build up transnational networks of their own' (Kohler-Koch 1994: 178). It is the ability to be present at all levels within a pluralised system of governance that allows such networks to gain agenda-setting access to the process of policy-making. But even the most powerful organised interests can accomplish this only if they are able to speak with one voice, avoiding contradictory positions at different government levels, as well as within their transnationally affiliated associations. Accordingly, it can be expected that 'big business' will take the lead, with European multinationals orchestrating consent, and, ultimately, 'a few leading business people managing the collective industrial interest representation in Europe' (Kohler-Koch 1996).

Others, such as labour unions, consumer groups and social movements in particular, will be able to exert influence within their specialised policy communities but hardly over the Community agenda as a whole. Functional differentiation of EU policy-making in the various component councils of the Council of Ministers as well as the Commission Directorates General has led to a proliferation of such policy communities. Interaction between organised interests and policy makers very much begins to resemble the American Congressional system, which is characterised by a compartmentalisation of the policy-making process in hundreds of sub-committees, offering each 'special-interest group its own special-interest sub-committee' (Parenti 1980: 226). At the surface, the multiple processes of log-rolling and package-dealing going on in this lobbyists' heaven resembles a true image of American pragmatism: you-win-some-and-you-lose-some. However, the reality is one of skewed influence. Only large corporate interests can be expected to afford presence at all stages and levels of policy formation.

As this comparison suggests, one should not hastily conclude that the presence of 'many policy communities' in Europe means that these will be generally able to 'exert great influence' over European public policy. And even more doubtful must appear the further assumption that such 'differentiation' necessarily 'reduces redistributive conflicts' (thus Peters 1992: 80-81). As in the American case, such assumptions are carried by faith rather than fact: specialised policy management at the European level is believed to be efficiency-driven and therefore leading to more acceptable and, presumably, equitable outcomes than policy management led by national politics.

More likely is that redistributive conflicts become obfuscated rather than reduced according to a classical strategy of *divide-and-rule*. The more policy fields and policy communities are functionally separated, the more a 'modernisation coalition' of dominant public and private interests can set the agenda. There can be little doubt as to its composition: 'policy entrepreneurs' in the Commission, managers of multinational corporations, and the governments of economically strong member states, with Germany at the apex (Cameron 1992; Kohler-Koch 1996). As has been pointed out for the United States quite some time ago, the fundamental flaw of such visions of a 'pluralist heaven' is that 'the heavenly chorus sings with a strong upper-class accent' (Schattschneider 1960: 35).

Another common yet equally questionable assumption about the transformation of governance in Europe is that the re-articulation of political space must inevitably lead to a weakening of nation state power and sovereignty. Competencies are given away to the Union above, and, perhaps as an inevitable corollary, organised away by the regions below. That the sandwiched state will inevitably be a weak(er) state, however, appears far from a foregone conclusion. European regulation may in fact free national governments from the 'suffocating embrace' (Kohler-Koch 1995: 10) of domestic opposition and welfare commitments in particular. EU governance in this sense resembles a multi-level game in which the more powerful players can more likely expect to maximise their interests by playing off one level against the other than can the less powerful. Limited interlocking at the European level becomes an additional arena for 'domestic problem-solving' (Kahler 1987: 301; Dyson, in this volume). Giving up domestic regulatory power may in such cases strengthen the state's 'overall autonomy' (see Wolf, in this volume).

This may help to explain why some governments are more vigorously pressing for regulatory Europeanisation than others. Embraced by strong unions and oppositional *Länder* governments, the German government, for example, may anticipate an increase in its overall autonomy in a deregulated European market environment from which the German economy, moreover, can be expected to benefit the most. The British government, on the other hand, may anticipate the opposite result, a decline of its overall autonomy in dealing with unions as well as regions, for example, which might further compound its relative weakness in the European marketplace. In other words, from a political economy perspective again, which attempts to determine the strength or weakness of states from the inseparable relationship between political and economic forces, one can presume, as in the case of regions and organised interests, that the re-articulation of political space brought about by the European transformation of governance is likely to strengthen the strong and weaken the weak (see Zinn 1989).[11] The universalist project does not appear to be embedded in a common commitment to political and social balance.

As long as this multi-level game remains tied to intergovernmental negotiation, and therefore exposed to national as well as transnational opposition, dominant actors will press for further regulatory autonomisation, i.e. a removal of entire policy fields from further political negotiation and public accountability. The result may be the transformation of an ever fragile and negotiable *acquis communautaire* into a stable and irreversible *fait accompli*. That, it must be suspected, is what the new constitutionalism is expected to accomplish.

The corner-stone of the new constitutionalism is the Single European Act, because it has established rules of market and capital mobility which can no longer be controlled politically by national governments, organised labour, or the European public at large (Camiller 1989). The European Monetary System (EMS), similarly, has insulated trade conditions from domestic monetary policy intervention (Lipietz 1992). But it is the anticipated creation of a European Central Bank (ECB) which stands out as the centrepiece of the new European economic constitutionalism, because it will write into constitutional stone the autonomy of European monetary policy from democratic scrutiny and control (Gill 1992). As a 'move from a "regime" approach to binding institutions', the progression from EMS to EMU (European Monetary Union) under the auspices of a fully independent ECB aims at 'doubling the level of decision-making' (Campanella 1995: 362). There is the level of continued political bargaining over the basic institutional and socio-economic direction of the integration process, which remains tied to democratic control, and there is the level of autonomised monetary policy, which appears removed from such control.

From both a Latin American and Eastern European perspective, such a scenario of dualised governance has been described as delegated market authoritarianism (Aznar 1994). Its characteristics are technocratic rule via executive bargaining and delegated decision-making power, from representative to semi-autonomous bureaucratic institutions. The carriers of this governing style and practice are to be found, on the one hand, in the interlocked directorships and ownership of transnational corporations and, on the other, in the networks of technically autonomous national and international institutions led by the World Bank and the IMF that dictate the terms of centre-periphery credit flow (Fields 1994). What is suggested, here, is a certain analogy between the role transnational corporations and international monetary institutions play in the dependent development of developing and post-communist countries, and the role a fully independent ECB will play in the further economic development of European member states.

Once established, the ECB can be seen as the 'first of a new family of regional institutions', that fit neither the realist assumption of national interest co-ordination nor the functionalist logic of interest linkage. The convergence criteria for third stage monetary union 'drawn up by the central bankers', for example, only make sense as disciplinary imposition on domestic public finance. They clearly challenge the 'communitarian balance' by making compliance the condition of core membership, instead of organising universal membership on the basis of negotiated compromise (Campanella 1995: 362-3). In other words, the logic and method of European integration begin to undergo fundamental change, from the original intention of defining and generating 'common public goods' through 'common European institutions' (Wallace 1996: 145), to a neoliberal regime of 'macroeconomic discipline' (Sandholtz 1994: 261) which may yet 'fragment into various tiers' (Cafruny 1997: 121) of uneven economic development and unequal access to the European process of governance.

Thus it would appear that the double tension built into the EU as a universalist project, between subsidiarity and solidarity within the political order, and then between that order and autonomous economic forces, translates logically into a dualised system of governance. On the one hand, the EU continues to function as a multi-level bargaining system, with core states, strong regions and powerful organised interests as its main actors.

On the other hand, these actors have already agreed upon the establishment of a market-oriented regulatory regime, which will now be secured through a new economic constitution aiming at the complete insulation of monetary policy from the political bargaining system. In so doing, they may succeed in disciplining domestic fiscal policy into compliance with overall monetary stability objectives, even when this runs counter to domestic objectives of economic competitiveness and social stability. It is exactly this new constitutionalism which makes visible the universalist nature of the European project. It sets the rules by which the bargaining game has to be played henceforth, externally as well as internally.

From a critical perspective of federalism, this would mean that consent requirement and mutual solidarity appear eclipsed from essential policy fields within the European system of pluralised governance. If one can say, therefore, that governance in the EU is carried by a new 'common understanding that governance is about co-ordinating multiple players in a complex setting of mutual dependence' (Kohler-Koch 1995: 16), then this understanding would appear ideologically captured by a 'new hegemonic discourse' of market efficiency, discipline and sound money (Gill 1992: 168). And it would also appear, in analogy to 'consensus formation' in the emerging new world order, that autonomised institutions of the ECB type are 'particularly important in defining the ideological bases of consensus, the principles and goals within which policies are framed, and the norms of 'correct' behaviour' (Cox 1987: 259). Governance, in other words, becomes framed by a *new governmentality*, which seeks to transform the federal consent *requirement* into regulatory consent *formation*.

While it appears plausible that the most powerful players might agree to institutional 'self-binding' in order to extend systemic control over a pluralised maze of self-interested states, regions, sectors and their policy communities, it is far less clear why the ideological capture works. If these pluralised players have understood that they have a chance to influence decisions by which they are directly affected, then why would they consent to play this game within the narrow confines of economic efficiency imperatives that might run directly counter to their self-interests?

A tentative answer has to return to the prior question of whether governance in the EU will enfold as a post-modern comedy of errors, or whether the EU constitutes a modernist drama of universalist proportions after all. What has been suggested throughout this chapter is, of course, that a significant pluralisation of governance has indeed taken place but that this transformation appears to remain caught, at least for now, in a larger project committed to a decisive modernisation push for the European economic and social space in its entirety. Modernisation in this context means 'the attempt to rationalise an entire society, make it conform to a model designed to impose the most efficient use of available means for the achievement of particular ends, such as reindustrialisation, military security, education for international competition, etc.' (Wolin 1983). This attempt, as has been suggested here with at least some degree of evidence, is driven by the persuasive powers of the dominant players among states, regions and organised interests. Compliance and conformity among a plurality of sub-plotters come with dependency on the decisions made or negotiated by these players.[12]

But most importantly, they may come from the establishment of seemingly 'neutral' institutions whose far-reaching powers are framed in a seemingly 'neutral' regulatory language. This language suggests that efficiency-oriented regulatory policy can be divorced from redistributive policy (see Jachtenfuchs and Kohler-Koch 1995: 21). This is the deceptive fallacy of the new constitutionalism which allows for ideological capture. Especially in a market-driven environment, the regulatory rationalisation of an entire society will always produce (relative) winners and losers, and will therefore always have redistributive consequences. These consequences may not be recognised at all in time by those directly and most negatively affected by them.

So it seems at least possible that the new European space will unfold as one of simultaneous homogenisation and fragmentation. On the one hand, there is a new governmentality committed to the transformation of the European space into one vast area of co-ordinated and interdependent economic efficiency. It is perhaps epitomised by a new denationalised European business class, staying in the same chain hotels, hanging out in the same chain coffee shops, reading the same newspapers and pursuing the same life-style in cities which begin to have more in common with one another than with the countries and regions in which they happen to be located. On the other hand, there are the European populations at large, far less mobile, and hoping to get a piece of the action without having to surrender their particular life-styles.[13] This double illusion may sustain the 'permissive consensus' which has accompanied the European project as a project of universalism.[14]

As one of the most profound voices of contemporary political geography observed, 'One of the principal tasks of the capitalist state is to locate power in the spaces which the bourgeoisie controls, and disempower those spaces which oppositional movements have the greatest potentiality to command' (Harvey 1989: 237).

The re-articulation of European political space can be interpreted in this sense as just such a relocation of power. While the definitive role of 'inner elite circles' in this process will certainly have to be established by further empirical testing (Liebert 1994: 162–3), one can at least make some predictions as to the presumable outcome. As a 'neo-liberal paradise' the new Europe will lead to the further 'pauperisation' of backward regions, as was the case in the *Mezzogiorno* after Italian unification or in the American south after the Civil War (Scharpf 1989).

The transformation from the limited pluralism of European government(s) to the pluralised diffusion of governance among public and private actors can therefore be expected to create a European society of winners and 'modernisation losers'. The question is whether it will be a relatively peaceful four-fifths society in which the conflicts of marginalisation can be contained, or whether it will be a two-thirds society increasingly haunted by 'street gangs' and a new right-wing populism erecting new barriers against trans-European social mobility (Enzensberger 1994). This may in turn very much depend on whether or not the one European tension, between subsidiarity and social solidarity, can be balanced so that the other tension, between political order and autonomous economic forces, does not get out of hand. As a project of universalism, in other words, the future of Europe can unfold either as a new type of federal order for the twenty-first century, a multi-level system of balanced power-sharing among a plurality of territorial as well as social actors, on the basis of mutual consent and solidarity, or as a desolidarised market-place which may repeat, on a European scale, what has been described as the essence of liberal capitalist state formation in the nineteenth century: an 'almost miraculous improvement in the tools of production, which was accompanied by a catastrophic dislocation of the lives of the common people' (Polanyi 1944: 33).

Notes

The revision of this paper has greatly benefited from suggestions by Beate Kohler-Koch. Helpful comments were also received from Ernst B. Haas (Berkeley), Markus Haverland (Utrecht), Oliver Schmidtke (Berlin) and Klaus-Dieter Wolf (Darmstadt). In addition, I learned a great deal from all workshop participants whom I also want to thank for their collegiality and friendship. I would like to dedicate this chapter to the memory of Thomas Ellwein who always laughed at me when my theoretical horses galloped too far from reality.

1 As Held points out in a footnote, he only substituted 'federal' with 'cosmopolitan' because he found that the former expression was not helpful due to the European federalism controversy.
2 Although contested (see Meadwell 1993), this is one of the classical explanations for the rise of regionalism in Quebec (see McRoberts 1988).
3 Jachtenfuchs and Kohler-Koch follow a formulation adopted by Fritz W. Scharpf (1992). Note that 'state' should not be understood as a singular sovereign action centre in the modern conventional sense, but as a plurality of action processes.
4 Non-majoritarian governance protects minority or single member interests through a sliding scale of measures, ranging from qualified majority voting to mutual veto power (see classically Lijphart 1977: esp. 36–8).
5 As has been pointed out already some time ago, this non-competitive style of policy-making is particularly typical for political processes characterised by a high degree of 'bureaucratic arbitration' (see classically Lehmbruch 1976: esp. 97).

6 This conceptualisation of subsidiarity and solidarity (for a more detailed exploration see Hueglin 1994) roughly corresponds to the analytical distinction of 'negative' and 'positive' subsidiarity in Article 3b of the Maastricht Treaty (Endo 1994).

7 The notion of a 'compact' denotes the assumption of an original treaty by which the participants establish a federal union on the basis of mutual agreement (cf. Abromeit 1996).

8 'Political economy of federalism' here means no more than giving expression to an analytical approach which, in analogy to 'international political economy', 'considers in a unified view political and economic determinants of the relations among markets, states (regions, provinces etc.) and institutions' in a multi-level system of governance (see Guerrieri and Padoan 1989: viii). Obviously, such a meaning challenges the conventional liberal separation of (political) state and (private) market spheres, because the analytical focus is on underlying social forces operating in both spheres (cf. Gough 1979).

9 As is well enough known, the Structural Funds now command about one third of the EU budget, but that budget still hovers at a paltry 1.5 per cent of the overall EU GDP.

10 A more cautious assessment comes to the conclusion that 'the distributional consequences of economic liberalization are contested and, above all, uncertain'. However, available data calling into question the inevitability of further spatial polarisation typically do not take into account intra-regional aspects of this dynamic (see Marks 1992: esp. 194–202).

11 As has been forcefully pointed out, any overall qualification of states and national economies as strong or weak needs to be differentiated further by a 'disaggregated' analysis of sectors, as well as the 'different levels – micro, meso, macro – at which the state confronts the economy' (Atkinson and Coleman 1989: 47).

12 Even Mitterand, as President of a country that can hardly be called peripheral within the Community context, complained with reference to German agenda-setting that 'we are not masters of our own policy' (quoted in Cameron 1992: 67–8).

13 This assumption certainly needs further empirical testing; at least one survey seems to confirm, however, that Europe's élites differ from the general public precisely in their perception of the EU as a vehicle for the promotion of economic growth (Commission 1996c: 5–6).

14 During the 1988 public hearings on the Free Trade Agreement between the United States and Canada, the Canadian novelist Margaret Atwood remarked that Canadians were hoping to gain access to American markets without having to give up the accomplishments of the Canadian social state, and she asked: what if *they* get *our* markets, and *we* get *their* social conditions? (Personal recollection of an incident widely reported by the media.)

15

GOVERNANCE IN THE EUROPEAN UNION

A comparative assessment

Rainer Eising and Beate Kohler-Koch

Introduction

The contributions in this volume explore whether a network mode of governance is emerging in the European Union (EU). They identify a complex mixture of different governance modes – networks, pluralism, corporatism and statism – at both European and member state levels as well as in different policy areas and sectors. This pattern and the overlap of elements reflect the dynamic character of the European Union and its heterogeneous composition on the one hand and area-specific variations on the other. Nevertheless, most of the studies have shown that most EC policy areas have network elements of governance which, in turn, have important transformational repercussions on the member states' own modes of governance.

Before outlining our conclusions we briefly discuss the choice of cases, the level of analysis and the methodology applied. The contributions to this volume certainly do not give a comprehensive account of European governance. They focus on the first pillar, the European Community (EC). Here, because of its supranational character, the interaction between Euro-level and member state level governance is most pronounced. Within the realm of the European Community, one chapter is devoted to the governance of system change, that is, the introduction of the Economic and Monetary Union. The main focus of the book is not constitutional politics; rather, it concentrates on how policy areas already under EC jurisdiction are governed and new policy regimes are developed. The chapters cover a broad range of issue areas, dealing with different aspects of the Internal Market Programme, such as sectoral regulation of production and supply (electricity) as well as services (banking, law and health-related services) on the one hand, and Community policies relating to transport, the environment and social affairs on the other hand.

As regards the level of analysis, most chapters analyse the repercussions of the European Community on the member states and the interaction between these two levels. This is particularly true in the case of the two chapters without a policy focus, but which instead give a general account of systems of interest mediation and the interaction of governance patterns in the European multi-level system (Schmidt, Sidenius, in this volume). The research presented does not include all member states, and some are only analysed in one or two policy areas. Nevertheless, a fair representation of the better-off large and small northern member states and of the poorer southern members has been achieved. In terms of policy cycles, most of the studies focus on policy formulation rather than policy implementation. The preferred approach has mainly been a comparative case study supplemented by surveys. This broad empirical coverage should provide a useful basis for some generalisations about the nature of EC-governance and its impact on the member states.

We will proceed in four steps. First, in the following section, we examine our core hypothesis, that we are currently witnessing a transformation towards a network mode of governance at the level of the European Community. The key elements and distinguishing characteristics of the EC's network system of governance will be highlighted. Second, we analyse the repercussions of EC governance on the member states' modes of governance, and third, we analyse the public-private intersection. Finally, our results are summarised in a brief conclusion.

Which mode of governance in the European Community?

The case for network governance

It is fashionable today to trace the emergence and perpetuation of modes of governance to the impact of institutional factors on the one hand, and of socio-economic dynamics on the other. Thus, a plethora of studies has provided evidence for changing patterns of governance in industrialised countries. The modernisation and functional differentiation of their polities and societies have paved the way for a blurring of the boundaries between public and private actors (e.g. Kooiman 1993, Mayntz 1992). More and more, governance is perceived as a 'sharing of tasks and responsibilities between private and public actors', as the guiding and steering 'efforts of social, political and administrative actors . . . in a more or less continuous process of interaction' (Sidenius, in this volume). Nonetheless, modes of governance seem to vary across different countries (Kenis and Schneider 1991, Van Waarden 1993). These differences are often attributed to specific national institutional configurations, and to the varying decision criteria and styles of public as well as private actors. In several analyses, these factors are regarded as crucial determinants of the national modes of governance (e.g. Kohler-Koch 1996). On the basis of these factors Vivien Schmidt (in this volume), for instance, identifies statism in Great Britain, France, and Italy, pluralism in the United States and a corporatist mode of governance in Germany.

To restrict the analysis to institutional configurations and socio-economic developments would mean neglecting the democratic quality of political associations as a critical variable for the evolutionary patterns of particular modes of governance. In the case of Western industrialised states, this does not constitute a severe problem, since they are similar systems in terms of democratic legitimacy. But this is not the case for the EC. We claim that the very fragility of its democratic legitimacy has important implications which, in combination with the EC's institutional properties, contributed to the emergence of a network mode of governance. The member states and the Community institutions accept *consociation* as the central ordering principle of their relations, and regard *interest* as the constitutive basis of the EC system.

The *EC's institutional set-up* differs markedly from that of the member state polities (Eising and Kohler-Koch 1994: 185–90, Kohler-Koch 1997a: 47–8). It is characterised by a multi-level structure, the combination of supranational and intergovernmental elements, and a strong role for the judiciary. During the policy cycle, the EC's actors are largely restricted to agenda-setting and policy formulation, whereas implementation is organised by the member states. Owing to the limited role of political parties and the predominance of the European Commission and the Council in decision-making, the EC is notorious for its technocratic decision criteria. A particular 'community method' (Wallace 1996: 32) has been developed, which is closely linked to the principles and norms of the overarching project of setting up an (Economic) Community. Nevertheless, the functional segmentation of the specialised Councils and the Commission's directorates gives rise to specialised sub-structures which – in the framework of the Community regime – develop their own rationality criteria.

Additional factors enhance the complexity of actor relations. The territorial and functional representatives of national interests come from fifteen widely differing systems. Therefore, actor constellations are remarkable for their heterogeneity and fluidity. Furthermore, the competencies of the political actors as well as the public and private participants vary according to different procedures and also change in different phases of the policy-making cycle. None of them enjoys complete control over either the process or the substance of decision making. Formal powers are overshadowed by multi-layered negotiations and consultations (Gottweis, in this volume).

Owing to these characteristics, it is almost inevitable that the European Community's mode of governance will be of the network type, which differs from ideal-type pluralism, statism, and corporatism (Kohler-Koch,

Pagoulatos, Schmidt, all in this volume). At the most general level, the interaction between public and private actors in the EC can be depicted as a negotiation process. The actors have different interests and they are 'mutually dependent, but at the same time autonomous' (Kohler-Koch 1996: 370). For EC actors, particularly the European Commission, the necessity to construct networks is turned into a virtue. The Commission's dependence on external expertise requires it to bring together the relevant political and societal actors. The integration of these actors into the decision process may be regarded as an attempt to mobilise support groups not only for certain policies but for the integration process as a whole. The EC's institutional segmentation and the restricted capacities of individual political actors make them very open to societal actors. Even the Commission cannot assert its oft-acclaimed position as process manager during all phases of the policy formulation process. The introduction of the 'Public Service' concept by the European Parliament and of the 'Single Buyer' model by the French Government during negotiations on the internal energy market (Eising, in this volume), as well as the complex and enduring negotiations during the formulation of the genetic engineering directive (Gottweis, in this volume), are good examples of this weakness on the part of the Commission. The individual actors' low degree of control over the political process augments the integration of socio-economic interest groups into EC decision-making.

But any system of governance can call on private actors for consultation, or institutionalise negotiations for private interest government. The purpose may be to bridge a decision-making gap or to avoid taking the blame for a contested policy move. Involving all affected interests is an approved strategy geared to restraining pressure group politics. Corporatist strategies have been praised for helping to mitigate the obstructive power of selfish interest groups and the cost arising from pluralist interest competition. In the context of the EC things are different. Public-private networks may well be institutionalised with a view to making decisions more expedient and acceptable. The Committee system, as well as the handling of interest group access by the Commission, increase the governability of the system. Nevertheless, the purpose is a different one; the aim is not to subdue 'interest group hedonism' (Caporaso 1974) and unwarranted demands, but to channel interest representation onto the European level. In a system in which the central actor for initiating and pursuing the formulation of policies (i.e. the Commission) lacks democratic accountability, and the Parliament has only a limited influence on the legislative process, functional representation gains in importance. The consent of societal organisations is a welcome substitute for democratic legitimacy. It is quite clear that the Commission is trying to introduce a 'mix' of legitimising elements of representation to make up for the Community's 'democratic deficit'.

Variations on a theme

If we shift the level of analysis, assumptions about the likelihood of EC network governance change. When the sub-systemic level is taken into account, it becomes evident that EC societal and political actors come from very different national settings and traditions. Therefore, European networks are characterised by an inbuilt rivalry over problem views and solutions which have to be accommodated (Héritier 1993: 438).

Furthermore, the concentration on just one part of the policy process, namely policy formulation, increases the degree of fluidity. EC policy networks do not have the same stability of actor constellations as at the national level, where routine processes in the implementation phase perpetuate relations. Network governance is not unambiguously dominant at EC level for yet another reason: EC decision-making does not start in a vacuum, but in a setting of varying national modes of governance. And precisely because the EC is still in its formative phase, the actors are struggling to introduce what they consider to be the most appropriate mode of governance.

The negotiation of Community policies is always a competition about modes of governance. In some policy areas, particular governing arrangements have been introduced without much opposition. In the area of EC social policy, elements of corporatism are present and the negotiations on EMU were characterised by a mode of statist governance controlled by government actors. This should come as no surprise, since corporatism and statism are the predominant modes of governance in the respective national policy areas. Their transfer to the EC level strengthened established national practices, by providing additional legitimacy among the actors involved. Wherever possible, member states aim to reduce their adaptation costs by transferring their national modes of governance to the European level. Therefore, competition among different national modes of governance at EC level and complex patterns of overlap will continue, despite the prevalence of the network mode. Vivien Schmidt (in this volume) argues that, for this very reason, the EC falls somewhere between the pluralist and the network modes and has developed a 'quasi-pluralist' mode of governance.

Does this assessment hold true, when the individual case studies are examined more closely? The chapters on policy regimes clearly revealed that decision procedures are open to a variety of fluctuating public and private actors, corresponding to either a network or a pluralist mode of governance. They point out that the mode of interaction shifts between attempts to construct 'minimum winning coalitions' and efforts to reach consensus among all concerned parties. Thus, in energy policy, after the initial clash over the Internal Energy Market, the mode of interaction between the Commission and the economic interest groups shifted to consensus formation. The Green Paper and the White Paper on the Common Energy Policy reflect the extensive debate between the member states, the European interest associations and the Commission. They take up all the various elements of the discussion but with a view to keeping them within the framework of what is regarded as legitimate by all of these actors. The adversarial mode of interaction which characterised the initial stages of the liberalisation programme has been overcome.

In the professional sector also, liberalisation brought about a 'flexible framework of both bilateral and multi-lateral linkages' between public and private actors engaged in the cooperative resolution of problems (Lovecy, in this volume). Again, in EC environmental policy, interaction is more often than not arranged in a consociational way. While this policy area had previously been characterised by an *ad hoc* 'appropriation' of the niches of environmental policy by the Commission, now traits of network governance are becoming more evident. The establishment of dialogue groups by the Commission reflects their intention to develop 'a mutual, cross national understanding'. They may also be regarded as an attempt to change attitudes (Lenschow, in this volume). And it is not only in these regulatory policy areas where a network mode of governance can be identified; it also figures prominently in distributive policy areas. The increase in structural funds and the reform of EC regional policy at the end of the 1980s have contributed to an upgrading of the European regions. The 'Community initiatives' in regional policy 'provide a fully fledged regime for co-operative governing, entailing principles, devising norms, rules and procedures that support, or even bring about, the institutionalisation of networks' (Kohler-Koch 1996: 373). Thus, there is evidence of the emergence of a network mode of governance in a broad range of EC policy areas, although it co-exists with other modes.

The *competing hypothesis* is that the European Community does not display an all-inclusive mode but variegated patterns of governance caused by the divergent properties of *different issues, policy areas and sectors*. At national level, a whole range of studies have pointed to such variations (e.g. Atkinson and Coleman 1992, Héritier *et al.* 1994, Hollingsworth *et al.* 1994). This finding may hold true for the EC as well. The high degree of organisational and functional segmentation is likely to trigger and perpetuate such variations because the political actors develop their own rationality criteria and decision styles in different areas.

Four examples illustrate this argument. First, Gerda Falkner (in this volume) has identified a quasi-corporatist mode of governance in the field of social policy. Social partnership along the lines of national neo-corporatism has been presented as 'good practice governance' by the Commission. Now the European employers' associations as well as the European trade union federation are given explicit competencies for associational self regulation. Second, due to its legalistic character, competition policy appears to be impermeable to relations organised around the principle of consociation (Allen 1996). In various instances of liberalisation, the Competition General Directorate (DG IV) has been keen to apply its legal powers under Article 90 (3) EC, which provides for a unilateral formulation of directives by the Commission. Such a proceeding is a significant deviation from the network mode of governance and iscloser to a statist pattern.

Third, in environmental policy, 'neither the impact of organisational and procedural innovations, nor the shift towards new policy instruments, nor the "constitutional" status of new governance elements are unambiguous' (Lenschow, in this volume). Andrea Lenschow regards the recorded innovations as extensions to, rather than replacements for, the established patterns of governance. Finally, the formulation of European Monetary Union falls definitely into the category of statism. Although societal actors are always affected and eager to be part of the game, and although the Commission usually has a vested interest in drawing in additional actors, in this case member governments have closed the arena.

What are the particular circumstances in which governing becomes a matter of negotiations between 'core executives' (Dyson, in this volume)? And what are the strategies to keep it that way? Negotiating the Economic and Monetary Union (EMU) is a good case to study. As at national level, monetary policy as a field is under the control of only a few actors with a heavy bias towards technocratic governance. It is of salient importance to the economic and social performance of a country. Establishing a monetary union with a single currency and a European Central Bank cuts deep into member states' sovereignty. The member governments considered it essential to keep the political process under their control and to avoid any domestic politicisation of the issue. One way to achieve this was through deliberate 'border politics'. There was consensus about defining the scope of monetary policy and the relevant actors in the field. 'The "territoriality" of the policy process expresses itself in a shared interest in retaining control of policy development within this narrow world' (Dyson, in this volume). The negotiation of EMU was not decision-making by networks, but intergovernmental negotiations in a traditional two-level game.

Vested interests are also important for *issue specificity*. Whenever the liberalisation of a sector or a profession touched upon well-organised vested interests, it met strong resistance. In particular monopoly firms and closed professional organisations resisted the opening-up of their markets. Negotiating the liberalisation process was a matter of hard bargaining and the actors had difficulties in agreeing on a common view. The market rationale was imposed on the incumbents. The regulatory reforms impinged directly upon the organisational viability and action capacities of the actors involved (see Aspinwall, in this volume). Therefore, interactions at EC level were unlikely to transform the actors' self interests. This was also very much the case during the neo-liberal regulatory reforms in Great Britain, France and Germany during the 1980s and 1990s (Foster 1992, Graham and Prosser 1991, Eising 1998). Such structural reforms do not lend themselves easily to consensual decisions, as they affect vital interests of powerful societal and economic actors be it at national or EC level. They lead to a significant redistribution of values by means of authoritative social or economic regulation, which scarcely allows for 'policy deliberation' (for this point see Majone 1993a) or consociational principles. The Commission's strategy of building up all-embracing policy communities was but a weak attempt to bypass sectoral opposition.

Thus, significant deviations from the network mode of governance can be recognised. However, even in these cases, its most important components can be identified. First, let us take a look at EC neo-corporatism. In several ways, the governance of EC social policy does not display the elements which characterised neo-corporatism during its heyday in the 1970s. The social dialogue at European level has been nourished by Commission support for several decades. It was the Social Agreement (see Falkner, in this volume) which first raised the standing of both sides of industry. In times of growing social pressure, it has contributed to an upgrading of the social partners and, by so doing, it has pushed forward the logic of functional representation. Employers and labour have become institutionalised as corporate social actors, and whenever their interests coincide, they gain a privileged position in EC policy-making. Mutual agreements are most likely to be transformed into a Commission proposal and, subsequently, a Council decision.

These provisions, however, do not set up a full fledged (neo-)corporatist system of governance for two reasons. Even though they managed to agree on several issues such as parental leave, in important areas of social policy and labour relations the social partners lack the cohesiveness to make binding decisions. In view of all the structural deficiencies and the imbalance in resources, neither trade unions nor the employers support corporatism as a legitimate system of governance at the European level. In other words, the functional scope of the neo-corporatist arrangements is rather limited. Since important structural prerequisites for neo-corporatism do not exist, the patterns of co-operation within the realm of the Social Protocol may be more adequately presented as a mode of network governance which emphasises the significance of associational self-regulation and functional subsidiarity. But the question of how this contributes to the penetration of system boundaries is also important. Empowering the representatives of labour and employers at European level is another step in the transformation of the multi-level system controlled by governments into an encompassing political space which allows societal actors room to intervene directly in EC policy-making.

Second, the prevalence of EC law will be examined. The legal process applied by the Competition Directorate General to bring about sectoral liberalisation ran into serious opposition from the European Parliament, the member states and economic actors. It was also resisted by the sectoral DGs responsible for energy, telecommunications and transport. In several instances, the use of the armoury for which EC competition law provides, 'was outvoted by the rest of the college of Commissioners' (Holmes and McGowan 1997: 180 on transport). The unilateral and strictly legal process implemented by the Commission pertaining to important reforms is even regarded as indecent when it runs counter to the market doctrine which, after all, is the most prominent 'rationality criterion' of the integration process (see Lepsius 1990). What actors are looking for, instead, is the construction of a broad consensus on policy principles and specific liberalisation measures. This is yet more proof that there is a predominant belief that networks and consensus formation are an appropriate way of governing the European Union. This is deeply rooted in political practice and daily routines. The Competition Directorate, with its marked case orientation and legalistic culture (Laudati 1996), is the single most important exception to this general pattern.

In sum, the central elements of the network mode of governance can be identified across a broad range of EC policy areas, although area and issue-specific variations remain. This mode of governance has gained broad acceptance among political, societal and economic actors, as it forms an attempt to safeguard the integration of the affected actors into the EC system. It thereby not only raises the legitimacy of the system as such but also the legitimacy of its various policies. It is regarded as the appropriate mode of governance because it is able to bridge the heterogeneity of the EC's members and compensate for the lack of democratic accountability by introducing elements of functional representation. When talking about a potential increase in the legitimacy of the EC system, the emphasis is on improving not so much input performance as output performance. However, the overall optimistic expectations that problem-solving capacity may be improved when negotiations take place in networks, have to be taken with a grain of salt. It is not clear that the network mode of governance leads to particularly efficient or effective problem-solving. In her analysis of EC environmental policy, Andrea Lenschow emphasises that different modes of governance may lead to equally (in-)appropriate results (see also Gerda Falkner, in this volume).

The importance of principles and concepts in EC governance

The main argument of this section is that, because of its institutional properties, the EC is open to and in need of guiding principles. Precisely because of its heterogeneous composition and complex institutional set-up, regimes around which actors expectations can converge are needed: the European Community puts a premium on the ability to provide convincing policy concepts and their interpretation. It requires 'the skilful manipulation of the highly entangled system of EC governance involving hundreds of actors' and of 'negotiations characterised by constant stalemates, reversals of positions, [and] the reshaping of actor coalitions' (Gottweis, in this volume).

There are two different kinds of regime.[1] First a specific set of principles, norms and rules may revolve around the 'community method' as such. Second, principles and concepts are developed which give direction to the Community's dealings in specific subject matters.

First, as argued in the previous section, EC governance is located in fundamental *belief systems about the appropriate mode of governance* in the European Community. The network mode of governance in the EC is 'well directed by shared beliefs about what constitutes the legitimacy of a political system and what supports the claim to make binding decisions' (Kohler-Koch, in this volume). In particular, the political actors' belief systems revolve around broad orientations of solidarity (Ebbinghaus and Kraus 1997: 350–1) and reciprocity. While the EC treaty now allows majority voting on a number of issues, decision-making in the Council is still characterised by a search for consensus (e.g. Hayes-Renshaw and Wallace 1995) to find political solutions regarded as legitimate by *all* the participants.

The preference for unanimous decisions within the Council is an important indicator for the validity of the consociational ordering principle. It points to the primordial importance of reciprocity criteria and the respect for the core idea of consociation (e.g. Rieger and König 1997: 32–3). Due to the EC's heterogeneous composition and their long-term co-operation across a broad range of policy areas, member state relations are marked by a multilateral and generalised reciprocity. In contrast to the specific reciprocity of market exchanges, the time horizon of generalised reciprocity is almost unlimited and its substantial elements are open and flexible (see Keohane 1984: 130). Often, no member state is obliged to transfer specific 'exchange resources' in EC negotiations. The mutual acceptance of the legitimacy and appropriateness of EC political programmes is more important.

Second, there are more specific principles, norms and rules which are important guiding posts within and across specific policy areas. It is not particularly satisfying, however, merely to ascertain that EC governance is marked by its strong reliance on regime formatting concepts. We therefore propose to differentiate between three types of concepts and principles, namely substantial, procedural, and distributive principles, each of which has its own characteristics.

Substantial concepts relate primarily to the content of a policy, the goals to be attained and the instruments to be employed. In environmental policy, the concept of 'sustainable development' provided a focal point for the convergence of expectations guiding political action (Lenschow, in this volume). In social policy (Falkner, in this volume), the emphasis on 'the social dimension of the internal market' fulfilled a similar function and gal-vanised agreement on the Social Protocol of the Maastricht Treaty. The chief characteristic of substantial concepts is that they are area-specific. The actors need not necessarily agree on 'all the definitions of the central problems', rather what is needed is 'sufficient overlap' for any policy concept to become a 'successful dominant approach' (Gottweis, in this volume).

Apart from this first set of guiding principles, there are general *procedural* and *distributive principles*. They pertain to the whole range of the EC system and to all of its policy areas. Procedural principles embody norms in terms of fair and efficient proceedings. Subsidiarity is viewed as a relevant criterion for an efficient allocation of competencies among the different levels of government (territorial subsidiarity) and to the public and private spheres (functional subsidiarity). While procedural principles refer to the appropriateness and efficiency of *processes*, distributive principles relate to the fairness of their *results*. Thus, the cohesion principle is meant to ensure solidarity between the northern and southern member states by means of transfer payments, opt-out provisions, and special programmes for the southern states.

The relationship between the procedural and distributive principles on the one hand, and the substantive principles on the other, is complex. Subsidiarity, reciprocity, and cohesion are important in all policy areas and shape the terms of the European political discourse. But their specific interpretation is, in turn, often shaped by the substantial principles in the contested policy area in question. This may be illustrated by two examples. First, during the liberalisation of the electricity sector (Eising, in this volume), the Commission, the member states and the sectoral actors related reciprocity to the principle of market integration. Reciprocity was meant to ensure that the opening up of the market was fair in terms of market outcomes. During the course of the policy debate, it was interpreted as an equal percentage of market opening in each of the member states. Second, the 'new approach' to harmonisation and mutual recognition is designed to ensure that the integration process is not impeded by the excessive harmonisation problems encountered in a heterogeneous context. Mutual recognition as a procedural principle is only conceivable against the background of market integration as the dominant rationality criterion of the European Community.

It is an inherent trait of principles and concepts that they are incapable of providing exact behavioural prescriptions; instead, they define rather broad normative standards and are open to interpretation. Therefore, their normative relevance as well as their prescriptive elements are often disputed and subject to divergent interpretations, as Thomas Hueglin has emphasised: 'It may indeed be the ideological hallmark of the integration process that it remains embedded in an open-ended conceptual discourse meant to conceal persistent dissent about goals and means rather than representing consent' (Hueglin, in this volume).

Alternative interpretations can be prevented by bringing them closer to a particular policy content. A context-specific interpretation will make principles, norms and rules more unequivocal. As interpretations narrow, policy choices and opportunities for deviant behaviour are also restricted: because common policies entail elements of both mutual interest and competing individual interests, actors will struggle for conceptual dominance. Therefore, one has to look for actors who will be able to provide and interpret principles and concepts, and for institutional settings which will give stability to some interpretations and will not accommodate others.

First, it should be borne in mind that interpretative margins vary with the different types of principles. *Prima facie*, there seems to be more latitude for the procedural and distributive principles because they display a higher degree of generality than the substantial principles. However, the procedural and distributive principles are more firmly embedded in institutions. Principles, such as cohesion and subsidiarity, have been written into the Treaties and are no longer open for immediate revision. They are now considered to be norms of a higher order and, when applied to specific areas and cases, they will be contested. Paradoxically, conflicts about application and interpretation tend to strengthen the principle. Even if actors only pay lip-service to them at first, they may turn into institutionalised reference points over time, shaping the discourse of EC governance. To the extent to which they are exercised and practised in daily routines they become part of the living constitution.

The definition and interpretation of substantial principles, on the other hand, looks more susceptible to the influence of socio-economic actors. They can bring in specialised expertise and mobilise political support for their views on the problem. As there is much to be lost and to be gained, resourceful actors will crowd the European arena and plead their cause. It is highly plausible to argue that 'a 'modernisation coalition' of dominant public and private interests can set the agenda. Thomas Hueglin claims that there can be little doubt as to its composition: '"policy entrepreneurs" in the Commission, managers of multi-level corporations, and the governments of economically strong member states with Germany at the apex' (Hueglin, in this volume). By calling it a 'modernisation coalition', the importance of particular contingencies is already being highlighted. These will usually be functional and task specific.

Even within the European Commission or individual member state governments, actors are in need of bridging concepts. Being responsible for different tasks within the administration, they identify with exclusive policy philosophies. Environmental policy is a good example of how a common denominator had to be found to break a deadlock. 'Sustainability' was the formula used by the environmentalists within the

Commission in order to present their strategies in a way which was also acceptable to their colleagues from other DGs whose task it was to keep the single market clear from what they called 'undue political interference' (see Jachtenfuchs 1996a, b). Similarly, the Environment Directorate General was able to define genetic engineering as a process technology and, through de-linking, was able to keep it away from highly contested areas like specific product regulations. The DG managed to construct a discursive network around this very definition, thereby shaping the content of the later directive on genetic engineering (Gottweis, in this volume). The concepts and definitions first formed the basis for a consensus within the Commission, and then among the member states and interest groups.

Both examples illustrate that, even within the EC institutions, the definition of policy concepts is highly contested; it is not necessarily driven by an economic logic but is decided according to the balance of power and interests of the actors involved.

EC governance and member state governance: towards convergence or diversity?

If we agree that there is at least a propensity to move towards network governance at the European level, how will this affect the modes of governance at member state level? Will a convergence in the way Europe is governed come about or will we be faced with quite distinct patterns? Can we tell when and why a transformation in national patterns of governance will take place? On the basis of the contributions in this volume, it is our contention that the impact of EC governance on the member states varies and hinges upon three variables:

- first, the very nature of EC governance
- second, the respective national patterns of governance and the degree of their institutionalisation
- and third, the cost-benefit ratio of adapting national patterns of governance to EC governance in terms of the costs of transformation and the benefits for future problem-solving capacities.

The conventional wisdom is that the ever-growing range of EC competence, covering more and more policy areas, and the frequency and depth of interference have a significant impact on the member states. Through our studies, we have amassed empirical evidence of such impacts, but they are neither clear-cut, nor do they point in any one direction. First, it is plausible to assume that the overlap of governance modes in several EC policy areas gives no clear direction to member states. Furthermore, the degrees of Europeanisation differ across and within individual policy areas. In addition, the legal instrument by which a policy is introduced at member state level matters. EC regulations leave less choice than EC directives, which allow for more flexibility in translating EC rulings into national law.

Second, the persistence of national patterns of governance varies across member states. The 'path dependency' of national institutional development is quite evident in many of the studies (e.g. Aspinwall, Lovecy, both in this volume). The way in which the interpenetrating of EC and national governing patterns will alter the established systems in the member states will depend on given national configurations. Apart from the overall national context, the sectoral political and social contexts must also be taken into account. In each case, the differential degree of institutionalisation is of great importance. Furthermore, in order to predict the likelihood and direction of change, those elements of the national modes of governance likely to be affected have to be analysed: the basic principles of the political processes, public and private relations, the national institutional configurations and the policy and decision-making styles.

Notwithstanding institutional persistence, the introduction of new substantial policy concepts leaves its mark on the national modes of governance. Taking the example of sustainable development and the primacy of the market doctrine, it is evident that it would be very difficult indeed to trace the origin of the concept and to evaluate their effect without taking note of their embeddedness in global economic and environmental discursive patterns. The acceptance of both concepts has, without doubt, been supported by the global discourse. Nevertheless, the EC is frequently an agent of change. Mark Aspinwall (in this volume) regards the 'liberalisation of the transport market' as 'a decision that many countries, particularly the Mediterranean ones, would not have made independently' of the Internal Market Programme. This argument also holds true for the liberalisation of many other sectors.

Andrea Lenschow argues in this volume that 'the clearest influence' of the EC on national patterns of governance is through the introduction of '*policy instruments*'. Devising and implementing EC policies clearly has less impact on the national *institutional configurations* then on national policies. In most of the member states, the co-ordination and negotiation of EC policies has been integrated into the established routines and practices (e.g. Mény *et al.* 1996, Sidenius, in this volume, Wessels and Rometsch 1996) and caused rather limited changes in formal structures and procedures. This holds true for single institutions, such as national parliaments (Norton 1996) and national executives (Wessels and Rometsch 1996) as well as for their routine interaction. Even the response of national actors to the 'judicialisation' of the political process through EC law and the European Court of Justice (ECJ) (Wincott 1996) varies widely and is subject to the existing national legal system and practices. In Great Britain, for example, where courts play hardly any role in the political process, cases were transferred to the ECJ four times less frequently than by Germany, which is characterised by its

'*Rechtsstaat*' tradition and the 'judicialisation' of political decision-making
(see Golub 1996: 366–7). This apparent continuity of national patterns and
practices could be misleading, and might deflect attention from changing
power relations within and between the national institutions in the new
multi-level framework (see below).

Finally, the costs of adaptation may be decisive for the national responses
to the EC mode of governance (see Lenschow; Pagoulatos; Sidenius;
Schmidt; all in this volume). In their comparative analyses, Vivien Schmidt
and Andrea Lenschow emphasise that it makes a difference when the network mode of governance at EC level encounters different national modes:
statism in France, Britain, Spain and Italy; corporatism in Germany; and
networks in the Netherlands. In their opinion, the least likely case in which a
network type of governance might be adopted is statism. Both systems are too
far apart: the EC networks are characterised by the inclusion of a multitude
of public and private actors. Their interaction revolves around substantial,
procedural and distributive principles. The individual actors have rather
low capabilities and their relationship is defined by interdependence. In
contrast, statism is characterised by a preference for autonomous action and
by a self-interested perspective of both private and public actors. The state
actors have high action capacities due to a high degree of organisational
concentration. The transition of this mode of governance to the network
mode of governance would be accompanied by high transaction costs and
a loss of autonomy for the public actors.

Nevertheless, it is interesting to note that, even in this case, the
responses are not uniform. In France – and also in Greece, Italy and Spain
– the 'loss of governmental autonomy in policy formulation has been largely
accepted'. On the one hand, France accepted it 'in exchange for greater
predominance in Europe'; on the other, Italy, Greece, and Spain accepted
it in exchange for political and economic modernisation programmes. Only
Great Britain has 'self-styled' its role as 'reluctant partner' (Schmidt, in this
volume). Apparently, apart from the 'clash' of the EC mode of governance
with the preponderant national mode of governance, the awareness of a
limited capacity to preserve national patterns and the ability to convince or
force others to adopt one's preferred mode of governance will influence
the national response. Weakness in terms of resources as well as in terms of
conceptual subordinance increases the propensity to learn and to adapt
(Pagoulatos, in this volume). Therefore, smaller and worse-off member
states may be more likely to accept the transformation of the national
modes of governance.

European governance also impinges upon the established actor constellations at national level. Several contributions highlight the 'explosion of
interest group activity' (Hueglin, in this volume) at EC level, and there is a
burgeoning amount of literature on this topic.[2] The growing range of EC
policies and the changes in EC decision rules since the Single European

Act have brought private actors into the game. It is widely assumed that multi-level networks break up the established national actor constellations and open up new opportunities for the pursuit of self-interests. The European Community offers a new space for the construction of transnational coalitions, the development of new cleavage lines, and the revival of dormant cleavages.

The way in which the European Community opens up an institutional arena which offers new legal and political opportunities for both private and public actors is highlighted in several contributions. In her analysis of the liberalisation of professional services, Jill Lovecy evaluates the impact of EC law and the European Court of Justice on the patterns of interest intermediation. In her opinion, access to the ECJ allowed 'policy outsiders' at the national level to come centre-stage at EC level, and has enabled individual members of the professions (or individual service recipients) 'to challenge and, when successful, overturn the kinds of entrenched national and sub-national restrictive practices which have been the product of alliance-building between those who are "policy-insiders" within the member states' sectoral governance structures'. The new practices of litigation caused a process of governance transformation 'by the back door' (Lovecy, in this volume).

However, while just one legal case may be sufficient to initiate political reforms, access to the political institutions and influence on political decisions are also a question of resources and of the congruence of the actors' perspectives on policy concepts and principles (Kohler-Koch 1996: 366). They therefore depend on the EC institutions' properties and outlook, as well as those of the member states and interest groups. Several studies have already pointed out that the EC system of interest representation is biased towards producer interests, due to the supremacy of the market doctrine and the superior organisational and informational resources of the economic interest groups (e.g. Schmidt, in this volume). Social interest groups, consumer associations, environmental groups and even organised labour not only command lower resources and organisational capacities (e.g. Young 1997), generally they also depend on the political support of just one 'sponsor' Directorate General and the less influential European Parliament. Even when they get such support, it is a 'coalition of the weak' because weak interest groups unite with Commission DGs with low standing and EP party groups which are often in minority positions. Economic interests, on the other hand, are often taken care of by several DGs.

Weak interest organisations can only gain when they conform to the policy concept of a dominant actor. A good example is provided by GEODE, a small European interest organisation founded by a few (Spanish and French) local electricity distributors. While almost all Continental European utilities opposed liberalisation of the electricity market, the GEODE members supported the EC proposals and were granted excellent access to the

Commission. Despite the fact that, in terms of capital and production share, they represent only a tiny fraction of the EC electricity sector, they were part of the winning coalition (Eising, in this volume). This case indicates that the economic weight of interest groups does not necessarily determine policy output. Influence might hinge upon the use of a coalition partner for the public actors in need of societal support for new policy ideas. The case again points to the importance of parallel interests and congruent belief systems (see Sabatier 1993).

The overall picture, however, confirms the well-known assertion that Europeanisation provides opportunities for resourceful actors. Talking about network governance, therefore, should not conceal the fact that *distributive justice* may suffer. One reason why actors depend so much on resources is that, in order for lobbying to be effective, interest groups have to be present both at EC and at national level. Niels Sidenius (in this volume) found that shifting policy-making responsibilities to the EC does not mean that relations between the national state actors and private actors are diminishing. On the contrary, several national interest groups even intensified their contacts with national institutions. Europeanisation has brought about the re-organisation of structures and strategies of interest mediation. Whether on balance private or public actors have gained in that process is difficult to assess. According to Edgar Grande, the very loss of autonomy incurred by public actors in the horizontal and vertical negotiations characteristic of EC decision-making may, at the same time, allow them to gain autonomy *vis-à-vis* private actors (Grande 1994). The strategy of 'self-binding' (Wolf, in this volume) may provide the means to turn down the demands of societal and economic interest organisations. This so-called '*paradox of weakness*' has been highlighted by several contributions (see Schmidt; Wolf, both in this volume).

Nevertheless, it is difficult to come to clear-cut conclusions about the relative influence of public and private actors in EC decision-making. On the one hand, easy access to Community institutions, the resource dependence of these institutions and their need for functional representation seems to tip the balance in favour of big private players. On the other hand, the complexity of the EC system and the centrality of the public actors in the decision-making process make it more difficult for interest groups to have a decisive impact. The cases of sectoral liberalisation analysed in this volume may be taken as 'crucial cases' (Eckstein 1992). Fundamental reforms were often decided on in the face of resistance from large and powerful economic actors with entrenched political ties to state actors. However, the success of these regulatory reforms cannot be attributed to the particular properties of the institutional structure alone. The awareness of global competition, global de-regulatory reforms and the hegemonic position of EC market integration all promoted sectoral liberalisation.

Making our conclusion on this point look even more tentative, we would like to contest the general relevance of the 'paradox of weakness'. The empirical validity of research undertaken thus far must be regarded as patchy. First, it is based on an empirical study of EC research and technology policy. It is now generally accepted that the co-operative information technology programme, ESPRIT (European Strategic Programme for Research in Information Technologies) was the forerunner of and catalyst for the later EC technology programs. ESPRIT was initiated by a coalition of the Commission and large European information technology firms against the initial preferences of the large member states' administrations (Sandholtz 1992, Sharp and Shearman 1987). The genesis of ESPRIT must therefore be regarded as a case in which national executives actually had to concede ground to large firms and to the Commission. Therefore, it is necessary to disaggregate the public and the private sectors, rather than referring to 'the' public sphere or 'the' private sphere alone. This would allow a more detailed analysis of who were the winners and who the losers. Within national governments, it is mainly the leading departments which will gain autonomy in relation to private actors and other national public actors. They are able to monopolise expertise and information in EC-level negotiations.

Taking a sub-systemic level approach reveals yet another point. *Internal* negotiation pressures presuppose that the positions of the public actors cannot be attributed to the influence of interest organisations. Taking the example of electricity liberalisation (Eising, in this volume), major policy concepts have been developed by national interest groups: the 'Single Buyer' concept was developed by Electricité de France and was then taken up by the French Industry Ministry and introduced to the EC level in a slightly modified version. The 'Negotiated Third Party Access' concept was promoted by German industrial energy consumers and accepted by the European Commission. Consequently, when negotiating at EC level, member state executives are not just involved in a genuinely internal debate, but may even find themselves responding to policy concepts promoted by national interest groups from other member states and may have to face transnational coalitions.[3]

When transposing EC directives into national law, member state administrations may even have to accept EC proposals which run counter to their own preferences but are supported by domestic interest groups. During the negotiations on the transposition of the EC directive on electricity liberalisation into German law, the leading German department, the Federal Ministry of the Economy, had to accept that the German *Stadtwerke* (municipal companies) insisted on the integration of the 'French' Single Buyer proposal into national law against the Ministry's opposition. This means that a proposal generated by Electricité de France and rather alien to the German economic culture may now become part and parcel of the German electricity sector.

Conclusion

The contributions assembled in this volume identified a complex mixture of governance modes at EC level which, however, display general characteristics. Despite the widely divergent member-state modes of governance and area-specific variations, most EC policy areas are marked by the preponderance of network governance. The fragility of the EC's democratic legitimacy and its complex and heterogeneous composition and set-up allow for this particular mode of governance. It is widely regarded as being able to bridge the heterogeneity of EC member states and socio-economic actors as well as compensating for the lack of democratic accountability by introducing elements of functional representation.

Thus, the network mode of governance in the EC is rooted in a general set of principles and norms about European decision-making: fundamental belief systems about appropriate ways of governing the EC form a major signpost for the state and private actors. Below this fundamental belief system, a second set of distributive, procedural and substantive concepts is of major importance in the multi-level networks and affects the formation of area-specific regimes.

The repercussions of EC governance on the member states and on public–private relations are not unequivocal, even though transformative pressures are implied. The signals emerging from Brussels are not always clear, as various modes of governance overlap and national modes of governance are often highly institutionalised. Most visible is the adaptation of policies and policy instruments to EC governance, while national institutional arrangements appear to be more impermeable. Member state responses to EC governance vary even if they are marked by the same national mode of governance, as the diverging responses of members with statist regimes have demonstrated. This highlights the trade-off between the national costs of adaptation and the perceived benefits accruing from a greater capacity for problem-solving in a collective endeavour.

Notes

1 The analytical distinction between principles, norms, rules – and procedures – is taken from the well-known debate on international regimes.
2 See Eichener and Voelzkow 1994b; Eising and Kohler-Koch 1994; Greenwood *et al.* 1992a; Greenwood and Aspinwall 1998; Kohler-Koch 1994; Mazey and Richardson 1993c; Van Schendelen 1993; Wallace and Young 1997.
3 The theoretical problems which must be faced when the autonomy of individual actors is analysed are treated by Klaus-Dieter Wolf in this volume.

BIBLIOGRAPHY

Abbott, A. (1988) *The System of Professions: An Essay on the Division of Expert Labor*, Chicago: University of Chicago Press.

Abromeit, H. (1996) *Decision-Making and Participation in Multi-Level Federations: A Model for Federalising the European Union*, paper, ECPR Joint Session of Workshops, Oslo (29 March – 3 April).

Aguilar, S. (1993) 'Corporatist and Statist Designs in Environmental Policy. The Contrasting Roles of Germany and Spain in the European Community Scenario', *Environmental Politics* 2, 2: 223–47.

Aguilar, S. (1997) 'Spain', in Weidner, H. (ed.) *Performance and Characteristics of German Environmental Policy. Overview and Expert Commentaries from 14 Countries*, Berlin: Wissenschaftszentrum für Sozialforschung, 58ff.

Alexander, E. R. (1995) *How Organizations Act Together: Interorganizational Coordination in Theory and Practice*, Amsterdam: OPA/Gordon and Breach.

Alexander, J. C. (1995) *Fin de Siècle Social Theory: Relativism, Reduction, and the Problem of Reason*, London: Verso.

Allen, D. (1996) 'Competition Policy: Policing the Single Market', in Wallace, H. and W. Wallace (eds) *Policy-Making in the European Union*, Oxford: Oxford University Press: 157–84.

Allison, G. (1971) *The Essence of Decision: Explaining the Cuban Missile Crisis*, Boston: Little, Brown.

Almond, G. A. (1958) 'A Comparative Study of Interest Groups and the Political Process', *American Political Science Review* 52, 2: 270–82.

Almond, G. A. and S. Verba (1965) *The Civic Culture: Political Attitudes and Democracy in Five Nations*, Princeton: Princeton University Press.

Andersen, S. S. (1993) 'Towards a Common EC Energy Policy', in Andersen, S. S. and K. Eliassen (eds) *Making Policy in Europe. The Europeification of National Policy-Making*, London: Sage: 133–54.

Andersen, S. S. and K. Eliassen (eds) (1993) *Making Policy in Europe. The Europeification of National Policy-Making*, London: Sage.

Anderson, J. (1979) *Public Policy-Making*, New York: Praeger.

Ansell, C. K. *et al.* (1995) *Dual Networks in the European Union*, paper, European Community Studies Association, Charleston, South Carolina (11–14 May).

Aspinwall, M. (1995) 'International Integration or Internal Politics? Anatomy of a Single Market Measure', *Journal of Common Market Studies* 33, 4: 475–99.

Atkinson, M. M. and W. D. Coleman (1989) 'Strong States and Weak States: Sectoral Policy Networks in Advanced Capitalist Economies', *British Journal of Political*

Science 19, 1: 47–67.

Atkinson, M. M. and W. D. Coleman (1992) 'Policy Networks, Policy Communities and the Problems of Governance', *Governance* 5, 2:154–84.

Averyt, W. (1977) *Agropolitics in the European Community: Interest Groups and the Common Agricultural Policy,* London: Praeger.

Axelrod, R. (1990) *The Evolution of Co-operation,* London: Penguin.

Aznar, L. (1994) *Democratic Societies at the Time of Market Authoritarianism,* paper, International Poltical Science Association, Berlin (21–25 August).

Badie, B. and P. Birnbaum (1983) *The Sociology of the State,* Chicago: Chicago University Press.

Barber, B. R. (1992) 'Jihad vs. McWorld', *Atlantic Monthly* 269, 3: 33–63.

Bauer M. (1989) 'The Politics of State-Directed Privatisation: The Case of France, 1986–88', in Vickers, J. and V. Wright (eds) *The Politics of Privatisation in Western Europe,* London: Frank Cass: 49–60.

Bennett, C. J. (1991) 'Review Article: What is Policy Convergence and What Causes It?', *British Journal of Political Science* 21: 215–33.

Benz, A. (1998) 'Ansatzpunkte für ein europafähiges Demokratiekonzept', in Kohler–Koch, B. (ed.) *Regieren in entgrenzten Räumen,* Opladen: Westdeutscher Verlag, Politische Vierteljahresschrift, Sonderheft 29: 345–68.

Bercusson, B. (1993) 'European Labour Law and Sectoral Bargaining', *Industrial Relations Journal* 24, 4: 257–72.

Boerzel, T. (1997) 'The Implementation of EU Environmental Policy in Spain and Catalunya', in Knill, C. (ed.) *Interim Project Report: The Implementation of European Environmental Policy. The Impact and Transformation of National Administrative Traditions, Annex,* Florence: EUI.

Bredima Savopoulou, A. and J. Tzoannos (1990) *The Common Shipping Policy of the European Community,* Amsterdam: North-Holland.

Bregnsbo, H. and N. C. Sidenius (1993) 'Denmark. The National Lobby Orchestra', in Van Schendelen, M. C. P. M. (ed.) *National Public and Private EC Lobbying,* Aldershot: Dartmouth: 187–206.

Bressers, H. (1997) 'The Netherlands', in Weidner, H. (ed.) *Performance and Characteristics of German Environmental Policy. Overview and Expert Commentaries from 14 Countries,* Berlin: Wissenschaftszentrum für Sozialforschung: 55–57.

Bröker, G. (1989) *Competition in Banking,* Paris: OECD.

Bruha, T. (1994) 'Das Subsidiaritätsprinzip im Recht der Europäischen Gemeinschaft', in Riklin, A. and G. Batliner (eds) *Subsidiarität,* Baden-Baden: Nomos: 373–410.

Buechler, Steven M. (1993) 'Beyond Resource Mobilization? Emerging Trends in Social Movement Theory', *Sociological Quarterly* 34, 2: 217–35.

Bulmer, S. (1992) 'Completing the European Community's Internal Market: The Regulatory Implications for the Federal Republic of Germany', in Dyson, K. (ed.) *The Politics of German Regulation,* Aldershot: Dartmouth: 53–78.

Bulmer, S. (1994) 'The Governance of the European Union: A New Institutionalist Approach', *Journal of Public Policy* 13, 4: 351–80.

Bundesministerium für Wirtschaft (1991) *Energiepolitik für das vereinte Deutschland,* Bonn.

Bundesministerium für Wirtschaft (1996a) *Gesetz zur Neuregelung des Energiewirtschaftsrechts,* Stand 30.04.1996, Bonn.

Bundesministerium für Wirtschaft (1996b) *Entwurf. Amtliche Begründung des Gesetzes zur Neuregelung des Energiewirtschaftsrechts,* Stand 17.05.1996, Bonn.

Bundesrat (1996) *Stellungnahme des Bundesrates. Entwurf eines Gesetzes zur Neuregelung des Energiewirtschaftsgesetzes*, Beschluß 806/96 vom 9.12.1996, Bonn: Bundesanzeiger.

Burley, A.-M. and W. Mattli (1993) 'Europe Before the Court: A Political Theory of Legal Integration', *International Organization* 47, 1: 41–76.

Burrage, M. and R. Torstendahl (eds) (1990) *Professions in Theory and History. Rethinking the Study of the Professions*, London: Sage.

Cafruny, A. W. (1997) 'Social Democracy in One Continent? Alternatives to a Neoliberal Europe', in Cafruny, A. W. and C. Lankowski (eds) *Europe's Ambiguous Unity: Conflict and Consensus in the Post-Maastricht Era*, Boulder: Lynne Rienner: 109–28.

Cameron, D. R. (1992) 'The 1992 Initiative: Causes and Consequences', in Sbragia, A. M. (ed.) *Euro-Politics: Institutions and Policymaking in the 'New' European Community*, Washington D.C.: Brookings Institution: 23–74.

Camerra-Rowe, P. (1994) *New Roads of Political Influence: The Response of German and British Road Haulage Firms to the 1992 Single European Market*, paper presented at the International Conference of Europeanists, Chicago.

Camiller, P. (1989) 'Beyond 1992: The Left and Europe', *New Left Review* 17, 5: 99–110.

Campanella, M. L. (1995) 'Getting the Core: A Neo-Institutionalist Approach to the EMU', *Government and Opposition* 30, 3: 347–369.

Campbell, J. L. and L. N. Lindberg (1991) 'The Evolution of Governance Regimes', in Campbell, J .L., J. R. Hollingsworth and L. N. Lindberg (eds) *Governance of the American Economy*, Cambridge: Cambridge University Press: 319–55.

Caporaso, J. (1974) *The Structure and Function of European Integration*, Pacific Palisades: Goodyear.

Caporaso, J., M. Green-Cowles and T. Risse (forthcoming) 'Introductory Chapter', in *Europeanization and Domestic Change*, Florence.

Cappelletti, M., M. Seccombe and J. Weiler (eds) (1986) *Integration through Law: Europe and the American Federal Experience, vol. 1*, Berlin/New York: de Gruyter.

Cassese, S. (1993) 'Italie: Privatisations Annoncées, Semi-Privatisations et Pseudo-Privatisations', in V. Wright (ed.) *Les Privatisations en Europe: Programmes et Problèmes*, Paris: Actes Sud: 161–85.

Cassina, G. (1992) 'La Dimension Conventionelle des Décisions de Maastricht', *Notabene* 67: 13–15.

Catenhusen, W.-M. and H. Neumeister (eds) (1987) Enquete-Kommission des Deutschen Bundestages, *Chancen und Risken der Gentechnologie. Dokumentation des Berichts an den Deutschen Bundestag*, München: Schweitzer Verlag.

Cawson, A. (ed.) (1985) *Organized Interests and the State. Studies in Meso-Corporatism*, London: Sage.

Christensen, J. G. (1978) 'Da centraladministrationen blev international. En analyse af den administrative tilpasningsproces ved Danmarks tilslutning til EF', in Amstrup, I. and I. Faurby (eds) *Studier i dansk udenrigspolitik*, Århus: Forlaget Politica: 75–118.

Christensen, J. G. (1981) 'Blurring the International–Domestic Politics Distinction. Danish Representation at EC Negotiations', *Scandinavian Political Studies* 4, 3: 191–208.

Christensen, J. G. (1991) *Den usynlige stat*, Copenhagen: Gyldendal.

Christiansen, P. M. (1993) *Det frie marked – den forhandlede økonomi*, Copenhagen: Jurist–og Økonomforbundets Forlag.

Christiansen, P .M. and N. C. Sidenius (1995) 'Korporatisme på retur?', *Politica* 27, 4: 436–49.

Christie, I. (1994) 'Britain's Sustainable Development Strategy. Environmental Quality and Policy Change', *Policy Studies* 15, 3: 4–20.

Coen, D. (1997) 'The Evolution of the Large Firm as a Political Actor in the European Union,' *Journal of European Public Policy* 4, 1: 91–108.

Cohen, M., J. March and J. Olsen (1972) 'A Garbage Can Model of Organizational Choice', *Administrative Sciences Quarterly* 17, 1: 1–25.

Coleman, W. D. (1994) 'Policy Convergence in Banking: A Comparative Study', *Political Studies* 42, 2: 274–92.

Coleman, W. and G. Underhill (eds) (1995) 'The Single Market and Global Economic Integration', special issue of *Journal of European Public Policy* 2, 3.

Commission (Commission of the European Communities) (1989) *Communication from the Commission Concerning its Action Programme Relating to the Implementation of the Community Charter of Basic Social Rights for Workers*, Brussels: COM (89) 568 final.

Commission (Commission of the European Communities) (1992) *The Future Development of Transport Policy*, Luxembourg: Office for Official Publications of the European Communities.

Commission (Commission of the European Communities) (1993a) *Towards Sustainability. A European Community Programme of Policy and Action in Relation to the Environment and Sustainable Development*, Luxembourg: Office for Official Publications of the European Communities.

Commission (Commission of the European Communities) (1993b) *Integrating the Environment into Other Policy Areas within the Commission*, Communication to the Commission from Mr Paleocrassas and Mr van Miert, Brussels.

Commission (Commission of the European Communities) (1993c) *Communication Concerning the Application of the Agreement on Social Policy Presented by the Commission to the Council and to the European Parliament*, Brussels: COM (93) 600 final, 6c.

Commission (European Commission) (1994a) *Growth, Competitiveness, Employment. The Challenges and Ways Forward into the 21st Century*, Luxembourg: Office for Official Publications of the European Communities.

Commission (European Commission) (1994b) *The Trans-European Transport Network*, Luxembourg: Office for Official Publications of the European Communities.

Commission (Commission Européenne) (1994c) *XXIIIe Rapport sur la Politique de Concurrence 1993*, Luxembourg: Office des Publications Officielles des Communautés Européennes.

Commission (European Commission) (1995a) *Report of the Group of Independent Experts on Legislative and Administrative Simplification*, Brussels: COM (95) 288fin (21 June 1995).

Commission (European Commission) (1995b) *Progress Report from the Commission on the Implementation of the European Community Programme of Policy and Action in Relation to the Environment and Sustainable Development 'Towards Sustainability'*, Brussels: COM (95) 624fin (10 January 1996).

Commission (European Commission) (1996a) *Communication from the Commission to the Council and the European Parliament. On Trade and Environment*, Brussels: COM (96) 54fin (28 February 1996).

Commission (European Commission) (1996b) *Annual Report on Monitoring and the Application of Community Law*, Brussels: COM (96) 600fin.

Commission (European Commission (1996c) *Top Decision Makers Survey: Summary*

Report, Brussels: Eurobarometer.

Commission (Commission of the European Communities) Directorate General for Economic and Financial Affairs (1992) *Country Studies: Greece,* Brussels.

Cooper, R. (1989) 'Modernism, Post Modernism and Organizational Analysis 3: The Contribution of Jacques Derrida', *Organization Studies* 10, 4: 479–502.

Council of the European Communities (1985) *Council Directive 85/384/EEC on the Mutual Recognition of Diplomas and Other Evidence of Formal Qualifications in Architecture Including Measures to Facilitate the Effective Exercise of the Right of Establishment and Freedom to Provide Services,* Brussels.

Cox, R. (1987) *Production, Power, and World Order: Social Forces in the Making of History,* New York: Columbia University Press.

Cram, L. (1997) *Policymaking in the European Union: Conceptual Lenses and the Integration Process,* London: Routledge.

Cremer, W. and A. Fisahn (1998) 'New Environmental Instruments in Germany', in Golub, J. (ed.) *New Instruments for Environmental Protection in the EU,* London: Routledge: 54–84.

Cronenberg, M. (1991) 'Energierechtsreform. Stand der Überlegungen aus der Sicht der Bundesregierung', in Baur, J. F. (ed.) *Reform des Energiewirtschaftsgesetzes. Eine Analyse der Änderungsvorschläge,* Baden-Baden: Nomos: 45–62.

Cunningham, F. (1987) *Democratic Theory and Socialism,* Cambridge: Cambridge University Press.

Curtin, D. M. (1997) *Postnational Democracy. The European Union in Search of a Political Philosophy,* The Hague: Kluwer Law International.

Czempiel, E.-O. (1981) *Internationale Politik: ein Konfliktmodell,* Paderborn *et al.,* Schöningh.

Czempiel, E.-O. (1991) *Weltpolitik im Umbruch: das internationale System nach dem Ende des Ost–West–Konflikts,* München: Beck.

Czempiel, E.-O. (1994) 'Vergesellschaftete Außenpolitik', *Merkur* 48, 1: 1–14.

Daly, G. (1994) 'Post–metaphysical Culture and Politics: Richard Rorty and Laclau and Mouffe,' *Economy and Society* 23, 2: 173–200.

Damgaard, E. (1992) 'Denmark: Experiments in Parliamentary Government', in Damgaard, E. (ed.) *Parliamentary Change in the Nordic Countries,* Oslo: Scandinavian University Press: 19–49.

Dashwood, A (1985) 'The European Parliament Wins Again', *European Law Review* 10, 3: 149–50.

Daugbjerg, C. (1994) 'Dansk industri og det Indre Marked. Policy–netværk i Bruxelles og København', *Politica* 26, 4: 458–73.

Davidson, S. (1989) 'Free Movement of Goods, Workers, Services and Capital', in Lodge, J. (ed.) *The EC and the Challenge of the Future,* London: Pinter: 111–28.

Davis, R. (1978) *The Federal Principle: A Journey through Time in Quest of a Meaning,* Berkeley: University of California Press.

De Crayencour, J.-P. (1982) *The Professions in the European Community: Towards Freedom of Movement and Mutual Recognition of Qualifications,* Brussels: Office of the European Communities.

Degli Abbati, C. (1987) *Transport and European Integration,* Luxembourg: Office for Official Publication of the European Communities.

Dehousse, R. (1992) 'Integration v. Regulation? On the Dynamics of Regulation in the European Community', *Journal of Common Market Studies* 30, 4: 383–402.

Dermine, J. (ed.) (1993) *European Banking in the 1990s,* Oxford: Blackwell.

Despicht, N. (1964) *Policies for Transport in the Common Market: A Survey of the National*

Transport Policies of the Six Member States of the European Economic Community and of the Implementation of the Transport Provisions of the Treaty of Rome, Sidcup, Kent: Lambarde.

Deutscher Bundestag (1997) *Gesetzesbeschluß des Deutschen Bundestages. Gesetz zur Neuregelung des Energiewirtschaftsrechts*, in Bundesrat. Drucksache 941/97, Bonn: Bundesanzeiger.

Diamandouros, N. (1994) *Cultural Dualism and Political Change in Postauthoritarian Greece*, working paper 1994/50, Madrid: Instituto Juan March de Estudios e Investigaciones.

Dicken, P. (1992) *Global Shift: The Internationalisation of Economic Activity*, London: Paul Chapman.

DiMaggio, P. J. and W. W. Powell (eds) (1991) *New Institutionalism in Organizational Analysis*, Chicago: Chicago University Press.

Dinan, D. (1994) *Ever Closer Union. An Introduction to the European Community*, London: Macmillan.

Donnelly, M. (1993) 'The Structure of the European Commission and the Policy Formation Process', in Mazey, S. and J. Richardson (eds) *Lobbying in the European Community*, Oxford: Oxford University Press: 74–81.

Doty, R. L. (1997) 'Aporia: a Critical Exploration of the Agent-Structure Problematique in International Relations Theory', *European Journal of International Relations* 3, 3: 365–392.

Dowding, K. (1995) 'Model or Metaphor? A Critical Review of the Policy Network Appoach', *Political Studies* 43, 1: 136–158.

Dunleavy, P. (1995) 'Reinterpreting the Westland Affair', in Rhodes, R. A. W. and P. Dunleavy (eds) *Prime Minister, Cabinet and Core Executive*, London: Macmillan: 181–218.

Dunleavy, P. and R. A. W. Rhodes (1990) 'Core Executive Studies in Britain', *Public Administration* 68: 3–28.

Dyson, K. (1977) *Party, State, and Bureaucracy in West Germany*, Beverley Hills: Sage.

Dyson, K. (1980) *The State Tradition in Western Europe. A Study of an Idea and Institution*, Oxford: Martin Robertson.

Dyson, K. (1992) *The Politics of German Regulation*, Aldershot: Dartmouth.

Dyson, K. (1994) *Elusive Union: The Process of Economic and Monetary Union in Europe*, London: Longman.

Dyson, K., Featherstone, K. and G. Michalopoulos (1995) 'Strapped to the Mast. EC Central Bankers, the Maastricht Treaty and Global Financial Markets', *European Journal of Public Policy* 2, 3: 465–87.

Ebbinghaus, B. and J. Visser (1994) 'Barrieren und Wege 'grenzenloser' Solidarität. Gewerkschaften und Europäische Integration', in Streeck, W. (ed.) *Staat und Verbände*, Opladen: Westdeutscher Verlag, Politische Vierteljahresschrift, Sonderheft 25: 223–55.

Ebbinghaus, B. and P. A. Kraus (1997) 'Die variable Geometrie der Subsidiarität: Zur Problematik territorialer und funktionaler Integration in Europa', in König, T., E. Rieger and H. Schmitt (eds) *Europäische Institutionenpolitik*, Frankfurt a.M.: Campus: 335–58.

Eckstein, H. (1975) 'Case Study and Theory in Political Science', in Eckstein, H. (1992) *Regarding Politics. Essays on Political Theory, Stability, and Change*, Berkeley: University of California Press: 117–76; reprinted from: F. I. Greenstein and N. W. Polsby (eds) *Handbook of Political Science*, Reading: 79–138.

Edelman, M. (1964) *The Symbolic Uses of Politics*, Urbana: University of Illinois Press.

Egan, M. (1994) *The Politics of European Regulation: Bringing the Firm Back In*, Paper presented to the International Conference of Europeanists, Council for

European Studies, Chicago, 31 March–2 April.

Eichener, V. (1996) 'Die Rückwirkungen der europäischen Integration auf nationale Politikmuster', in Jachtenfuchs, M. and B. Kohler-Koch (eds) *Europäische Integration*, Opladen: Leske und Budrich: 249–80.

Eichener, V. and H. Voelzkow (1994a) 'Europäische Integration und verbandliche Interessensvermittlung. Ko-Evolution von politisch-administrativem System und Verbändelandschaft', in Eichener, E. and H. Voelzkow (eds) *Europäische Integration und verbandliche Interessenvermittlung*, Marburg: Metropolis: 9–27.

Eichener, V. and H. Voelzkow (eds) (1994b) *Europäische Integration und verbandliche Interessenvermittlung*, Marburg: Metropolis.

Eidenmüller, H. (1990) 'Deregulating the Market for Legal Services in the European Community: Freedom of Establishment to Provide Services for EC Lawyers in the Federal Republic of Germany', *Modern Law Review* 53, 5: 604–8.

EIRR. *European Industrial Relations Review* (monthly) London: Andrew Brode.

Eising, R. (1998) *Liberalisierung und Europäisierung: Die regulative Reform der Elektrizitätsversorgung in Großbritannien, der Europäischen Gemeinschaft und der Bundesrepublik Deutschland*, Mannheim: unpublished dissertation.

Eising, R. and B. Kohler-Koch (1994) 'Inflation und Zerfaserung. Trends der Interessenvermittlung in der Europäischen Gemeinschaft', in Streeck, W. (ed.) *Staat und Verbände*, Opladen: Westdeutscher Verlag, Politische Vierteljahresschrift, Sonderheft 25: 175–206.

Elazar, D. J. (1987) *Exploring Federalism*, Tuscaloosa: University of Alabama Press.

Ellwein, T. (1990) 'Die Fiktion der Staatsperson – Eine Skizze', in Ellwein, T. and J. J. Hesse (eds) *Staatswissenschaften: Vergessene Disziplin oder neue Herausforderung?*, Baden-Baden: Nomos: 99–110.

Emmerich, V. (1978) *Ist der kartellrechtliche Ausnahmebereich für die leitungsgebundene Versorgungswirtschaft wettbewerbspolitisch gerechtfertigt?*, Gutachten, erstellt für das Land Niedersachsen. Hannover.

Endo, K. (1994) 'The Principle of Subsidiarity: From Johannes Althusius to Jacques Delors', *Hokkaido Law Review* XLIV, 6: 553–652.

Enzensberger, H. M. (1994) 'Der große Bürgerkrieg und die Grenzen der Verantwortung', in Kohler, G. and M. Meyer (eds) *Die Folgen von 1989*, München, Wien: Carl Hanser: 17–25.

Erdmenger, J. (1983) *The European Community Transport Policy: Towards a Common Transport Policy*, Aldershot: Gower.

Esping–Andersen, G. (1990) *The Three Worlds of the Welfare Capitalism*, Cambridge: Polity.

Esser, C. (1994) *Die Haltung der EVS hinsichtlich der geplanten Deregulierungsvorhaben im Energiesektor und unternehmensstragische Maßnahmen zu ihrer Bewältigung*, paper presented at the International Conference on Competition Policy and Electricity Generation in Britain and Germany, 17–19 November 1994, Tübingen.

Esser, J. (1995) 'Germany. Challenges to the Old Policy Style', in Hayward, J. (ed.) *Industrial Enterprise and European Integration: From National to International Champions in Western Europe*, Oxford: Oxford University Press: 48–75.

EURELECTRIC (1991) *What Form of Competition for the Electricity Supply Sector in Europe? Position of the Continental Members of EURELECTRIC*, Brussels.

Europäisches Parlament (1993a) 'Legislative Entschließung mit der Stellungnahme des Europäischen Parlaments zu dem Vorschlag für eine Richtlinie des Parlaments und des Rates betreffend gemeinsame Vorschriften für den Erdgasbinnenmarkt (KOM (91)0548 – C3–0443/93)', *Amtsblatt der Europäischen*

Gemeinschaften no. C 329/182ff.

Europäisches Parlament (1993b) 'Legislative Entschließung mit der Stellungnahme des Europäischen Parlaments zu dem Vorschlag für eine Richtlinie des Parlaments und des Rates betreffend gemeinsame Vorschriften für den Elektrizitätsbinnnemarkt (KOM (91) 0548–C3–0442/93) *Amtsblatt der Europäischen Gemeinschaften* no. C 329/150.

European Court of Justice (1974) *Commission of the European Communities v. the French Republic*, Case 167/73, 4 April 1974.

European Court of Justice (1985) *European Parliament v. Council of the European Communities*, Case 13/83, 22 May 1985.

European Court of Justice (1986) *Ministère Publique v. Asjes et al.* Cases 209–13/84, 1986.

European Parliament/Council of the European Union (1996) 'Directive 96/92/EC of the European Parliament and of the Council of 19 December 1996 Concerning Common Rules for the Internal Market in Electricity', *Official Journal of the European Communities* 40 (1997) 27: 20–30.

Evans, P. B., H. K. Jacobson and R. D. Putnam (eds) (1993) *Double-Edged Diplomacy: International Bargaining and Domestic Politics*, Berkeley: University of California Press.

Evers, H.-U. (1983) *Das Recht der Energieversorgung*, Baden-Baden: Nomos.

EWI (Energiewirtschaftliches Institut an der Universität Köln) (1995) *TPA and Single Buyer Systems, Producers and Parallel Authorizations, Small and Very Small Systems*, Cologne.

Falkner, G. (1991) 'EG-Sozialcharter. Feierlich erklärt ist nicht gewonnen', *Österreichische Zeitschrift für Politikwissenschaft* 1991, 3: 289–300.

Falkner, G. (1993) 'Sozialdumping im EG-Binnenmarkt. Betrachtungen aus politikwissenschaftlicher Sicht', *Österreichische Zeitschrift für Politikwissenschaft* 1993, 3: 261–77.

Falkner, G. (1996a) 'The Maastricht Social Protocol: Theory and Practice', *Journal of European Social Policy* 1: 1–16.

Falkner, G. (1996b) 'European Works Councils and the Maastricht Social Agreement. Towards a New Policy Style?', *Journal of European Public Policy* 2: 192–208.

Falkner, G. (1997) 'L'accord Européen sur le Congé Parental: vers un Corporatisme dans la Politique Sociale Européenne?, *Politiques et Management Publiques* 15, 1: 171–93.

Falkner, G. (1998) *EU Social Policy in the 1990s: Towards a Corporatist Policy Community*, London and New York: Routledge.

Favoino, M. (1997) *Integrating Policies and Sharing Reponsibilities. Implementing Structures for EU Commission 5th Environmental Action Programme*, paper presented at the EUI spring workshop on the implementation of the EU environmental policy, 10–11 April.

Fields, A. B. (1994) *Can there be Political Democracy Without a Democratic Economy? Is a Democratic Political Economy Possible?*, paper presented at the International Poltical Science Association, Berlin (21–25 August).

Fokkema, T. and P. Nijkamp (1994) 'The Changing Role of Governments: The End of Planning History?', *International Journal of Transport Economics* 21, 2: 127–45.

Foster, C. D. (1992) *Privatisation, Public Ownership and the Regulation of Natural Monopoly*, London: Blackwell.

Freeman, G. (1985) 'National Styles and Policy Sectors: Explaining Structural Variation', *Journal of Public Policy* 5, 4: 467–96.

Freestone, D. (1991) 'European Community Environmental Policy and Law', in Churchill, R., J. Gibson and L. M. Warren (eds) *Law, Policy and the Environment*, Oxford: Blackwell: 135–54.

Friedrich, C. J. (1968) *Trends of Federalism in Theory and Practice*, London: Pall Mall.

Frohlich, N., J. Oppenheimer, J. and O. Young (1971) *Political Leadership and Collective Goods*, Princeton: Princeton University Press.

Fuchs, G. (1994) 'Policy-making in a System of Multi-level Governance. The Commission of the European Community and the Restructuring of the Telecommunications Sector', *Journal of European Public Policy* 1, 2: 177–94.

Garrett, G. (1992) 'International Cooperation and Institutional Choice: The EC's Internal Market', *International Organization* 46, 2: 533–60.

Gehring, T. (1994) 'Der Beitrag von Institutionen zur Förderung der internationalen Zusammenarbeit. Lehren aus der institutionellen Struktur der Europäischen Gemeinschaft', *Zeitschrift für Internationale Beziehungen* 1, 2: 211–42.

General Secretariat of the European Union (1996) *Consolidated Text. Amended Proposal for a Directive of the European Parliament and of the Council Concerning Common Rules for the Internal Market in Electricity*, 21 June 1996, Brussels.

George, A. L. and R. O. Keohane (1980) 'The Concept of National Interests: Uses and Limitations', in George, A. L. (ed.) *Presidential Decisionmaking in Foreign Policy*, Boulder: Westview: 217–37.

Giavazzi, F. and A. Giovannini (1987) 'Models of the EMS: Is Europe a Greater Deutschmark Area?', in Bryant, R. and R. Portes (eds) *Global Macroeconomics: Policy Conflict and Cooperation*, New York: St Martin's Press: 237–72.

Giddens, A. (1984) *The Constitution of Society: Outline of the Theory of Structuration*, Berkeley: University of California Press.

Gieryn, T. F. (1995) 'Boundaries of Science', in Jasanoff, Sh. *et al.* (eds) *Handbook on Science, Technology and Society*, Newbury Park, Cal.: Sage: 393–443.

Gill, S. (1992) 'The Emerging World Order and European Change', in *Socialist Register*, London: Merlin Press: 157–96.

Glasbergen, P. and P. Driessen (1994) 'New Strategies for Environmental Policy: Regional Network Management in the Netherlands', in Wintle, M. and R. Reeve (eds) *Rhetoric and Reality in Environmental Policy: the Case of the Netherlands in Comparison with Britain*, Aldershot: Avebury: 25–39.

Goetz, K. H. (1995) 'National Governance and European Integration. Intergovernmental Relations in Germany', *Journal of Common Market Studies* 33, 1: 91–116.

Goffman, E. (1974) *Frame Analysis: An Essay on the Organization of Experience*, New York: Harper and Row.

Gold, M. (ed.) (1993) *The Social Dimension. Employment Policy in the European Community*, London: Macmillan.

Gold, M. and M. Hall (1994) 'Statutory European Works Councils: The Final Countdown?', *Industrial Relations* 25, 3: 177–86.

Golub, J. (1996) 'The Politics of Judicial Discretion: Rethinking the Interaction Between National Courts and the European Court of Justice', *West European Politics* 19, 2: 360–85.

Gorges, M. J. (1993) 'Interest Intermediation in the EC after Maastricht', in Cafruny, A. and G. Rosenthal (eds) *The State of the European Community, vol. 2. The Maastricht Debates and Beyond*, Boulder: Longman: 73–90.

Gottweis, H. (1997) 'Genetic Engineering, Discourses of Deficiency, and the New Politics of Population', in Taylor, P., S. Halforn and P. Edwards (eds) *Changing Life: Genomes, Ecologies, Bodies, Commodities*, Minneapolis: University of Minnesota Press.

Gottweis, H. (1998) *Governing Molecules. The Discursive Politics of Genetic Engineering in Europe and in the Unites States*, Cambridge, Mass.: MIT Press.

Gough, I. (1979) *The Political Economy of the Welfare State*, London: Macmillan.

Graf, W. D. (ed.) (1992) *The Internationalization of the German Political Economy: Evolution of a Hegemonic Project*, London: Macmillan.

Graham, C. and T. Prosser (1991) *Privatizing Public Enterprises: Constitutions, the State and Regulation in Comparative Perspective*, Oxford: Clarendon Press.

Grande, E. (1994) *Vom Nationalstaat zur europäischen Politikverflechtung. Expansion und Transformation moderner Staatlichkeit – untersucht am Beispiel der Forschungs– und Technologiepolitik*, unpublished dissertation, University of Konstanz.

Grande, E. (1996a) 'The State and Interest Groups in a Framework of Multi-Level Decision-Making: The Case of the European Union', *Journal of European Public Policy* 3, 3: 318–38.

Grande, E. (1996b) 'Das Paradox der Schwäche. Forschungspolitik und die Einflusslogik europäischer Politikverflechtung', in Jachtenfuchs, M. and B. Kohler-Koch (eds) *Europäische Integration*, Opladen: Leske und Budrich: 373–400.

Grande, E. (1997) *Post–nationale Demokratie. Ein Ausweg aus der Globalisierungsfalle?*, Technische Universität München, Institut für Sozialwissenschaften Lehrstuhl für Politische Wissenschaft, Working Paper 2/97.

Grant, C. (1994) *Delors: Inside The House that Jacques Built*, London: Nicholas Brealey.

Green Cowles, M. (1995) 'The European Round Table of Industrialists: The Strategic Player in European Affairs', in Greenwood, J. (ed.) *European Casebook on Business Alliances*, Hemel Hempstead: Prentice Hall: 225–36.

Greenwood, J. (ed.) (1995) *European Casebook on Business Alliances*, Hemel Hempstead: Prentice Hall.

Greenwood, J. and M. Aspinwall (eds) (1998) *Collective Action in the European Union: Interests and the New Politics of Associability*, London: Routledge.

Greenwood, J., J. R. Grote and K. Ronit (eds) (1992a) *Organized Interests and the European Community*, London: Sage.

Greenwood, J., J. R. Grote and K. Ronit (1992b) 'Conclusions', in Greenwood, J., J. R. Grote and K. Ronit (eds) *Organized Interests and the European Community*, London: Sage: 238–76.

Greenwood, J. and K. Ronit (1992) 'Established and Emergent Sectors: Organized Interests and the European Level in the Pharmaceutical Industry and the New Biotechnologies', in Greenwood, J., J. Grote, and K. Ronit (eds) *Organized Interests and the European Community*, London: Sage: 69–98.

Greenwood, J. and K. Ronit (1994) 'Interest Groups in the European Community: Newly Emerging Dynamics and Forms', *West European Politics* 17, 1: 31–52.

Gregory, R. (1989) 'Political Rationality or 'Incrementalism'?', *Policy and Politics* 17, 2: 139–53.

Grieco, J. M. (1990) *Cooperation among Nations. Europe, America, and Non–tariff Barriers to Trade*, Ithaca/London: Cornell University Press.

Grieco, J. M. (1995) 'The Maastricht Treaty, Economic and Monetary Union and the neo-realist research programme', *Review of International Studies* 21, 1: 21–40.

Grier, K. (1989) 'On the Existence of a Political Monetary Cycle', *American Journal of Political Science* 33, 2: 376–89.

Grimm, D. (1995) 'Does Europe Need a Constitution?', *European Law Journal* 1, 3: 282–302.

Grinspun, R. and R. Kreklewich (1994) 'Consolidating Neoliberal Reforms: "Free Trade" as a Conditioning Framework', *Studies in Political Economy* 43: 33–61.

Gröner, H. (1975) *Die Ordnung der deutschen Elektrizitätswirtschaft*, Baden-Baden: Nomos.

Guerrieri, P, and P. C. Padoan (1989) *The Political Economy of European Integration:*

States, Markets and Institutions, New York: Harvester Wheatsheaf.

Gwilliam, K. M. and P. J. Mackie (1975) *Economics and Transport Policy,* London: Allen and Unwin.

Haas, E. B. (1958) *The Uniting of Europe. Political, Social and Economic Forces, 1950–1957,* Stanford: Stanford University Press.

Haas, E. B. (1964) *Beyond the Nation-State. Functionalism and International Organization,* Stanford: Stanford University Press.

Haas, E. B. (1990) *When Knowledge is Power. Three Models of Change in International Organizations,* Berkeley: University of California Press.

Haas, P. (ed.) (1992) 'Knowledge, Power and International Policy Coordination', *International Organization* 46, 1 (special issue).

Haggard S. and R. Kaufman (1992) 'Institutions and Economic Adjustment', in Haggard, S. and R. Kaufman (eds) *The Politics of Economic Adjustment: International Constraints, Distributive Conflicts, and the State,* Princeton: Princeton University Press: 3–37.

Haigh, N. (1990) *EEC Environmental Policy and Britain, 2nd edn.,* Harlow: Longman.

Haigh, N. and C. Lanigan (1995) 'Impact of the European Union on UK Environmental Policy Making', in Gray, T. S. (ed.) *UK Environmental Policy in the 1990s,* Basingstoke: Macmillan: 18–37.

Hajer, M. A. (1992) *Furthering Ecological Responsibility through Verinnerlijking: The Limits to a Positive Management Approach,* working paper 39, Leiden: Rijkuniversiteit Leiden.

Hajer, M. A. (1995) *The Politics of Environmental Discourse: Ecological Modernization and the Policy Process,* Oxford: Oxford University Press.

Hall, P. (1986) *Governing the Economy: The Politics of State Intervention in Britain and France,* Cambridge: Polity.

Hall, P. (1993) 'Policy Paradigms, Social Learning, and the State: The Case of Economic Policymaking in Britain', *Comparative Politics* 26, 2: 275–96.

Hall, P. (1995) *The Political Economy of Europe in an Era of Interdependence,* paper for a Seminar on the State and Capitalism since 1800, Center for European Studies, Harvard University.

Hancher, L. (1994) 'Infringement Proceedings Force ECJ to Rule on Key Legal Issues', *EC-Energy Monthly* 69/5.

Hantrais, L. (1995) *Social Policy in the European Union,* London: Macmillan.

Harms, W. (ed.) (1987) *Atomstrom aus Frankreich? Zur Schaffung eines europäischen Binnenmarktes für Strom,* Cologne: Heymann.

Harvey, D. (1989) *The Condition of Postmodernity: An Inquiry into the Origins of Cultural Change,* Oxford: Blackwell.

Hasenclever, A., P. Mayer and V. Rittberger (1997) *Theories of International Regimes,* Cambridge: Cambridge University Press.

Hassard, J. and M. Parker (1993) *Postmodernism and Organizations,* London: Sage.

Haverland, M. (1997) *Two Worlds of Environmental Policy and Government–Industry Relations. Implementing Producer Responsibility for Packaging Waste in the United Kingdom and the Netherlands,* paper presented at the ECPR workshops in Bern, 27 February – 4 March.

Hayes-Renshaw, F. and H. Wallace (1997) *The Council of Ministers,* London: Macmillan.

Hayes-Renshaw, F. and H. Wallace (1995) 'Executive Power in the European Union: The Functions and Limits of the Council of Ministers', *Journal of European Public Policy* 2, 4: 559–82.

Hayward, J. (1991) 'The Policy Community Approach to Industrial Policy', in Rustow, D. and K. Erickson (eds) *Comparative Political Dynamics: Global Research Perspectives,* New York: Harper Collins, pp. 381–407.

Hayward, J. (1995a) 'Introduction: Europe's Endangered Industrial Champions', in

Hayward, J. (ed.) *Industrial Enterprise and European Integration: From National to International Champions in Western Europe*, Oxford: Oxford University Press: 1–20.

Hayward, J. (1995b) 'Organized Interests and Public Policies', in Hayward, J. and E. C. Page (eds) *Governing the New Europe*, London: Polity: 224–56.

Heinelt, H. (1998) 'Zivilgesellschaftliche Perspektiven einer demokratischen Transformation der Europäischen Union', *Zeitschrift für Internationale Beziehungen*, 5, 1: 79–107.

Heinz, J. *et al.* (1993) *The Hollow Core. Private Interests in National Policy Making,* Cambridge, Mass.: Harvard University Press.

Held, D. (1992) 'Democracy: From City-States to a Cosmopolitan Order', in Held, D. (ed.) *Prospects for Democracy,* Oxford: Blackwell: 13–52.

Held, D. and A. McGrew (1993) 'Globalization and the Liberal Democratic State', *Government and Opposition* 28, 2: 261–88.

Heller, H. (1934) *Staatslehre,* Leiden: A.W. Sijthoff.

Hellmann, G. (1994) '"Einbindungspolitik". German Foreign Policy and the Art of Declaring 'Total Peace', in Callies, J. and B. Moltmann (eds) *Die Zukunft der Außenpolitik. Deutsche Interessen in den internationalen Beziehungen* (Loccumer Protokolle 67/94) Rehburg-Loccum: Evangelische Akademie Loccum: 86–127.

Her Majesty's Government (1990) *This Common Inheritance,* London: HMSO.

Héritier, A. (1993) 'Policy-Netzwerkanalyse als Untersuchungsinstrument im europäischen Kontext: Folgerungen aus einer empirischen Studie regulativer Politik', in Heritier, A. (ed.) *Policy-Analyse. Kritik und Neuorientierung*, Opladen: Westdeutscher Verlag: 432–47.

Héritier, A. *et al.* (1994) *Die Veränderung von Staatlichkeit in Europa. Ein regulativer Wettbewerb: Deutschland, Großbritannien und Frankreich in der Europäischen Union,* Opladen: Leske und Budrich.

Héritier, A., C. Knill, S. Mingers (1996) *Ringing the Changes in Europe. Regulatory Competition and Redefinition of the State. Britain, France, Germany,* Berlin/New York: de Gruyter.

Hildebrand, P. M. (1993) 'The European Community's Environmental Policy, 1957 to "1992". From Incidental Measures to an International Regime?', in Judge, D. (ed.) *A Green Dimension for the European Community. Political Issues and Processes,* London: Frank Cass: 13–44.

Hirschman, A. (1970) *Exit, Voice, and Loyalty. Responses to Decline in Firms, Organizations, and States,* Cambridge, Mass.: Harvard University Press.

Hirschman, A. (1982) *Shifting Involvements: Private Interest and Public Action,* Oxford: Blackwell.

Hirst, P. and G. Thompson (1996) *Globalisation in Question: the International Economy and the Possibilities of Governance,* London: Polity.

Hix, S. (1994) 'The Study of the European Communities: The Challenge to Comparative Politics', *West European Politics* 17, 1: 1–30.

Hix, S. (1998) 'The Study of the European Union II: The "New Governance" Agenda and its Rival', *Journal of European Public Policy* 5, 1: 38–65.

Hoffmann, S. (1966) 'Obstinate or Obsolete? The Fate of the Nation-State and the Case of Western Europe', *Daedalus* 95, 3: 862–915.

Hogwood, B. and L. Gunn (1984) *Policy Analysis for the Real World,* Oxford: Oxford University Press.

Hollingsworth, J. R., P. C. Schmitter and W. Streeck (1994) 'Capitalism, Sectors, Institutions, and Performance', in Hollingsworth, J. R., P. C. Schmitter and W. Streeck (eds) *Governing Capitalist Economies. Performance and Control of Economic Sectors,* New York/Oxford: Oxford University Press: 3–16.

Hollingsworth, J. R., P. C. Schmitter and W. Streeck (eds) (1994a) *Governing Capitalist Economies. Performance and Control of Economic Sectors,* New York/Oxford:

Oxford University Press.

Hollingsworth, J. R. and W. Streeck (1994) 'Countries and Sectors: Concluding Remarks on Performance, Convergence, and Competitiveness', in Hollingsworth, J. R., P. C. Schmitter and W. Streeck (eds) *Governing Capitalist Economies. Performance and Control of Economic Sectors*, New York/Oxford: Oxford University Press: 270–300.

Holmes, P. and F. McGowan (1997) 'The Changing Dynamic of EU–Industry Relations: Lessons from the Liberalization of European Car and Airline Markets', in Wallace, H. and A. R. Young (eds) *Participation and Policy-Making in the European Union*, Oxford: Clarendon: 159–84.

Hood, C. (1995) 'Emerging Issues in Public Administration', *Public Administration* 73, 1: 165–83.

Hooghe, L. and G. Marks (1997) 'The Making of a Polity. The Struggle over European Integration', *European Integration online Papers* (EIoP) 1, 4 (http://eiop.or.at/eiop/texte/1997–004a.htm).

Hooghe, L. and M. Keating (1994) 'The Politics of European Union Regional Policy', *Journal of European Public Policy* 1, 3: 367–93.

Hornung-Draus, R. (1994) 'Euro–Betriebsräte. Praxistauglichkeit auf dem Prüfstand', *EuroAS* 12, 1: 4–6.

Hueglin, T. O. (1986) 'Regionalism in Western Europe: Conceptual Problems of a New Political Perspective', *Comparative Politics* 18, 4: 439–58.

Hueglin, T. O. (1990) *A Political Economy of Federalism*, Kingston: Institute of Intergovernmental Relations, Queen's University.

Hueglin, T. O. (1991) *Sozietaler Föderalismus: Die politische Theorie des Johannes Althusius*, Berlin: de Gruyter.

Hueglin, T. O. (1994) 'Federalism, Subsidiarity and the European Tradition: Some Clarifications', *Telos* 100, 1: 37–55.

Hull, R. (1993) 'Lobbying Brussels: A View from Within', in Mazey, S. and J. Richardson (eds) *Lobbying in the European Community*, Oxford: Oxford University Press: 83–92.

Ikenberry, J. G. (1988) 'Conclusion: an Institutional Approach to American Foreign Economic Policy', *International Organization* 42, 1: 219–43.

Ikenberry, J. G., D. A. Lake and M. Mastanduno (1988) 'Introduction: Approaches to Explaining American Foreign Policy', *International Organization* 42, 1: 1–14.

Immergut, E. (1990) 'Institutions, Veto Points and Policy Results: A Comparative Analysis of Health Care', *Journal of Public Policy* 10, 4: 391–416.

Jachtenfuchs, M. (1995) *Theoretical Perspectives on European Governance*, MZES working paper, Mannheim: Mannheimer Zentrum für Europäische Sozialforschung.

Jachtenfuchs, M. (1996a) 'Regieren durch Überzeugen: Die Europäische Union und der Treibhauseffekt', in Jachtenfuchs, M. and B. Kohler-Koch, *Europäische Integration*, Opladen: Leske und Budrich: 429–454.

Jachtenfuchs, M. (1996b) *International Policy-Making as a Learning Process. The European Union and the Green House Effect*, Aldershot: Avebury.

Jachtenfuchs, M. (1997) 'Democracy and Governance in the European Community', *European Integration online Papers* (EIoP) 1, 2 (http://eiop.or.at/eiop/texte/1997–002a.htm).

Jachtenfuchs, M. (1999) *Ideen und Integration. Verfassungsideen in Deutschland, Frankreich und Großbritannien und die Entwicklung der EU*. Unpublished dissertation, University of Mannheim.

Jachtenfuchs, M. and B. Kohler-Koch (1995) *The Transformation of Governance in the European Union*, MZES AB III Arbeitspapier no. 11, Mannheim: Mannheimer Zentrum für Europäische Sozialforschung.

Jachtenfuchs, M. and B. Kohler-Koch (eds) (1996a) *Europäische Integration*,

Opladen: Leske und Budrich.
Jachtenfuchs, M. and B. Kohler-Koch (1996b) 'Regieren im dynamischen Mehrebenensystem', in Jachtenfuchs, M. and B. Kohler-Koch (eds) *Europäische Integration*, Opladen: Leske und Budrich: 15–44.
Jänicke, M. and H. Weidner (1997) 'Germany', in Jänicke, M. and H. Weidner (eds) *National Environmental Policies. A Comparative Study of Capacity Building*, Berlin/Heidelberg: Springer: 133–155.
Jenkins-Smith, H. and P. Sabatier (1994) 'Evaluating the Advocacy Coalition Framework', *Journal of Public Policy* 14, 2: 175–203.
Jessop, B. (1990) *State Theory: Putting the Capitalist State in Its Place*, Cambridge: Polity.
Jobert, B. and P. Muller (1987) *L'Etat en Action. Politiques Publiques et Corporatismes*, Paris: Presses Universitaires de France.
Joerges, C. and J. Neyer (1997) 'From Intergovernmental Bargaining to Deliberative Political Processes: The Constitutionalisation of Comitology', *European Law Journal* 3, 3: 273–99.
Jordan, G. and Schubert, K. (eds) (1992) 'Policy Networks', *European Journal of Political Research* 21, 1–2 (special issue).
Josselin, D. (1996) 'Domestic Policy Networks and European Negotiations: Evidence from British and French Financial Services', *Journal of European Public Policy* 3, 3: 297–317.
Junne, G. (1996) 'Integration unter den Bedingungen von Globalisierung und Lokalisierung', in Jachtenfuchs, M. and B. Kohler-Koch (eds) *Europäische Integration*, Opladen: Leske und Budrich: 513–30.
Kahler, M. (1987) 'The Survival of the State in European International Relations', in Maier, C. S. (ed.) *Changing Boundaries of the Political. Essays on the Evolving Balance between the State and Society, Public and Private in Europe*, Cambridge: Cambridge University Press: 287–319.
Kassim, H. (1994) *The Development of the Common Air Transport Policy: Implications for Existing Theories and Future Theorising*, unpublished paper, Birkbeck College, London.
Katzenstein, P. J. (1987) *Policy and Politics in West Germany: The Growth of a Semisovereign State*, Philadelphia: Temple University Press.
Katzenstein, P. J. (ed.) (1989) *Industry and Politics in West Germany: Toward the Third Republic*, Ithaca: Cornell University Press.
Kazakos, P. (1991) *Greece Between Adjustment and Marginalisation*, Athens: Diatton (in Greek).
Keating, M. (1994) 'Regions and Regionalism in the European Community', *International Journal of Public Administration* 18, 10: 1491–511.
Keating, M. and Hooghe, L. (1996) 'By-Passing the Nation State? Regions and the EU Policy Process', in Richardson, J. (ed.) *European Union: Power and Policy-Making*, London/New York: Routledge: 216–229.
Keller, B. (1993) 'Die soziale Sicht des Binnenmarktes. Zur Begründung einer euro–pessimistischen Sicht', *Politische Vierteljahresschrift* 4, 4: 588–612.
Keller, B. (1995) 'Perspektiven europäischer Kollektivverhandlungen – vor und nach Maastricht', *Zeitschrift für Soziologie* 4, 4: 243–62.
Kenis, P. and V. Schneider (1991) 'Policy Networks and Policy Analysis: Scrutinizing a New Analytical Toolbox', in Marin, B. and R. Mayntz (eds) *Policy Networks: Empirical Evidence and Theoretical Considerations*, Boulder: Westview: 25–59.
Keohane, R. O. (1984) *After Hegemony. Cooperation and Discord in the World Political Economy*, Princeton: Princeton University Press.
Keohane, R. O. and S. Hoffmann (1991) 'Institutional Change in Europe in the 1980s', in Keohane, R. and S. Hoffmann (eds) *The New European Community: Decision-Making and Institutional Change*, Boulder: Westview: 1–39.
Kerremans, B. (1996) 'Do Institutions Make a Difference? Non-Institutionalism,

Neo-Institutionalism, and the Logic of Common Decision-Making in the European Union', *Governance* 9, 2: 217–40.

Kielmansegg, P. Graf (1996) 'Integration und Demokratie', in Jachtenfuchs, M. and B. Kohler-Koch (eds) *Europäische Integration*, Opladen: Leske und Budrich: 47–71.

King, P. (1982) *Federalism and Federation*, Baltimore: Johns Hopkins University Press.

Klöcker, I. A. (1985) *Hauptprobleme der Zusammenschlußkontrolle in der Versorgungswirtschaft*, Pfaffenweiler: Centaurus-Verl.-Ges.

Knight, J. (1992) *Institutions and Social Conflict*, Cambridge: Cambridge University Press.

Knill, C. (1995) 'Staatlichkeit im Wandel. Großbritannien im Spannungsfeld nationaler Reformen und europäischer Integration', *Politische Vierteljahresschrift* 36, 4: 655–80.

Knill, C. (ed.) (1997) *Interim Project Report. The Implementation of European Environmental Policy. The Impact and Transformation of National Administrative Traditions*, Florence: EUI.

Knill, C. and A. Héritier (1996) 'Neue Instrumente in der europäischen Umweltpolitik. Strategien für eine effektivere Implementation', in Lübbe-Wolff, G. (ed.) *Der Vollzug des europäischen Umweltrechts*, Berlin: Erich Schmidt: 209–34.

Knodt, M. (1996) *Der 'verhandelnde Staat' auf regionaler Ebene – politikrelevanter Paradigmenwechsel oder Mogelpackung?*, MZES AB III Arbeitspapier no. 18, Mannheim: Mannheimer Zentrum für Europäische Sozialforschung.

Knoepfel, P. and H. Weidner (1983) 'Implementating Air Quality Control Programs in Europe. Some Results of a Comparative Study', in Downing, P. and K. Hanf (eds) *International Comparisons in Implementing Pollution Laws*, Boston/The Hague: Kluwer-Nijhoff: 191–211.

Kohler-Koch, B. (1992) 'Interessen und Integration', *Politische Vierteljahresschrift* Sonderheft 23: 81–120.

Kohler-Koch, B. (1994) 'Changing Patterns of Interest Intermediation in the European Union', *Government and Opposition* 29, 2: 167–80.

Kohler-Koch, B. (1995) *The Strength of Weakness. The Transformation of Governance in the EU*, working paper, Mannheim: Mannheimer Zentrum für Europäische Sozialforschung AB III/Nr. 10.

Kohler-Koch, B. (1996) 'Catching Up With Change. The Transformation of Governance in the European Union', *Journal of European Public Policy* 3, 3: 359–80.

Kohler-Koch, B. (1997a) 'Organized Interests in European Integration. The Evolution of a New Type of Governance?', in Wallace, H. and A. Young (eds) *Participation and Policy-Making in the European Union*, Oxford: Oxford University Press: 42–68.

Kohler-Koch, B. (1997b) *Interactive Governance: Regions in the Network of European Politics*, paper presented at 5. ECSA conference, Seattle.

Kohler-Koch, B. (1998a) 'Die Europäisierung nationaler Demokratien: Verschleiß eines europäischen Kulturerbes?', in Greven, M. T., *Demokratie – eine Kultur des Westens. DVPW–Kongreßband (1997)* Opladen: Leske und Budrich: 263–88.

Kohler-Koch, B. (1998b) 'Europäisierung der Regionen: Institutioneller Wandel als sozialer Prozeß', in Kohler-Koch, B. (ed.) *Interaktive Politik in Europa. Regionen im Netzwerk der Integration*, Opladen: Leske und Budrich: 13–31.

Kohler-Koch, B. and J. Edler (1998) 'Ideendiskurs und Vergemeinschaftung: Erschließung transnationaler Räume durch europäisches Regieren', in Kohler-Koch, B. (ed.) *Regieren in entgrenzten Räumen*, Opladen: Westdeutscher Verlag, Politische Vierteljahresschrift, Sonderheft 29: 169–206.

Kohler-Koch, B. and M. Jachtenfuchs (1996) 'Regieren in der Europäischen Union – Fragestellungen für eine interdisziplinäre Forschung', *Politische Vierteljahresschrift* 37, 3: 537–56.

Kommission (Kommission der Europäischen Gemeinschaften) (1988) *Der Binnenmarkt für Energie* (Arbeitsdokumente der Kommission) Brussels: KOM

(88): 238 – ende.

Kommission (Kommission der Europäischen Gemeinschaften) (1991) *Vorschlag für eine Richtlinie des Rates betreffend gemeinsame Vorschriften für den Elektrizitätsbinnenmarkt; Vorschlag für eine Richtlinie des Rates betreffend gemeinsame Vorschriften für den Erdgasbinnenmarkt,* Brussels: KOM (91): 548 – ende. – SYN 384–5.

Kommission (Kommission der Europäischen Gemeinschaften) (1993) *Abgeänderter Vorschlag für eine Richtlinie des Europäischen Parlaments und des Rates betreffend gemeinsame Vorschriften für den Elektrizitätsbinnenmarkt; Abgeänderter Vorschlag für eine Richtlinie des Europäischen Parlaments und des Rates betreffend gemeinsame Vorschriften für den Erdgasbinnenmarkt,* Brussels: KOM (93): 643 – ende.

Kooiman, J. (ed.) (1993) *Modern Governance. New Government–Society Interactions,* London: Sage.

Kooiman, J. (1993a) 'Social-Political Governance. Introduction', in Kooiman, J. (ed.) *Modern Governance. New Government–Society Interactions,* London: Sage: 1–6.

Kooiman, J. (1993b) 'Governance and Governability. Using Complexity, Dynamics and Diversity', in Kooiman, J. (ed.) *Modern Governance. New Government–Society Interactions,* London: Sage: 35–48.

Koppen, I. (1992) *The Role of the European Court of Justice in the Development of the European Community Environmental Policy,* Working Papers of the European University Institute, SPS 92 (18).

Krasner, S. D. (1978) *Defending the National Interest,* Princeton: Princeton University Press.

Krasner, S. D. (1984) 'Approaches to the State: Alternative Conceptions and Historical Dynamics', *Comparative Politics* 16, 2: 223–46.

Kreile, M. (1992) 'Einleitung', in Kreile, M. (ed.) *Die Integration Europas,* Opladen: Westdeutscher Verlag, Politische Vierteljahresschrift, Sonderheft 23: vii–xix.

La Spina, A. and G. Sciortino (1993) 'Common Agenda, Southern Rules: European Integration and Environmental Change in the Mediterranean States', in Liefferink, J. D., P. D. Lowe and A. P. J. Mol (eds) *European Integration and Environmental Policy,* London/New York: Belhaven Press: 217–36.

Laclau, E. and C. Mouffe (1985) *Hegemony and Socialist Strategy: Toward a Radical Democratic Politics,* London: Verso.

Ladrech, R. (1994) 'Europeanization of Domestic Politics and Institutions: The Case of France', *Journal of Common Market Studies* 32, 1: 69–88.

Lange, P. and M. Regini (1989) 'Conclusion', in Lange, P. and M. Regini (eds) *State, Market, and Social Regulation: New Perspectives on Italy,* Cambridge: Cambridge University Press: 249–72.

Laski, H. (1925) *A Grammar of Politics,* London: George Allen and Unwin, repr. 1957.

Latour, B. (1993) *We Have Never Been Modern,* Cambridge, Mass.: Harvard University Press.

Laudati, L. (1996) 'The European Commission as Regulator: The Uncertain Pursuit of the Competitive Market', in Majone, G., *Regulating Europe,* London/New York: Routledge: 229–263.

Le Blansch, K. (1996) *Milieubezorg in Bedrijven. Overheidssturing in het perspectief can de verinnerlijkingsbeleidslijn,* Amsterdam: Thesis.

Le Nestour, C. and B.-M. Zinow (1994) 'Rechtsfragen des "Service Public"', *Recht der Energiewirtschaft* no. 4: 129–33; no. 5: 170–4.

Lehmbruch, G. (1967) *Proporzdemokratie: politisches System und politische Kultur in der Schweiz und in Österreich,* Tübingen: Mohr.

Lehmbruch, G. (1976) *Parteienwettbewerb im Bundesstaat,* Stuttgart: Kohlhammer.

Lehmbruch, G. (1982) 'Introduction: Neo-Corporatism in Comparative Perspective', in Lehmbruch, G. and P. Schmitter (eds) *Patterns of Corporatist Policy Making,* London/Beverly Hills: Sage: 1–27.

301

Lehmbruch, G. (1984) 'Concertation and the Structure of Corporatist Networks', in Goldthorpe, J. (ed.) *Order and Conflict in Contemporary Capitalism*, Oxford: Oxford University Press: 60–80.

Lehmbruch, G. (1987) 'Administrative Interessenvermittlung', in Windhoff-Héritier, A. (ed.) *Verwaltung und ihre Umwelt. Festschrift für Thomas Ellwein zum 60. Geburtstag*, Opladen: Westdeutscher Verlag: 11–43.

Lehmbruch, G. (1991) 'The Organization of Society, Administrative Strategies, and Policy Networks', in Czada, R. and A. Windhoff-Héritier (eds) *Political Choice – Institutions, Rules and the Limits of Rationality*, Frankfurt a.M.: Campus: 121–58.

Lehmbruch, G. and P. Schmitter (1982) *Patterns of Corporatist Policy-Making*, Beverly Hills: Sage.

Leibfried, S. and P. Pierson (1995) 'Semisovereign Welfare States: Social Policy in a Multitiered Europe', in Leibfried, S. and P. Pierson (eds) *European Social Policy: Between Fragmentation and Integration*, Washington D.C.: Brookings Institution: 43–7.

Lenschow, A. (1996) *Institutional and Policy Change in the European Community. Variations in Environmental Policy Integration*, New York: New York University, unpublished Ph.D. dissertation.

Lenschow, A. (1997a) 'The Implementation of EU Environmental Policy in Germany', in Knill, C. (ed.) *Interim Project Report: The Implementation of European Environmental Policy. The Impact and Transformation of National Administrative Traditions*, Annex 1, Florence: EUI.

Lenschow, A. (1997b) 'Variation in EC Environmental Policy Integration: Agency Push Within Complex Institutional Structures', *Journal for European Public Policy* 4, 1: 109–27.

Lepsius, R. M. (1990) 'Die Europäische Gemeinschaft: Rationalitätskriterien der Regimebildung', in Zapf, W. (ed.) *Modernisierung moderner Gesellschaften. 25. dt. Soziologentag 1990 in Frankfurt*, Frankfurt a.M.: Campus: 309–17.

Levin, M. and H. S. Strauss (1991) 'Introduction: Overview of Risk Assessment and Regulation of Environmental Biotechnology', in Levin, M. and H. S. Strauss (eds) *Risk Assessment in Genetic Engineering*, New York: McGraw-Hill.

Lewin, L. (1992) *Samhället och de organiserade intressena*, Stockholm: Norstedts.

Lewis, P. and R. Abel. (eds) (1989) *Lawyers in Society, vol. 3: Comparative Theories*, Berkeley: University of California Press.

Liebert, U. (1994) 'Netzwerke und neue Unübersichtlichkeit. Plädoyer für die Wahrnehmung politischer Komplexität', in Leggewie, C. (ed.) *Wozu Politikwissenschaft?*, Darmstadt: Wissenschaftliche Buchgesellschaft: 155–69.

Lijphart, A. (1977) *Democracy in Plural Societies: A Comparative Exploration*, New Haven: Yale University Press.

Lijphart, A. (1985) 'Non-Majoritarian Democracy: A Comparison of Federal and Consociational Theories', *Publius* 15, 2: 3–15.

Lindberg, L. N. and S. A. Scheingold (1970) *Europe's Would-Be Polity*, New Jersey: Prentice-Hall.

Lindberg, L. N. and J. L. Campbell (1991) 'The State and the Organization of Economic Activity', in Campbell, J. L., J. R. Hollingsworth and L. N. Lindberg (eds) *Governance of the American Economy*, Cambridge: Cambridge University Press: 356–95.

Lindberg, L. N., J. L. Campbell and J. R. Hollingsworth (1991) 'Economic Governance and the Analysis of Structural Change in the American Economy', in Campbell, J. L., J. R. Hollingsworth and L. N. Lindberg (eds) *Governance of the American Economy*, Cambridge: Cambridge University Press: 3–34.

Lindblom, C. (1979) 'Still Muddling, Not Yet Through', *Public Administration Review* 39, 6: 517–26.

Linstead, S. and R. Grafton-Small (1992) 'On Reading Organizational Culture', *Organization Studies* 13: 331–55.

Lipietz, A. (1992) *Towards a New Economic Order,* Oxford: Oxford University Press.

Lodge, J. (1995) 'The European Parliament and the Authority-Democracy Crisis', - *Annals of the American Academy* 531: 69–83.

Lovecy, J. (1994) *The Single European Market and Professional Self-Regulation. Doctors, Lawyers and the Dynamics of Managed Mutual Recognition,* paper presented to the Conference on the Evolution of Rules for a Single European Market, University of Exeter.

Lovecy, J. (1995) 'Global Regulatory Competition and the Single Market for Professional Services: The Legal and Medical Professions in France and Britain', *Journal of European Public Policy* 3, 3: 514–34.

Lowi, T. J. (1964) 'American Business, Public Policy, Case Studies, and Political Theory', *World Politics* 16, 4: 677–715.

Lübbe-Wolff, G. (1996) 'Stand und Instrumente der Implementation des Umweltrechts in Deutschland', in Lübbe-Wolff, G. (ed.) *Der Vollzug des europäischen Umweltrechts,* Berlin: Erich Schmidt: 77–106.

McFarland, A. (1992) 'Interest Groups and the Policymaking Process: Sources of Countervailing Power in America', in Petracca, M. (ed.) *The Politics of Interests: Interest Groups Transformed,* Boulder: Westview: 58–79.

McGowan, F. (1993) *The Struggle for Power in Europe – Competition and Regulation in the EC Electricity Industry,* London: Royal Institute of International Affairs.

McLaughlin, A. and G. Jordan (1993) 'The Rationality of Lobbying in Europe: Why are Euro-groups so Numerous and so Weak? Some Evidence from the Car Industry', in Mazey, S. and J. Richardson (eds) *Lobbying in the European Community,* Oxford: Oxford University Press: 122–61.

McLaughlin, A., G. Jordan and W. Maloney (1993) 'Corporate Lobbying in the European Community', *Journal of Common Market Studies* 31, 2: 191–212.

McRoberts, K. (1988) *Quebec: Social Change and Political Crisis,* Toronto: McClelland and Stewart.

Maier, C. (1984) 'Preconditions for Corporatism', in Goldthorpe, J. (ed.) *Order and Conflict in Contemporary Capitalism,* Oxford: Clarendon: 39–59.

Majone, G. (1991) *Market Integration and Regulation: Europe after 1992,* Working Papers of the European University Institute, SPS No.91/10.

Majone, G. (1992) 'Regulatory Federalism in the European Community', *Government and Policy* 10, 2: 299–316.

Majone, G. (1993a) 'Wann ist Policy-Deliberation wichtig?', in Héritier, A. (ed.) *Policy-Analyse. Kritik und Neuorientierung,* Politische Vierteljahresschrift, Sonderheft 24, Opladen: Westdeutscher Verlag: 97–115.

Majone, G. (1993b) 'The European Community between Social Policy and Social Regulation', *Journal of Common Market Studies* 31, 2: 153–75.

Majone, G. (1994) 'The Rise of the Regulatory State in Europe', *West European Politics* 17, 3: 77–101.

Majone, G. (1996) *Regulating Europe,* London: Routledge.

Mancini, G. F. (1991) 'The Making of a Constitution for Europe', in Keohane, R. O. and S. Hoffmann (eds) *The New European Community. Decisionmaking and Institutional Change,* Boulder: Westview: 177–94.

Maravall, J.-M. (1993) 'Politics and Policy: Economic Reforms in Southern Europe', in Pereira, L. C. B., J. M. Maravall and A. Przeworski (eds) *Economic Reforms in New Democracies: A Social-Democratic Approach,* Cambridge: Cambridge University Press: 77–131.

March, J. and J. Olsen (1989) *Rediscovering Institutions: The Organisational Basis of Politics,* New York: Free Press.

March, J. and J. Olsen (1994) *Institutional Perspectives on Political Institutions,* Arena paper 2, Oslo.

March, J. and J. Olsen (1995) *Democratic Governance*, New York: Free Press.

Markert, K. (1996) 'Die Rolle des Bundeskartellamtes bei der 'Regulierung' der deutschen Strom– und Gasversorgung', in Sturm, R. and S. Wilks (eds) *Wettbewerbspolitik und die Ordnung der Elektrizitätswirtschaft in Deutschland und Großbritanien*, Baden-Baden: Nomos: 281–94.

Marks, G. (1992) 'Structural Policy in the European Community', in Sbragia, A. M. (ed.) *EuroPolitics: Institutions and Policymaking in the „New" European Community*, Washington D.C.: Brookings Institution: 191–224.

Marks, G. and D. McAdam (1996) 'Social Movements and the Changing Structure of Political Opportunity in the European Union', in Marks, G. *et al.* (eds) *Governance in the European Union*, London: Sage: 95–120.

Marks, G. *et al.* (1996) 'Competencies, Cracks and Conflicts: Regional Mobilization in the European Union', in Marks, G. *et al.* (eds) *Governance in the European Union*, London: Sage: 40–63.

Marks, G., L. Hooghe and K. Blank (1995) *European Integration since the 1980s: State-Centric versus Multi-Level Governance*, Paper presented at the American Political Science Association Meeting, Chicago, 31 August – 3 Sept. 1995.

Marsh, D. and R. A. W. Rhodes (1992) 'Policy Communities and Issue Networks. Beyond Typology', in Marsh, D. and R. A. W. Rhodes (eds) *Policy Networks in British Government*, Oxford: Clarendon Press: 249–287.

Martinelli, A. (1991) *International Markets and Global Firms. A Comparative Study of Organized Business in the Chemical Industry*, London: Sage.

Mastanduno, M., D. A. Lake and J. G. Ikenberry (1989) 'Toward a Realist Theory of State Action', *International Studies Quarterly* 33, 4: 457–74.

Mathis, C. (1995) 'Vorschläge für eine Neuorientierung der Elektrizitätswirtschaft in Frankreich. Der "Rapport Mandil"', *Energiewirtschaftliche Tagesfragen* 45, 1/2: 54–58.

Mattera, A. (1991) 'Les Principes de "Proportionnalité" et de la "Reconnaissance Mutuelle" dans la Jurisprudence de la Cour en Matière de Libre Circulation des Personnes et des Services: de l'Arrêt "Thieffry" aux Arrêts "Vlassopoulou", "Mediawet" et "Dennemeyer", *Revue du Marché Unique Européenne* 4: 191–204.

Mavrogordatos, G. (1988) *Between Pityokamptes and Prokroustes: Professional Organisations in Greece Today*, Athens: Odysseas (in Greek).

Mayntz, R. (1992) 'Modernisierung und die Logik von interorganisatorischen Netzwerken', *Journal für Sozialforschung* 32, 1: 19–32.

Mayntz, R. (1993) 'Policy Netzwerke und die Logik von Verhandlungssystemen', in Héritier, A. (ed.) *Policy Analyse. Kritik und Neuorientierung*, Opladen: Westdeutscher Verlag, Politische Vierteljahresschrift, Sonderheft 24: 39–56.

Mayntz, R. and Scharpf, F. W. (1995) 'Steuerung und Selbstorganisation in staatsnahen Sektoren', in Mayntz, R. and F. W. Scharpf (eds) *Gesellschaftliche Selbstregelung und politische Steuerung*, Frankfurt a.M./New York: Campus Verlag: 9–38.

Mazey, S. (1995) 'The Development of EU Equality Policies: Bureaucratic Expansion on Behalf of Women?', *Public Administration* 73, 4: 591–609.

Mazey, S. and J. Richardson (1993a) 'Introduction', in Mazey, S. and J. Richardson (eds) *Lobbying in the European Community*, Oxford: Oxford University Press: 2–26.

Mazey, S. and J. Richardson (1993b) 'Environmental Groups and the EC: Challenges and Opportunities', in Judge, D. (ed.) *A Green Dimension for the European Community: Political Issues and Processes*, London: Frank Cass: 109–128.

Mazey, S. and J. Richardson (1993c) *Lobbying in the European Community*, Oxford: Oxford University Press.

Mazey, S. and J. Richardson (1996) *Influencing the EU's agenda: Interest Groups and the 1996 IGC*, paper for the 24th ECPR, Joint Sessions of Workshop, Oslo 29 March – 3 April.

Meadwell, H. (1993) 'The Politics of Nationalism in Quebec', *World Politics* 45, 2: 203–41.

Mearsheimer, J. J. (1990) 'Back to the Future. Instability in Europe after the Cold War', *International Security* 15, 1: 5–56.

Meinecke, F. (1963) *Die Idee der Staatsräson in der neueren Geschichte*, Munich: Oldenbourg (first pub. 1924).

Mény, Y., P. Muller and J.-L. Qermonne (1996) 'Introduction', in Mény, Y., P. Muller and J.-L. Qermonne (eds) *Adjusting to Europe. The Impact of the European Union on National Institutions and Policies*, London/New York: Routledge: 1–24.

Meyer, M. W. and Associates (1978) *Environments and Organizations*, San Francisco: Jossey Bass.

Mingst, K. A. (1995) 'Uncovering Missing Links: Linkage Actors and their Strategies in Foreign Policy Analysis', in Neack, L., J. A. Hey and P. J. Haney (eds) *Foreign Policy Analysis. Continuity and Change in its Second Generation*, Englewood Cliffs: Prentice Hall: 229–42.

Molle, W. (1990) *The Economics of European Integration*, Aldershot: Dartmouth.

Moon, B.E. (1995) 'The State in Foreign and Domestic Politics', in Neack, L., J. A. Hey and P. J. Haney (eds) *Foreign Policy Analysis. Continuity and Change in its Second Generation*, Englewood Cliffs: Prentice Hall: 187–200.

Moran, M. (1984) *The Politics of Banking. The Strange Case of Competition and Credit Control*, London: Macmillan.

Moran, M. (1994) 'The State in Western Europe and the Financial Services Revolution', *West European Politics* 17, 3: 158–77.

Moravcsik, A. (1991) 'Negotiating the Single European Act: National Interests and Conventional Statecraft in the European Community', *International Organization* 45, 1: 19–56.

Moravcsik, A. (1993a) 'Introduction: Integrating International and Domestic Theories of International Bargaining', in Evans, P., H. Jacobson and R. Putnam (eds) *Double-Edged Diplomacy: International Bargaining and Domestic Politics*, Berkeley: University of California Press: 3–42.

Moravscik, A. (1993b) 'Preferences and Power in the European Community: A Liberal Intergovernmentalist Approach', *Journal of Common Market Studies* 31, 4: 473–524.

Müller, E. (1989) 'Sozial–liberale Umweltpolitk. Von der Karriere eines neuen Politikbereichs', *Aus Politik und Zeitgeschichte* B 47–48/89: 3–15.

Müller, W. and V. Wright (1994) 'Reshaping the State in Western Europe: The Limits to Retreat', *West European Politics* 17, 3: 1–11.

Nedergaard, P. (1994) *Organiseringen af Den Europæiske Union*, Cobenhagen: Handelshøjskolens Forlag.

Nentwich, M. (1995) '*Citizens' Involvment in European Politics: Towards a More Participatory Democracy?*, paper prepared for the Fourth Biennial International Conference of the European Community Studies Association (Charleston, South Carolina, 11–14 May).

Nettl, J. P. (1968) 'The State as a Conceptual Variable', *World Politics* 7, 4: 559–92.

Neunreither, K. (1993) 'Subsidiarity as a Guiding Principle for European Community Activities', *Government and Opposition* 28, 2: 206–17.

Nicolaïdis, K. (1993) *Legal Precedent and Political Innovation in the European Community: Explaining the Emergence of Managed Mutual Recognition*, paper presented to the ECSA Conference, Washington D.C., May 1993.

Nordhaus, W. (1989) Alternative Approaches to the Political Business Cycle, *Brookings Papers on Economic Activity* 2, 1: 1–68.

Nordlinger, E. A. (1981) *On the Autonomy of the Democratic State*, Cambridge, Mass.: Harvard University Press.

North, D. (1990) *Institutions, Institutional Change and Economic Performance*,

Cambridge: Cambridge University Press.

Norton, P. (ed.) (1996) *National Parliament and the European Union*, London: Frank Cass.

Nugent, N. (1989) *The Government and Politics of the European Community*, Durham: Duke University Press.

Nugent, N. (1991) *The Government and Politics of the European Community*, London: Macmillan.

Nugent, N. (1992) 'The Deepening and Widening of the European Community: Recent Evolution, Maastricht and Beyond', *Journal of Common Market Studies* 30, 3: 311–28.

Nugent, N. (1995) 'The Leadership Capacity of the European Commission', *Journal of European Public Policy* 2, 1: 603–23.

Obradovic, D. (1995) 'Prospects for Corporatist Decision-Making in the European Union: The Social Policy Agreement', *Journal of European Public Policy* 2, 2: 261–83.

OECD (1992) *Regulatory Reform, Privatisation and Competition Policy*, Paris: OECD.

Offe, C. (1981) 'The Attribution of Public Status to Interest Groups: Observations on the West German Case', in Berger, S. (ed.) *Organizing Interests in Western Europe: Pluralism, Corporatism, and the Transformation of Politics*, Cambridge: Cambridge University Press: 123–58.

ORGSPSS4 (1994) *Interest Associations Resources, Structure, Tasks and Contact with Public Authorities*.

Orzack, L.H. (1991) 'The General Systems Directive and the Liberal Professions', in Hurwitz, L. and C. Lequesne (eds) *The State of the European Community. Policies, Institutions, and Debates in the Transition Years*, London: Longman: 137–52.

Padgett, S. (1990) 'Policy Style and Issue Environment: The Electricity Supply Sector in West Germany', *Journal of Public Policy* 10, 2: 165–93.

Padoa-Schioppa, T. *et al.* (1987) *Efficiency, Stability and Equity: A Strategy for the Evolution of the Economic System of the European Community*, Oxford: Oxford University Press.

Pagoulatos, G. (1996) 'Governing in a Constrained Environment: Policy-Making in the Greek Banking Deregulation and Privatisation Reform', *West European Politics* 19, 4: 744–69.

Pagoulatos, G. and V. Wright (forthcoming, 1999) 'The Politics of Industrial Privatization: Spain, Portugal and Greece in a European Perspective', *Revista Trimestrale di Diritto Pubblico*.

Papaioannou, R. and D. Stasinopoulos (1991) 'The Road Transport Policy of the European Community', *Journal of Transport Economics and Policy* 25, 2: 203–8.

Parenti, M. (1980) *Democracy for the Few*, New York: St. Martin's Press.

Pedersen, O. K. *et al.* (1992) *Privat Politik*, Copenhagen: Samfundslitteratur.

Pelkmans, J. (1990) 'Regulation and the Internal Market: an Economic Perspective', in Siebert, H. (ed.) *The Completion of the Internal Market*, Tübingen: J. C. B. Mohr: 91–117.

Perraton, J. *et al.* (1997) 'The Globalisation of Economic Activity', *New Political Economy* 2, 2: 257–77.

Peters, B. G. (1992) 'Bureaucratic Politics and the Institutions of the European Community', in Sbragia, A. M. (ed.) *Euro-Politics. Institutions and Policymaking in the "New" European Community*, Washington D.C.: Brookings Institution: 75–122.

Peters, B. G. (1995) *The Politics of Bureaucracy*, New York: Longman.

Peters, G. (1986) *American Public Policy*, Chatham N.J.: Chatham House.

Peterson, J. (1995) 'Playing the Transparency Game: Consultation and Policy Making in the European Commission', *Public Administration* 73, 3: 473–92.

Petit, P. (1994) 'Les Relations de Services et l'Internationalisation des Economies: Vers une Globalisation Différenciée', in De Bandt, J. and J. Gadrey (eds) *Les*

Relations de Service, Paris: CNRS.

Pierson, P. (1996) 'The Path to European Integration: A Historical Institutionalist Analysis', *Comparative Political Studies* 19, 2: 123–63.

Polanyi, K. (1944) *The Great Transformation*, Boston: Beacon Press, repr. 1957.

Pollack, M. (1996) 'The New Institutionalism and EC Governance: The Promise and Limits of Institutional Analysis', *Governance* 9, 4: 429–58.

Pridham, G. (1996) 'Environmental Policies and Problems of European Legislation in Southern Europe', *South European Society and Politics* 1, 1: 47–73.

Putnam, R. (1988) 'Diplomacy and Domestic Politics: The Logic of Two-Level Games', *International Organization* 42, 3: 427-460.

Rasmussen, H. (1986) *On Law and Policy in the European Court of Justice. A Comparative Study in Judicial Policymaking*, Dordrecht: Martinus Nijhoff.

Raworth, P. (1994) 'A Timid Step Forwards: Maastricht and the Democratization of the European Community', *European Law Review* 19, 1: 16–33.

Reed, M. and M. Hughes (1992) *Rethinking Organization. New Directions in Organization Theory and Analysis*, London: Sage.

Rhodes, C. and S. Mazey (eds) (1995) *Building a European Polity?*, Boulder: Lynne Rienner.

Rhodes, R. A. W. (1988) *Beyond Westminster and Whitehall. The Sub–Central Governments of Britain*, London: Unwin Hyman.

Rhodes, R. A. W. (1997) *Understanding Governance. Policy Networks, Governance, Reflexivity and Accountability*, Buckingham: Open University Press.

Rhodes, R. A. W. and D. Marsh (1992) 'Policy Networks in British Politics. A Critique of Existing Approaches', in Rhodes, R. A. W. and D. Marsh (eds) *Policy Networks in British Government*, Oxford: Clarendon Press: 1–26.

Rhodes, R. A. W. and P. Dunleavy (eds) (1995) *Prime Minister, Cabinet and Core Executive*, London: Macmillan.

Richardson, J. (1993) 'Interest Group Behavior in Britain: Continuity and Change', in Richardson, J. J. (ed.) *Pressure Groups*, Oxford: Oxford University Press.

Richardson, J. (1994) 'Doing Less by Doing More: British Government 1979–1993', *West European Politics* 17, 3: 178–97.

Richardson, J. and A. G. Jordan (1979) *Governing Under Pressure: The Policy Process in a Post-Parliamentary Democracy*, Oxford: Martin Robertson.

Richter, M. (1995) *Sektorale Transformationsprozesse der ostdeutschen Ökonomie am Beispiel des Umbaus von Strom- und Gaswirtschaft*, Konstanz.

Rieger, E. and T. König (1997) 'Einleitung: Perspektiven und Probleme europäischer Institutionenpolitik', in König, T., E. Rieger and H. Schmitt (eds) *Europäische Institutionenpolitik*, Frankfurt a.M.: Campus: 11–41.

Riker, W. H. (1962) *The Theory of Political Coalitions*, New Haven: Yale University Press.

Risse-Kappen, T. (1994) 'Ideas do not Float Freely: Transnational Coalitions, Domestic Structures, and the End of the Cold War', *International Organization* 48, 2: 185–214.

Rocher, F. and M. Smith (1995) 'Introduction', in Rocher, F. and M. Smith (eds) *New Trends in Canadian Federalism*, Peterborough: Broadview Press: 7–20.

Rorty, R. (1989) *Contingency, Irony, and Solidarity*, Cambridge: Cambridge University Press.

Rosenau, J. N. (1969) 'Pre-Theories and Theories of Foreign Policy', in Farrell, R. B. (ed.) *Approaches to Comparative and International Politics*, Evanston: Northwestern University Press: 27–92.

Rosenau, J. N. (1988) 'Patterned Chaos in Global Life: Structure and Process in the Two Worlds of World Politics', *International Political Science Review* 9, 4: 327–64.

Rosenau, J. N. (1992) 'Governance, Order, and Change in World Politics', in Rosenau, J. N. and E. O. Czempiel (eds) *Governance without Government: Order and Change in World Politics,* Cambridge: Cambridge University Press: 1–29.

Rosenau, J. N. and E. O. Czempiel (eds) (1992) *Governance without Government: Order and Change in World Politics,* Cambridge: Cambridge University Press.

Ross, G. (1995a) *Jacques Delors and European Integration,* Oxford: Polity.

Ross, G. (1995b) 'Assessing the Delors Era and Social Policy', in Leibfried, S. and P. Pierson (eds) *European Social Policy: Between Fragmentation and Integration,* Washington D.C.: Brookings Institution: 357–88.

Rueschmeyer, D. (1989) 'Comparing Legal Professions: A State-Centred Approach', in Lewis, P. and R. Abel (eds) *Lawyers in Society, vol. 3: Comparative Theories,* Berkeley: University of California Press: 289–321.

Ruggie, J. G. (1993) 'Territoriality and Beyond: Problematizing Modernity in International Relations', *International Organization* 47, 1: 139–74.

Sabatier, P. A. (1993) 'Advocacy-Koalition, Policy-Wandel und Policy-Lernen', in Héritier, A. (ed.) *Policy-Analyse. Kritik und Neuorientierung,* Politische Vierteljahresschrift, Sonderheft 24, Opladen: Westdeutscher Verlag: 116–48.

Sandholtz, W. (1992) *High-Tech Europe. The Politics of International Cooperation,* Berkeley: University of California Press.

Sandholtz, W. (1993) 'Choosing Union: Monetary Politics and Maastricht', *International Organization* 47, 1: 1–39.

Sandholtz, W. (1994) 'Choosing Union: Monetary Politics and Maastricht', in Nelsen, B. F. and A. C.-G. Stubb (eds) *The European Union: Readings on the Theory and Practice of European Integration,* Boulder: Lynne Rienner: 257–90.

Sandholtz, W. and J. Zysman (1989) '1992: Recasting the European Bargain', *World Politics* 42, 1: 95–128.

Sbragia, A. M. (1992a) 'Introduction', in Sbragia, A. M. (ed.) *Euro-Politics. Institutions and Policymaking in the 'New' European Community,* Washington D.C.: Brookings Institution: 1–22.

Sbragia, A. M. (1992b) 'Thinking About the European Future: The Uses of Comparison', in Sbragia, A. M. (ed.) *Euro-Politics. Institutions and Policymaking in the 'New' European Community,* Washington D.C.: Brookings Institution: 257–91.

Sbragia, A. M. (1993) 'The European Community: A Balancing Act', *Publius* 23, 3: 23–38.

Scharpf, F. W. (1985) 'Die Politikverflechtungs-Falle: Europäische Integration und deutscher Föderalismus im Vergleich', *Politische Vierteljahresschrift* 26, 4: 323–56.

Scharpf, F. W. (1988) 'The Joint Decision Trap: Lessons from German Federalism and European Integration', *Public Administration* 66, 3: 239–78.

Scharpf, F. W. (1989) 'Regionalisierung des europäischen Raums' and 'Diskussion', *Cappenberger Gespräche* 23, Cologne: Kohlhammer: 7–51.

Scharpf, F. W. (1991) 'Political Institutions, Decision Styles, and Policy Choices', in Czada, R. and A. Windhoff-Héritier (eds) *Political Choice – Institutions, Rules and the Limits of Rationality,* Frankfurt a.M.: Campus: 53–86.

Scharpf, F. W. (1992) 'Die Handlungsfähigkeit des Staates am Ende des Zwanzigsten Jahrhunderts', in Kohler-Koch, B. (ed.) *Staat und Demokratie in Europa, 18. Wissenschaftlicher Kongreß der DVPW,* Opladen: Leske und Budrich: 93–115.

Scharpf, F. W. (ed.) (1993) *Games in Hierarchies and Networks. Analytical and Empirical Approaches to the Study of Governance Institutions,* Frankfurt a.M.: Campus.

Scharpf, F. W. (1994) 'Community and Autonomy: Multi-level Policy-Making in the European Union', *Journal of European Public Policy* 1, 2: 219–42.

Scharpf, F. W. (1996) *A New Social Contract? Negative and Positive Integration in the Political economy of European Welfare States,* Working Papers of the European University Institute, RSC No.96/44.

Scharpf, F. W. (1997) *Games Real Actors Play. Actor-Centred Institutionalism in Policy Research,* Boulder: Westview.

Scharpf, F. W., B. Reissert, and F. Schnabel (1978) 'Policy Effectiveness and Conflict Avoidance in Intergovernmental Policy Formation', in Hanf, K. and F. W. Scharpf (eds) *Interorganizational Policy Making. Limits to Coordination and Central Control*, London: Sage: 57–114.

Schattschneider, E. E. (1960) *The Semisovereign People: A Realist's View of Democracy in America*, New York: Holt, Rinehart and Winston.

Scherzberg, A. (1994) 'Freedom of information – deutsch angewendet: Das neue Umweltinformationsgesetz', *Deutsches Verwaltungsblatt* 109, 13: 733–745.

Schiffer, H. W. (1995) *Energiemarkt Bundesrepublik Deutschland*, Cologne: Verl. TÜV Rheinland.

Schmidt, V. A. (1995) *Democracy at Risk? The Impact of European Integration on National Patterns of Policymaking*, paper for the IV. Biennial International Conference of the ECSA, Charleston, South Carolina: University of Massachusetts, Boston.

Schmidt, V. A. (1996a) *From State to Market? The Transformation of French Business and Government*, Cambridge/New York: Cambridge University Press.

Schmidt, V. A. (1996b) 'Loosening the Ties that Bind: The Impact of European Integration on French Government and its Relationship to Business', *Journal of Common Market Studies* 34, 2: 223–54.

Schmidt, V. A. (1997a) 'European Integration and Democracy: The Differences among Member-States', *Journal of European Public Policy* 4, 1: 128–45.

Schmidt, V. A. (1997b) 'European Integration and Institutional Change: The Transformation of National Patterns of Policy Making', in Göhler, G. (ed.) *Institutionenwandel*, Leviathan, Sonderheft 16/97, Opladen: Westdeutscher Verlag: 143–180.

Schmitter, P. C. (1979) 'Still the Century of Corporatism?', in Schmitter, P. C. and G. Lehmbruch (eds) *Trends Toward Corporatist Intermediation*, London: Sage: 7–52.

Schmitter, P. C. (1981) 'Interest Intermediation and Regime Governability in Contemporary Western Europe and North America', in Berger, S. (ed.) *Organizing Interests in Western Europe: Pluralism, Corporatism, and the Transformation of Politics*, Cambridge: Cambridge University Press: 287–330.

Schmitter, P. C. (1989) 'Corporatism is Dead! Long Live Corporatism!', *Government and Opposition* 24, 1: 54–73.

Schmitter, P. C. and G. Lehmbruch (1979) *Trends Toward Corporatist Intermediation*, Beverly Hills: Sage.

Schneider V. (1992) 'The Structure of Policy Networks', *European Journal of Political Research* 21, 1–2: 109–29.

Schulz, O. (1996) *Maastricht und die Grundlagen einer Europäischen Sozialpolitik: der Weg – die Verhandlungen – die Ergebnisse – die Perspektiven*, Cologne: Heymann.

Séché, J.-C. (1988) *Le Guide des Professions Libérales dans l'Optique du Grand Marché*, Document de la Commission des Communautés Européennes, Brussels.

Sharp, M. and C. Shearman (1987) *European Technological Collaboration*. London/New York: Routledge and Keagen Paul.

Sidenius, N. C. (1982) 'Industrielle interesseorganisationer i den politiske beslutningsproces', *Politica* 14, 4: 43–74.

Sidenius, N. C. (1984) 'Dansk Industripolitik – Beslutningsformer, Interesser og Statens Relative Autonomi', in Olsen, G. R, M. Ougaard and N. C. Sidenius, *Stat, Statskundskab, Statsteori*, Århus: Forlaget Politica: 118–64.

Sidenius, N. C. (1989) *Dansk Industripolitik – Nye Løsninger på Gamle Problemer*, Århus: Hovedland.

Sidenius, N. C. (1994) 'Danish Industry Facing the Internal Market', in Lundqvist, L. and L. O. Persson (eds) *Northern Perspectives on European Integration*, Stockholm: NordREFO: 148–59.

Sidenius, N. C. (1995) 'EU på Organisationernes Dagsorden: Aktivitet og Konsekvenser', *Samfundsøkonomen* 1995, 2: 33–40.

Sidenius, N. C. (1997) 'Problems Searching a Solution: The Role of the Folketing in Danish European Community Politics', in Isaksson, G.-E. (ed.) *Inblickar i Nordisk Parlamentarism*, Åbo: Åbo Akademi: 193–220.

Sidenius, N.C. (1998) 'A Collective Action Problem? Danish Interest Associations and Euro–Groups', in Greenwood, J. and M. Aspinwall (eds) *Collective Action in the European Union: Interests and the New Politics of Associability*, London: Routledge: 81–107.

Simon, H. (1954) 'A Behavioral Theory of Rational Choice', *Quarterly Journal of Economics* 69, 1: 99–118.

Simonis, G. (1972) 'Außenpolitischer Handlungsspielraum und politische Autonomie', in *Gesellschaftlicher Wandel und politische Innovation, Politische Vierteljahresschrift*, Sonderheft 4/1972 (im Auftrag der DVPW): 282–314.

Simonis, U. (1994) 'Environmental Policy in the Federal Republic of Germany: Curative and Precautionary Approaches', *WZB Schriftenreihe FSII*: 94(406).

Skocpol, T. (1979) *States and Social Revolutions: A Comparative Analysis of France, Russia, and China*, Cambridge: Cambridge University Press.

Smart, B. (1992) 'Foucault, Sociology, and the Problem of Human Agency', *Theory and Society* 11, 2: 121–41.

Smith, T. T. Jr. and R. D. Hunter (1992) 'The European Community Environmental Legal System,' *Environmental Law Reporter* 22: 10106–35

Sotiropoulos, D. A. (1995) *The Remains of Authoritarianism: Bureaucracy and Civil Society in Post-Authoritarian Greece*, working paper 1995/66, Madrid: Instituto Juan March de Estudios e Investigaciones.

Spaargaren, G. and A. P. J. Mol (1992) 'Sociology, Environment, and Modernity: Ecological Modernization as a Theory of Social Change', *Society and Natural Resources* 5, 4/5: 323–44.

Steinmo, S., K. Thelen and F. Longstreth (eds) (1992) *Structuring Politics: Historical Institutionalism in Comparative Analysis*, Cambridge: Cambridge University Press.

Strange, S. (1985) 'Interpretations of a Decade', in Tsoukalis, L. (ed.) *The Political Economy of International Money: In Search of a New Order*, London: Sage: 1–43.

Streeck, W. (1995a) 'Politikverflechtung und Entscheidungslücke. Zum Verhältnis von zwischenstaatlichen Beziehungen und sozialen Interessen im europäischen Binnenmarkt', in Bentele, K. and F. W. Scharpf (eds) *Die Reformfähigkeit von Industriegesellschaften. Fritz W. Scharpf – Festschrift zu seinem 60. Geburtstag*, Frankfurt a.M./New York: Campus: 101–28.

Streeck, W. (1995b) 'Neo-Voluntarism: A New European Social Policy Regime?', *European Law Journal* 1, 1: 31–59.

Streeck, W. and P. C. Schmitter (1991) 'From National Corporatism to Transnational Pluralism: Organized Interests in the Single European Market', *Politics and Society* 19, 2: 133–65

Suleiman, E. N. (1987) *Private Power and Centralization in France*, Princeton: Princeton University Press.

Tarrow, S. (1988) *Democracy and Disorder: Protest and Politics in Italy, 1965–1975*, Oxford: Oxford Unversity Press.

Taylor, P. (1991) 'The European Community and the State: Assumptions, Theories and Propositions', *Review of International Studies* 17, 2: 109–25.

Tesier, R. (1993) 'Ethique Environmentale et Théorie du Fait Moral chez Durkheim', *Social Compass* 40: 437–49.

Thelen, K. and S. Steinmo (1992) 'Historical Institutionalism in Comparative Politics', in Steinmo, S., K. Thelen, and S. Longstreth (eds) *Structuring Politics, Historical Institutionalism in Comparative Analysis*, Cambridge: Cambridge University Press: 1–32.

Thomson, J. E. (1995) 'State Sovereignty in International Relations: Bridging the Gap between Theory and Empirical Research', *International Studies Quarterly* 39, 2: 213–33.

Tilly, C. (ed.) (1975) *The Formation of National States in Western Europe*, Princeton: Princeton University Press.

Tinbergen, J. (1965) *International Economic Integration*, Amsterdam: Elsevier.

Torstendahl, R. (1992) *State Theory and State History*, London: Sage.

Traxler, F. and P. C. Schmitter (1995) 'The Emerging Euro-Polity and Organized Interests', *European Journal of International Relations* 1, 2: 191–218.

Tschannen, O. and F. Hainard (1993) 'Sociologie et Environment: Tropismes Disciplinaires ou Nouveau Paradigme?', *Schweizerische Zeitschrift für Soziologie* 19, 2: 421–43.

Tsoukalis, L. (1993) *The New European Economy: the Politics and Economics of Integration*, Oxford: Oxford University Press.

Tsoukalis, L. (1994) *The European Union and Global Economic Interdependence*, paper, International Poltical Science Association, Berlin (21–25 August).

UNCED (1992) *The Global Partnership for Environment and Development: A Guide to Agenda 21*, Geneva: UNCED.

UNCTAD (1994) *World Investment Report*, New York/Geneva: United Nations.

Unger, B. and F. van Waarden (1995) 'Introduction: An Interdisciplinary Approach to Convergence', in Unger, B. and F. van Waarden (eds) *Convergence or Diversity? Internationalization and Economic Policy Response*, Aldershot: Avebury: 1–35.

UNICE Letter to the Secretary General, Council of Ministers of the EC, 14 March 1991.

Van der Straaten, J. and J. Ugelow (1994) 'Environmental Policy in the Netherlands: Change and Effectiveness', in Wintle, M. and R. Reeve (eds) *Rhetoric and Reality in Environmental Policy. The Case of the Netherlands in Comparison with Britain*, Aldershot: Avebury: 118–44.

Van Schendelen, M. P. C. M. (1993) *National Public and Private EC Lobbying*, Aldershot: Dartmouth.

Van Schendelen, M. P. C. M. and R. Pedler (eds) (1994) *Lobbying the European Union: Companies, Trade Associations and Issue Groups*, Aldershot: Dartmouth.

Van Waarden, F. (1992) 'Dimensions and Types of Policy Networks', *European Journal of Political Research*, 21, 1–2: 29–52.

Van Waarden, F. (1993) 'Über die Beständigkeit nationaler Politikstile und Politiknetzwerke. Eine Studie über die Genese ihrer institutionellen Verankerung', in Czada, R. and M. G. Schmidt (eds) *Verhandlungsdemokratie, Interessenvermittlung, Regierbarkeit. Festschrift für Gerhard Lehmbruch*, Opladen: Westdeutscher Verlag: 191–212.

Van Waarden, F. (1995) 'Persistence of National Policy Styles: A Study of their Institutional Foundations', in Van Waarden, F. and B. Unger (eds) *Convergence or Diversity? Internationalization and Economic Policy Response*, Aldershot: Avebury: 333–72.

VDEW (1993) *VDEW–Arbeitsbericht 1993*, Frankfurt.

VIK (various years) *Tätigkeitsbericht*, Essen.

Vincent, D. and D. Stasinopoulos (1990) 'Developments in Transport Policy: The Aviation Policy of the European Community', *Journal of Transport Economics and Policy* 24, 1: 95–100.

VKU (1994) *Stellungnahme des VKU–Bundesvorstandes vom 26. Januar 1994 zum Konzept des Bundeswirtschaftsministeriums für eine Reform des Ordnungsrahmens für Strom und Gas und zum Entwurf eines Gesetzes zur Neuregelung des Energiewirtschaftsrechts vom 20. Oktober 1993*, Cologne.

Vogel, D (1986) *National Styles of Regulation: Environmental Policy in Great Britain and the United States*, Ithaca: Cornell University Press.

Wägerbaur, R. (1992) 'Regulating the European Environment: The EC

Experience', *University of Chicago Legal Forum* 17: 17–39.

Wallace, H. (1996) 'Die Dynamik des EG-Institutionengefüges', in Jachtenfuchs, M. and B. Kohler-Koch (eds) *Europäische Integration*, Opladen: Leske und Budrich: 141–63.

Wallace, H. and A. R. Young (1997) 'The Kaleidoscope of European Policy-Making: Shifting Patterns of Participation and Influence', in Wallace, H. and A. R. Young, *Participation and Policy-Making in the European Union*, Oxford: Clarendon Press: 235–50.

Wallace, W. (1983) 'Less than a Federation, More than a Regime: the Community as a Political System', in Wallace, H., W. Wallace and C. Webb (eds) *Policy Making in the European Communities*, 2nd edn, Chichester: John Wiley: 403–36.

Wallace, W. (1996) 'Government without Statehood: The Unstable Equilibrium', in Wallace, H. and W. Wallace (eds) *Policy-Making in the European Union*, 3rd edn, Oxford: Oxford University Press: 439–460.

Waltz, K. N. (1959) *Man, the State and War: A Theoretical Analysis*, New York: Columbia University Press.

Waltz, K. N. (1979) *Theory of International Politics*, Reading: McGraw-Hill.

Warne, E. J. D. (1993) *Review of the Architects (Registration) Acts 1931–1969*, London: Department of the Environment.

Watson, P. (1993b) 'Social Security', in Gold, M. (ed.) *The Social Dimension. Employment Policy in the European Community*, London: Macmillan: 153–71.

Weale, A. (1992) *The New Politics of Pollution*, Manchester/New York: Manchester University Press.

Weale, A. (1997) 'Great Britain', in Jänicke, M. and H. Weidner (eds) *National Environmental Policies: A Comparative Study of Capacity Building*, Berlin: Springer: 88–107.

Weidner, H. (1995) '25 Years of Modern Environmental Policy in Germany. Treading a Well Worn Path to the Top of the International Field', *WZB Schriftenreihe FSII:* Berlin: 95/301.

Weidner, H. (1996) 'Umweltkooperation und laiternative Konfliktregel-ungsver-fahren in Deutschland. Zur Entstehung eines neuen Politknetzwerkes', *WZB Schriftenreihe FSII:* Berlin: 96/302.

Weidner, H. (ed.) (1997) 'Performance and Characteristics of German Environ-mental Policy. Overview and Expert Commentaries from 14 Countries', *WZB Schriftenreihe FII:* Berlin: 97/301.

Weiler, J. (1991) 'The Transformation of Europe', *Yale Law Journal* 100: 2403–83.

Weiler, J. (1996) 'The ECJ and Political Integration', in Bulmer, S. and A. Scott (eds) *Economic and Political Integration in Europe: Internal Dynamics and Global Context*, Oxford: Blackwell: 131–160.

Wendt, A. (1994) 'Collective Identity Formation and the International State', *American Political Science Review* 88, 2: 384–96.

Wessels, W. and D. Rometsch (1996) 'Conclusion: European Union and National Institutions', in Rometsch, D. and W. Wessels (eds) *The European Union and Member States: Towards Institutional Fusion?*, Manchester: Manchester University Press: 328–65.

West, A. (1991) 'Reforming the French Legal Profession: Towards Increased Competitiveness in the Single Market', *Legal Studies* 11, 2: 189–203.

Wheale, P. and R. McNally (1990) 'UK Government Control of the Release of Genetically Engineered Organisms into the Environment. A Critical Evaluation', in Leskien, D. and J. Spangenberg (eds) *European Workshop on Law and Genetic Engineering*, Bonn: BBU Verlag: 53–62.

White, R. (1991) *A Guide to the Courts and Legal Services Act 1990*, London: Fourmat.

Whitelegg, J. (1988) *Transport Policy in the EEC*, London: Routledge.

Wildavsky, A. (1975) *Budgeting: A Comparative Theory of Budgetary Processes*, Boston:

Little, Brown.

Williams, S. (1991) 'Sovereignty and Accountability in the European Community', in Keohane, R. O. and S. Hoffmann (eds) (1991) *The New European Community. Decisionmaking and Institutional Change*, Boulder: Westview: 155–76.

Wincott, D. (1995) 'The Role of Law or the Rule of the Court of Justice? An 'Institutional' Account of Judicial Politics in the European Community', *Journal of European Public Policy* 2, 4: 583–602.

Wincott, D. (1996) 'The Court of Justice and the European Policy Process', in Richardson, J. (ed.) *European Union. Power and Policy-Making*, London: Routledge: 170–86.

Winters, L. A. (1993) *The European Community: A Case of Successful Integration?*, Centre for Economic Policy Research, London: Discussion Paper no. 755.

Wolf, K.D. (1995) 'Was sind 'nationale Interessen'? Versuch einer begrifflichen Orientierungshilfe im Spannungsfeld von Staatsräson, vergesellschafteter Außenpolitik und transnationalen Beziehungen', in Callies, J. and B. Moltmann (eds) *Die Zukunft der Außenpolitik. Deutsche Interessen in den internationalen Beziehungen*, Rehburg-Loccum: Evang. Akademie: 248–68.

Wolin, S. S. (1983) 'From Progress to Modernization: The Conservative Turn', *Democracy*: 9–21.

Woolley, J. T. (1992) 'Policy Credibility and European Monetary Institutions', in A. M. Sbragia (ed.) *Euro-Politics: Institutions and Policymaking in the "New" European Community*, Washington D.C.: Brookings Institution: 157–96.

World Commission on Environment and Development (WCED) (1987) *Our Common Future*, Oxford/New York: Oxford University Press.

World Society Research Group (1996) 'In Search of World Society', *Law and State* 53/54: 17–41.

Wright, D. (1991) 'EC Environmental Policy. Coping with Interdependency', *Futures* 23: 709–23.

Wright, S. (1994) *Molecular Politics. Developing American and British Regulatory Policy for Genetic Engineering, 1972–1982*, Chicago: Chicago University Press.

Wright, V. (1994a) 'Industrial Privatization in Western Europe: Pressures, Problems and Paradoxes', in Wright, V. (ed.) *Privatization in Western Europe: Pressures, Problems and Paradoxes*, London: Pinter: 17–43.

Wright, V. (1994b) 'Reshaping the State: Implications for Public Administration', *West European Politics* 17, 3: 102–34.

Wyplosz, C. (1993) 'Macro-Economic Implications of 1992', in Dermine, J. (ed.) *European Banking in the 1990s*, Oxford: Blackwell: 423–48.

Young, A. R. (1994) *Ideas, Interests, and Institutions: The Politics of Liberalisation in the EC's Road Haulage Industry*, Working Paper no. 9, Sussex European Institute.

Young, A. R. (1997) 'Consumption without Representation? Consumers in the Single Market', in Wallace, H. and A. R. Young (eds) *Participation and Policy-Making in the European Union*, Oxford: Clarendon Press: 206–34.

Zangl, B. (1994) 'Politik auf zwei Ebenen', *Zeitschrift für Internationale Beziehungen* 1, 2: 279–312.

Zinn, K. G. (1989) 'BRD: Europäische Hegemonialmacht oder Opfer sozialer Sklerose?', in Steinkühler, F. (ed.) *Europa '92: Industriestandort oder sozialer Lebensraum*, Hamburg: VSA: 61–78.

Zürn, M. (1995) 'The Challenge of Globalization and Individualization: A View from Europe', in Holm, H.-H. and G. Sorensen (eds) *Whose World Order? Uneven Globalization at the End of the Cold War*, Boulder: Westview: 137–163.

Zürn, M. (1996) 'Über den Staat und die Demokratie im europäischen Mehrebenensystem', *Politische Vierteljahresschrift* 37, 1: 27–55.

INDEX

www.ingramcontent.com/pod-product-compliance
Ingram Content Group UK Ltd.
Pitfield, Milton Keynes, MK11 3LW, UK
UKHW020400010325
455677UK00021B/558